Superheroin
and the Epic Jou

Superheroines and the Epic Journey

Mythic Themes in Comics, Film and Television

VALERIE ESTELLE FRANKEL

Foreword by TRINA ROBBINS

McFarland & Company, Inc., Publishers
Jefferson, North Carolina

LIBRARY OF CONGRESS CATALOGUING-IN-PUBLICATION DATA

Names: Frankel, Valerie Estelle, 1980– author.
Title: Superheroines and the epic journey : mythic themes in comics, film and television / Valerie Estelle Frankel ; foreword by Trina Robbins.
Description: Jefferson, North Carolina : McFarland & Company, Inc., Publishers, 2017. | Includes bibliographical references and index.
Identifiers: LCCN 2016051332 | ISBN 9781476668789 (softcover : acid free paper) ∞
Subjects: LCSH: Comic books, strips, etc.—United States—History and criticism. | Women superheroes in literature. | Women superheroes in motion pictures. | Women superheroes on television.
Classification: LCC PN6725 .F67 2017 | DDC 741.5/3522—dc23
LC record available at https://lccn.loc.gov/2016051332

BRITISH LIBRARY CATALOGUING DATA ARE AVAILABLE

ISBN (print) 978-1-4766-6878-9
ISBN (ebook) 978-1-4766-2801-1

Cover illustration © 2017 Gazometr/iStock

Printed in the United States of America

McFarland & Company, Inc., Publishers
  Box 611, Jefferson, North Carolina 28640
  www.mcfarlandpub.com

Table of Contents

Foreword

The Heroine with a Thousand Faces
by Trina Robbins

My second grade schoolteacher mother taught me to read at the age of four, and I have been reading comics ever since. I started with the comics my mother bought me: Raggedy Ann, Our Gang, Donald Duck and Uncle Scrooge, but as soon as I was old enough to cross two streets, I went regularly to Mr. Itskowitz' candy store with a dime clutched in my hot little hand, and made my own choices. Without having to think twice about it, I gravitated to any comic that starred a woman or girl. This was the era of Timely's teen titles: Patsy Walker, Millie the Model, Tessie the Typist, and a seemingly endless line of comics about teenagers and career girls. Archie comics didn't move me. Sure, they co-starred Betty and Veronica, but the blonde and brunette spent their time fighting over Archie, while the Timely teen girls had their own adventures.

It was only a matter of time before I discovered superheroines—yikes! Mary Marvel, Miss America, Moon Girl—and Wonder Woman! I loved them all, but there was something about Wonder Woman that resonated most deeply within my skinny little girl heart. I had never before heard of Amazons, and weren't they wonderful? They lived on an island where there were no boys allowed, a refreshing change from my real life world, were everything said No Girls Allowed, including the presidency. And there was something else, something indefinable that made Princess Diana special. I couldn't understand it, but I could feel it.

Fast forward 40 years. It's June 1988, and I am suffering from a mysterious ailment that manifests itself in a constant fever and pain in my joints. (I later discovered it was mononucleosis.) Too feverish to even read, all I can do is recline in front of the TV. What a cosmic coincidence! What should be running on public television but a six-part series called *The Power of Myth*, featuring immortal mythologist Joseph Campbell, interviewed by journalist Bill Moyers. Too weak to even comment, I can only grunt with epiphany as, in an altered state, I watch Joseph Campbell explain to me why I so love Wonder Woman.

Suddenly everything is clear to me! Starting with her creation, by a virgin mother and a deity, Princess Diana is the universal hero, called to her journey when Steve Trevor's plane crashes on her mystical island, venturing forth to heal America, the wounded land battling the Axis forces of evil—wow!

Now, along comes Valerie Estelle Frankel's *Superheroines and the Epic Journey*, saying that not just my beloved Wonder Woman, but a world of superheroines, from Marvel comics to Egypt and India, from the Golden Age Black Widow to Promethea, from Joss Whedon's Buffy to Whedon's unmade Wonder Woman film, are all universal heroes, and she shows us how in these pages.

My favorite section has to be the one on costume. Joseph Campbell says, "You're in another transformation … you put on a uniform, you're another creature." Marla Drake dons the magical panther skin that her explorer uncle brought back from Africa, and her adventures as Miss Fury begin. Princess Diana's starry skirt and eagle-emblazoned bustier have power, too. The princess wins her outfit in the Amazon Olympics. And only when she dons it does she become Wonder Woman. So clothes really do make the woman! In fact, all those male cartoonists who've drawn Wonder Woman in the past, who've taken away her iconic costume and dressed her in everything from white catsuits to leather jackets and combat boots, are they attempting to take away her power? Does this explain my love of fashion?

So here we are, simple flesh-and-blood mortals. We can't fly, bullets don't bounce off us, we're not fast enough to play bullets and bracelets. But isn't every birth a small miracle? Shouldn't we follow our bliss? And when the call for help comes, shouldn't we heed it? I think of my favorite David Bowie line: *we can be heroes*. We can *all* be heroes.

Trina Robbins has been writing books, comics, and graphic novels for more than 40 years. Her books Nell Brinkley and the New Woman in the Early 20th Century *(McFarland, 2001) and* Tarpe Mills and Miss Fury *(2011) were nominated for Eisner and Harvey awards. Her 2013 graphic novel* Lily Renee: Escape Artist *was awarded a gold medal from Moonbeam Children's Books. After her* Pretty in Ink *(2013), her definitive history of women cartoonists, she was voted into the Will Eisner Comic Book Hall of Fame.*

Introduction

Considering Superheroes and Heroines

Joseph Campbell's hero's journey has long been linked with superheroes. As Campbell describes his monomyth, also called the chosen one plot, in *The Hero with a Thousand Faces*: "A hero ventures forth from the world of common day into a region of supernatural wonder: fabulous forces are there encountered and a decisive victory is won: the hero comes back from this mysterious adventure with the power to bestow boons on his fellow man" (23).

The hero, with epic birth and awesome powers (whether from the gods or a radioactive spider bite), accepts his destiny and rides off to battle. Campbell scholar Christopher Vogler explains, "The hero is presented with a problem, challenge, or adventure to undertake. Once presented with a Call to Adventure, she can no longer remain indefinitely in the comfort of the Ordinary World" (15). On a deeper level, the call signals "the awakening of the self," an eagerness to become something more. After mentorship, friends and trials, he descends into death itself where he faces his own dark side. After, he returns with a new understanding he uses to enrich his community. Thus Superman, in the darkest place of all, battles his Bizarro self, or the archetypally-named Darkseid, or his Kryptonian relatives, or Doomsday itself. This makes the epic plot fans most adore.

Though movie makers haven't brought it in nearly as much, the heroine's journey is not so different. The heroine has different gifts, a weapon that's often more chalice, ring, or magical cord than sword (Supergirl's ship, Vixen's totem, the Witchblade gauntlet, Wonder Woman's bracelets, girdle, tiara, and lasso). Often, she trains with the wicked witch rather than the more modern fairy godmother or the boy's kindly Obi-Wan/Dumbledore mentor. While the hero meets the mystical goddess for his mate, the heroine's lover is the shapeshifter, always transforming, never fully trustworthy (it's no accident that film Black

Widow falls for the Hulk). The immature heroine too descends to death and faces her shadow, but this is the wicked witch, killer of the innocent that the heroine quests to protect. She returns to life with new wisdom, finally prepared for the challenges of adulthood. (All this appears in more detail in my *From Girl to Goddess: The Heroine's Journey in Myth and Legend*.)

"The immanence of an alternative and implicitly feminist mythology in the stories of female superheroes is one of the unexplored aspects of these comics" (Robinson 6). There is much hidden within the superheroine epics about the female experience and mystical growth, far beneath the monster smashing. She's on a quest to realize her personal power and claim it, whatever society says. The heroine's journey needs some amending, of course, when the superhero takes it. Her talisman is replaced by or augmented with a superpower, often a classically feminine one. This need not be gentle invisibility or empathy—some heroines use the power of the natural world to topple the greatest patriarchs. As the hero or heroine learns to master new abilities, this represents adolescence with its new physical changes and responsibilities.

Accepting the call involves a disguise (though often a slapdash or derivative costume mimicking someone else as Supergirl, Batgirl, Batwoman, Donna Troy, and both Ms. Marvels do). Significant moments include self-naming as well as a wilderness journey where she finds her identity. External forces trying to stop her include the patriarchy (often as the government or the heroine's calculating creator) and a world of misogyny. Meanwhile, many action heroines, raised in a world of warriors like Batwoman and Batgirl, find themselves seeking their lost feminine side on a quest for the mother. By contrast, those raised by only mothers like Wonder Girl and Wonder Woman herself seek independence. Other relationships—with the sister or child—are especially momentous, as they represent aspects of the self. As with the traditional heroine's journey, rescuing the surrogate daughter, a metaphor for her own innocence, is paramount.

The heroine's journey, like the myths that created it, offers a template for how to grow up. Campbell feels that the old myths no longer work as "what were thought to be the vices of the past are the necessities of today" (Campbell and Moyers 16). As religion becomes less of a cultural institution, stories from *Star Wars* to *The Hunger Games* are becoming our cultural touchstones, our way of transmitting behavioral standards. Superheroes, gaining popularity each year, take their place among them. "Anyone who is familiar with standard religious stories (of virtually any religion) immediately recognizes a similarity between superheroes' abilities and activities and the lives and times of sacred characters" (Packer 75).

Superheroes represent a distinctly American form of storytelling that builds on the traditions of epic myth. Richard Reynolds in *Super Heroes: A*

Modern Mythology lists seven steps that define the superhero genre, especially the origin story:

1. The hero is marked out from society. He often reaches maturity without having a relationship with his parents.
2. At least some of the superheroes will be like earthbound gods in their level of powers. Other superheroes of lesser powers will consort easily with these earthbound deities.
3. The hero's devotion to justice overrides even his devotion to the law.
4. The extraordinary nature of the superhero will be contrasted with the ordinariness of his surroundings.
5. Likewise, the extraordinary nature of the hero will be contrasted with the mundane nature of his alter-ego. Certain taboos will govern the actions of these alter-egos.
6. Although ultimately above the law, superheroes can be capable of considerable patriotism and moral loyalty to the state, though not necessarily to the letter of its laws.
7. The stories are mythical and use science and magic indiscriminately to create a sense of wonder [16].

Here, protecting the community is a vital factor, as is a devotion to true justice, beyond earthly laws. Superpowers of course are central. While mythic heroes frequently celebrate their gifts, the superheroes' powers come from deep trauma and they often long for normalcy. "It's always the ones that can fly and juggle tanks that have the self-confidence problems," Huntress tells Power Girl, who retorts, "And it's the ones that can't that have psychological ones" (Conner, *Power Trip*).

Sharon Packer, author of *Superheroes and Superegos: Analyzing the Minds behind the Masks*, adds to the list of superhero qualities that there is a humanitarian mission, a costume, secret identity, and often a theme to the character, a cast of supporting characters and repeat nemeses, and finally an origin story that includes changing tragedy into good deeds (77–78). Superheroines have all this, but there is often more to their stories as they seek the deep mystical side of female experience, not only physical success through punching.

Depending on one's definition, the world is brimming with not just male superheroes but also superheroines. Consider the Powerpuff Girls, Sailor Moon, Sharkboy and Lavagirl, Witchblade, Sabrina the Teenage Witch, Dark Angel, Alias, Dollhouse, Red Sonja, Agents of S.H.I.E.L.D., Agent Carter, the Bionic Woman, Birds of Prey, Wonder Woman, Charmed, Lara Croft, Crouching Tiger Hidden Dragon. This says nothing of the superheroines with arcs in *Smallville*, *Arrow*, *Heroes*, *Powers*, *Sky High*, the *Batman* films, *The Avengers*, and so forth.

Certainly, there are the big superheroines: Wonder Woman, Batgirl, Super-girl, Harley Quinn, Power Girl, Black Widow, Captain Marvel, Sue Storm, She-Hulk, Jean Grey and a host of other X-Men, with villainesses like Catwoman, Poison Ivy, Elektra, and Mystique. Of course, there are thousands more as authors write new ones each day.

Coming from comic books seems an unfair definition. Many comics are fantasy-based (as in elves, dwarves, and magic), yet contain a superheroine in costume like Jane Yolen's *Foiled*. Gaiman's famous *Sandman* skirts the edge, with his mythic characters like Lady Death intermarrying with Marvel super-heroes. Thanks to today's movies and shows, more people are likely familiar with Black Widow, Mystique, Gamora, or even Catwoman from their films, rather than the comics. (Significantly, all these heroines starred in male-centric movies, emphasizing how the industry still hasn't pulled off a true well-made superheroine film at the time of writing.)

There are also a few (rare) superhero novels and short story collections. The anthology *Masked* by Lou Anders, *The Amazing Adventures of Kavalier and Clay* by Michael Chabon, *Wild Cards, Nobody Gets the Girl, Fortress of Solitude, Soon I Will Be Invincible*, many franchise and film tie-ins…. Among these, how-ever, ones featuring a woman make a much smaller subset: *DC Super Hero Girls, The She-Hulk Diaries*, and *Chicks in Capes* rank high, along with Seanan McGuire's beloved webseries *Velveteen Versus*. Many self-published series are joining them on the shelves, breaking traditions of race, age, and orientation to tell stories with no gatekeepers where truly anything is possible.

The heroine's journey was easier. As well as appearing in nearly all super-heroine comics, it involves a descent into death or a representation thereof, then emerging strong in a metaphor for growing up or overcoming life's trials. Some stories were easy to pick—*The Dark Phoenix Saga, Witchblade, Wonder Woman: Odyssey*. Others were more nebulous—Catwoman from her own film, from *Batman Returns*, from the comics—which made the greatest impression? What of Elektra? Or Supergirl?

I explored numerous independent comics, sources of some really inter-esting material like Terry Moore's Echo with armor melded to her body or *Priya's Shakti*, starring an anti-rape activist filled with goddess power. The 1940s offered a Canadian Inuit superheroine comic called *Nelvana of Northern Lights* (now recently reprinted). *Womanthology* broke ground with many short comics all by women. At the same time, I tried to include all the stories with the truly iconic superheroines. I tried to vary authors and time periods, though the past couple years have offered a renaissance of female heroes, from DC's New 52 with Harley Quinn, Birds of Prey, Batgirl, Batwoman, Teen Titans, and so on to Marvel's female Thor and multiple Spider-Women, scientist Mockingjay,

Pakistani Ms. Marvel, undefeatable Squirrel Girl, and several lineups of Avengers and X-Men. I found fascinating things on the shelf—who knew girl power novelist Tamora Pierce had taken on the female White Tiger? Or that superheroines historian Trina Robbins had written the children's comic *Go Girl!*? Brilliantly, *Promethea* by Alan Moore delves into the mystical side of superheroing and a level of perception below the typical human senses.

Ideally, I would have had a great deal of racial diversity and many comics written by women. Sadly, the sampling on both is limited. Female comic book creators make up about 10 percent of the creators, total, over time, with the numbers at around 20 percent at the time of writing. Today, there are celebrated female creators like Amanda Conner, Marguerite Bennett, Chelsea Cain, Kelly Sue DeConnick, Marjorie Liu, and Gail Simone, while new heroines explore every aspect of girl power and womanly strength. Some decades like the 50s, 60s, and 90s had a far smaller sampling of empowered and diverse female creators or even characters, while the 40s, 80s, and 2000 on brimmed with interesting storylines for many lesbian, handicapped, racially mixed and other often-sidelined characters. Feminism and other minority issues have always been linked, and in recent times, more writers are coming to realize this:

> One of the most important differences between Second and Third Wave feminism is the latter's awareness of intersectionality, or the ways in which various social markers, such as race, class, age, ability, body type, gender identity, and sexuality converge with sex and gender to restrict and police privilege. Intersectionality recognizes that sexism is connected to many other manifestations of prejudice and that the struggles of seemingly disparate groups for fair treatment are actually intertwined. A Feminist Hero's Journey, therefore, should not only grapple with topics relating to sex and gender, but other social hierarchies as well [Kyle 141–142].

With hundreds and hundreds of comics and films to choose from, I decided to limit myself to true superheroes—costumes and secret identities and/or hero names rather than just the tough action heroines. Diana Prince, Secret Agent doesn't fulfill the criteria, but Wonder Woman does. Xena and Buffy, like Lara Croft and Sarah Connor, were close, but not strictly superheroes with nicknames and costumes.

Older television shows like *Wonder Woman*, *The Secrets of Isis*, *Electra Woman and Dyna Girl*, *Sabrina the Teenage Witch*, and *The Bionic Woman* are episodic rather than arcing, so they don't lend themselves well to a study of this kind of plot. Likewise, children's shows like *DC Super Hero Girls*, *Justice League*, *Super Friends*, *Legion of Super Heroes*, *Teen Titans*, *Steven Universe*, *Avengers Assemble*, *Spider-Woman*, *Burka Avenger*, *Mighty Morphin' Power Rangers*, *Cybergirl*, *She-Ra: Princess of Power*, *Kim Possible*, and *The Powerpuff Girls* mostly share this episodic structure (though all offer valuable examples of girl power). Other shows, including *Powers* and *Heroes*, as well as George R.R. Martin's *Wild Cards* book series, are more crime dramas and political thrillers than stories that follow the superhero classic plot.

At the same time, there are some delightful heroine's journey arc shows like *Marvel's Jessica Jones, Birds of Prey, Witchblade, Agent Carter, Dark Angel,* and *Agents of S.H.I.E.L.D.* Male-centric shows like *Smallville* and *Arrow* have superheroine arcs for Lana Lang, Supergirl, Watchtower, Speedy, and Black Canary, though the hero is the central focus. *Vixen* deserves points for starring a Black female superhero in the *Arrow/Flash* universe, though it's only a half hour online cartoon in contrast with 22 hours per season each of *Arrow* and *Flash*. Finally, *Supergirl* (2015), breaking ground as a girl power superheroine show, has finally hit prime time. Still, her origin as Superman's sidekick lingers since her actions are always compared to the big man in blue.

Comic books offer most of these great heroine epics. However, many fans are surprised to hear there are girl power comics at all. For too many decades, Superman, Batman, Spider-Man, and Wolverine have dominated, with far more acclaim than their female counterparts. This is the biggest problem—comics have spent so many decades as a boys' only world that when everything changes, readers are slow to pick up on it. Greg Rucka notes, "Superhero comics—and I specify superhero comics—are a sexist medium. They are directed primarily, even to this day, at a fictional adolescent readership that is now in its forties! But they're still guys" ("An Interview with Greg Rucka").

The art is another significant factor—too many comics focus on the heroine's posterior or cleavage, drawing her in increasingly problematic outfits. When the base costume for Ms. Marvel or Wonder Woman is already a bathing suit, showing more skin gets worse and worse. Black Widow spends too much time dressing and undressing, often in her car backseat while instructing her driver not to look. This book focuses on story arcs, rather than examining the heroine's outfit in each. Certainly in many the posture, from the anatomically impossible "broken back" that emphasizes bust and bottom to the camera angles centering on the heroine's body parts, often detracts from her strength. Let it suffice to say, sometimes the heroine is dressed more powerfully, with muscles and actual pants, and sometimes she saves the world with a top that barely stays up. Male heroes rarely have this problem.

Explaining the way to conduct a feminist reading of comic books, Jennifer K. Stuller, author of *Ink-Stained Amazons,* suggests examining women's depiction—how bad is the "gaze" on exaggerated body parts and skimpy outfits? Also, how do the heroines relate to other women and do they deal with real women's issues of the time? ("Feminism" 240). Are they sidekick girlfriends or central characters?

A related tool for measuring feminism is the Bechdel Test (named for comic strip creator Alison Bechdel). It insists that a film or show must include at least two women who have at least one conversation about something other than a man or men. Thus it emphasizes that fictional women should form bonds and work as a team, rather than competing over boyfriends or functioning only as villainesses. Sidekick token females like Batgirl or Hawkgirl have significant problems in this area, especially if they are the only "girl." Of course, there are many excellent female team-ups, not just limited to *Birds of Prey*. Famous female friends have included Wonder Woman's Holliday Girls in the 40s and extensive circles of surrogate family in the 80s, as well as adoptive superhero sisters Donna Troy and Wonder Girl. Post-2012, Captain Marvel is seen calling Spider-Woman or Jessica Jones, just for time with friends.

Gail Simone's term "Women in Refrigerators" is another famous tool for considering feminism. As Simone discovered when she began categorizing, countless comic book females, especially love interests, were killed, maimed or depowered, most often as props to hurt the hero. The term references the shocking incident in *Green Lantern* #54 (1994), in which the hero comes home to find that his girlfriend, Alex DeWitt, has been killed and literally stuffed in a refrigerator. Female Robins and Batgirls have fared especially cruelly. Granted, since she observed the trend in 1999, matters have improved. According to Yabroff, "Simone says she sees a change since she wrote her 'refrigerator' rant 10 years ago. 'At that time, the trend was towards grim stories where female characters were killed,' she says. 'We only had a handful of female characters to look up to. Today we're not seeing those stories so much'" (Yabroff).

So what are the ingredients of the truly epic superheroine, whether in comics or film? Certainly, take her on the heroine's journey, putting something truly important at stake and having her grow through the experience. Give her more to battle than the evil makeup company of *Catwoman* the movie and more to battle in than stripper clothes. She also needs the full emotional range, including the humor and fun of Peter Quill and the genius of Tony Stark. A female friend or two. And of course, the epic plot detailed here.

◆◆◆ 1 ◆◆◆

Growing Up

Hero Birth: Wonder Woman (DC Comics, 1941)

One of the earliest heroines was also the most enduring. To many, Wonder Woman is the first and only superheroine (though far more have followed in her shining boots).

> Wonder Woman's emergence and success in the 1940s was unparalleled by any other woman in comic books during that time or since. Her continued success has defied the odds, though changes in the structure of the comic books helped to welcome young female readers. By and large, women as well as men were drawn to the 1970s television series. Since Wonder Woman's spectacular beginnings, she has become an icon for female empowerment, as well as a term for any woman who can multitask with finesse or show abilities that transcend traditional norms [Knight 314].

Thus this book begins with Wonder Woman, the ultimate archetypal heroine, and her divine birth. Mythic heroes have no ordinary parentage—most are half god and half human. Baby Hercules strangled snakes in his cradle, and his father Zeus disguised himself as rain, a swan, a bull, and a further pantheon of creatures to seduce his many paramours. All this marks the hero for a life of distinction at the tale's beginning. It also introduces the world of the magical, where superpowers, gods and destiny transform the mortals of earth. Marco Arnaudo adds in the critical work *The Myth of the Superhero*, "The superhero universe, so charged in tone and action, fosters the possibility of seeing the struggle between the basic forces of the human soul behind its stories, whether in terms of archetypes in the psychological sense or, more broadly, in the sense of narrative form" (118).

Young Diana stands out for her female-only creation by the goddesses and world of women. In the original origin story from the 1940s, Aphrodite, goddess of love, desires "women who will conquer your strongest warriors," as she tells Ares, the masculine war god and her rival. *Wonder Woman* #1 explains,

"Wonder Woman's story is the history of her race. It reaches back into that Golden Age when proud and beautiful women, stronger than men, ruled Amazonia and worshipped ardently the immortal Aphrodite, goddess of Love and Beauty." Of course, the author William Moulton Marston's use of Aphrodite complicates this imagery, as he believed women would one day conquer the world through the power of love. As he added:

> Frankly, Wonder Woman is psychological propaganda for the new type of woman who should, I believe, rule the world. There isn't love enough in the male organism to run this planet peacefully … what woman lacks is the dominance or self-assertive power to put over and enforce her love desires. I have given Wonder Woman this dominant force but have kept her loving, tender, maternal, and feminine in every other way [qtd. in Daniels 22–23].

Tenderly, Aphrodite sculpts the Amazons from clay, emphasizing their independence as she procreates without a man. She leads the Amazons to an island where they will live in peace forever, as long as no man ever steps there. It is a "promised haven of peace and protection," with a city "which no man may enter—a Paradise for women only" (*Wonder Woman* #1). Feminist Gloria Steinem, famously a great Wonder Woman fan, describes the mythic Amazon prehistory as an important part of women's cultural memory, now mostly erased by the patriarchy:

> Once upon a time, the many cultures of this world were all part of the gynocratic age. Paternity had not yet been discovered, and it was thought (as it still is in some tribal cultures) that women bore fruit like trees—when they were ripe. Childbirth was mysterious, it was vital and it was envied. Women were worshipped because of it, were considered superior because of it. Men prayed to female gods and, in their religious ceremonies, imitated the act of birth (as many tribesmen still do). In such a world, the only clear grouping was that of mothers and children. Men were on the periphery—an interchangeable body of workers for, and worshippers of, the female center, the principle of life [209].

Thus Wonder Woman and her Amazons hail back to such a time and emphasize the utopian perfection a world of women can create. Superheroines are in many ways the goddesses of today, bringing apocalyptic powers like Storm or Dark Phoenix. As Poison Ivy cries in *Batman & Robin* (1997) as she staggers from the transforming jungle: "Let the flames touch the sky. For I am nature's arm, her spirit, her will. Hell, I am Mother Nature. The time has come for plants to take back the world so rightfully ours. Because it's not nice to fool with Mother Nature."

After centuries pass for the Amazons, Queen Hippolyte desires a child. With Athena's guidance, she sculpts a small statue in her studio and prays until Aphrodite brings the baby to life. This is once more the fantasy of the gynocracy, where women do not need men. "The fairy tale elements of the story of

Wonder Woman's birth show the effort made to appeal to young female readers with a taste for magical, escapist fantasies, while also creating a world where women could live unhampered by the brutish, small-minded ways of men," explains Mike Madrid, author of the critical work *The Supergirls* (37). Once more, the powerful woman of the story gives birth absent of men, controlling her own choices as well as procreation. It's a magical moment, sacred and beautiful. The arrival of the Divine Child represents creativity manifested and a new level of consciousness. Clay, too, is the *prima materia*, often associated with the earth mother and the lifecycle. Diana is the primordial woman, shaped by the most basic source of creation.

Gifted by the gods, the child Diana possesses the wisdom of Athena and the beauty of Aphrodite, is faster than Mercury and stronger than Hercules. Newly awakened, the wonder child leaps into her mother's arms. On her island, it's implied that the women aren't magical, only exceptionally trained, to the point where they can bounce bullets off their bracelets. Diana, Steinem notes, "had come to her many and amazing powers naturally. Together with her Amazon sisters, she had been trained in them from infancy and perfected them in Greek-style contests of dexterity, strength, and speed. The lesson was that each of us might have unknown powers within us, if we only believed and practiced them" ("Introduction" 7). Thus the magical fantasy girl, created in a way no human of earth could imitate, becomes nonetheless an empowering role model for girls everywhere.

The birth of the divine child offers unity for her tribe, a moment of completion as individuals become a family. When Crystal and Quicksilver's daughter Luna is kidnapped, all the Avengers go to war. Storm notes, "A child links us to one another. Her very existence serves as a reminder that our histories are not as disparate as we would first believe." This child already bridges Avengers and Inhumans, and now inspires an X-Man to recover her.

Likewise, *Angela: Asgard's Assassin: Priceless* begins with the birth of the divine child as Freya has a daughter. Angela, her other, long-estranged daughter, returns to the home of her birth to see her, and Freya insists, "Now we have a future. Our republic will be built on this ground. All grudges forgotten between Vanir and Asgardian and even the mystical angels." However, Angela steals the child, teleporting away. The child, apparently, is also one of darkness. "A weapon, a bomb, a monster." Angela, the doer of dirty work, knows she must take the baby away from their galaxy. She plunges the baby into divine fire and purges the evil from her before sending her home and facing her own punishment. Here, Angela acknowledges the universal joy at her magical sister's birth, but approaches it with skepticism, fighting to reveal the truth.

X-Men: The End begins with a prophecy of the girl destined to be the next

Majestrix of the alien Shi'ar. "The Stars shall be her home and earth her destination. Mothered by War, her father's her Salvation" (Claremont). She is the daughter of Deathbird, the older sister of the current Majestrix, and thus has an awesome lineage. As the comic begins, "There are a lot of ways to tell this story. The best way starts with a girl. And a prophecy (in stories like this, there's always a prophecy). She didn't much care about that, really. Her name was Aliyah Bishop, after her paternal grandmother. What she cared about, all she wanted out of life, was to find the father she'd never seen. Such a simple dream…." Aliyah, who's been raised alone on a spaceship after her mother's death, accordingly goes seeking her father, X-Man Bishop. This is set against an epic Shi'ar-X-Men war, though her personal struggle and sweetness remain a current throughout. In the end, she claims the throne and thus creates peace between their worlds.

Most superheroines lack this kind of mystical birth—they are born ordinary girls to superpowered or ordinary parents, then develop abilities around puberty (Rogue, Kitty Pryde, Black Canary) or train heavily (Black Widow, Batgirl) or encounter supernatural forces that empower them (Mary Marvel, Invisible Woman, Captain Marvel, She-Hulk, White Tiger). However, a few sparkle from their first moments of creation, emphasizing the truly divine power they will hold.

Baby Hope has a destined birth in *X-Men: Messiah Complex*—she is the first mutant born after the devastation of House of M, which deprived most mutants of their powers. At once, several factions attack her hometown and slaughter most of the inhabitants, while everyone embarks on a quest to find the child. It's Cable, the warrior from the future, who must tell the X-Men she won't be safe in their time, with everyone hunting her. Professor X agrees and tells the X-Men's leader, "You can't control the future, Scott. You can only allow it to be born." He reluctantly gives Hope to Cable, who carries her to the future and trains her to be a warrior beside him. This way, Hope will have the option to choose a destiny for herself. After, more mutants are born, and it's revealed the girl is the only one who can stabilize "Generation Hope." She's become a savior in truth (Brubaker).

As she grows up on Paradise Island, Diana is the best of the elite Amazons, beating her sisters at every test. She is strong, fast, and nearly invulnerable. Other major powers include languages, telepathy with animals, astral projection, magic resistance, and mental communication—the number of mental gifts suggest a brilliant and enlightened young woman, far ahead of ordinary mankind. Similarly, Diana invents and flies an invisible plane and has invented the purple healing ray—making her the equal or more of any American man of the time. She can ride a horse, swim, and play American sports like hockey.

Steinem explains, "This beautiful Amazon did have some fantastic gadgets to help her … but she still had to get to the plane, throw the lasso with accuracy, and be agile enough to catch bullets on the steel-enclosed wrists" ("Introduction" 1). Once more, these are skills earth girls can master with practice, or so the story suggests.

As someone who can do everything, like Superman, she is an ideal figure, more god than mortal. As Marston explained in *The American Scholar*:

> Not even girls want to be girls so long as our feminine archetype lacks force, strength, power. Not wanting to be girls they don't want to be tender, submissive, peace-loving as good women are. Women's strong qualities have become despised because of their weak ones. The obvious remedy is to create a feminine character with all the strength of a Superman plus all the allure of a good and beautiful woman ["Why" 42–43].

Some of the themes here are problematic as Marston believed women should have power because of their goodness and loving nature—a form of objectification. Still, his paragon went out and captivated generations of girls with the knowledge that they could be anything without relying on men. In *Sensation Comics* #7 (July 1942), Wonder Woman announces her mission is to spend her time "defending America from the enemies of democracy and fighting fearlessly for downtrodden women and children in a man-made world."

In contrast with the absent mothers of weak-willed Disney princesses, Hippolyte protects her daughter with strength and prepares her for the savage outside world. She's also a great power. Steinem adds admiringly: "Queen Hippolyte founds nations, wages war to protect Paradise Island, and sends her daughter off to fight the forces of evil in the world" ("Introduction" 2).

A herald of these forces arrives in the person of Captain Steve Trevor of American Army Intelligence, who crashes his plane near Paradise Island. Sympathetically, Princess Diana rescues him, "carrying the full-grown man as if he were a child" in a loving gender reversal lest his feet touch the ground of the Amazons' homeland, as is forbidden (*All Star Comics* #8). Aphrodite and Athena order Hippolyte: "American liberty and freedom must be preserved! You must send with Capt. Trevor your strongest and wisest Amazon—the finest of your wonder women!—for America, the last citadel of democracy, and of equal rights for women, needs your help!" Hippolyte agrees, saying that her chosen one will save the world: "She shall go forth to fight for liberty and freedom and all womankind" (*All Star Comics* #8). Diana wins Hippolyte's tournament through her training and superior skill, setting off to defend the free world on 70 years of adventures. This is an achievement of choice, not birth, emphasizing that the heroine excels through both.

Another Golden Age heroine, the first from Canada, has a mystical birth story straight from myth. Nelvana of Northern Lights, created by Adrian Dingle, debuted in *Triumph-Adventure Comics* #1 (1941). The daughter of a mortal Inuit woman and Koliak the Mighty, King of the Northern Lights, she is imbued with power as well as a tie to the human community. When the god wed a mortal woman, the other gods were outraged and cursed him into invisibility. He vanished, only appearing to mortal eyes as the Northern Lights above. His son Tanero inherited this curse and became invisible ... at least, to white men. However, Nelvana discovers she can draw on her father's powers to turn invisible, disrupt radio communications, shapechange, or speed along the Northern Lights' rays and fight super-powered Nazi agents.

To her people, she is a figure of myth who will "cause the caribou to roam again and the seal to once more feed and clothe us." Even as the local chief promises this, "the earth is lighted by a blazing aura and the awe-stricken people look up to see a beautiful vision appearing." Nelvana descends to earth in a blaze of light, like a goddess from on high, and rides out (on her brother—now transformed into a dog, making it clear who's in charge). She summons down the Northern Lights, magnetizes them, and drags bombs out of the ocean to save her people and all the wildlife.

Whether Nelvana, Diana, Hope, or the other heroines that followed, the young champion has been blessed by the gods, and she grows into an adolescent of beauty, courage, and power. Next she must grow out of childhood and leave her safe world, to discover the stirrings of strength welling up from within.

Ordinary World: *After the Golden Age* (Novel, 2011)

After the Golden Age by Carrie Vaughn is a superhero novel—unusual in itself. It stars Celia West, born to her world's two greatest superheroes, though she has no powers herself. Each day in Commerce City is a struggle—she's a simple accountant while her parents, secret identities revealed long ago, live in their millionaire penthouse and fly about the city dealing out justice. They are Captain Olympus (Warren West)—mighty and invulnerable—and his fiery wife Spark (Suzanne West).

Beginning her story, Celia dwells in a rut. When supervillains kidnap her to get to her parents, she can't even muster the enthusiasm of terror. She knows her parents or the rest of the Olympiad, Arthur Mentis and the Bullet, will save her every time ... and they do. She has her gal pal, a superheroine named Typhoon who's really her college pal Analise. She begins dating a police officer, the mayor's son. But every moment is one in which she's judged by the lives of her parents. As she explains, "Your parents are the greatest superhumans Commerce City has ever known, but you ... you can't even ride a bicycle straight.

You can't win a swim meet. You can't fly or read minds or tell the future, or pyrokinetically manipulate pasta sauce. And your parents can't hide their disappointment. Tell me, what do you do then?" (150).

They in turn have always been disappointed as she's never lived up to their legacy by having powers. Her father gives in to his super-rage all too often, and Celia's mother hesitates to support her. Her father has never accepted her life and doesn't call or compliment her, ever. Everyone around her idolizes her parents, so they judge her as the failure and envy her for her relationship with them ... though the truth is, it's nearly nonexistent. Her boyfriend's parents wonder if their grandchildren will be freaks and ask about her parents' strategies. Total strangers psychoanalyze her life. And Celia just wants to be free of it all.

"The actual process of individuation—the conscious coming-to-terms with one's own inner center (psychic nucleus) or self—generally begins with a wounding of the personality and the suffering that accompanies it," explains Jungian scholar Marie-Louise Von Franz (*Individuation* 169). Much of the story is told in flashback, as her past actions largely influence her present ones. All the city is consumed with the trial of its biggest supervillain, the Destructor. However, Celia keeps secret that as a rebellious teen, she aided the Destructor in his quest for ultimate power. As Mentis explains to her parents, "Celia is not evil. She isn't even bad, really. She's only trying to find her own way in the world, and is doing it by getting as far away from you as she possibly can" (34). A moody goth teen, she went too far and nearly became a criminal, though when she returned to goodness, the records were sealed. To the dismay of Mark, her police boyfriend, these details come out during the trial. Instantly, Celia is dumped, suspended from work, and abandoned by Analise.

She lies around her house in despair, harassed by the press and surrounded by judgmental news. "Rather than confront the glass ceiling that holds her down, the hero decides not to stand up. She uses her creativity to make do with her situation and avoid the truth that she lives in a world that works against her growth as a person" (Schmidt, *45 Master Characters* 200). The heroine must break out, whether to a new state of being as a superheroine or to a new place where she can live in freedom. In fact, Mentis arrives and suggests she find a new path for her life instead of giving in. Miserable and judged by everyone, Celia fights to establish her own identity with her new life far from her parents. She begins investigating a new crime wave everyone is certain is the Destructor's work from within his prison cell. However, using only her smarts, she discovers a very different trail indeed.

Meanwhile, as Celia follows up on the crime spree, she meets a startling informant. The Hawk, a superhero who vanished 50 years before, comes to her and says he suspects the mayor. He also spins her world around when he points out he never had powers but still fought for truth and justice.

Thus inspired, Celia breaks out of her rut. On a crashing bus hijacked by a gun-wielding driver, she strangles him and drives the bus to a stop before it sinks into the river. Afterwards, Mentis tells her she's a hero and saved 40 people, while she insists she simply didn't want to die. Her ordinary heroism continues as she confronts her parents and finally follows clues to the Mayor's secret base, where he's attempting to create an army. She averts doomsday with ordinary human strength, proving that superpowers aren't necessary to save the day. However, without breaking free she would have spent all her life in a holding pattern, unable to grow beyond her parents' enormous influence.

Admittedly, the Ordinary World is often anything but, as Black Widow grows up training as an assassin in the Red Room and Hit-Girl's childhood is similarly vicious. Some heroines grow up in alt-worlds, some in the hideously warped Gotham, surrounded by the mad. But many live ordinary lives until they lose a friend or hear a cry for help—then they don their masks and head off into danger, relying on human abilities to save the day. The Spider Queen from 1941 was once "plain Shannon Kane." When her husband is suddenly murdered, she decides, "I'll have to carry on somehow!" She takes his formula and constructs bracelets that shoot "spiderweb fluid" and uses them to fight crime decades before Spider-Man (Madrid, *Divas* 78).

On the Marvel television show *Agents of S.H.I.E.L.D.*, all the characters are supposed to be normal humans, the Avengers' cleanup crew in a sense. However, the orphan Skye begins investigating her parents and discovers there's a great secret behind her childhood in scattered foster homes. After a dozen episodes of redacted files, Agent Coulson, Skye's boss and mentor, finds someone willing to tell the truth: Baby Skye was an unknown alien object, one that "the entire village had died trying to protect" ("Seeds" 112).

After this spectacular origin, with a baby who literally fell from the sky (giving extra weight to her self-chosen name), Coulson feels he must share this story with his protégé. In an instant, she transforms from ordinary girl to supernatural mystery. To his surprise, she accepts it with faith and optimism rather than terror. As Coulson notes proudly, Skye finds goodness in her origin:

> Her whole life, she thought she wasn't wanted, that she didn't belong, that every family that took her in didn't want her to stay, didn't care. But all that time, it was S.H.I.E.L.D. protecting her, looking after her. That's what she took away from the story—not the family she'll never have, but the one she's always had. Here I am, telling her something that could destroy her faith in humanity, and somehow she manages to repair a little piece of mine.

The world is full of evil and lies and pain and death, and you can't hide from it-you can only face it. The question is, when you do, how do you respond? Who do you become? ["Seeds" 112].

This is the story of a girl who was cherished by an entire village, as was her mother the healer. Her birth was considered a blessing and though it brought death, it was a sacrifice made to protect her. This legacy follows Skye through the series as her new surrogate family takes devastating risks to protect her as well. She continues questing for family, and finally meets her lost mother, just as Diana and heroines like her seek separation and independence. For all these questing heroines, the yearnings of adolescence lead them outward, seeking the part of the self they lack.

Still others, like Marie in the first X-Men film, lean in to kiss a boy and suddenly have superpowers erupt, forcing them onto a far more terrifying path as they flee their homes, transformed forever by the burden of puberty....

Adolescence: Ms. Marvel (Marvel Comics, 2014)

Fans were delighted by 2014's new Ms. Marvel by G. Willow Wilson and Adrian Alphona, a Pakistani girl who embodied an immigrant experience that connected with everyone, much like *My Big Fat Greek Wedding*. Maya K. comments on this moment of racial change in comics, noting:

[As an adolescent] I rarely saw my experiences reflected in mass media. This was somewhat isolating because at that age you don't understand that no matter the skin color, gender, sexual orientation, or heritage there is a common human experience called adolescence. Having diverse characters not only speaks to the minority child but to the majority child too. A white teen reading Ms. Marvel learns that the so called diverse character isn't really that different from themselves and, in fact, they are more similar than one would think. The straight teen reading about the LGBT teen sees themselves in the fears and alienation and then understands they are them. This narrows the divide between the "us" and the "them."

Half Afro-Brazilian and half Chilean Marvel artist Natacha Bustos notes, "A greater number of readers are looking for characters they can identify with, and above all, with the aim that any reader, whatever their background or lifestyle, is capable of transcending their own identities to see themselves in a mirror of entertainment for 20 or 30 minutes without any difference" (Towers, "Meet Marvel's Newest").

Kamala Khan of Jersey City adores the Avengers to the point of writing fanfic, but as a 16-year-old Pakistani girl trying to fit in, she thinks, "My chances of becoming an intergalactic super hero are even slimmer than my chances of becoming blond and popular" (Wilson, *Ms. Marvel: No Normal*). Kamala's restrictive parents have her life mapped out—staying home every night, perfect grades, med school, then marriage to a man of their choice and many children. Wishing to be normal for just one night, Kamala sneaks off to a forbidden party. This moment of rebellion, a departure from the normal world for one of excitement, signals her rocky adolescence, a desire to grow beyond her parents' confines. Thus it is matched by the coming of her powers. "In the first stage of this kind of adventure, the hero leaves the realm of the familiar, over which he has some measure of control, and comes to a threshold" (Campbell 146). Kamala crosses over, and everything changes, forever.

"It is no accident that superhero stories appeal most to those who are in the midst of change themselves. Pubescents and early adolescents, whose bodies are changing, were the audience of the first superhero comics" (Parker 125). Penelope Parker of Earth-11 (bitten by a radioactive spider) worries she'll be even more of a social pariah, then realizes, "No, wait ... I'm a pariah because I'm an 11-year-old that uses words like 'pariah.' This is just another weirdo thing. I can do this." She thus realizes she's gone from weird to "weirdo-er." She decides to save those in danger but immediately gets shy and flustered. Holding a rescued boy in her arms, she panics and turns red behind her brown bag mask in an uncertain adolescent response (Cook, "Penelope Parker"). Another young superheroine, Stature (Ant Man's daughter), shrinks to the size of her cereal bowl when accused of wrecking Iron Man's car, then grows to room-filling anger when she realizes he's tricked her. Thus her mood swings are incorporated visually into her superpowers (Knisley). "The mutant's constant struggle to contain and discipline his body adds an emotional and melodramatic element to the obvious male power fantasy and pubescent metaphor that is an enduring theme for the superhero genre" (Brown, "Supermoms" 186). This also works for the young women.

When Kamala storms out of the party, embarrassed by her overprotective friend Bruno, she finds herself engulfed by a strange mist. She passes out in it and has a vision of her idol, Ms. Marvel. The superhero tells her, "You're about to get the kind of reboot most people only dream about.... It's not going to turn out the way you think" (Wilson, *Ms. Marvel: No Normal*). In this scene, she receives a mentor and superpowers, all in a burst of transformation.

Waking, Kamala finds herself trapped in a casing of black stone. When she smashes out of her cocoon, literally and metaphorically, she discovers she's become Ms. Marvel—blonde hair, white skin, and signature outfit. Maya K. adds: "It doesn't surprise me that her Ms. Marvel persona is currently a white young woman because it reflects her wish to look like everyone else." Kamala wonders, "This is what I asked for, right? So why don't I feel strong and confident and beautiful? Why do I just feel freaked out and underdressed?" Her body is transforming, taking her towards adulthood, but like most adolescents, she feels gawky and misshapen, even in an outfit that makes other women look perfect.

Kamala transforms back to herself, but when she hears mean girl Zoe calling, she turns back into Ms. Marvel, thinking, "As soon as Zoe shows up I feel uncomfortable. Like I have to be someone else. Someone cool." Only by putting on Ms. Marvel's brave, assured outward persona does Kamala feel confident. When Zoe tumbles off the dock, Kamala recites her father's lesson from the Koran about saving lives and reaches into the water. Her hand expands to the size of a boat and she easily saves the other girl. Teens gather to beg "Ms. Marvel," as they think, for her autograph and she flees.

These growing limbs signal the "all arms and legs stage" as well as increased agency in the world. Now Kamala has the power to save a girl with a single scoop of her fingers—she need only decide how to use her new ability. There is even more happening beneath the surface. As she thinks, "It's like I have a completely new sense. It's not sight or taste or touch—it's something much weirder. Something almost—Inhuman." This too is a metaphor for adolescence, with new drives and sources of perception. The Terrigen Mist that transforms her is only an outward representation of her inner change. As Joseph Campbell describes it:

> What's running the show is what's coming from way down below. The period when one begins to realize that one isn't running the show is called adolescence, when a whole new system of requirements begins announcing itself from the body. The adolescent hasn't the slightest idea how to handle all this, and cannot but wonder what it is that's pushing him— or even more mysteriously, pushing her [Campbell and Moyers 142].

"Maybe this is what I've been *waiting* for," Kamala thinks, making a giant fist. "Maybe I'm finally part of something … bigger." At this moment, she throws off her imitation of Ms. Marvel. She leaves behind the blonde hair and black bathing-suit costume as Kamala finds a way to be a superhero as herself, with her own more modest and youthful style.

On returning home, Kamala runs for the fridge. As she says, "I'm hungry in a way I've never been hungry before. Ravenous. Starving. Seriously, I need a thesaurus. It's the healing I think, it feels like I skipped a night of sleep—like the healing power comes straight out of my life force." This too is a mark of both adolescence and transformation. However, she is also caught by her parents. As her father cries, "Tell me why my precious Kamala has suddenly become a reckless, disobedient girl I barely recognize," she is becoming a teenager, feeling dissatisfaction with an obedient life of childhood, before enlightenment hits.

When her father tells her she's named Kamala because it means perfection and she's perfect the way she is, she decides to become the best self that she can. She trains and learns "how to work with this new body instead of against it" and discovers what she can accomplish through her more mature physical self. As Kamala grows and shrinks, she considers how she's growing out of old parts of her life and no longer fits them.

She creates a costume from her burkini (a modest swimsuit with long arms and legs plus a tunic), emphasizing that she will cover up far more than the original Ms. Marvel. However, she adds a lightning bolt as an homage to the character and takes her old name (as Carol Danvers is now Captain Marvel, of course). "Maybe the name belongs to whoever has the courage to fight," she decides. When she's shot defending her friend Bruno from a robber (actually his punk brother Vick in disguise), she heals instantly, but Bruno discovers her secret. She uses her smarts and video game training as well as superpowers like a giant fist to sneak into the gang that is holding Bruno's brother and free him. Significantly, a fist is a symbol of agency and choice.

As she saves those around her (starting with her friends then expanding outward), she begins to take pride in her new identity as well as her old one, blending the two into a cohesive whole. As she announces: "This guy thinks he can threaten us where we live? Ms. Marvel has a message for him. This is Jersey City. We talk loud, we walk fast, and we don't take any disrespect. Don't mess." Nonetheless, she must soon rush off to her cousin's wedding as she balances responsibilities to superheroing and family. Thus ends the first collection, *No Normal.*

Ordinary teen life in Jersey City is a large part of the story, with Kamala's high school based on real high school McNair Academic High School (though it is renamed Coles Academic High School, after the actual street McNair is on). Further, as she grows from saving friends and family to defending her community, Kamala champions her generation. As the corrupt adult called the Inventor persuades teens their only value is in being human batteries, Kamala protests, "We're not the ones who messed up the economy or the planet. Maybe [adults] do think of us as parasites, but they're not the ones who are gonna have to live with this mess—" (Wilson, *Ms. Marvel: Generation Why*). She tells the teens not to give up on their generation and throw their lives away but to find a way to save the earth.

By the end of 2014, Kamala was guest-starring in *The Amazing Spider-Man* and soon joined the Avengers. With her cross-cultural appeal praised for drawing female Muslim readers into comics, many critics started calling her the new Spider-Man, teen icon for the current generation. Maya K. concludes: "This country has changed drastically in the almost 50 years (!!) since I was born. Almost half the population under 5 years old is not white. This is huge on so many levels because it means our mass media will change to reflect the demographic. It will have to because the market will demand it." With African American characters starring in *Fantastic Four*, *The Flash*, and *Spider-Man*, comics are expanding to reflect the modern audience.

While *Spider-Man* is the famous comic of the teen experience, there are others that star girls. Arriving in *Uncanny X-Men* #129 (1980), Kitty Pryde was created to be the younger generation. As she runs away from home and protests unfair teachers, she mirrors her teen readers. "She was, perhaps, the first realistic teenage superhero ever seen in comics, with all of the flaws and charms that come with youth—spunky, brilliant, courageous, while also insecure, flighty, and immature" (Madrid, *Supergirls* 232). Her power is disappearing—a clear metaphor for the wallflower student at the school—though writers Chris Clare-mont and Joss Whedon both find ways to turn this power into a formidable strength. Claremont's *Kitty Pryde and Wolverine* (1984–1985) in particular sees her growing to fight off a demon's influence and finally choosing who she wants to become. Memorably, Wolverine convinces her to save herself without her teacher's aid. As he warns, "If you run away to Charley, it doesn't matter if the cure's successful, you'll never be as strong again. You'll always be dependent on Xavier, always subconsciously turn to him when things get rough. Ogun will have broken your spirit—crippled the fundamental you—in a way that'll never heal." She takes his advice and trains, then fights to save herself.

The *X-Men* films by Bryan Singer also focus on young people as Rogue flirts with Iceman and learns to bring her new powers to their relationship. She is the first film's connection with teen vulnerability as Rogue runs away from home and desperately seeks a place to belong. By the third film, she's terribly constrained by her powers, a metaphor for her changing body. Caught in a love triangle as Iceman flirts with Kitty, Rogue must choose between love and power, in a heartbreaking decision.

On the run from their families, Marvel's Runaways are all teens, growing into their suddenly-acquired powers. Their saga follows them discovering romance and sexual identities as well as the blossoming of new abilities and priorities. Most of all, they grow from obedient children following the com-mands of their evil parents to those making their own moral choices. Through it all comes a sense of frustration, shared by Kamala, that they aren't taken seri-ously in the world of adult superheroes. As they travel to the past and intervene in an intergalactic war, the point comes up over and over that adults cause the wars and teens are the ones to die in them. In one arc, they travel to the 1900s, where Chase notes, "Nobody [treated] us like kids. For once, we got to be equals, not babies. Could use more of that in the twenty-first. Age doesn't make grown-ups" (*Runaways: Dead End Kids*). In a world where superpowers develop at puberty and teens are the top comic book readers, it seems the Runaways are right.

Eleven-year-old Molly spends the first *Runaways* comic asking parents and friends about changes in her body with "all this gross stuff happening" ... to their surprise, it isn't puberty but mutant strength. This metaphor echoes through many superhero comics, as the powers reflect new abilities and transformation. In *Avengers Academy*, Hasmat's powers erupt on the threshold of her first sexual encounter. "They said the trigger event for my powers was probably the excitement of my first time with Greg," Jenny relates. By becoming so toxic that she nearly kills Greg, she retreats from thus critical moment and shields herself metaphorically—no boy will touch her again (Gage, *Avengers Academy: Permanent Record*).

In the short comic "Becoming" by Mariah McCourt, a teen begins the story curled up on her bed thinking, "It figures that I would get mine later than everyone else I know." This is not menarche, but superheroism. Despite her misery, she dreams of flying over the city and protecting it in a dark cape and mask. As she climbs out of bed, she finds herself floating and realizes that growing up is not as terrible as she expected, but brings new powers she can use to transform her world. Likewise, in the children's comic *Power Pack*, Julie, on the verge of adolescence, complains to her mother that everything's changing. Her mother replies, of course, with the platitudes "Nothing ever stays the same ... not really. It may be a pain in the neck, but it's what life—and growing up— are all about!" She adds that if her daughter sprouted wings and flew she would love her just the same. Julie is struggling, of course, with this very issue (Simonson, *Power Pack*).

Transforming into an adult offers new terrors as world-saving powers may come at great cost. The independent *All Fall Down* sees 13-year-old Sophie Mitchell hit puberty and unknowingly steals the powers of every superhero and -villain on the planet. As the world's only remaining superhero, Siphon, the responsibilities of saving the world from every crisis are all down to only her. Worse yet, several former superheroes band together to take her down and restore their own powers. As she becomes an adult, she must defend herself in adult competition, with all the world's problems squarely on her shoulders. Of course, this reflects how growing up often feels.

"What's so scary about 12-year-old girls? They're shapeshifters. Not quite one thing or another. How can we have a meaningful dialogue with adolescent girls when we live in a culture that still can't talk about tampons? It's weird, right?" With this thought, Chelsea Cain and Kate Niemczyk's Mockingbird offers empathy to a girl who's just developed superpowers. Meanwhile, as an idiot policeman tries to tempt the girl with a juice box, she shoves him off the roof with an electric shock. Her t-shirt, ironically, reads "girl power" (#3). Mockingbird saves the man (who's complaining that he was never trained to talk to a 12-year-old girl), catches the juice box and drinks it, tells the head detective to recycle it for her, and heads up to talk to the preteen. She connects with her by understanding what she really feels—frustrated with adults but desperate to save the friends everyone thinks she's holding hostage. Thus Mockingjay emphasizes the need for a new kind of savior.

Another metaphor that appears is the acceptance of peers and finding a refuge. Kamala finally finds the Inhumans, who give her Lockjaw the super-powered dog. The other superheroes team up with her, embracing her as one of them. In *The Birth of Generation Hope*, the five new X-Men mutants have powers flashing out of control until their peer Hope comes and touches their hands. Hope describes the problem as "You're stuck between who you were and who you're going to be." One young woman named Laurie protests, "I don't want to be like this anymore. Everything hurts and everything is awful and—and I don't want to be a freak anymore and—" She's experiencing wild hair and skin changes, reflecting her transformation. When she bursts out, "How can anyone possibly help a freak like me!" and jumps off a roof, Hope grabs her. All at once, the new superheroine Transonic transforms into a force of beauty and power ... and flies (Fraction). While Hope's touch is the trigger, her generous acceptance and camaraderie is what they're really seeking.

Call to Rescue: *Go Girl!* (Dark Horse Comics, 2002)

"If you saw a truck bearing down on a child, would you stand there and let it happen?" Supergirl asks, defining heroism by deeds (David, *Supergirl*). The Call to Adventure for the heroine is usually one to save the innocent—family, friends, or sometimes strangers that suggest the most vulnerable, child-like part of the self. It's the central theme of the heroine's journey: "To become man's saviors and protectors, the rescuers of their children, the guardians of family, and thus, of the entire country and cosmos" (Frankel, *From Girl to Goddess* 317).

The Trina Robbins children's comic *Go Girl!* is a delightful play on super-hero stories with many calls to adventure. Robbins created the comic after meeting Anne Timmons, a talented artist who wasn't getting hired because her comics were drawn in a very feminine style, and the women decided to try a joint project together (Stuller 149). Robbins explains in the comic's introduction that the comic "is a dream come true and our chance to prove that girls—

and the boys who like them—will read comics, when there are comics for them to read."

As the tale begins, teen Lindsay Goldman learns her mother was the superhero Go Go Girl in the 1970s, complete with miniskirt. The pair lead an ordinary life. However, when Lindsay's best friend Haseena Ross is kidnapped, Lindsay promptly digs out her mother's costume and boots. Flying to the rescue (an inherited superpower), Lindsay tracks the kidnap car and crashes into the room where her friend is being held. She charges in and punches the kidnapper … though she fails to realize until almost too late that the elderly woman in a wheelchair is the ringleader. When Haseena, helping to trip the villains, shouts, "Go, Girl!" the new superheroine has a nickname.

Lindsay flies her friend to safety, but her mother suddenly arrives to tell her, "A superheroine never runs away!" Haseena, in the best friend role, has called for backup. After they all defeat the bad guys, Lindsay fears being sidelined. However, her mother tells her, "You could've gotten killed in there!" then adds in a disarming reversal, "You have to know how to fight! Being a superheroine takes more than just the ability to fly." Thanks to Lindsay's devotion to her friend, and her mother's understanding, her training has begun.

As critic Brandi L. Florence notes, Go Girl "is basically still a teenager at heart." More importantly, the comic is designed for actual girls, not pin-up fans. "Each issue features colored mini-posters, paper dolls, and artwork and letters from readers. With superheroines like these finally beginning to gain in popularity, perhaps the big publishing houses will begin to focus their attentions on strong characters and begin to write comics that do not pander to their audiences" (61).

A series of short adventures follow. In the next, an *It's a Wonderful Life*-style sequence, Lindsay saves several ungrateful strangers, and then wonders why she bothered. Promptly, a time traveler from the future whisks Lindsay to another dimension where she never existed. She discovers the boy she stopped from shoplifting lives on the street, the ungrateful girl she saved from a truck is in a wheelchair, and her mother sits in a park consumed by despair. When Lindsay discovers Haseena has been kidnapped and was never rescued, she rushes to save her best friend and helps the despairing community, doing her best to fix this other world. When she returns home, she's rewarded with as surprise party where her friends and family show they value her.

Often the heroine must guard those less fortunate, rescuing loved ones from the dark underworld of despair or confinement. If this lost soul is not her child or young brother, it may be her rationality (father) or her animus and emotional warmth (lover). Sometimes it may be an animal helper, one who offers an outside, thoughtful perspective. In each case, she is not just reuniting her family. She is reuniting her self [Frankel, *From Girl to Goddess* 151].

Likewise for Lindsay, saving everyone around her has led to a celebration, emphasizing that her complete self (symbolized by all the family) is united. Each innocent life means a healing of the community and thus her world.

The *It's a Wonderful Life* adventure has shown her how important saving strangers can be. In 2010's "Holiday Story," even the morally ambiguous Poison Ivy saves eco-tourists in the South American jungles, after reflecting that introducing their children to the rainforests was a noble thing to do. By intervening, she becomes a force for good in the world, expanding from protecting her forest to safeguarding those who visit it.

Saving one's loved ones is more common for superheroines. In *Kitty Pryde & Wolverine*, Kitty follows her kidnapped father to Japan so she can protect him. Sara Lance (Black Canary) spends Season Two of *Arrow* protecting her father and sister from a distance. She only reveals herself to persuade her father to leave town before the League of Assassins comes for both of them ("League of Assassins" 205). The kids of *Power Pack* go on a mission into space to rescue their parents, kidnapped by aliens. (Simonson, *Power Pack*). The Powerpuff Girls and their father-creator Professor Utonium genuinely love each other as well—though the girls give up in despair in the film, they rally to save him from a giant monkey attack. Donna Troy, Wonder Girl of the New Teen Titans, exclaims in "Clash of the Titans": "I love my mother, and if you hurt her or even try I will make you suffer" (Wolfman). Other heroines go seeking a vanished heritage. Amanda Conner's Power Girl bemoans having "no history. No family. No connection to anything or anybody that people cared about," so she sets out on her quest. The *Witchblade* television show likewise follows Sara on her search for her ancestry.

Amazing Spider-Man #8 sees Ms. Marvel and Spider-Girl each saving a baby in danger. Both children are symbolically connected to them—Ms. Marvel's has just emerged from a cocoon and has inhuman powers as she does. After she returns the baby to its parents, she worries how the family will deal with the child's new abilities—her own everyday conflict. Meanwhile as Mayday's father Spider-Man is dying in battle, her mother hands May her baby brother and tells her, "He's your responsibility now. Your greatest responsibility." The Spiderverse event begins and both siblings are whisked into the battle for the universe (Slott).

Wonder Woman of DC's New 52 is on a mission to protect the baby Zeke, whom the gods, especially the dreaded Firstborn, are trying to destroy. Even *Suicide Squad Volume 1* has Harley Quinn and her teammates discovering a baby is the cure to a zombie infestation. Escaping, they must keep the child safe. In the short story "Switchback," 16-year-old Mimi must protect her younger brother, age three, and teach him to hide his own superpowers.

"He's got to hide it, or they'll get him. You know that," she insists (Nocenti 241).

When the heroine saves little children, she finds she's healing the lost part of herself in need of care and attention. Rogue returns to Dodson, Mississippi. There they find a mutant who can unknit reality. Confronted by her devastating power, Rogue thinks, "I doubt it's intentional. Poor kid may not even realize she's the cause. Must be flat-out terrified." As she adds to herself, "I've been her." She coaxes the girl Lauren out with gentleness and empathy. As she thinks, "A little girl—okay, a little mutant girl—lets out a yelp for her momma and I go all weak in the knees. So is that what this is about? Me tryin' to help this kid the way folks never helped me?" (Rodi, *Rogue: Going Rogue*).

Of course, Go Girl isn't done rescuing. Next comes evil teacher Ms. Steele, who won't let her take tests when she's tardy and chips away at her self-esteem. Lindsay soon discovers she's been replacing the football players at school with simulacra and keeping the real ones locked in her basement. Ms. Steele plans on summoning demons to consume their bodies while she takes their souls and uses them to make herself young and beautiful once more. As the demonness gloats about sapping Go Girl's self-worth, she charges in, shouting, "I'm so over that," and punches the villainess. As Go Girl realizes, "All I had to do was believe in myself and her magic didn't work over me!" in a clear metaphor for self-determination. Her mother comes to rescue her, only to find Go Girl has handled it herself.

Go Girl has no particular love for the football players, but finds herself expanding from those close to her to her casual acquaintances as soon as they need saving. Campbell describes lifesaving as "the breakthrough of a meta-physical realization, which is that you and the other are one, that you are two aspects of the one life" (Campbell and Moyers 138). By saving others, Go Girl acknowledges the ties binding them all.

Soon enough, a group of girls at Lindsay's school set themselves up as rival superheroes, making her feel inferior. Suddenly, adult villainess Chatty Catty the Feline Fury kidnaps the superheroines because of how much she's always hated Go-Go Girl. When Go Girl arrives, Chatty Cathy happily plans a grandiose revenge, beginning with putting them all in the meat grinder. The girls shamefacedly reveal that they never had superpowers—they've only been hiring actors to defeat. However, Go Girl swings down from the chandelier and catches Chatty Catty, encouraging her rivals to join in and forming a larger bond of sisterhood with her classmates. Empowering others is an important step, emphasizing that saving people means their inner well-being as well as the outer.

Next they visit Go-Go Girl's old partner, Right-On Sister, who now owns a dude ranch. Their hostess reveals that her cattle have been vanishing and she needs Go Girl's help. Branching out to her mother's friend and the larger public, Lindsay agrees. She catches the cattle rustlers only to discover the bigger culprit behind them—visiting aliens taking the cattle and leaving one of their own in return. Thus she moves beyond the problems of earth to even help intergalactic tourists in trouble.

Her final adventure comes when her mother goes to see her old flame and partner Wowman, who's substantially less impressive than he thinks he is. Go Girl must tell him, "A superhero doesn't fight bad guys for *money!* We do it 'cause we're superheroes and—and that's what we do!" A bomber bursts in, but mother and daughter save the day, while Wowman admits he can no longer fly and has been faking his powers for years. Lindsay ends the series of shorts by making a friend of the runaway Marnee and founding the team Girls United Against Pushy Parents, or GUPPIES. With the start of her own team, she can save the world with many more adventures to come.

Superheroines, even more than superheroes, are protectors of life. Steinem says of Wonder Woman: "This was an Amazon super-hero who never killed her enemies. Instead, she converted them to a belief in equality and peace, to self-reliance and respect for the rights of others. If villains destroyed themselves, it was through their own actions or some unbloody accident" ("Introduction" 9). Through her adventures, from Golden Age to modern times, Diana empowers young women, teaching them to be strong. "You see girls, there's nothing to it," she explains while lifting a boulder in *Wonder Woman* #13 (1945). "All you have to do is have confidence in your own strength!"

The film tie-in *Suicide Squad: Most Wanted Deadshot and Katana* #1 has Katana going to Markovia to save important scientist Dr. Helga Jace from warlords, only to be confronted by a crowd of frantic villagers, some pregnant or surrounded by children. "Perhaps my instincts are in league with the demons in my sword," she thinks, but she agrees to help as long as they follow her orders. The warlords' leader Lady Eve brandishes her claws and cries, "Die, knowing your alleged savior, Katana, has abandoned you, to save herself!" Katana, however, attacks from the shadows. She wins the day and only leaves to draw off the enemies' violence. She has saved everyone, including, of course, the little girl and her cat (Barr).

One of the funnier characters in Gail Simone's *Welcome to Tranquility* is the Pink Bunny, Suzy Fury. A young man sneaks up on her as she showers, and she tackles him, flinging him across the room, then preparing him to punch him on her pink-curtained bed, noting, "Let me show you *another* fun thing a man and woman can do in bed, Mister." When he begs for mercy, and she recognized the boy she once took in and helped, she makes him breakfast and he explains that the Hellkitten ordered him to murder her in return for the antidote for the poison she gave him. However, he dies rather than hurt Suzie.

Enraged, Suzie goes after Rosario Munez, also known as "Hellkitten." She thinks (in pink thought bubbles), "Maria, you evil bitch. You killed this poor sop just to hurt me. Well, guess what—I know where you live." In pink bunny outfit with an incongruous pistol, she drives to the evil woman's mansion and punches the guard in the face, then tears apart the steel gate. As the women argue and fight, the bunny turns the Hellkitten's poisoned glove on her, with the taunt "Stop hitting yourself." She dies and the bunny smirks that she can "laugh it up in hell."

Later an older Pink Bunny defends her students at the school from a zombie attack. As one girl notes, "Pink Bunny, Suzy, she's been like a mom to me. Way more than my real mom! We can't leave her with those things." The two girls Pink Bunny sacrifices herself to save (one in flower decorated pigtails) unleash a swarm of power against the zombies. Thus by being protected, the next generation gains awesome power. Passing on this strength allows superheroines to expand their ethics of caring, spreading new saviors throughout their community.

Refusal of the Call: *X-Men* (Film, 2000)

The Bryan Singer film *X-Men*, despite its title and its framing of Wolverine as a main character, is absolutely a heroine's journey epic. It follows young Marie from the start, as the X-Men describe how the mutation of superpowers suddenly spring into life during moments of great stress. The film superimposes Marie having her first kiss. This moment plunges the boy she kisses into a coma and triggers her flight into the world. Clearly, she can protect her family and friends by keeping her dangerous superpower away from them.

She's next seen hitchhiking through the northern wilderness, clearly penniless as she sits hopelessly at the bar. She has no clear destination, only "away." Whenever she touches someone, she drains them of energy, so she keeps herself distant, untouchable. However, just as one boy triggered her journey, another launches her on the next stage. Wolverine is equally lacking a destination, but cut off from the past as well. The two aimless adventurers cling to each other as Marie stows away with Logan and they find comradeship on their travels. If Marie is the sweet, harmless adolescent, Wolverine is adult competence, savagery and rage.

Soon enough, Magneto's forces attack and Professor Xavier's X-Men rescue the heroes and carry them to the metaphorical magical world. In this instance, it is Professor X's school, a world in which the "Gifted" students can grow and flourish without mistreatment from the "normal world." There, Marie, now calling herself Rogue, thrives and makes friends, especially with Bobby Drake, Iceman. He of course represents the sweet romantic urges fluttering within her, even as she fears to open herself again.

Her gift is arguably the most powerful of all, as she can borrow the gift from any mutant. Seeking Logan, she bursts into his bedroom and, dreaming, he impales her on his claws. She steals his lifeforce and heals herself. In this moment, she claims the power of the Wolverine, deliberately using her gift in her greatest extremity. However, doing so terrifies her and she flees the school. This is a second refusal of the call, a denying of the magical world and all it offers and rejection of her own power. Terrified, she prefers the ordinary world that will never accept her to a haven where she can become a heroine. In her gently-brought up world, nice girls don't seek power and certainly don't tear it from mighty men. Rogue has transgressed, and thus fears herself. It's Logan who comes and persuades her to return. Thus he acts as her animus, the masculine guiding force from within that encourages her to claim her powers, the role model she wishes to become.

Several other young superheroines refuse their calls. Lunella Lafayette, Moon Girl, is a nine-year-old young science whiz and inventor who's frightened that she might suddenly transform into an Inhuman. Tinkering with Kree gadgets, she's desperate to control the circumstances of her transformation, reflecting her finding power over her own life. Thus her mission becomes one to prevent having powers and symbolically avoid growing up. She also sees her smarts as her real superpower—she doesn't want another one. Assistant editor Emily Shaw explains: "The character lives in this world where people don't really get her ... that her brain just works a little differently than all of the other kids her age really resonated with us, and that idea of feeling sort of isolated and on your own during that very early time of life we thought was really compelling, and could really resonate with a lot of readers. That's what really gave the story its heart at the beginning" (Towers, "Meet Marvel's Newest").

While the heroines may struggle, often for good reasons, inevitably they're drawn into the fight.

In another adventure, 12-year-old Idie Okonkwo of Nigeria suddenly becomes a mutant with powers over heat and coolness. As she huddles in a church and prays, the people of her village tell her, "God will not protect you from us. You are a witch child and God will not listen to you.... There is nothing you touch that does not suffer and die!" When the X-Men come for her, Storm tells her God only gives people burdens they can carry and bids her be her own shepherd. As Storm calls her "a treasure," they talk her down from the brink of suicide and show her she can make a difference. She later names herself for the goddess Oya (Fraction, *Birth of Generation Hope*). Later, fighting beside the X-Men, the teen becomes a killer, mercilessly slaughtering the enemy. "Once you accept that you're a monster, being a murderer doesn't bother you quite so much," she says. At this, Wolverine breaks from Scott Summers's Utopia and leads Idie and many of the children to safety at their old school. This too is a retreat, though a brave stand in the face of the unending violence. When Idie worries that the X-Men have shattered because of her, Wolverine replies, "You helped lead us *home*" (Aaron, *X-Men: Schism*). Often recalling why they chose the mission can be the key, and running can be a braver choice than fighting.

Sometimes a parent is the force holding back the heroine. Kortni of *DC Bombshells* discovers her real father is a British lord. When she finds him, he offers her dolls and ponies, every imaginable luxury. However, when she hears a call to battle from her sister Supergirl, her father clutches her determinedly, insisting, "I can't lose you again." He actually has his manservant chloroform her so he can tuck her into bed in a room he's decorated with stuffed animals. "You're only seventeen! A little girl ... I have to keep you safe," he insists. This is a great fantasy, to have one's parents' protection. In this case, however, this imprisoning will keep the heroine from fulfilling her destiny, and she flees (Bennett, *DC Bombshells* #25).

The great patriarch of the X-Men, the professor, encourages Rogue to master her terrifying gifts and stay with the X-Men. However, the one who truly makes her claim her power is the story's villain.

Magneto's great plan involves forcing Rogue to wield his own power to destroy the human government's superiority, transforming the leaders of the UN into mutants. By using Rogue ostensibly as a pawn he forces her to realize that she is the most powerful of all—for one night she can even be Magneto.

Rogue is very much a "girl," a teen runaway as heroine who soon falls for a teenage boy though she has "a little crush" on her older male mentor Wolverine. Magneto kidnaps her and chains her in something that might as well be a tower ... all he would have to do is threaten to marry her to complete the fairy-tale pattern. In fact, his great scheme will drain her to the point of death.

In the wake of this plan, the superheroes band together to save her, but they are not truly a rescue from without. They can be seen as embodying aspects of her psyche, like Dorothy's heart, brain and courage gathering to sneak into the witch's lair and aid her. Wolverine, the strongest of them, makes it to Magneto's machine, but there he can only save her by surrendering to her power—holding her close and using her own gift to save her. In fact, he sacrifices his own power and nearly his life for that chance, emphasizing his yielding to her will. It's Rogue's power there that saves the day.

She ends the story secure in her place at the school, finally a superheroine, marked by a touch of white hair that indicates maturity and wisdom—she has finally grown up. Logan leaves the school seeking his past, launching himself on an adventure that is more about him, as this film has truly explored its central heroine.

Rogue's inability to be touched is a defensive barrier—in fact, those who touch her fall into comas or die. As one novelization explains, "She had to admit, there was a fundamental safety in her power. Her body was absolutely her own, and no one could lay a hand on her without suffering the consequences. Could she handle being vulnerable?" (Claremont, *X-Men: The Last Stand* 183). Thus it resembles the barrier of thorns surrounding Sleeping Beauty or the ring of fire around Brunhilda. The virginal heroine is unready for men, so her world creates a powerful force of armor around her. Only when she matures (shown in the comics by Rogue's secondary mutation) does the shield lower at last.

Of course, the third film sees her deliberately giving up her power, taking the cure so she can touch and be touched at last. The clinic resembles an abortion clinic, emphasizing her own rights to her body. In the novelization (most likely based on an early version of the script), she can't go through with it and continues as an X-Man. It explains, "Being a mutant, that was fate's fault, or nature's, or God's; you could vent against those higher powers all you pleased. The cure, however, was all on you" (Claremont, *X-Men: The Last Stand* 182). Still, it's implied that Leech's powers of negating X-Men's abilities can offer her a natural, more temporary solution (286). In the film, she makes the choice she feels is best for herself, taking the cure, which will allow her to finally connect with others. While this is a loss of superhuman power, it also suggests growing up.

Making the Choice: Runaways (Marvel Comics, 2003–2008)

The Runaways are a delightful Marvel team created by Brian K. Vaughan that comprise many backgrounds and certainly embody the coming of age experience—especially because they're all teens. They are Nico, a Japanese American Catholic goth girl; Alex Wilder, an African American gamer; Gert, overweight with purple hair; and blond slacker Chase Stein. Added to this are Molly Hayes, the only preteen at age eleven, and Karolina Dean, a pale lesbian vegan, who are both far from helpless damsels. Later on they pick up Victor Mancha, a half-Mexican cyborg who's the son of Ultron.

Their call to adventure is not to save someone, but, as the title suggests, to run away. After they watch their parents gather for their annual secret ritual and murder a teenage girl, all the children are shocked. "Whoever they are, we have to stop them," Alex Wilder insists. The teens discuss it and find themselves divided on calling the police. Nico finally says, "We're talking about our parents. Mine aren't perfect, but they're not monsters. They never were to me, anyway. But I keep thinking about that girl. She wasn't much older than us, y'know? If nothing else, we should try getting to the bottom of this for her" (Vaughan, *Runaways: Pride and Joy*). When the police dismiss their claims, the teens decide to search their houses and find proof.

At this point, they are just sneaking around at night, trying to solve the mystery. However, their parents are determined to shut down their investigation. Without warning, they threaten to kill Molly to control the teens. "This is where the coping strategy the character has chosen falls apart. It no longer works for her, and her whole life and everything she believes in has changed" (Schmidt, *45 Master Characters* 207). As the group debates running or surrendering, Alex suggests they charge in and rescue their friend. Nico points out that they have to take care of each other, and the Runaways go to battle. This moment of leaving home is a profound transition. Campbell notes, "All children need to be twice born, to learn to function rationally in the present world, leaving childhood behind" (Campbell and Moyers 9).

The transition is instantly rewarded. When they rescue Molly, she surges with mutant strength as her powers suddenly awaken. Likewise, as they investigate, Gert finds Old Lace, the telepathic dinosaur her parents have left her, and Chase finds his inventor parents' fire-throwing gloves. Karolina removes her confining med-alert bracelet and discovers she's an alien with powers of flight and rainbow light. While fighting her own parents, Nico is shocked when the magical Staff of One leaves her mother and bonds with her. For all of them, the decision to find independence metaphorically and literally triggers their abilities and they become superheroes. "Traumas that fell most people transform the superhero into someone bigger and better, stronger and smarter" (Parker 129). Going independent has given them their power.

Chase leads them to a cave in Griffith Park as they become runaways in truth. They name it "The Hostel" as it's a shattered mansion buried beneath the earth, a hidden place of safety where the teens can hide (Vaughn, *Runaways: Pride and Joy*). Underground represents the subconscious and the underworld. It's a place of buried secrets and desires, where the savage goddesses reign, while up above the pale princess does her duty. Thus heroines flee to the forest or the underground world and there discover their strength and hidden identity. Campbell notes:

All these different mythologies give us the same essential quest. You leave the world that you're in and go into a depth or into a distance or up to a height. There you come to what was missing in your consciousness in the world you formerly inhabited. Then comes the problem either of staying with that, and letting the world drop off, or returning with that boon and trying to hold onto it as you move back into your social world again. That's not an easy thing to do [Campbell and Moyers 129].

On arriving, the teens immediately choose nicknames, emphasizing that they are no longer their parents' children but superheroes. They travel the town performing good deeds like stopping robberies, before they finally enter the lion's den to confront their parents and end their evil schemes. Through it all, well-meaning adult heroes like Captain America or Cloak and Dagger function as threshold guardians—forces that try to stop the heroes from escaping their restrictive lives and pursuing their destinies. Each time the children must battle the voices of adulthood and find salvation in one another.

After their adventure, they're all put in foster homes. However, when they break out for a reunion, Chase reveals he's found Old Lace. After rescuing her from a Stark holding area, Gert says, "I'm not going back…. I thought I'd be able to put up with being controlled by know-nothing adults again … but I can't. Not after everything we've been through" (*Runaways: The Good Die Young*). Karolina craves the freedom to fly. When Chase finds his parents' leapfrog airship, they all take off.

Karolina has a separate call to adventure in *Escape to New York*. She kisses Nico and gets rejected, then feels utterly miserable. She moans, "I thought I'd finally figured out who I was, but now I know I don't know *anything*." As she calls herself a freak as well as an alien, she feels that being lesbian means she will never fit in on any planet. She feels increasingly out of place, a misfit even among her superpowered friends. She insists she doesn't belong with the Runaways or anywhere. As she wishes on a star that she'd never been born, Nico alerts her that the star is crashing.

A spaceship lands, and a handsome, dark-skinned young man tells her, "I know you better than anyone." He reveals that he is her fiancé, come to take her away from backwater earth. As she defensively unleashes her power on him, he calls her abilities "glorious" and simply admires all she is. He adds that he is an alien Skrull. Though he attacks her friends and threatens to blow their ship out of the sky, Karolina finally meets with him when he asks to talk, especially when he tells her that her own planet is at stake.

He explains that he is the prince of one planet, and his parents and Karolina's agreed their children should wed. Now the two planets are locked in battle. As he adds, touchingly, "This is a mindless conflict being fought between the adults of each world, but there are youths on both sides who have known nothing but bloodshed their entire lives, and they are eager for an end to the war." He hopes their dynastic marriage can bring peace. Karolina sadly refuses, adding, "I can't do it because it'd be a lie." As she shamefacedly adds, "I like girls."

To her surprise, Xavin tells her this is no problem, as Skrulls are shapeshifters. He transforms into an equally hot girl, and begs Karolina to at least see their homeworlds and consider the marriage. Karolina agrees, because, as she says, "people are dying," and she's committed to fixing her parents' mistakes. More than that, however, is the promise of not having to hide her rainbow light or her attraction to women, but have both celebrated by a planet of her own people. She need no longer be a freak and alien but can go home (Vaughan, *Runaways: Escape to New York*).

> The heroine's journey takes her from birth through the world of life. This can also be called the external world of society and manners, the world of common day, one of homework and agendas and crying babies and muddy floors. By contrast, the underworld below the horizontal split is the realm of the unconscious, of magic, of desires made manifest with a wish, and, yes, of death. This is the woman's traditional sphere of power—the world of emotion and spirit [Frankel, *From Girl to Goddess* 176].

Though Karolina has never fit in on earth, alien worlds are her true realm of destiny and power.

The magical land is most often a reflection of the heroine—the mystical place where she truly belongs. In 2010's "Holiday Story," Poison Ivy visits the South American jungles and reflects, "Down here, I'm not a freak, an oddity to be unfairly judged and locked away. In this land I'm a goddess." Thus surrounded by the plant world, she leaves behind her human identity if only for a time. Similarly, the penultimate season ten episode "Prophecy" on *Smallville* sees Supergirl take the Legion of Super-Heroes Ring, and fly off to find her own people and lost Kandor. On the show *Birds of Prey*, teen Dinah has visions of the warrior team and travels to Gotham to find them. There she finds a true home among metahumans like herself. A place with soul-friends or a true home, where all one is fits perfectly, is the ultimate goal.

> Not all adventures are so profound; one can attempt something new, like skydiving or running for office. Or one can quest to reclaim one's lost childself, the most innocent and playful part of the personality. One may seek true love, or quest to destroy the evil demons of one's soul. This is a questioning, a setting forth, an opening of one's attention to the forces of the universe and the faint whisper of the unconscious from deep within [Frankel, *From Girl to Goddess* 19].

Nonetheless, the biggest, most epic stories see the heroine cross time and space to find her great love, home, or destiny. On a time-travelling journey to

1907, the Runaways find two girls like themselves in need of saving. Victor falls for Lillie McGurty, "the Spieler," who can dance on air. The two soar into passionate, adoring love. Victor asks her to come to the future, but Lillie is afraid. Victor finally gives her a note passed to him by an old woman in the future: "This is your last dance. Your chance to change your fate. Leave this world for a better one or waste your days in regret." For all the decades after, Lillie sits alone, regretting not going with Victor and the Runaways, waiting until she can send this message back in time. Nonetheless, young Lillie refuses. "Here I'm brave! Now! In the future? What if I don't like it! What if you don't like me? What if I can't dance?" She stays behind and time continues to loop, as each time she waits a century to send herself back a message, and each time she refuses (Whedon, *Runaways: Dead End Kids*).

Saving the workers at a destroyed factory, Karolina finds one victim, Klara, grew a trellis of roses and climbed down it. The next day, Karolina discovers an older man is abusing the girl, so she goes to see Klara with Molly in tow. Karolina tells her, "I just thought you might want to know there are other people like you, and that ... you don't have to hide, or let people push you around ...." Molly, eager for a friend her own age, invites her to join them. Klara reveals that the older man is not her father but her husband. The girls are horrified and insist on spiriting her away. Klara in turn is horrified by Karolina and Xavin's lesbian relationship, which according to her religion is forbidden. Molly angrily calls her "just another grown-up" and leaves her. As the Runaways are about to return to the future, Klara reconsiders and comes running, covered in fresh bruises from her husband. The Runaways embrace her and carry her to the future (Whedon, *Runaways: Dead End Kids*). One turn-of-the-century young woman refuses the challenge, but the other crosses over and finds herself in a world of modern wonders.

Crossing into a new adventure, to a different time and space is especially scary. Nonetheless, the young heroes face the threshold with courage, determined to find freedom and adventure with teens like themselves. The search for a place to fit in is paramount here, as all are young teens seeking a community without the control of the corrupt grown-up world.

The transition often appears when the heroine stands at a significant crossroad. On the day of her wedding, Susan Murphy is struck by a meteorite that makes her suddenly grow over 50 feet in height in Pixar's *Monsters vs. Aliens*. Symbolically, she is bursting out of the ceremony she knows is wrong for her, as her powers manifest themselves. Usually a wallflower, this is her strength and desire to be seen, slamming into the forefront at last. As she says later, "All that talk about us—'I'm so proud of us,' 'Us just got a job in Fresno'—there was no us, it was just Derek. Why did I have to get hit by a meteor to see that?"

♦♦♦ 2 ♦♦♦

Superhero Tools

Superpowers: *Wild Cards* (Book Series, 1987–)

Long before his *Game of Thrones* television series became famous, author George R.R. Martin used to play the role-playing game *Superworld* with some of his science-fiction friends. Their campaign evolved into an ongoing book series, in which many authors wrote about their own characters. Melinda M. Snodgrass is co-editor, and many top science fiction and fantasy authors have contributed chapters.

The series is quite large, with 12 initial volumes from Bantam between 1987 and 1993, then five more from other publishers, then five from Tor, with more scheduled. Though the series exists largely under the pop culture radar (despite the recent success of both *Game of Thrones* and superheroes) it's surprisingly long-lasting. A television show is in the works.

On an alt-world earth, in 1946, an alien virus spreads. It kills 90 percent of those who come into contact with it, while 9 percent mutate into deformed creatures (Jokers) and the remaining 1 percent gain superpowers (Aces). Some heroes, known as Deuces, have rather useless powers like changing color or producing fire from their hands. Others, usually the Jokers, have their powers pushed to their disturbing conclusions—Chrysalis has transparent skin displaying all her organs, and Caitlyn is beautiful, but her eternal youth leads to stiffness from stonelike calcification.

This series offers an unusual view of superheroes beyond its already unusual prose format. Much like the stars of *Heroes*, these characters span races and nationalities. There are grandmothers, toddlers, and successful businessmen, mostly just trying to live ordinary lives. The majority are not precisely superheroes as they don't go around saving the day, but their spectrum of powers is intriguing as the authors have unlimited freedom to break down barriers.

Many superpowered women stand out in the series, permanently transformed by their powers. Radha Valeria O'Reilly, Elephant Girl, can switch to her elephant form and even fly, as can the flashy and beloved winged woman Peregrine. Arachne can weave silk from her own body into beautiful scarves. Bagabond, a homeless woman, uses thousands of animals as spies and helpers. These bonds with all of nature or specifically flying creatures and spiders all come from feminine symbolism, emphasizing intuition and connection with nature.

Ana Cortez, Earth Witch, has always earned a living through ditch-digging and helping with gardening projects. To Ana's shock, a priest tells her to give her astounding earth powers up.

> "Then here is your penance. If you are truly sorry for what happened, and you seek true forgiveness from God, then you will never use your ace again. You must abandon your power."
>
> She held her breath, forgetting to inhale. Whatever she had expected to hear, that wasn't it. Not use her ace? Might as well tell her heart to stop beating, it was that much a part of her.
>
> "Can you do that, Ana?" Father Gonzales continued. "Scripture tells us that if our eye offends us, we must pluck it out. Your power has wrought harm. Therefore, you must renounce it. Do you understand?" [Vaughn, "Nuestra Señora"].

Her father tells her that the priest is wrong and adds, "Your power comes from God, and from the mother of God." Ana has inherited this great feminine power, and should use it to save those in need. Her grandmother had her own nature powers, as her father explains: "They say she is like a vine, that her skin is green, and instead of limbs, branches grow from her. But Ana, what I haven't told you is that she is also holy. A great *curandera. La Curandera de Las Flores.* Because flowers bloom from her, and she plucks these flowers from her own body, dries them, and makes medicines from them. She cures thousands of people" (Vaughn, "Nuestra Señora"). Ana travels to meet her grandmother and thus explores her own inner magic.

The earth is intrinsically feminine, though only a few heroines (Skye from *Agents of S.H.I.E.L.D.*, Power Girl's apprentice Terra, X-Man Petra, Lavagirl of *Sharkboy and Lavagirl*) take its world-transforming powers. The novel *The Strange Adventures of Rangergirl* features true believer Jane getting earth powers. She explains, "I can break down doors, gouge my way through walls. Mud can be soft debris, or it can be dried and fired and made solid as bricks. It can ooze through the tiniest cracks, or it can fall down a hillside and destroy a village" (Pratt 86). Thus Ana's power is one of the greatest ancient goddesses, though it can also be subtle and flexible.

Ana travels with several superheroines in the book *Busted Flush.* The

Amazing Bubbles is nearly indestructible—when she's hit, she grows enor-mously fat, and can even turn the fat into rubbery bubbles that are her weapons and tools. Her Korean girlfriend, Ink, can make her thoughts appear as text on her skin. There's Kate Brandt, Curveball. Midnight Angel has a flaming sword and wings. The Canadian heroine Simone Duplaix, Snowblind, can blind every-body within a certain radius. Jerusha Carter, Gardener, can grow plants quickly. Though the women are in many ways more interesting, the men include Drum-mer Boy, Holy Roller, Toad Man, Lohengrin, Rustbelt, and The Llama. The leader, John Fortune, carries the female Ace Sekhmet inside his head, giving him some gender flexibility as he transforms into a fire-breathing lioness, yet struggles with the destructive goddess inside him. There's also Noel Matthews, Double Helix, born a hermaphrodite, who can also transform into the alluring spy Lilith or the tough guy Bahir. Using these three bodies, Noel has many bosses, playing a double and triple agent to steer the course of the world. Together they call themselves the Committee.

Their team has a great deal of tension, especially in romance. Cameo can channel the dead through their material possessions. When she's asked to rein-carnate Aliyah Malik, she discovers the woman was the Ace Simoon, with an incredible tornado power. However, there's some awkwardness for Aliyah at being among her still-living friends. The two women begin a love triangle with Jonathan "Bugsy" Tipton-Clarke, who can turn into a wasp swarm. Eventually they find a balance, but only when the lifecycle continues by Aliyah's returning to death.

The Committee investigates the totalitarian People's Paradise of Africa, where they get drawn into a Nigerian civil war. As the poster-child Dolores cures others by taking their pain and injury into herself, she considers the state secret that led to her creation. "And if she mentioned the experimental injection she and the others received there … even her sudden heroine status wouldn't save her" (127). Young women whose superpowers are forced on them by the patriarchy make a common trope in superhero fiction, stressing their exploita-tion. Tom Weathers, the Radical, who's the chief enforcer for her country, has her killed so she won't reveal that he started the war, but he has her preserved forever as a martyr and hero of the people. Added to the mix is another victim, the Texan teen Drake Thomas, cruelly nicknamed Little Fat Boy since he can cause nuclear explosions. The People's Paradise wants him as a pawn. The Committee tries to protect him, but the government organization SCARE wants him dead.

Juggling all these plots, Earth Witch, Gardener, Bubbles, and Cameo/ Simoon end up in New Orleans, trying to protect the city from a flood. There they plant trees and raise embankments in a straightforward intervention. After, however, they're drawn into the dark, mystical side of the city as they meet the mysterious Hoodoo Mama, who can animate the dead and use them as her tools.

This young woman, Joey Hebert, has a horrific past. When her mother died and her mother's boyfriend raped her, Joey's power awoke and her mother rose from the grave to literally rip the man's head off, screaming that he'd promised to protect her daughter. Symbolically, Joey was channeling her mother's spirit and actions in her own life. Joey continued raising more zombies. "And the more zombies Joey raised, the stronger she felt. And Mommy was proud of her" (Spector 991). However, her mother finally crumbled and Joey had to accept she was dead. Nonetheless, she took over the criminal underworld of New Orleans. "Joey was a queen in this world and her justice against men who hurt women was swift and terrible" (Spector 691). From her mother's protective strength, she developed her own power.

The last heroine of *Busted Flush* is Niobe. Named for the woman of Greek myth who lost all her children, she has the power of birthing clutch after clutch of superpowered babies. In fact, they *are* her superpower, as each has gifts that can aid her. They're born intelligent and aware, and completely in love with her. In one scene, she escapes from the detainment facility where she's being studied. Her child Zane camouflages to get to the elevator and work the controls while Zenobia floats up to get the keys. Meanwhile, Zoe sings a song over the intercom that's so mesmerizing that everyone starts wandering aimlessly. Thus they make their escape (Martin, *Busted Flush* 162–167). Niobe makes it her mission to rescue Drake (Little Fat Boy), as she decides she will save one child who won't inevitably die in a few hours. Her children act as empowered parts of herself—the friends and companions that save her and allow her to save others in turn. Noel, Double Helix, finds and protects her and Drake, building a tiny unconventional family with Niobe far from the world's chaos.

When the People's Paradise capture Drake, they provoke him to go nuclear, but Bubbles bravely contains the explosion. She relates, "I felt my body instantly expand to its maximum size. The power raged into me like molten lead. It burned and sang and made me want to bubble forever. The concrete cracked under us as I became heavier and heavier" (439). Often the heroine's true superpower is endurance and preservation, here pushed to epic levels. Bubbles is left comatose and has gained so much mass that she cannot be moved. Ink and Hoodoo Mama spend the next year keeping vigil and defending her. Meanwhile, the destruction goddess Sekhmet leaves John Fortune and bonds with Drake, to guide him toward mastering his power.

After this, the heroes invade the People's Paradise and discover the thousands of children they've murdered to create just a few brainwashed Aces.

These children suck the life from people with unstoppable hunger or poison, symbolizing how starved they've been of love and real morality. Bubbles, guided by a child's voice calling her telepathically, saves little Adesina from a pit of corpses, while Hoodoo Mama sends the dead children against their murderess. Gardner rescues another group of children and leads them to safety, feeding and defending them with her trees.

Rustbelt leads the heroes against Tom Weathers, who transforms into a 70-foot monster with a literal "hard-on for everything that lived" (*Suicide Kings* 415). Lighting gathers at his pointy horns and he can shoot more of it from his fingers. Thus the heroes aren't just fighting the murderess of the innocent, but also the all-consuming patriarchy. Bubbles fights him physically, but as they exchange blows, the pair just grow ever-larger and more monstrous. In the midst of battle, Cameo resurrects Dolores. She proclaims, "This is no day for healing. This is a day for the ending of things. Tom Weathers has killed me. Let him take the pain that I carried" (*Suicide Kings* 425). She shares it with him and the agony of all his victims kills him. Thus all-out war is not the answer, but the quieter feminine power of healing and death. She returns him and herself to the lifecycle that they've denied for so long with their superpowers. Likewise, Gardener is killed, but in her death, gives life to a beautiful grove that provides the villagers with dazzling fruits.

In the *Wild Cards* universe, not all the adventures are this epic. There are also the quiet mental powers or gifts of invisibility common to early Marvel heroines. Pop Tart works in film stunts, as she can cheaply make things appear and disappear ... though she turns her talents to criminal behavior. Brain Trust can harmlessly absorb other people's minds and memories. The Syrian Kahina is clairvoyant. Topper can do magic. Moonchild is a master Korean martial artist who can turn invisible when in shadow or in darkness. Zelda, the Bodysnatcher, can jump from body to body. Rosa Loteria can turn into the character that she draws from her lotería card deck. Wraith has shadowcat powers of insubstantiability. Cordelia Chaisson can cause cardiac arrest, or revive someone having it. Water Lily can extract the water molecules from anything ... or anyone. While these are quiet, subtle powers, they can of course have devastating effect.

All these powers—animals, invisibility, water, energy/light, magic, and even death are in fact classic for superheroines. Throughout comics and other media, superheroine powers fall into several categories: There's disappearing from sight or becoming insubstantial like Sue Storm, Kitty Pryde, Monica Rambeau (the 80s Captain Marvel), Veil (*Avengers Academy*), Phantom Girl (*Legion of Super Heroes*), Martian Girl (*DC Super Hero Girls*), Becky Taylor (*Heroes*), Lieutenant Farah Nazan (*Heroes Reborn*), and Violet Parr (*The Incredibles*)—

a self-effacing power that actually becomes world-saving protection as the characters grow. "While her ability to phase through solid objects initially may make her seem like a mysterious wallflower when she disappears through barriers, with this power, Pryde actively challenges notions of stability at their most basic, physical level" (Galvan 47). She can whisk away people in danger, or reach into computers and short them out.

Related to this is shapechanging or flexibility (Mystique, Ms. Marvel 2014, Giganta, Gypsy, Chimera, Elastigirl, Mary Marvel, Vixen, Connie Logan from *Heroes*), along with illusion—Candice Willmer (*Heroes*), Princess Projectra, Dani Moonstar, or Gypsy. Emily Sung is Element Woman, a DC superhero with the power to transmutate objects and materials. Like DC's Vixen, Monstergirl, Rita Lopez, can transform into animals, monsters and humans with no restriction. Black Thorn from Checkmate is a master of disguise. Rita Farr of *Doom Patrol* is a Hollywood actress who can alter her size. All of these demonstrate flexibility but also a lack of identity in the male-dominated world.

In Ann Nocenti's short story "Switchback," Mimi, who can invade another's mind and control him or her, is enacting her psychological issues. Her brother notes, "She doesn't like her own skin, so she tries on everyone else's" (288). In fact, her smile is lopsided after an accident, and she lacks empathy, so she invades people's minds in an attempt to find it. This storyline in which trauma causes a particular ability is common of course. More to the point, her skin-hopping is a tool used to reject her own life and find another's.

Velveteen, in the short story series by Seanan McGuire, brings stuffed animals to life. These can be seen as a metaphor for affecting the world with a kind of intensified nature magic. As Velveteen's story adds, "Did you ever wonder how Velveteen's powers worked? How she was able to give life where there wasn't any? … She gave them her life. She shared her own energy with the things she animated" (McGuire, *Velveteen vs. The Multiverse*). Life Lass from the *Legion of Super-Heroes* can also animate objects. "Tat Master" by Naomi Hirahara features a girl whose Japanese tattoos do what she writes. She learns to protect those in danger but also defend herself when her ex-boyfriend arrives. Like Monica Dawson from the television show *Heroes*, Daredevil's girlfriend Maya Lopez can replicate any action she sees. DC's Soseh Mykros, Nemesis, has a related power. These suggest exaggerated intuition.

Unlike weaponry, built-in armor is defensive, even passive. Characters so-gifted include Echo, X-Men's Armor, Bulleteer, Emma Frost, Witchblade, and Illyana. Women thus often find alternatives to super weapons. Medusa of the Inhumans has prehensile hair, much like DC's Godiva and X-Man Lorelei Travis. This is the feminine made a force on the world, but still a more passive force than a blade. Medusa is joined by the children's book *The Adventures of Moxie Girl*, a comic about a Black girl who hates her hair until she uses a magical shampoo that turns her curls into superfighting Afro puffs. (The book was inspired, designed and co-written by seven-year-old Natalie McGriff to combat her self-esteem issues.) Likewise, in a story about owning her own superpowered hair salon, Marvel's Molly Fitzgerald notes in *Girl Comics*, "Super powers means super hair and it doesn't take a whole lot of talent to deal with it." Nonetheless, the little visiting cousin with no superpowers knocks the evil Trapster out with a hair dryer (Immonen).

For many heroines, there's a nature bond: Storm, Poison Ivy, Squirrel Girl, Mera, Rhosyn "Rose" Forrest, Tsunami (Miya Shimada), Cascade (Sujatmi Sunowaparti), Isis, Layla from *Sky High*, Arsenic and Rose Red from *Runaways*. On *Heroes Reborn*, Phoebe Frady releases a cloud of darkness and Alice Shaw and Malina can manipulate weather.

More specifically, the feminine nature imagery often takes the form of cat (Catwoman, Tigress, Hellcat, Wildcat, Miss Fury, the Cheetah, the Kitten, Catgirl, Catania, Catspaw, White Tiger, Catseye, the Black Cat, The Jaguar, Supergirl's super-cat Streaky). Jil DeSmoot in *Nexus* is a Felim, while Tamaranians like DC's Starfire are descended from tree-dwelling flying cats. Rosabelle Mendez, also known as Pantha, is one of the Teen Titans, and the heroine of *Dark Angel* has cat DNA. Greer Grant of Marvel's *The Cat* has "her intensified perceptions … like an embodiment of that mythical quality known as human intuition." Spider imagery is also common for women (Black Widow, Spider-Woman, Silk, Spider-Girl, Spider Gwen, Madame Web, Spider Widow). "Association of the Great Goddess with the spider occurs in myths of both the Old World and the New" (Walker 419). Symbolically, both of these mystically knowing animals have been tied to women and a deeper perception.

Flying aligns with spirituality as many women (and admittedly men) have bird or related imagery, including Owlwoman, Raven, Dawnstar, Lolita Canary, Firehawk, Lady Lark, Lady Blackhawk, Flamebird, Hummingbird, Deathbird, Songbird, Mockingbird, Dove, Harpy, Silver Swan, and Hawkgirl. Black Canary, originating in 1947, falls into this pattern but has a disturbing gender metaphor—a voice so shrill it can shatter glass and knock out the foe (or perhaps a feminine voice so *powerful* it can do the same). Other fliers include Wonder Woman, Donna Troy, Wonder Girl, Captain Marvel, Starfire, Bumblebee, Wasp, Pixie, Isis, and Lucy in the Sky from *Runaways*.

For a more amorphous nature bond, there's the invisible power of energy. Like Katie of *Power Pack*, Mike Brennan's Electric Girl shocks everything she touches. There's the related *Electra Woman and Dyna Girl* with their gadgets. Monica Rambeau, Captain Marvel, can transform herself into any form of energy within the electromagnetic spectrum. DC's Chandi Gupta (Maya) can project energy and manifest a mystical bow. Jade, daughter of Green Lantern, also has energy powers and can control the mystical Starheart; DC's Livewire is an energy-channeling villain. Finally, Phoenix's energy was something new in its cosmic destruction:

> Comic book heroines prior to Phoenix didn't have this sort of poise and self-sufficiency. In the Marvel Universe, they tended to have secondary powers—witchery, prehensile hair, becoming invisible (known in real life as fading demurely into the background). Jean Grey was an example of the type: She had a telekinetic power that moved things around and she left the heavy lifting to the boys. Phoenix is on a whole different level, yet she doesn't simply borrow the fighting style and strength of a superhero. She's a whirlwind rather than a missile. In spite of her explosive birth, Phoenix's force isn't phallic. It's a spreading force-field, a cosmic tsunami [Rose].

Likewise, Doctor Light channels near-unlimited energy through the Vega Energy Conduit, allowing her to absorb light. With this power she can also fly, cast illusions, phase, and make force fields. Dazzler and Jubilee of the X-Men and Dagger of *Cloak and Dagger* have light powers, while the new Phantom Lady has technology that allows her control over the light spectrum. Light Lass (*Legion of Super-Heroes*) has a flight ring that invokes her super-light form. Meanwhile, Linda Tavara from *Heroes* can also manipulate auras, in her case, to steal powers and lives. Also on *Heroes*, Emma sees sound waves as beautiful lights and produces amazing music by merging her emotions into her power, enticing everyone who hears it. However, this is not only a soft and sweet power: when she's frightened, she can force the lights into a concussive blast powerful enough to leave a scar in her apartment wall.

There's also simple combat, and the skills like healing, strength, and tracking that accompany it—admittedly often going to someone with no metaphysical power at all, though others have superhuman strength, endurance, or reflexes (Elektra, Huntress, Batgirl, Batwoman, Aurora West, Kate Bishop, Jessica Jones, Hit-Girl, Black Widow, Stargirl, Flamebird, Angel Dust, Gamora, Onyx, Katana, Liberty Belle, Ravager, Rampage, DC's Vigilante, Artemis, White Tiger, Danger Girl, Lady Shiva, Witchblade, Manhunter, Spy Smasher, Lady Blackhawk). This creates a warrior woman who's undoubtedly tough—it's said of Ms. America, America Chavez: "She's beauty, she's grace, she'll punch you in the face" (Bennett, *A-Force: Warzones*). Or there's enhancements in all areas (Wonder Woman, Supergirl, Power Girl, Lady Thor, Big Barda, Buffy the Vampire Slayer). "The Magician from Mars" (1940) could use one hundred percent of her brain, fly, reshape reality, and remain eternally young and lovely. Patsy Walker (aka Hellcat), is, according to her writer Kate Leth, "a superhero martial-arts wiz [who] can sense mystical energy! She learned how to fight on the moon, so you *know* she's good" (Errico). Thus she combines fighting skills and superhuman sensitivity, incorporating both sides of the spectrum.

There are many other specifically feminine powers:

- Telepathy/Mind control/telekinesis: Jean Grey, Emma Frost, Cassandra Nova, Madame Mirage, Malice, Maxima, Luna Maximoff, Emma de Lauro (*Mutant X*), Betty Clawman, Gypsy, Faith, *Teen Titans'* Raven, The Legion of Super-Heroes' Saturn Girl, Kelly Bailey from *Misfits*.
- Clairvoyance: Omen of *Teen Titans*, X-Men's Negasonic Teenage Warhead, Layla Miller, Destiny and Blindfold, Raina (*Agents of S.H.I.E.L.D.*), Molly Walker (*Heroes*), Angela Petrelli (*Heroes*), Bridget Bailey (*Heroes*), Garnet (*Steven Universe*), Julia Carpenter (*Spider-Woman*), Mary Marvel, Dream Girl (*Legion of Super Heroes*), Alisha Daniels (*Misfits*), Madame Web
- Sex powers: Poison Ivy, Circe, Wallflower, Crimson Fox, Alisha Daniels from *Misfits*
- Death: Lady Death, *Pretty Deadly*, Death (*Sandman*), Dr. Mirage, Ida May Walker (*Heroes*), *Smallville*'s Chloe Sullivan, Dead Girl
- Magic: Scarlet Witch, Zatanna, Illyana Rasputin, Janissary, Madam Mirage, Enchantress, Silver Sorceress, Nico Minoru (*Runaways*), *Black Magick*, *Rachel Rising*

The intuitive mental powers are gentle and insubstantial, at least superficially. Sex powers are also one of the more empathetic skills, admittedly one written into female characters by male writers, but also a way of connecting with the deeper self. Death, meanwhile, is the feminine realm of spiritual power and wisdom, as is spellcasting. Scarlet Witch thinks, "I've often heard the spells I cast referred to as chaos magic but in actual fact, they're far from chaotic—their power and intensity are linked to the energy of the earth and womankind, revered by ancient pagan faiths, feared by men. Its name is witchcraft" (Robinson, *Scarlet Witch: Witch's Road*). More physical power—fire, lasers, speed, strength—tend to be more classically masculine. Nonetheless, the feminine powers, wielded cleverly, can offer an awesome wellspring of power.

Talisman: *Witchblade* (TV, 2001–2002)

Superheroines have had a tough time breaking into television outside of team cartoons. The first in America, before *Wonder Woman* and *The Bionic Woman*, was *Isis*, now called *The Secrets of Isis* (1975–1977). On an archeological dig, teacher Andrea Thomas discovers an amulet of Queen Hatshepsut's. As the opening narration explains: "'O my Queen,' said the Royal Sorcerer to Hatshepsut, 'with this amulet, you and your descendants are endowed by the Goddess Isis with the powers of the animals and the elements. You will soar as the falcon soars, run with the speed of gazelles, and command the elements of sky and earth.'" With these many powers, Andrea can use the amulet and transform into "Isis, dedicated foe of evil, defender of the weak, champion of truth and justice!" For her and many superheroes, it's a talisman like Thor's hammer that gives them the power ... though they must be worthy.

Decades after this show, the independent comic *Witchblade* became something rare—another female-centric superhero show that lasted for two entire seasons. In flashback, the mysterious Kenneth Irons tells his apprentice, Ian Nottingham.

> It is written that no man has ever successfully won the Witchblade. That only the chosen women can wear it. And though I tried for all my force of will, I could not keep it on my hand. The gauntlet burned me. Seared my flesh until I had to rip it from my wrist. But even my brief exposure was enough to bind me to it forever. To make me a part of it. To allow me to see some of what it sees, but not all.
>
> That is my blessing and my curse. I understand the way it thinks, I know what it wants. And what does it want? It wants something that cannot be explained in words. To know what it wants, one must directly experience the Witchblade [1.1].

He shows off a pair of interlocked rings on his hand. Gloves and circles are particularly feminine symbols. Gauntlets and wristbands like Wonder Woman's bullet-bouncing bracelets accentuate the acts of the hands—symbol of active power. Sasha Martin, She-Hulk's temporary ward, has an alien gauntlet permanently fixed over her left hand, which conjures giant hands made out of Hard Light (Wilcox, *She Hulks: Hunt for the Intelligencia*).

"Men may quest for the grail, but each woman already bears the feminine deep within, and only needs evoke it. Her talisman helps her do so, but this token of her inner femininity cannot be a sword" (Frankel, *From Girl to Goddess* 46). The heroine's talisman is often a circle or a container like Lucy's healing potion in Narnia or Dorothy's slippers in Oz. Donna Troy has the History of the Universe Orb plus a divine earring and bracelet; Black Widow has her stinging "Widow's bite" bracelets. Wonder Woman's lasso, bracelets, belt, and tiara all fall into the category of round items. With her own magical necklace, Amy Winston could transform from an American 13-year-old to the fully-grown Princess of Gemworld, Amethyst. All these are also women's adornments like the original Batwoman's purse of gadgets, projected outward as a source of power. A finger slipping into a glove or ring suggests sex, since women are symbolically tied to the circle of life. Roundness indicates the self-perpetuating lifecycle as well as a community unbound by male hierarchy, only friendship.

> Along with rings, Freud links women with images of the home, forests and flowers, jugs, and bowls. Jung lists ploughed fields, gardens, magic circles, mandalas, caves, springs, wells, "various vessels such as the baptismal font, or vessel-shaped flowers like the rose or the lotus." As he adds, "Many things arousing devotion or feelings of awe, as for instance the Church, university, city or country, heaven, earth, the woods, the sea or any still waters, matter even, the underworld and the moon, can be mother-symbols." Flowers are delicate fertility symbols, while forests and potions bear the dark mystery of the unconscious. Water evokes the deep feminine, interconnectivity and flexibility [Frankel, *From Girl to Goddess* 51].

There's also the symbolic totem, as Captain Marvel visits Ms. Marvel, Kamala Khan, and tells her she's doing a good job. She offers the younger woman a pendant with the captain's star and Kamala's lightning bolt superimposed along with a locator. She tells Kamala, "I wanted you to have something you could hold. To remind you that you don't have to do all this alone" (Wilson, *Last Days*).

From DC, Mari Jiwe McCabe, Vixen, arrived in *Action Comics* in 1981. Born in Africa, she is the daughter of the Reverend Jiwe. He bestowed on her the magical Tantu Totem, supposedly created by Anansi the Spider, which could give a mortal his powers. While she moved to New York and became a model, she finally returned to Africa to reclaim the totem. The CW's cartoon adaptation, premiering summer 2015, has everyone she meets trying to take her necklace, turning her adventures into a battle to protect her identity. Using it, she wields the powers of panther, hawk, elephant, or anything she chooses, dramatically depicted onscreen.

In J.J. Marreiro's comic series from Brazil, Stunning Woman was once schoolteacher Carol Rosas. When an extra-terrestrial crashed, she saved an alien's life and it offered her the Medallion-Stunning, a cosmic amulet that gave her strength, speed, and invulnerability (*International Catalog*).

Certainly, a heroine can wield a gun or sword (though a surprising number like Xena wield a feminine chakram instead). Distance weapons in particular were popular with ancient goddesses, who fought at a remove: "Unlike delicate Venus, war goddesses travel armed, though rarely with swords. Artemis has her silver bow, and Hecate a whip, both distance weapons. Pele needs only the devastating power of her lava" (Frankel, *From Girl to Goddess* 48–49). Likewise, Catwoman has a whip, Wonder Woman a lasso, Batgirl, batarangs. "My skateboard is my Mjolnir," one punk kid insists (Harrison, "Defect"). She need not be a classic warrior, but a hero of wit and speed. *Mystery Men* features the Bowler (Janeane Garofalo), whose hurled bowling ball outshines all their more masculine weaponry.

Diana's Lasso of Truth is symbolically a mythic weapon "created in divine realms" and imbued with the power "to penetrate the human soul" (Arnaudo 126). In ancient myth, cords bound the earth to the heavens and people's minds to reason. The Fates spun a lifeline for each person, and goddesses like Hathor bound miscreants in glowing ribbons. Ropes thus emphasize interconnection and bonds between body and spirit. They can also represent the umbilical cord, connecting each person with the divine mother. In Egypt, cords represented matriarchal law, in service to Maat, goddess of justice. In Greece, "Ariadne's thread leading Theseus through the Labyrinth (into the darkness and out again) represented the rebirth journey" (Walker 130).

Like Red Sonja, Katana has a sword (with her dead husband's soul in it!). However, when this happens, the symbolism suggests this is a warrior woman who is separating herself from the feminine and following the men's path.

> A woman who craves guns and swords can be seen as envying men rather than celebrating her womanhood. One who suppresses all emotion can be seen agreeing that women are hysterical and choosing to forego all traces of "womanly weakness" to find strength, here synonymous with masculinity.
>
> Unfortunately, American culture (and indeed world culture) tends to agree with these stereotypes so much so that only masculine forms of strength are seen as valid, while attempts to problem-solve, talk things out, comfort others, deal with women's issues from abortion to relationships, have children, value emotions, look beautiful, or protect others are considered the weaker, feminine side [Frankel, *Empowered* 17–18].

Characters like Wonder Woman who find strength through gentleness and love of life, or through feminine symbols like the lasso are thus celebrating the feminine on a deep level rather than abandoning it as "weakness."

The show *Witchblade* attempts to find a balance as Sara Pezzini, a cop, wields the Witchblade itself, a magical gauntlet that can transform from a full set of armor to a simple bracelet, It's a shield, a tool of transformation, and one that enhances perception. As such, it's a perfect feminine symbol down to its name. While she begins by using it as a weapon, the Witchblade also connects Sara with her ancestors and channels her into levels of deep spirituality. "The Witchblade is an unwieldly if sexy extrusion of warring gendered anxieties, symbols, and powers, both masculine and feminine in form and affect, it refuses one gendered identity. Does the Witchblade grant Sarah toughness, or does her toughness manifest itself as the Witchblade?" (Greven 126).

As the first episode starts, Sara follows the crimelord Gallo into a museum where the gauntlet catches her eye. As she stares, a red eye on the gauntlet's back opens and stares back. She has been chosen. In fact, the eye is another feminine symbol, expressing perception as well as roundness. Symbolist Barbara Walker considers the eye the first method of mother-child bonding, and adds, "Because the eye of the Goddess was so often the eye of judgment, patriarchal societies feared it and tended to describe it as the evil eye" (309). The witch frightens people because she can shift shape—thus creating perpetual uncertainty about her true identity. She is the all-engulfing, terrifying matriarch.

The crimelord's men surround Sara and start shooting. She shoots back as she dodges, but her gun is shot from her hand. Suddenly, the gauntlet flies through the air to land on her outstretched arm. Bullets bounce off it and the glove protects her. A suit of armor watches her from across the room, and suddenly everything explodes.

Sara miraculously escapes, only to find herself sitting in the ambulance, stroking a strange silver bracelet with a red oval stone. She staggers home, still dazed. "I don't know why I keep pushing the envelope. Something's gotta change. I've gotta change," she decides. That night, she dreams of Joan of Arc burning at the stake. She sees Cleopatra, other warriors and heroes. The red stone zooms in on her like a staring eye, choosing her for her destiny.

The next morning, wearing her bracelet, Sara stares at a photo of a murder victim and finds herself reliving the woman's life. At the crime scene, she sees another vision. She and her partner Danny follow Gallo to the theater he plans to buy, but they are spotted. Gallo kills Danny, but when he aims for Sara, she has more visions of the red eye. The bracelet expands into a gauntlet. Bullets bounce off it and hit the goons around her. Only Gallo escapes.

When she wears the bracelet at Danny's funeral, Danny appears to her and says: "I'm here to tell you there's a lot more happening around you than you think. Things are a lot more connected. Open those doors of perception. There's people knocking, you'll see...." He acts as a spirit guide and also an indication of a new level of awareness. Danny "functions as the uncanny Other who provides Sarah with insights, heightened perception" (Greven 146). As he adds: "You don't even know who you are. All I can say is you're from a line going back through time and forward into the future. Part of a wave, a force. A warrior bloodline. You're the inheritor of something unique and powerful. And I think that deep down, you know it." It is his job to tell the heroine things she senses but cannot put into words—his speech sends Sara on a quest in which she finds out she's adopted and comes from the Witchblade heritage. Danny also foreshadows the mentor who is to follow.

Her case takes her to billionaire Kenneth Irons, who donated the entire wing of medieval artifacts to the museum. He tells her that he does not own the bracelet—if anyone does, it's her. As he shows her his wing devoted to art and study of the Witchblade, Sara gazes at paintings of great heroines from India, Egypt, China, Europe. All wield a bracelet or gauntlet, though each is different. All the women cover their faces. Irons tells her: "It's written that Joan's sword seemingly came to life during her battles. After her capture at Compiégne, a weapon disappeared from her hand. The Witchblade has a way of slipping from its wielder's grasp just when it is needed most. You're wearing it now."

"Able to link to and synthesize all the great women warriors throughout time, the Blade is a controlling metaphor for the intermittent outbursts of formidable, militaristic female fury throughout history" (Greven 128). It's symbolically a key to female power and inner magic. Irons' servant Ian Nottingham in "Conundrum" tells Sara that women wear the Witchblade because they can withstand the pain of childbirth. "The Witchblade enables Sara to embody essential female sexual power while wielding phallic male strength" (Greven 129).

When Sara asks why only women can wear the Witchblade, Irons tells her: "Women are more elemental. They're closer to nature than men. The Witchblade finds them superior." Certainly, female superheroes and fictional witches find themselves with more natural powers and fewer technological ones—Poison Ivy or Storm is a more likely role for a woman than Iron Man. This isn't meant to be a weaker path (or wasn't in ancient myth) but is instead parallel, emphasizing the woman as Mother Nature.

> IRONS: I do want to help you, Sara. I can help you solve the mystery. The Witchblade has powers. Many powers. But only the person who wields it can truly know them all. Haven't you felt different since it's found you?
> SARA: That's an understatement. Yes, in fact, I feel like I'm losing my mind.
> IRONS: And yet you can't tell anyone about your predicament. Anyone but me. Why do you think that is?
> SARA: Look, Mr. Irons, the bottom line is I don't want this thing. You can have it back.
> IRONS: You loved your father very much, didn't you?
> SARA: Yes, I did.
> IRONS: You can use the Witchblade to pierce the veil of the senses. To see in an entirely new way. To extract more information from the universe than the normal human sensorium allows. You already have.

Perception is one of the most common gifts for women, with magic mirrors, eyeglasses, and crystal balls for the questor. Wonder Woman's mother Hippolyte has a Magic Sphere which allows her to "know what has gone on and is going on in the other world, and even, at times, to forecast the future" (*All Star Comics* #8). Through it, she teaches Diana art, science, and the world's languages. The Golden Age Phantom Lady's weapon was a black light ray that would shroud the focus of its beam in darkness, changing others' vision. Catwoman is obsessed with mirrors. Oracle, Chloe Sullivan, and Felicity Smoak, data geniuses on their television shows, all watch the world through computer screens. For a far more prosaic and geeky contrast, Squirrel Girl's tools of wisdom are her "Deadpool's Guide to Supervillains" trading cards, which inform her of whom she faces.

Moon Girl from 1947 came from a long line of women who had been unbeatable in battle. In the 13th Century, the Princess of the Moon, the greatest warrior of her people, fought and slew the wizard Ka-Zhan, taking his prize, the Moonstone. She passed it down through the female line, until finally, Moon Girl's mother passed it down to her. However, with it, she could not be defeated, and could not accept a spouse weaker than herself. Taking her family heirloom, she left her home and traveled to America to fight crime. There, the moonstone served her as a tracking device and a scrying mirror (Gaines, *The Happy Houlihans* #1).

Philippine superheroine Darna is much like Wonder Woman with flight, superstrength and indestructability. This heroine arrived in 1950, as the Philippines, post–World War II, needed an icon. She's appeared in many films and cartoons and maintains a steady popularity. Her origin story concerns a magical stone falling from the sky. The ordinary girl Narda discovers that she can transform when she swallows the magic White Stone of the Adranika, assuming she's acting unselfishly. Its opposite, the Black Stone of the Anomalka, is held by Braguda, Queen of Darkness. Whoever has both can conquer any planet (*International Catalog*). This, a round symbol of light or darkness, links the heroine with the heavens as well as the powers of the earth.

Irons tells Sara she was destined to wear the Witchblade and adds: "The gauntlet has chosen you. You must accept it. Use it or lose it. And if you don't deserve it, if you don't earn it, it will abandon you." Talking to him, she has visions of a moon, medieval warriors, the red eye. He adds that the Witchblade has clearly chosen her as she has a mark of linked circles. "The circles represent the light and dark powers of the Witchblade." She protests that it's a scar from shrapnel during a SWAT team raid 11 months earlier. When he persists, she panics and runs away.

A showdown comes between herself and Gallo, and the Witchblade fights for her once more. Sara advances on Gallo, seeing flashes of the red eye and also of herself in full, concealing armor. She claims its power and all the painted faces in the gallery look up. However, she backs away from a final brutal revenge. Though she's driven to kill the man, Sara finally lowers her gauntlet and its sword blade to arrest him by the book. As she concludes the episode: "And that's the story of how I came to have this strange thing on my hand called the Witchblade. I still don't know exactly what the Witchblade is or how to use it. Every day I gain a bit more control but this control requires will, and vigilance. I think of Danny a lot. He was right. Everything and everyone is more connected than we realize. So there is no pat ending, no neat finale, no single final image." "The tough woman, especially in her metahuman deviance of even categorization by species, serves as a helpful example of the fluidity of sexual and gendered roles in our 'posthuman' moment" (Greven 125). She breaks boundaries and resists classification.

The Magdalena, a reoccurring guest star in the *Witchblade* comics, with other crossovers and one-shots, got her own series in 2010. The heroine, Patience, gets her powers from her bloodline as well as Christ's Spear of Destiny. With these comes the gift to see into the human heart and show people their sins so they can change. Here the masculine weapon blends with feminine perception to create a heroine both warrior and woman.

In the same tradition, Joss Whedon's Fray, a slayer far in the apocalyptic future, receives the slayers' mystical death scythe from her demonic mentor Urkonn. He tells her, "It is your sword and scepter. Let it proclaim you the hero—and the monster—that you will need to be." Thus he acknowledges her duty to deal death as well as life, and echoing "the destructive and creative powers of the Great Mother" (Cooper 146). While the scythe itself is an image of the death that brings new life, another cycle is reflected in her goddess triple crescent tattoo, suggesting three ages of womankind (mother, maiden, crone), as well as the feminine polarity of the universe (Whedon, *Fray*).

As both a blade and a bracelet, the Witchblade melds feminine and masculine imagery. "Armored and sensual, phallic and feminine, the Witchblade-wielding Sara is an ingenious compromise between the normatively reproductive tied to Nature and the Western, phallic masculine hero" (Greven 129).

Irons takes over the internet in the series finale, "Ubique" (212). He tells Sara, "You see, Sara, with the Witchblade upon your wrist, you had infinite potential to win people's hearts. You had no idea how powerful you were, but once the Witchblade abandoned you I was able to start winning their minds." Thus he casts himself as her equal and opposite—she has the path of emotion and he has the one of power. To defeat him, Sara faces him on the astral plane as soon as he tries claiming the Witchblade. Dressed in an armor breastplate with a long flowing white sheer robe and loose hair, she tells him, "The Witchblade is a state of mind and a state of the heart. My dear Irons, can't you see this is where the real battle is fought? And you have already lost." There she kills him, tranquilly, knowing she possesses all the power of the glove and the realm of the spirit. They are united at last.

Self-Naming: Captain Marvel (Marvel Comics, 1977–2012)

In the superhero world, one's codename is essential, a way of defining one's purpose. It's also a symbol of casting off the old identity and forming a new one, particularly when poised at a significant life transition. Campbell describes the custom of changing one's dress and even name while passing from one lifestage to another (Campbell and Moyers 88).

Ms. Marvel #1 from 1977 (written by Gerry Conway and a later-credited Carla Conway and penciled by John Buscema) begins with her foiling a bank robbery in Manhattan. She takes the bad guys down with flight, super-strength, and her "seventh sense." She also cultivates a sense of mystery, flying off with a "My apologies, gentlemen. I have business elsewhere" in her black mask, stomach-revealing shirt, and briefs. The crowd watches, stunned by this new heroine, and a little girl tells her mommy that she wants to be just like her when she grows up. Ms. Marvel "totally represented the new, liberated, upbeat spirit" that Marvel Comics wanted to represent (Lee, *The Superhero Women* 84).

Across town, J. Jonah Jameson hires Carol Danvers as the new editor of *Woman Magazine*. Her first assignment? The mystery heroine. She takes the job but reminds him it's *Ms.* Carol Danvers and he can forget recipes and diet plans for the articles. Chatting with Mary Jane Watson, Carol describes her love of writing, only to be struck by a terrible headache and pass out. Thus begins her transformation to her alternate identity.

Previously, Carol and the alien captain Mar-vell were kidnapped by the evil Colonel Yon-Rogg then caught in the explosion of a Kree Psyche-Magneton device, which could turn thought into reality. At that moment, Carol wished to be a superhero instead of just the damsel in distress, and Carol's genetic structure melded with the dying Mar-vell's, making her a Kree-human hybrid, complete with his memories (*Captain Marvel* #18).

Carol Danvers is the ordinary woman side, the concealing human mask over her superhero self. However, Carol doesn't realize the power that dwells within. This outer face can be one of self-delusion as well as propriety: "One could say, with a little exaggeration, that the persona is that which in reality one is not, but which oneself as well as others think one is" (Jung, "Concerning Rebirth" 123). Carol's human life is an illusion, one she willingly buys into.

As she flies about the city fighting crime, she has flashes of déjà vu around the Daily Bugle and thinks, "I'll need all my concentration and all my Kree-born skill" only to be confused by this declaration. When the villain Scorpion asks, "Who on earth are you?" she replies, "That's a better question than you know." As she fights, she realizes her powers do come from the Kree and her star-emblazoned uniform mimics Captain Marvel's for a reason. However, she has total amnesia and her identity is a blank.

She defeats the villain despite this handicap, and tells his hostage J. Jonah Jameson he can call her Ms. Marvel. "The costume ties me to Captain Marvel in a way I don't yet understand. 'Till I do understand, I'll need a name," she concludes. This of course sets her in a category of 50s heroines like Batwoman and Supergirl who name themselves as counterparts to a male hero. Updating it to Ms. changes little. She sets out on a mission to "find out who I am and where I come from." Teasingly, she tells the sexist Jameson not to prejudge her and leaves him safe but still handcuffed.

Back at the office, Carol Danvers is surprised at Jameson's new hatred for Ms. Marvel. She's been having blackouts, and apparently compartmentalizes her double identity. As she thinks, "Which is the greater enigma? The woman named Carol Danvers? Or the warrior we all call Ms. Marvel?"

Continuing to have blackouts, Carol goes to her friend and psychologist Michael Barnett for help. Dr. Barnett uses hypnosis to learn her story. In trance, she recalls the battle between Captain Marvel and Yon-Rogg, and absorbing an explosion that engulfed them both, then waking unharmed in a hospital. Finally, she recalls transforming into the stronger, larger Ms. Marvel. Though the doctor doubts her, he's convinced when she passes out and transforms once more. At last, Ms. Marvel goes to cover a story on the first woman astronaut. After surviving a journey into space, she follows her impulses to the cave where she was reborn. Her split memories begin to unite, and she understands who she is. "Both men and women need to dissolve the ego to awaken. Women come into their power to realize their authentic goal and connectedness, whereas men let go of their power to realize their authentic goals and connect-edness" (Schmidt, 45 Master Characters 194). Ms. Marvel discovers her real power and thus claims her superhero self.

Nonetheless, this character will change her name several more times, each time signaling a fundamental identity shift or acceptance of new responsibilities. Rogue drains her abilities and the new powerless Carol becomes a secret agent for Professor X. When out in space, she's supercharged with the Brood's evolutionary ray that triggers her latent potential. She renames herself Binary, a simple superhero without complex memories and identity. Most of all, however, Binary links her with energy-rich stars. As Binary, she wears a white leotard with white thigh-highs and gloves accented by blazing red skin and flaming head. Without any earth ties, the new hero goes off to explore the heavens with the spacefaring Starjammers. When the Avengers encourage her to return, she spends months recovering at Avengers Mansion before she finally rejoins them.

In *Avengers* vol. 3 #4, Beast tells Carol, "Your powers have definitely decreased. From these readings, I doubt you'll even be able to shift into your Binary form again." She confesses she's been feeling that way for weeks and considers piloting a Warbird. He tries to console her by pointing out she's gone from "phenomenally powerful to merely incredibly powerful." When he realizes she feels disconnected from her old self, he suggests names like Warrior Woman or Regalia, in a long list of ludicrous codenames. She finally chooses Warbird, indicating a new set of powers and purpose. Her plain body suit emphasizes that her Binary powers are indeed gone, along with the need to accessorize them. Jessica Jones similarly rejects her sweet superhero name of Jewel—she still has her powers but is no longer the spunky, costumed superheroine after her abuse at the hands of the Purple Man. Now she's a "normal" private investigator (Bendis, *Alias*).

Names are an indication of pride, or identity. In Gail Simone's *Red Sonja*, Sonja determinedly names herself in a fighting arena, where all the slaves have lost their names. Even chained in the darkness, it's the one thing she clings to. However, to save a village of innocents, Sonja kneels to her enemy, Dark Annisia, and surrenders. Annisia tells her, "You are no longer Sonja, the devil. You are nothing. You are no one. Someone *mark* this wretch." With the shadow of a dark bird painted over her eyes, Sonja goes into exile up in the mountains.

While dealing with a drinking problem and court martial, Carol finally becomes Ms. Marvel again through events like *Civil War*, *Secret Invasion*, and *Dark Reign*. In the *House of M* storyline, the altered reality shows Carol what life might have been like if she were the top of the world's heroes. In this, she is the House of M's greatest heroine, Captain Marvel, basking in fame and celebrity with her press conference. When the X-Men reveal the world as a sham, Carol thinks, "I know that, all appearances to the contrary, I am *not* the best superhero on earth. I am not the best of the best." However, she comes to the realization that she could be, and ends the comic resolving to do just that.

With this thought, she reboots her *Ms. Marvel* series and heads off on more adventures. She begins *Ms. Marvel* #1 (2006) as a competent air force pilot and superhero, throwing around cars with incredible strength. Still, she's concerned not only with her image but her purpose. As she tells a publicist, "I feel like I've been goofing around the last few years. Like I've never really gone above and beyond. Never really *earned* my way." Struck by dizziness on a solo rescue mission, she refuses to call for help, thinking, "Nobody else is coming, Carol. It's up to you." Her thought, "No more being dizzy for you now, okay?" seems a callback to the earlier series and an affirmation that this time will be different.

Back in 1977, Conway hoped that readers "might see a parallel between her quest for identity, and the modern woman's quest for raised consciousness, for self-liberation, for identity…" but adds an apology that the book was written by a man because "for whatever reason (right or wrong), at the moment there are no thoroughly trained and qualified women writers in the superhero comics field…. There should be, no denying it, but there aren't" (qtd. in Robbins 126). As the series reached a new reimagining, a woman finally took the helm.

In *Captain Marvel* #1 (2012), the series was rebooted by Kelly Sue DeConnick with art by Dexter Soy, with a promotion for the heroine. The captain struggles over her name as well as what it means to her.

> "My pitch was called 'Pilot' and the take can pretty much be summed up with 'Carol Danvers as Chuck Yeager,'" says DeConnick. "Carol's the virtual definition of a Type A personality. She's a competitor and a control freak. At the start of our series, we see Carol pre–Captain Marvel, pre–NASA even, back when she was a fiercely competitive pilot. We'll see her meeting one of her aviation heroes and we'll see her youthful bravado, her swagger. Then over the course of the first arc we're going to watch her find her way back to that hungry place. She'll have to figure out how to be both Captain Marvel *and* Chuck Yeager—to marry the responsibility of that legacy with the sheer joy being nearly invulnerable and flying really [expletive] fast [Beard, "WonderCon"].

Captain Marvel notes that her biggest hero was a pilot named Helen Cobb with 15 speed records ... but as a superpowered being, Carol can't compete that way anymore—it wouldn't be fair. Most of all, she regrets losing the risk that came with being fully human. Squabbling with Captain America, he points out, that with her new uniform she ought to take on a new name. When Carol protests, "Captain Marvel is dead, Steve. He was a good man and a *real hero.* Too many things were taken from him. I won't take one more—" Steve must remind her he was actually Captain Mar-Vell "and I don't mean to be unkind here, but you took his name a long time ago." As he adds, "It was his mantle. Now, it's his legacy. And he wanted *you* to have it." He tells her that now that she's led the Avengers, she shouldn't be an adjunct but should take the role of superhero.

> "Carol has an incredible respect for Mar-Vell, as a person and as an icon," notes DeConnick. "It's on Captain America to help her understand that Captain Marvel wasn't his name, it was his mantle. And he would have wanted her to have it. As for the rest of the Marvel Universe, well, I expect the opinions probably vary person to person, but I imagine the overwhelming attitude would be one of, 'What took her so long?'" [Beard, "WonderCon"].

Carol flies into space and considers her lost humanity, a hangup that has been holding her back from accepting the title. She's lost the risk that made her fully human, but as she reflects, many humans would give anything to reach out and touch the edge of space as Carol can. She goes into freefall and hits the atmosphere at Mach 3. She thinks, "Cue adrenaline rush. This ... this is what lucky looks like. Decision made.... I'm keeping the damn name."

Other memorable characters also have significant moments of transformation. After being psychologically tortured by visions of failing her team and her family, Sue Storm strikes back against her attacker Psycho-Man, stealing his control box and rendering him impotent. "You defiled me, Psycho-Man.

And now you are going to be punished," she announces. At the comic's end, she notes that she's been neglecting working on growing up. "He forced me to look into the deepest corners of my *soul*, forced me to confront who I am, what I have become." She adds that gaining their superpowers meant losing her child-like naiveté. After Psycho-Man's attack she is no longer innocent. "There is no Invisible Girl anymore, Reed. She died when the Psycho-Man twisted her soul. From now on, I am the Invisible Woman" (*Fantastic Four* #284).

Lois and Clark: Ultrawoman has Superman's powers accidentally trans-ferred to Lois. Clark names her (as she did him early in the series) calling her "Ultrag—woman! Ultrawoman." His tough reporter partner, he knows, won't stand for anything less. Like Lois, superheroes are often named by others, in scenes that are sometimes empowering and sometimes condescending and silly. Sue Storm is revolted in her first film when her brother names her "Invis-ible Girl" (though the Thing is far angrier). Catwoman in the Halle Berry film hates that a guard names her "Cat-broad." In "Velveteen vs. The Isley Crayfish Festival," the superheroine is given her name by the terrible corporation that demands a monopoly on superheroes. After they adopt her, much of her life is dictated by their marketing department.

> "This is just a fascinating hero name we've picked for you, Miss Martinez," said the man from Marketing, smiling benevolently over his clipboard. Velma squashed the urge to send her Barbie to scratch the eyes out of his smug face. "And why do you think we chose that name for you?"
> "Cause I bring toys to life, and they said that 'The Puppeteer' and 'Bride of Chucky' had negative connotations."

Agents of S.H.I.E.L.D.'s Skye mentions the orphanage named her "Mary Sue Poots," a silly name (and also a nod to Mary Sue fanfiction characters that are all-powerful, ridiculous stand-ins for the writers) ("The Only Light in the Darkness" 119). She names herself Skye in its place. This is a defiant one-word hacker name and also a hint of where she is going—her destiny as a powerful Inhuman, in touch with the elements but forever living on the S.H.I.E.L.D. air-plane. Later she renames herself again, asking her friends to call her Daisy, her birth name. Even though the parents who chose it became supervillains, they still loved her.

If the superhero side (like the hacker side in *The Matrix*) is the "true self," rejecting one's human name acknowledges this. Mystique in the film *X-Men: The Last Stand*, asserts that the name her parents gave her is her "slave name," and Callisto insists all of their kind get tattoos to mark them as special. They and their friends in the Brotherhood all reject their human labels. Gert of *Runaways* takes a similar approach. She wants to be called Arsenic after she flees her evil parents, noting Gert is "the name *they* gave me" (#6). Most of her teammates agree, though Alex insists he can redeem his family name by keeping it.

The normal high schoolers try being superheroes in *Glee*: "Dynamic Duets" (4.7). The McKinley kids name themselves for aspects of their personality they want to highlight including wealthy Sweet 'n' Spicy (Sugar), cruel Queen Bee (Becky), the Human Brain (Brittany) and the very Professor X-like wheelchair-bound Dr. Y (Artie). Granted, many of their powers are frivolous, but they're interested in exploring new sides of themselves. Coach Beiste explains, "Putting on a mask is like getting up on stage. It gives you the freedom to be the person you secretly aspire to be." Her power is sex-change, one she in fact enacts later with a real surgical sex-change. Meanwhile, Ryder learns he's dyslexic, and struggles with feeling like it's his own secret identity. Kitty, the mean girl, is ordered to team up and sing with terrified Marley. However, when Marley, who's struggling with bulimia, names herself Wallflower, Kitty (dressed as a catlike Femme Fatale with a whip), gives her a lecture on confidence:

> MARLEY: I can't. I look ridiculous.
> KITTY: I'm sure that's not true. Come on, I won't judge.
> [She comes out in gold spandex.]
> KITTY: Uncross your arms. I don't get it. What's WF?
> MARLEY: It's supposed to be Wallflower.
> KITTY: Wallflower?
> MARLEY: Your alter ego's supposed to reflect how you feel about yourself, right? When I looked in the mirror, this is what I saw.
> KITTY: Well, get over here, so Femme Fatale can tell you what she sees. Stand up straight. Shoulders back. You look H-O-T-T, hot…. But first things first. Marley Rose, you are Wallflower no more. You are Woman Fierce, and we are going to kill this song.

They sing Bonnie Tyler's "Holding Out for a Hero" and Marley gains confidence, strutting in her spandex and swirling her cape. She and Kitty work together, perfectly coordinating their dance and working side by side, confident bad girl and shy good one.

Kitty Pryde in a memorable moment renames herself not as the lighthearted Ariel or Sprite but the more serious Shadowcat, a nod to her powers, in *Kitty Pryde and Wolverine* #5. Gazing at herself, she mulls over her choices— a normal life or a superpowered one. "Except normal people don't skydance. I can't give that up. Even without any superpowers, I'll never settle for what society—or my parents—expect of me. I'm not a Kitty anymore, much as I wish differently, I've grown up. I'm a cat. And I like the shadows a whole lot more than the daylight." "Just as she previously dispenses with the identities that parents or society lined up for her, here she rejects previous codenames given to her by her fellow teammates and fashions her own moniker out of the bits and pieces of herself. Discarding these nominal ties allows her to draw greater strength from within herself" (Galvan 56).

Kitty's teammate, Hisako Ichiki, can create a devastating shield from the strength of her ancestors. In Joss Whedon's run, he whisks his new teen character off on a trip with the X-Men. She and Wolverine crash on a planet together, and, as she breaks down, Wolverine orders her to throw away her uniform and adds, "You wanna cry on my bubbling, skinless shoulder? You're in that suit 'cause you're an X-Man. You're an X-Man 'cause I seen you fight and I want you on the team. But if I'm wrong, if you're just a whining teenager gonna freak out on a hostile alien planet and cost me time, then lose the suit and go die. We got worlds to save" (Whedon, *Astonishing X-Men: Unstoppable*). Her response, "Armor," tells him that she's decided to be a hero and name herself at last.

Secret Identity: Supergirl (DC Comics, 1959)

Superheroes "have multiple identities, with many that alternate between being a regular person and a hero. This narrative device can be perceived as a symbolic reflection … of the radically different stages that an individual can go through" (Arnaudo 134). Of all the transformations heroes undergo, the one who's changed the most is likely Supergirl. Unlike Ms. Marvel, she's mostly done so under a single nickname.

Supergirl came from the nebulous period between Golden and Silver Ages when superheroes were waning. Supergirls were entering the mode, less competent sidekicks who smiled from the pages. The ultra-feminine Batwoman spent her time trying to wrangle Batman into marriage, just as Lois Lane was doing to Superman. Wonder Woman spent all her time gushing over Steve Trevor, *Superman's Girlfriend Lois Lane* was a popular comic, and Supergirl herself became an adorable young cousin for Superman, whose "adventures often focused less on adventure and more on a quest to find love," explains Mike Madrid (*Supergirls* 86). Supergirl was "sweet," but not particularly assertive or effective as she deferred to her older cousin in all things. Nonetheless, Supergirl represents an important cultural moment as she remains the only "important and long-lasting superheroine from the 1950s" (Robbins 104).

In 1959, she burst from her ship in *Action Comics* #252, a pretty blonde in a short skirt. On finding she was his little cousin, Superman adopted her and placed her in an orphanage, promising to watch over her "like a big brother." In a world of supermen, Supergirl was one of the many "girls" like Mary Marvel or Batgirl who were considered proper role models for female readers. "'Girl' meaning not yet woman, not quite mature, not entirely whole. Girls *could* have careers, as long as they were culturally appropriate for their generation, but grown women were married and homemakers" (Stuller, *Ink-Stained Amazons* 13). When Superman introduced her to the world, he commented, "Physically, she's the mightiest female of all time! But at heart, she's as gentle and sweet and as quick to tears—as any ordinary girl!"

On finding Superman is her cousin and promises to take care of her, she embraces him and cries, choking, "You mean I'll come and live with you?" (Binder, *Action Comics* #252). He instantly backpedals, protesting that this would endanger his secret identity. He tells his little cousin to become Linda Lee at the Midvale Orphanage, and she does, hiding her blonde hair under a brown braided wig to appear more ordinary. He doesn't bother adopting her himself, though he keeps her handy as his backup. When she requests to reveal herself, Superman responds, "No Supergirl! I have many cunning enemies! If I'm ever in a bad trap, you're the only one who could rescue me!" (Binder, *Action Comics* #252). "Superman, despite being raised by caring parents who taught him everything he needed to know, actively deprived Supergirl of a loving home. To Superman, Supergirl was little more than a tool" (Hanley 121). His occasional visits are tests or requests for help, rather than loving family time. When Supergirl befriends Krypto the Superdog, Superman scolds her for risking her identity and exiles her to an asteroid (as a rather cruel test, as it turns out) in *Action Comics* #258.

She has all the powers of Superman but not the authority. In fact, when she arrives on earth in May 1959, Superman bars her from using her powers until he judges that she can use her "super-powers properly" (Binder, *Action Comics* #252). She's allowed to perform Super-feats "as long as nobody sees me" as she puts it (Binder, *Action Comics* #253). Thus she's stuck using them in secret (often to aid her cousin), following the literal pronouncement only. Superman can lift a rocket into space publically; for Supergirl, it must appear a nebulous "miracle" (*Action Comics* #254). As such, she appears scattered with imperfect control of her powers, mostly because of Superman's restrictions:

> In her earliest adventures, written primarily by Otto Binder or Jerry Siegel, Supergirl is to Superman as Streaky the Supercat is to Supergirl herself: "cute but a problem" ("World's Mightiest Cat" 192/2). Like Streaky, she is difficult to control, and she threatens to expose and to weaken her guardian. That is, whatever one makes of her various transformations— or lack of them—over the ensuing half-century, Supergirl's earliest adventures play out the complexities of gender performance in the age of Betty Friedan's "feminine mystique" [Link].

In the essay "The Secret of Supergirl's Success," Alex Link explains, "Her unique success is attributable in part to the way in which she presents a rich and subtle critique of mid-twentieth century American idealizations of femininity." Link adds that Supergirl's readers are "invited to emulate her efforts to secure limited freedom while under the ever-watchful gaze of patriarchy."

Girls of the time were supposed to be sweet and wholesome. They were told to play with dolls and grow up into homemakers who would use their brains and strength to mop kitchen floors in high heels, dress beautifully, and play jacks with their children. They were also meant to support their husbands in everything, making them feel like real men who could protect their little women. Betty Friedan's *The Feminine Mystique* protested the gender roles of the time, showing how women were forced to present an artificial mask of weakness rather than glory in their abilities. Superman orders Supergirl to fall in line.

> As a powerful female using her extraordinary abilities to perform meaningless tasks, such as dusting her room with her "super-breath" ("Supergirl From Krypton" 46/3), or creating rainbows to comfort a crying child ("The Day Supergirl Revealed Herself" 173/1–4), Supergirl literalizes Friedan's description of the conventional American woman as little more than a special kind of domestic appliance, and hyperbolizes the untapped potential of so many American women. By trying to live within Superman's restrictions, Supergirl literalizes Friedan's sense that American women are forbidden "to use [their] own abilities in the world" (297), and forbidden to "accept or gratify their basic need to grow and fulfill their potentialities as human beings" (133) [Link].

Heating a fellow orphan's iron with heat vision and refreezing her ice cream just isn't a good enough outlet for her powers.

Though Supergirl sabotages possibilities of her own adoption, knowing she can't have a normal life, she secretly aids other children, helping Timmy Tate as an assistant in his magic show, or fixing Frank Cullen's golf game with superbreath. Tellingly, she helps Eddie Moran, a boy orphan, appear to have saved a drowning man. The man adopts heroic Eddie, and Supergirl is left on the sidelines once more.

One outlet for Supergirl's powers is carnivals and magic shows. As the assistant in Timmy Tate's magic act, she can burst her steel chains and float but allow the man in charge to take the credit (Binder, *Action Comics* #253). In "Supergirl's Foster Parents!" (*Action Comics* #254) the Dales adopt Linda Lee. Touring with their carnival act, she can "prove" that their strength tonic works and once again misdirect her true source of power. She lifts an elephant, but when her foster father guzzles the drink, she must give him the illusion of powers as well, immediately sidelined by another male superman. These sideshow acts emphasize the illusions she uses in a well-crafted screen over so many aspects of her life that she can never be herself except when acting a part. Other times, she assists her cousin behind the scenes, allowing the public and Superman himself to think he did it all. This was the 50s' girl's job.

On dropping her at the orphanage, Superman tells her, "Someday the outside world will hear of you as Supergirl! But for a long time to come, you'll live here quietly as an ordinary girl" (Binder, *Action Comics* #252). As the narrator says, in "The Day Supergirl Revealed Herself!" in response to Supergirl's despair that the world will never know of her existence, "But we know, Supergirl!" This was the 50s' quiet undertone—that women, who had been so powerful in the 40s, might be again, but "not now, not today." Any heroic deeds had to be understated, dismissed, the credit given to a man. This is Supergirl's true secret identity—one she shared with all 50s girls. Link adds, "Supergirl's shared secret with readers is not the specific identity of her mundane alter ego—as with readers who know Superman's secret identity—but that any mundane girl might be more powerful than she seems."

Superheroes maintain an artificial persona, the polite daylight self so different from the powerful, buried raging shadow side—the Jekyll and Hyde in all of us. However, superheroes display their shadows as the more real selves. "In general, we can say superheroes reverse the usual order of '*persona*, outside, *shadow*, inside.' They turn the shadow inside out and show us the inside first" (Packer 135). In this case, Jekyll is a thin façade over the more authentic Hyde—"Clark Kent" or "Diana Prince" is the artificial persona donned in order to fit in. Both characters struggle with how to live an ordinary life, which identity deserves the time put in and which most craves the love and approval of others.

Of course, the public superhero is another kind of persona, iconic and larger than life, who must always appear perfect. "The interchangeability between *shadow* and *persona*, and secret self and super self adds to the allure of the superhero" (Packer 135). Oracle directs people as an androgynous green mask, revealing nothing of herself. No one knows of her personal history, her disability, or her past as Batgirl. Thus the mask allows her to reinvent herself as none of these things—only the flawless power of information.

Poor Supergirl, however, is trapped in double secret identities as she buries Kara and Supergirl under unloved orphan Linda. She longs only to be loved and admired for her true self. Still, every mistake she makes, big or tiny, gives Superman an excuse to prolong her anonymity. In February 1962 (Siegel, *Action Comics* #285), Superman finally decides the time has come. Of course, Superman dictates terms: Supergirl must tell her foster parents, then he will announce Supergirl's arrival to the city. The poor heroine can only utter, "Superman's such a dear! I realize now how wise he was to delay announcing my existence until I was really ready!"

As it turns out, the entire world reacts with sexism, from the admiring woman who "love[s] her hair" to the jealous actress, to the powerful men who resent a "snip of a child" and "young girl" who can outcompete them. Perhaps Superman is right that 1959 couldn't handle a supergirl, though 1962 is little better. "Readers both female and male watched her mature as a heroine and a woman. For the first time in a generation, young girls had a new superheroine to emulate. Yet Supergirl's appeal wore thin over time. Attempts to expand her personality beyond her original naivete failed, and she died—valiantly, at least, while saving the world—in *Crisis on Infinite Earths* #7 (1985)" (Misiroglu 534–535).

Heroines today often make different choices. Squirrel Girl explains, "I'm not one to try and hide. Hiding just makes people not trust you. People look at me and they don't know what to think. And I'm pretty okay with that because I'm not hiding anything." Other college students stare at her swishing tail, and she only smiles (Bendis, *New Avengers* #15).

Thus original Supergirl's mundane identity was a product of her era and uniquely a reflection of women's issues, as many superheroines' identities were not. Wonder Woman's Diana Prince identity of the 1940s and of the 1970s television show were basically identical to Clark Kent's—a bumbling geek ignored by the love interest.

> Both Clark Kent's and Wonder Woman's alter ego, Diana Prince, wore glasses to obscure their appearance, to signify weakness (both superheroes had perfect vision), as well as to project the stereotypical persona of the smart but socially awkward person (nowadays known as the geek). Prince began as a nurse and then was promoted to military intelligence. She was depicted as weak and inhibited, and frequently positioned as a damsel in distress. Trevor, who preferred the powerful figure that was Wonder Woman, was not attracted to her [Knight 307–308].

Lois Lane and Steve Trevor were, of course, completely dazzled by the superpowered alien in the flashy costume—the hero's "real self" or "best self," which is far from ordinary. This became a popular story pattern, emerging in many comics that followed.

In *Womanthology's* "Meanwhile! On Tethys, Orbiting Saturn…" human Jeremy is shocked to realize that Sunwoman, the alien superhero rescuing him, is really "mousy, mild Penny Peraje." She's thrilled he worked it out. "On my home planet, we strive for a true meritocracy," explains the young Black woman in a mask—marginalized on earth across all her categories. One is the world of family and social status while the other is one's chosen path "where you get your real recognition from society. It's remarkably similar to the superhero-secret identity," she adds. She explains to her boyfriend that she can only marry him when he sees through her everyday normal persona to the superhero within and recognizes both sides (Fortuner). This is the hero's common quest—to be loved for both sides, both flashy and quiet.

Supergirl's quandary in 1959 is more difficult. Her Supergirl side can only emerge in secret, hidden even from her cousin. While superheroes are occasionally thrown out of town and must operate beneath the government radar, some specifically female ones are ordered to reign in their joie de vivre (She-Hulk), burgeoning superstrength (Pepper Potts in *Iron Man 3*), total power (Dark Phoenix), or entire identity (Supergirl). Thus the secret identity can be a prison as much as a tool for societal acceptance.

Costume: Miss Fury (Timely Comics, 1941)

One of the first costumed superheroines reveled in her alt-identity as it gave her power and freedom. Miss Fury (1941) was the first female superhero created and drawn by a female cartoonist, June Tarpé Mills. Sadly, she had to keep her own identity secret. As the cartoonist noted in an interview, "It would have been a major let-down to the kids if they found out that the author of such virile and awesome characters was a gal" (qtd. in Tarpe 8). "Miss Fury feared no man, slapping and scolding bad guys, even whipping them with her tail. Her adventures were written and drawn by a real-life woman of wonder: Tarpé Mills, one of the first successful female creators to render superheroines for the printed page. Mills was, like her character, glamorous. *Miss Fury* was a popular strip, enjoyed by both sexes, and Mills basked in the glow of celebrity its acclaim brought her" (Misiroglu 532).

As the comics open, rich socialite Marla Drake discovers another young woman will be wearing the same outfit as she is to a costume party. This is a horror for the young socialite, one that emphasizes the frivolity of her life. At once, she rips up her costume and refuses to attend. Her housemaid, Francine, suggests she instead wear the panther skin from her deceased uncle, who himself acquired the ceremonial robe from an African witch doctor. Marla Drake's friend, Albino Joe, warns her against wearing it, as it's cursed with strange powers and can actually work miracles. However, it fits her precisely. Wearing it connects Marla with the deep mystical, ancient traditions—all her partying lifestyle lacks (#1). Her uncle apparently insisted that she never part with the skin. As she thinks, "He believed whoever wore it would be able to accomplish almost anything!" but as Albino Joe warned her, "With every favor gained through black magic, go two misfortunes."

Thus equipped, she heads off for the party, but instead finds herself foiling an escaped murderer. In the process, however, the police come to suspect her. Newspaper coverage of the event dubs the mystery woman "Black Fury." After a few weeks, Drake corrects them that she should instead be called Miss Fury.

She continues wearing the disguise as necessary, a tool in her crimefighting, though it never subsumes her identity.

> Marla didn't play the wilting flower in order to cover up her secret identity of Miss Fury. She was a strong, determined woman who lived her life the way she wanted. Her Miss Fury persona was a means to an end rather than the answer to her dreams, and one that she didn't particularly enjoy. If anything, Marla was less like herself when events forced her to assume the disguise of Miss Fury. "Somehow, I've had nothing but misfortune since my uncle left me the black leopard skin! If the things that happened to me are blessings, they certainly have been well disguised!" [Madrid, *Supergirls* 9].

Some comic book characters wear the same thing every day, while others vary their clothing. Miss Fury resembles a fashion model in endless lacy evening gowns and day dresses with wide shoulder pads, as well as lingerie and sportswear. "Miss Fury ran for a very respectable ten years, outlasting most of its superhero rivals but also courting controversy. In the strip's later years ... one 1947 costume was so daring that 37 newspapers canceled the strip" (Misiroglu 349).

> Though she started off in comic strips, Miss Fury soon made the slide into comic books. The comic books were apparently intended for a female audience, as issue #4 included a page of paper dolls. By selling more than a million copies during the war, Miss Fury had taken America by storm. A poll taken showed that one hundred percent of men and ninety percent of women were fans of the cat-suited heroine (Robbins 21). Miss Fury was apparently popular enough that she was brought back in 1991 by Adventure Comics [Florence 20–21].

Wonder Woman wore the same outfit for countless decades before, in the Pérez era, she began playing with a wide variety of outfits, suggesting that as an ambassador or lounging at home, she might prefer something other than red and starry blue. Rucka put her in jeans. On her 70s television show, she varied her starry uniform with a formal cape for visiting the White House and a Western version in "The Bushwhackers" (112) with long-sleeved red shirt and white calf-length trousers.

> When the television series emerged in the 1970s, Wonder Woman received several new additions to her wardrobe. She had a Wonder Wet Suit, a Wonder Biker costume, a Wonder Skateboard suit, and a cape. These outfits not only made her more effective at her job but demonstrated that Wonder Woman was an active, athletic woman. Wonder Woman excelled in activities that were normally attributed to masculinity [Knight 307].

Like Miss Fury, several Marvel characters reveal a love of lavish clothes. In *Marvel Her-oes*, the Wasp explains, "I can only use my own clothes because my dad's treated the fabric to shrink with me." At the same time, she discovers her talent and dreams of being a fashion designer (Randolph). The adult Wasp designs many variants for herself as well as Ms. Marvel's lightning bolt suit.

Sue Storm creates her team's uniforms and Reed, trying on his suit, praises the design: "Say! This isn't half bad, Sue! You ever think of working for Dior?" (*Fantastic Four* #3). Adolescent Molly of *Runaways* makes costumes, though she is the only one of their exasperated group to do so. Ryan North, writer of *Squirrel Girl*, adds:

> One of the first things Erica [Henderson] did was redesign Squirrel Girl's costume: she came up with maybe 10 different options, and they all had these really great elements in them. And I wanted to use them all, so we decided that Squirrel Girl would be tweaking her own costume all the time, trying out different outfits to see how well they work. I'm excited for that: in real life people change their clothes every day—hopefully—and their looks pretty regularly: why should super heroes be any different? Especially super heroes in college, which is where you go to reinvent yourself? [Beard].

Michael Carroll's novel *Super Human* has superstrong Abby, who also has metal controlling power, don clothes she's carefully assembled—heavy boots from an army surplus store, plus a discarded leather biker's jacket and jeans she's modified with hundreds of steel washers threaded on wire to create her own chain mail (47–48). Many heroes and heroines create the first outfit from scrounged materials around them, only later upgrading to a proper supersuit. Cassie, Wonder Girl, assembles a realistic teen outfit including a black t-shirt with the Wonder Woman "W" crest, a black leather jacket, gloves, red shorts, goggles, and a black wig to hide her identity. Penelope Parker makes a costume from leg warmers from failed gym and a tutu from failed ballet, emphasizing how she's shaped by her past (Cook, "Penelope Parker"). Silk weaves her costume from her own powers.

Clothes control how others see us, emphasizing one's inner power like the panther suit or functioning as concealing disguise. Of course, the costume allows the heroine to break out of her everyday world and perform superhuman feats as another self.

> Superhero comic books are considered genre fiction. It highlights the thesis that costumes—not just uniforms or fashion—are a vital element of a superhero persona. More vital, even, than the moniker. You can call yourself "Batman" all you want, but if you run around in a tracksuit, no one will make the connection. Take away the cowl and the cape, and it's not Batman. It's Bruce Wayne in a tripped-out tracksuit, most likely made by Armani. By the same token, Captain America can't wear what every other American soldier does, because he's not every other American soldier. He has to stand out. Comics are a visual medium, and costumes are key [Milik].

Barbara in the film *Batman & Robin* (1997) appears a sweet schoolgirl, complete with uniform. "By day she is a refined private-school teen, dressed in tartan skirt and blazer. By night, she wears leather, rides motorbikes, racing deadly hoods through the back streets of Gotham" (Mainnon and Ursini 135).

She tells Dick Grayson it's her release, though it's gotten her kicked out of school:

> BARBARA: I started racing after my parents died. There was something about the speed, the danger, that took me out of myself, that made the hurt go away. You wouldn't understand.
> DICK: You'd be surprised.

Having hung up her own costume, May, elseworld daughter of Spider-Man, thinks, "I just began my junior year at Midtown High and I discovered I really like being a normal teenager." She has better grades and time to spend with friends. However, she finds herself moonlighting in a hoodie, stopping crooks out of a need for adventure. "I promised my parents I wouldn't become Spider-Girl—but we never discussed Red Hoodie Girl," she thinks (DeFalco, *Amazing Spider-Girl* #1). This is how many early superheroines started: The Woman in Red, the first ever to don a costume, arrived in Standard Comics' *Thrilling Comics* #2 (March 1940). "She was actually police officer Peggy Allen, but by night she sported a crimson hood, mask, and cloak—as well as a revolver—to mop up crime without the judicial restraints that tied her hands in her day job" (Misiroglu 532).

> Making her debut in 1947, Black Canary was the archetype of the new Film Noir era heroine…. A gorgeous blonde in a low cut black swimsuit, bolero jacket and fishnet tights, Black Canary was actually Dinah Drake, a florist who wore her black hair tied in a bun, and sensible, high-necked blouses. When trouble brewed, Dinah slipped into her fishnets and pinned on a blonde wig to become the gutsy, karate chopping Black Canary. But Dinah had another incentive to lead a secret life. A roguishly handsome private detective named Larry Lance became a frequent customer in Dinah's florist shop. He had a knack for getting into trouble, and Dinah would usually end up switching into her Black Canary guise to rescue him [Madrid, *Supergirls* 24].

Miss Fury only wears her panther suit on occasion, more often relying on her wits, reflexes, and detective work, even at night. The skin has claws over the knuckles and possibly a weighted "tail" for smacking guns out of people's hands. At the same time, the costume gives her freedom to operate outside her everyday respectability and prowl through buildings at night. "The form-fitting suit apparently offers ease of movement—a must when trouncing Nazi officers, and its cursed properties allow her to go about with the padded feet of a panther, which is conducive to the martial arts style fighting that she appears to prefer…. She is obviously fighting evil, and appears fully capable of handling herself" (Florence 21).

Wearing the costume, Miss Fury doesn't display any occult powers, but instead they free her from her life of dullness. For the New-York-bound creator, Miss Fury must have likewise seemed an "other self" of pure escapism—this is why Marla Drake is an exact copy of her artist. Miss Fury went on wild adventures in Brazil, solved crimes, had men fight over her, and showed off a fabulous wardrobe.

There's additional significance to Miss Fury's costume. Her panther suit clearly reflects her beloved sidekick—an actual cat. Though Persian cat Peri-Purr seems a simple pet, he is known to leap on villains and scratch and claw them. When Miss Fury is replaced by an imposter, the cat suspects and reveals the truth. In another storyline, Marla releases her cat into a house so she can sneak in and reclaim her costume, thus linking the animal with her superhero self.

Miss Fury's costume links her with her greatest adversary and finally her child. Her greatest nemesis, Baroness Erica Von Kampf, is glamorous and blonde … though with a chilling swastika branded on her forehead. She is a femme fatale, with a son named Darron, whom she's abandoned to be raised by mad scientist Diman Saraf. Darron escapes Diman and comes seeking Marla—attracted from the first to her leopard skin, which he identifies as a "cat." Marla finds him endearing, and is saddened when Diman carts him away. However, Marla considers following. As she thinks, "I could climb that wall with this black leopard skin but, as Albino Joe said, it's accursed…" (Tarpe 60). As she begins to talk herself out of it, she hears Darron scream. On goes the costume. Investigating in her catsuit, Marla discovers to her horror that Diman intends to kill the boy in a vicious experiment (Tarpe 50). She scales ropes to enter his lair, wraps the toddler in her cape, and loads him on her back. With Darron sharing her liberating costume, they escape together. After, Marla tries to adopt little Darron, but like many women in her war era, she is denied because she is single. Nonetheless, she perseveres, and after years of work, finally gains custody and returns with Darron to the U.S.

As Marla once loved Erica's husband Gary Hale, then loves and raises her son, Marla and Erica seem two halves of the same character—one moment the bad mother, the next, the good. They almost never encounter each other directly, emphasizing their shared personhood. During the women's only meeting, Marla is on the run from the police in her catsuit, as they think she's a burglar. While she's stealing Marla's clothes (which she offers to pay for) the women get into an extensive catfight and Erica attempts to kill her, before Marla escapes in her clothes, becoming the Baronness in truth (Tarpe 12). This is known as the Jungian shadow—one's dark side brought to life, and a staple of the hero's and heroine's journey, with the many evil twins of comics. Their shared outfit provides the link, like walking in the other person's shoes. Marla adopting Erica's child is an even greater connection.

So many heroes use their costumes to express how they want to be perceived:

The Fantastic Four and X-Men wear uniforms. Joining an army, putting on a uniform means "giving up your personal life and accepting a socially determined manner of life in the service of the society of which you are a member" (Campbell and Moyers 15). The Green Lanterns, Star Sapphires, and so on, wear uniforms that reflect the colors of their powers.

Janet Van Dyne (the Wasp) insists that in a hundred years all people will remember is "what we did and what we looked like," as she adds, "Our uniforms are as much a part of our legacy as anything we'll ever do" (Bendis, *The Pulse* #11). Thus the many fashions of the decades are tied into the costumes:

> The 70's were about sensation and pleasure; the 80's craved alienation and suppressed emotion. Storm used her new leather and studs fashion and the accompanying harsher attitude to build a wall around herself, to keep the world out. "The difference is not cosmetic ... my appearance is an expression of something deep within me.... I find myself casting aside the precepts and beliefs that gave my life meaning—and hardly missing them once they are gone," Storm tells Professor X, as she tries to cope in a world grown cold and forbidding [Madrid, *Supergirls* 230].

For most heroes, the colors and symbols are created in homage. There are animal costumes for Miss Fury, Catwoman, the Cheetah. Like many Golden Age heroes, Wonder Woman, Captain America, and Superman have patriotic colors. When Batwoman's father presents her with her costume, he calls it "red and black ... the colors of war" (Rucka, *Batwoman: Elegy*). He adds a bat symbol "so everyone knows whose side you're on." Power Girl notes that people always ask why she has her "boob window" in her plain white costume. As she explains, she wanted a symbol like Superman's. As she adds poignantly, "I just ... I couldn't think of anything. I thought, eventually, I'd figure it out. And close the hole. But I haven't" (Conner, *Power Girl: Power Trip*). Of course, Batgirl, Supergirl, Hawkgirl, Wonder Girl, and so forth dress to mirror the central heroes of their stories. The film *Sky High* half-jokingly explains that sidekicks must color coordinate their costumes with the heroes for maximum effectiveness.

Still, it's hard to ignore that while Green Lanterns wear full-length uniforms, their feminine counterparts the Star Sapphires (armed with the power of love) wear basically two thin strips of cloth over their breasts.

> When looking at superheroines in the comic books, it is difficult to see the justification behind their costumes. If one is going to be flitting about the sky while battling villains, why wear a miniskirt (Supergirl, Mary Marvel)? If one's profession requires extensive range of motion, why wear a corset (Lady Rawhide)? If running after bad guys is in the job description, what is the point of wearing stiletto heels (Zatanna)? How did the battle thong (Vandala, Chastity) get approved as appropriate demon-fighting attire? Many superheroines, especially those of recent years, are attired in costumes that seem more appropriate for dancing on tables than for saving the world [Florence 54].

Only in the film *Deadpool*, itself a parody of superheroing, does the villainess's impractical corset pop open in combat. A few other stories deconstruct the outfits. In *Seven Soldiers*, one superheroine becomes an erotica star. "Women wear cleavage-baring costumes, men pay good money for pictures of bullets bounding off heroines' ample chests, and superhero team-ups are presented as euphemisms for more intimate liaisons" (Singer 238). Emma Frost of *X-Men: Origins* actually *is* a stripper, explaining her corset costume. On *Powers*, Retro Girl describes how much baby powder is needed for her to wear her old costume. She-Hulk wears tight bodysuits, to her alter-ego's dismay. Her human side Jennifer explains: "Superheroes have a different dress code, too. Shulky's PVC, Lycra, leather, sequined, and studded ensembles crammed the guest closets. She always dumps her clothes on the floor, expecting me to put away her thigh-high boots, spangled bikini bottoms, and chain-mail bras" (Acosta, *The She-Hulk Diaries* 17).

In another story, Wonder Woman tries many outfits, disgusted that as she puts it, "someone instagrammed my butt last month during the Mexican earthquake relief." She describes everyone tweeting about her cellulite and interviewing her about her hair. "You know, there's an entire kink subculture of people who want to be punched and slapped by me," she adds (De Campi, *Venus Rising*). She accepts their fees and donates the money to charity, in a problematic storyline. There are also all the scenes where the women change clothes in the panels.

> One study conducted by Jessica H. Zellers shows an examination of how women are depicted in eighteen graphic novels. She finds that "of the suggestively clad, partially clad, or naked individuals, about three times as many were women (296) than men (107)." From the graphic novel sample where there were 1,768 male characters and 786 female characters, only 6% of all males were suggestively clad, partially clad, or naked; while of all the females, 38% were suggestively clad, partially clad, or naked. Additionally, of all males, 2% were naked, while of all females, 24% were naked. Zellers writes: "It is incredible that almost one out of every four females was, at some point, depicted in the nude" [qtd. in Jehanzeb].

Jenette Kahn, president of DC Comics, acknowledges that comic books are based on "male fantasies even if the character is supposedly female. This dependence on male fantasies is also self-perpetuating. Since most comics are based on male fantasies, few women read them; since few women read them few women are interested in the comic book industry, comics are based on male fantasies" (qtd. in Florence 55).

A few 40s and 50s costumes were modest to the point of full-length suits, like Batwoman's. Nonetheless, most heroines' costumes, rooted in 40s "good girl art" with shorts and halter tops or slinky gowns, grew briefer and briefer.

Power Girl is accustomed to everyone staring at her giant cleavage to the point where she thinks she'll never need a mask (Conner, *Power Trip*). In *Wonder Woman* #153, Wonder Girl asks Arrowette to give her a makeover with a starry miniskirt, though she insists, "A super-heroine's IQ should be bigger than her chest measurements." Superboy assures her he liked her before, and she realizes "You don't need lipstick and hot pants to like yourself." Wonder Woman writer Phil Jimenez insists:

> This is my argument for the "bathing suit" costume—that costume is all about sex, sexual power, sexual defiance, body freedom and absence of shame. Of course it's not "practical"; no superhero costume is. It's a symbol of something else. Thus, the constant need to modify it, to make it battle-ready, to make it "practical" rather defeats the whole purpose of the original costume. This was, originally, a character that was full of fun and light; who saw crime fighting as an adventure; who had no shame about her body; who was a skilled enough athlete and fighter she'd never need armor in the first place (and while she used a sword here and there over her first few decades, it was rare with her, because really, with her power and speed, wouldn't that just be cheating? Where would the fun, and self-betterment be in that?) [Illidge].

It's an ongoing debate from the 40s through today, with occasional twists on presuppositions. For instance, on *Smallville*, season seven's Clark Kent plays surrogate parent to the newly arrived Supergirl. "She's a young teenager ... she's a little rebellious," notes Kara's actress Laura Vandervoort. "She knows what she wants and she goes after it" ("Supergirl: The Last Daughter"). Rebelling against her "uptight" cousin, she dons a red bikini and parades around the house in it to his embarrassment, as she prepares for the Corn Pageant. Though this is certainly problematic, it seems a wave to 90s girl power: "Girl power heroines, while strong, are also thoroughly feminine, wearing short skirts and makeup not to please society but *because they want to.* This era of feminism has been designated "third-wave": Unlike the 1970's second-wave demands for equality, third-wave feminism believes in choice, in multiple paths to feminist empowerment" (Frankel, *Buffy* 12).

"Today's women can be strong and sexy and they don't have to apologize for it," adds producer Alfred Gough ("Supergirl: The Last Daughter"). Kara reminds Clark that he too was gender-clichéd as a teen, and refusing to let her be a beauty queen as he was an equally stereotyped quarterback is hypocritical.

Another answer creators find is flipping the exploitation, acknowledging the sexy nature of comics by stripping the men for the eyes of female viewers. On the big screen, Thor, Wolverine, and Captain America show lots of skin, which the women of the films admire with frank admiration. Arrow's constant shirtlessness on his own show is something of a running joke. Some comic book artists highlight Nightwing's posterior (often paired with his acrobatics) in a way usually reserved for female characters. And Namor, in his swim trunk costume, is often highly sexualized. "Ad Vice" by Abby Denson and Emma Vieceli has Marvel's top heroes lounging in speedos as Mary Jane contemplates them as dating prospects. *Mockingbird* (2016) has the fully-dressed heroine rescuing Hawkeye and Lance Hunter, who have both been stripped to their underwear.

Of course, the main reason to wear the superhero costumes is power—self-expression and a statement of heroism. This is why many women cosplay superheroines at conventions—Wonder Woman or Supergirl's strength, not their cleavage. It's a symbol that the person in the suit can do miraculous feats.

> Melissa Benoist, the star of the upcoming television series *Supergirl*, felt a range of emotions the first time she put on her signature leotard and cape to play Kara Zor-El—but most of all she felt empowered. "It's impossible not to feel empowered when you put it on," the former *Glee* cast member told *Entertainment Weekly*. "I feel like a different person almost. It really is an alter ego, where I feel inspired, hopeful and empowered" [Rhodan].

Shadow Side: *Savage She-Hulk* (Marvel Comics, 1980)

"I am a bright and accomplished woman—so why do I always slip up and revert to being a six-foot-seven, jade-green party girl/superhero?" Jennifer asks poignantly (Acosta, *The She-Hulk Diaries* 17). In fact, she's repressed, a lawyer who rarely dates and takes no time out for fun. This is when the shadow comes to play.

In She-Hulk's famous origin story by Stan Lee and John Buscema, Bruce Banner visits his mousy lawyer cousin Jennifer Walters, seeking a confidante. However, when he hears which criminals she's been taking on as a lawyer, he warns her that they could kill her. She laughs off his fears, responding, "Those things only happen in movies."

Immediately, however, the pair enter a fantastical world more like fiction than reality. Nicholas Trask, a crime boss at war with her father, Los Angeles County Sheriff William Morris Walters, has operatives who shoot Jennifer as a pawn in their struggle. Banner, in this case cast as her helpful best friend, carries her to a doctor's office and gives her a transfusion of his blood.

Jennifer wakes in the hospital and discovers her bones are tingling—she's on the edge of transformation. As she thinks, "I'd better forget Doc [Banner] for a while and figure a way to prove Trask is guilty! If only I weren't so frail, so powerless…."

As she ponders this, the goons break into her room, disguised as doctors.

Under threat, her dark frightening side bursts out. She turns giant, green, ragged, savage. She-Hulk, like Medusa or the Furies from Greek myth, is the force of female rage, the power that women keep bottled up in order to act "nice" and civilized. However, in the comic, "a burning, blazing all-consuming *rage* flows through her veins like hot seething lava." Describing her transformations, Jennifer Walters explains:

> I felt the roar of She-Hulk's personality—the bravado, the swag, and sexiness. There was a sharp moment when we coexisted, when I was She-Hulk and She-Hulk was Jennifer Walters, and it always felt amazing, like pure shimmering joy, like utter rightness and balance and perfection, and the universe stopped for that moment.
> Then it was gone and I existed like a shadow within her [Acosta, *The She-Hulk Diaries* 72].

The shadow is all civilization deems unacceptable—all the individual has buried deep within. "The shadow cast by the conscious mind of the individual contains the hidden, repressed and unfavorable (or nefarious) aspects of the personality." However, it is not evil, only too primal and unmannerly for everyday life. "Just as the ego contains unfavorable and destructive attitudes, so the shadow has good qualities—normal instincts and creative impulses" (Henderson 110).

The thugs in terror call her a "She-Hulk," and she responds: "You called me a She-Hulk! And a She-Hulk I'll be!" If she is to be condemned as a monster for releasing her powerful side, she may as well revel in it. She hurls the iron bed at them and they scamper. While the proper, law-abiding Jennifer tried to prosecute them as criminals, Savage She-Hulk is sick of the rules and rips the elevator car apart, yelling, "I'll get them" over and over. She is sick of following the rules while men break them to attack her. This lashing out indicates a welcoming of all the fury and terror buried deep within, an embracing of her dark hidden strength.

> For the individual, one of the major tasks in the process of psychological development is to recognize, acknowledge, and accept those rejected aspects of the self (the shadow). The process of integration through acknowledging and accepting the shadow aspects of our personalities gives us depth and access to a greater range of expression. Oftentimes the shadow will hold hitherto unknown powers and capabilities [Von Franz, *Individuation* 170–171].

"I never felt like this before! I can doing anything!" She-Hulk marvels. "I'm throbbing with power." In fact, her first act is to terrorize the goons into confessing Trask is a murderer, then to turn them over neatly to the police. She-Hulk is seen aiding Jennifer Walters' professional life, using her strength to aid her other self's "day job." She ends the comic thinking, "From now on, whatever Jennifer Walters can't handle—the She-Hulk will do." She has discovered a valuable tool.

The young adult novel *The She-Hulk Diaries* features Jennifer's frustration with her alter-ego. Comparing the more powerful side of herself to a sloppy roommate, she always fights for control. More tellingly, she considers her a separate person. Meanwhile, She-Hulk leaves her notes and gifts like flyers for singles' events, encouraging her to let loose a little in her everyday life. She-Hulk is also protective, to the point where Jennifer thinks, "I knew that Shulky wouldn't tolerate anyone spanking me, not even Dr. Stunning" (Acosta 232). However, Jennifer channels She-Hulk into enormous strength. At book's end, she decides, "I'm her and she's me, and we may as well stop treating one another like annoying roommates" (Acosta 314).

The monster is an essential psychological figure, acting as the catalyst for personal growth. "To encounter the monster by engaging it in combat or by taming it implies action originating from the [hero] but engulfment implies action by being acted upon…. But this transformation, insofar as it passes through symbolic death, also means a new beginning" (Beaudet 221). Having the monster burst from Jennifer challenges her to recognize the strength waiting to emerge from her and transform.

> She-Hulk, as a character, should give everyone the strength to be who they are, despite what our culture's gender norms dictate. She-Hulk is unashamed of her femininity just like we should all be unashamed of who we are. She just has *fun* and finds *joy* in her life, which she lives on her own terms. Masculine, cisgender males get this type of affirmation in nearly every sitcom that exists; Sam Malone is the default macho protagonist while Diane Chambers has her intellect turned into a punchline…. She-Hulk is important in the Marvel Universe because she proves that everything we've deemed feminine is not laughable; it's viable, powerful, and worthy of celebration [White].

In a multi-part adventure in *Superman's Girlfriend Lois Lane* #70–71 (1966), Catwoman forces Lois into one of her catsuits, hypnotizing her to think she *is* Catwoman and loading her up with gadgets. Unexpectedly, Lois revels in this. Surrounded by lions and tigers, she cries, "Snarrrlll! I'm not afraid of them!" (Dorfman). Thanks to Catwoman's catnip, they become her willing subjects. She turns them on Clark Kent, a do-gooder and thus Catwoman's enemy. The beasts tear at his clothes, exposing his secret identity … something the real Lois has always desired. Meanwhile, Catwoman takes Lois's role, convincing Superman she's Lois and beguiling him into kissing her, something she considers "Dee-lish" and "the Cat's Meow." With Superman off coddling Catwoman-as-Lois, the real Lois, coming out of her hypnosis, rescues herself from a cage in a daring feat of acrobatics. In Catwoman's car, she charges in to save Superman, only to discover Catwoman has transformed him into a cat (well, a super-cat) and locked him in a kryptonite cage. Lois saves him from it and cares for him until she can figure out a way to restore him. Her adventure leaves her delightfully powerful as she revels in the bad girl's strength.

This power, of course, lurks within everyone. Emir Ribeiro's Brazilian hero Velta can transform into a seven-foot tall Amazonian who can fire electricity and concussive force from her fists (or anywhere else) and has strong healing powers as well. She clearly represents the heroine's best, most powerful self. She fights crime, enjoying the thrills and the spotlight as She-Hulk does (*International Catalog*).

Nonetheless, it often comes with a touch of darkness. Scarlet Witch tells Jennifer, "I know how it feels when your life is out of control, Jennifer. My mutant ability is to create chaos. To make the improbable a certainty. Sometimes, all of this negative energy sends my head spinning too. Sometimes I feel as if I can do nothing but perpetuate the unnatural." She reminds her that they both have friends in the Avengers who will help them (Johns, "The Search for She-Hulk").

At a party in *Avengers* #291–294, the guest Avenger Marrina begins devouring everything in sight. "Once before I saw Marrina behave with such violence … when she was drawn to her genetically encoded mate," her teammate Namor thinks. When he tries to stop her, she transforms into a ferocious fanged sea creature. She dives into the water and her husband dives after her. Notably Captain Marvel and She-Hulk protest killing her, while the men believe she will have to die, as she threatens the innocents around her. Harkening back to ancient goddesses, she's described as "a grim and awesome specter, recalling an ancient time before the age of men when monsters held dominion over all the earth." Finally, Namor is forced to slay her. "We dared to love though we were of two worlds, and this is our fate," he notes tragically. While her shadow here is terrifying, it represents her greed and overwhelming hunger tearing from her to take over all aspects of her life, having been repressed for far too long. "The qualities we have renounced and tried to root out still lurk within, operating in the shadow world of the unconscious," as Vogler puts it (71). On occasion, they will burst from where they lie suppressed and take over the personality. Only by dragging them into daylight can the heroes understand themselves as full individuals. Or not, if the male characters promptly kill her.

Unlike in some monster comics, Jennifer's savage shadow is gorgeous. "She-Hulk wows the men with a body that is the epitome at once of sexiness and of superheroic strength" (Robinson 100). Everyone admires her and wants to date her. Her fanmail, especially, from fans "mostly presenting themselves as terminally horny adolescent boys—provide monthly reinforcement of the notion that Shulkie, as she is nicknamed, is not only the top female in the comics, but also the most desirable woman on (at least) this planet" (Robinson 100).

> She-Hulk is an important character because she is everything that is feminine in a way that Hulk is everything that is masculine, and she's a character that owns it. She's a character that shows that, yes, you can be invested in your looks while also being a take-no-prisoners lawyer. You can enjoy shopping, and you can also be an A-list Avenger. She's a role model for young girls that says, "You can be as girly as you want to be—and that *is awesome*" [White].

Eventually She-Hulk gains control of her transformations. Following this, Jennifer decides that she is going to retain her She-Hulk form permanently—having discovered the freedom, confidence, and assertiveness that it gives her. Like only a few superheroes, Jennifer ends up without a human side—she is tall and green day and night. As a metaphor, this suggests not fitting in, but also taking pride in her inner savagery, owning it and displaying it like a badge. After her own comic ran 25 issues, she joined the Avengers and Fantastic Four, then regained a solo series in 1989, called *The Sensational She-Hulk*. Half was written and drawn by John Byrne who famously made the character self-aware, adding a new dimension to her shadow powers.

Superheroes display their shadow self proudly, unlike most fictional characters and real people. The shadow is what's unacceptable in polite society—the crazy inventor side or unsightly squirrel tail—all the qualities "normal people" don't display. Some series have the character frantically passing as normal, bundling his wings under a big coat like Angel in *X-Men: The Last Stand*. However, when he unfurls those wings and flies, the world stands in awe of his hidden glory, finally revealed. Superheroes "separate their secret selves from their super selves and rarely express conflicts about this schism" (Packer 133). They have a superhero identity with new name and costume, all giving prominence to the normally unacceptable self.

Outside superhero fiction, the heroine is more likely to meet her shadow as a foil—a person who reminds her of all she suppresses in herself and secretly wishes she could be. In *Witchblade:* "Ubique" (212), the long-dead Lucrezia Borgia confronts Sara on the astral plane and takes the Witchblade from her. The stone changes from blue to red, indicating an opposite purpose. As Sara's friend Gabriel puts it, "Look, legend has it that there is an alternate line of Witchblade users. Ones who are uhm … how should I put it, Sara, not so principled as you." She is Sara's inverse, using the glove for savagery not justice and truth. As Lucrezia notes, "It's true; The Witchblade enhances pleasure from sex and violence," so that's how she uses it, finally battling Sara and impaling her with the blade.

Spitfire, a World War II pilot turned vampire, has powers of speed and immense agility. A trail of fire follows her when she runs. Beginning her own arc, she faces a vampire who calls her a novice and tells her, "You'll only just be starting to realize what living this long is like. What the weight of all this meaningless history will do to you." Spitfire is struck by the shared experience. "I could have been you," the vampire screams in fury as Spitfire stops her (Cornell).

Battling her shadow Circe, Diana might be speaking to her own savage dark side. "Are you so incapable of functioning in a world where people respect, love, and treat each other as equals? By my gods—are you that afraid?" Circe responds, "I hate your hypocrisy and your pointless niceties—preaching values the Amazons and the Olympians barely comprehend—standing as a pinnacle for people who are as naïve as you." Here she voices the frustration boiling beneath Diana's surface as she tries to set a good example but knows she goes unheard and harbors dark thoughts like these in her heart. Driven to rage, Diana pulls back a fist, then refuses, noting, "I won't let you take my compassion from me" (Jimenez, *Paradise Found*). This is the shadow battle, one the heroine wins by acknowledging the power of the dark side, yet remaining true to herself.

◆◆◆3◆◆◆

Family Foils

Grandmother-Mentor: Miss Harkness (Marvel Comics, 1970–1989)

"For those who have not refused the call, the first encounter of the hero-journey is with a protective figure (often a little old crone or old man) who provides the adventurer with amulets against the dragon forces he is about to pass" (Campbell 69). More often of course, young women have female mentors. The little old woman in the woods, a benevolent grandmother figure like Cinderella's (rather modern) fairy godmother, is a purely helpful influence on the heroine's journey. She doesn't fear being supplanted by the competitive daughter and instead happily guides her. Jung explains that the daughter grows up identifying completely with her mother. As she develops her own personality,

> all the fabulous and mysterious qualities attaching to her image begin to fall away and are transferred to the person closest to her, for instance the grandmother. As the mother of the mother, she is "greater" than the latter; she is in truth the "grand" or "Great Mother." Not infrequently she assumes the attributes of wisdom as well as those of a witch. For the further the archetype recedes from consciousness and the clearer the latter becomes, the more distinctly does the archetype assume mythological features. The transition from mother to grandmother means that the archetype is elevated to a higher rank [Jung, "Psychological Aspects of the Mother Archetype" 102].

In *Ms. Marvel: Generation Why*, teachers appear for teen Kamala as Wolverine helps her battle giant sewer alligators. He tells Medusa, queen of the Inhumans, about her, and Medusa sends Kamala the giant teleporting dog Lockjaw and tutors her from afar. Medusa, of course, is a ruling queen and leader, all the young Inhuman Kamala might someday become.

Despite Medusa's power, the true grandmother mentor of Marvel is

Agatha Harkness. The white-haired woman is first introduced as little Franklin Richards' governess in *Fantastic Four* #94. Seeking a safe refuge for the child, the Fantastic Four take the baby to a house "that looks like Dracula's dream house," as Ben Grimm puts it. She greets them, imperious in blue-black and gold with a high Victorian collar. With skull-like shadows on her face, she escorts them all to rooms so they can stay the night in her manor. Of course, closeness with death and the mysteries is the ancient mentor's role.

Despite her elderly exterior, she easily fends off the Frightful Four when they try to kidnap the boy. As they climb the stairs, she warns them, "Come no further!" Ignoring her, they advance, only for her cat Ebony to transform into a panther and fling one villain out the window. "Surely you wouldn't threaten a frail lady like myself," Miss Harkness asks, hair flying wildly as she gathers mystic power and unleashes it. The Sandman and Trapster attack as well, but she turns the Sandman's body into rock and uses her magic to terrify the Trapster until he faints. When the Fantastic Four finally come running, it's to find Miss Harkness, now tidy, peacefully knitting by the sleeping baby's crib.

She finally hints to the Fantastic Four, then later tells them outright, that she is a practicing witch. After, Miss Harkness becomes Franklin's permanent governess. More than that, she's a source of extra perception for the team. While the heroes fight, Miss Harkness contacts them to warn them of danger, and occasionally directs their powers. She functions as the Fantastic Four's external senses, calling them telepathically when Franklin's powers manifest, and saving Reed from the Negative Zone. She finally wields little Franklin's developing powers, focusing them with adult control to destroy Ultron.

Through the actions of the warlock Nicholas Scratch, her son, her past is finally revealed. Once, she was leader of the New Salem, Colorado, a colony of witches. When her son takes over the community, he kidnaps his mother and puts her on trial in *Fantastic Four* #185–186. On the spot, he convicts her of treason for fraternizing with the outside world and sentences her to death. Clutching young Franklin, Miss Harkness decides, "I am old—I have seen my fair share of years! Whatever happens to me now does not matter! But nothing must happen to the child! … Thus I must act…. NOW!" She unleashes a deadly wall of flames, but not to fight, only to alert the Fantastic Four where they are.

There, the Fantastic Four fight Salem's Seven as Scratch's children are called. Thus they are Miss Harkness's own evil grandchildren. In this instance, the grandchildren are under the sway of their father, uniting with him to destroy the benevolent grandmother. This is an unusual twist, as the grandmother is normally a force of positive guidance for the youngest generation.

Thomasina Lindo, nonsuperpowered sheriff of the superhero town of

Tranquility, goes to see her mentor "the spirit of the jungle, the smartest and most powerful woman in the entire world. Witches come from all over the world to study at her feet." She is Salabal, a beautiful African woman and "jungle princess" as well as Tommy's grandmother. She takes her student into the hidden past through astral protection to reveal the source of their battle and gives Tommy a lion amulet that transfers her power to the younger woman (Simone, *Welcome to Tranquility*).

> Usually, when the hero is at the nadir of despair, a nurturing, strong, and independent woman appears to her. Although the hero associates this figure with her biological mother, often the actual mother is more captor than rescuer. The powerful and heroic woman whom she encounters may be a surrogate mother figure. Unlike the male seducer who claims that he can slay the dragons for her, the female rescue figure tells the hero that she is capable of saving herself [Pearson and Pope 184].

In a patriarchal world, this figure awakens the hero's own buried sense of self-determination, like an encouraging voice from within.

Likewise, when Katana's sword is broken, she takes it to the elderly woman rumored to be the only one able to fix it. She gives Katana grouchy but wise advice that trying to clean what is corrupt will only corrupt the doer (Nocenti, *The New 52: Katana*). Though Katana is mostly guided by her husband's soul in her sword, she still seeks feminine traces in her life.

Witchblade: "Periculum" (107) sees Sara undergo initiation. The Witchblade takes her into a dream state where she meets three previous holders of the weapon. Wearing her face, they tell her they are her—time is cyclical, not linear. They challenge her to become a warrior, defend herself with the Witchblade, cleanse the impurity from people's hearts. Through their counseling her on faith, love, and the nature of time, she gains a deeper understanding of women's magic and her ancestral gift. She accepts her mission and wakes from initiation with a new sense of purpose.

Miss Harkness ends her guardianship of Reed and Sue's son in *Avengers* #128, adding to Scarlet Witch, "My dear, I know of a desire in you … a desire to *be* more than you *have been*." Thus she appears to find a better fit for herself—tutoring the young woman in her growing power rather than safeguarding the life of a little boy. The Scarlet Witch eagerly accepts the offer to become a witch in truth. However, Miss Harkness's first assignment is that "you do *not* leave my side for the *slightest second* until the cock crows!"

They spend the night battling Necrodamus, who seeks to capture their souls. When Miss Harkness falls, the Scarlet Witch steps in. She fights him until all her spellcasting strength is expended; however, as Miss Harkness's cat's familiar eyes glow, she manages an unprecedented fourth strike. With the villain banished, Miss Harkness reveals that she was well the whole time and that this was a test. "But Wanda it was you who overcame Necrodamus ... you who drew upon your unconscious reserves of inner strength," she adds (Englehart, *Avengers* #128). Her stepping back allows the heroine to grow. "In this way, the mentor's qualities transmit to her goddaughter in an act more magical and divine than a mother's qualities transferring genetically.... The mentor offers different wisdom than the parents, but wisdom that is no less valuable" (Frankel, *Girl to Goddess* 37).

Later, Scarlet Witch explains, "It took Agatha Harkness's teachings to make me comfortable in my body, with its extra mutant power! Not that it ever seemed so strange to me, but other people were always reacting, always throwing me off balance" (Hembeck, *Vision and Scarlet Witch* #3). This is why, as she thinks, she fell for the Vision. With this new guide, she understands herself, and thus her true powers.

Eventually Salem's Seven take over the New Salem community again. They capture Agatha and burn her at the stake, apparently killing her. In the battle, a mental image of the deceased witch tells Wanda to not just funnel the energy of the fight but to use it. Wanda draws the power inward to help herself become pregnant with the Vision's children. In *Vision and Scarlet Witch* #12, she gives birth to twin boys. Thus the eldest generation dies, but her passing allows the birth of the new.

Another fascinating mentor is Madame Web, blind paraplegic Cassandra Webb, who lives on a weblike life support system. She guides Spider-Man as she can see much, attuned to the "web of life." When Madame Web sees her own death is coming, she joins Norman Osborn in an arcane ritual called the Gathering of the Five: The five participants will each receive knowledge, power, immortality, insanity, or death. She appears to die, but actually receives immortality, and finds herself much younger and healthier (Byrne, *Spider-Woman* #9). In this and other tales, the crone is the mistress of the gates of death, and, like Kali, also of rebirth and new life. Meanwhile, Mattie Franklin takes her frightened father's place in the ceremony and gets power as a new Spider-Woman, soon launching her own comic with 1999's *Spider-Woman* Volume 3. As the old woman loses her gravitas, the next generation is empowered.

Later, Madame Web mentors several Spider-Women, helping them take down her own evil granddaughter, the fourth Spider-Woman, Charlotte Witter. Using "torture, sensory deprivation and starvation," Doc Ock has given her powers, then forces her to kill other Spider-Women and finally Spider-Man. Charlotte's a killer of men, literally feeding off them after she stuns them. When Charlotte attacks the prior three Spider-Women, she absorbs their powers into herself (Slott, *Amazing Spider-Man* #6). The Spider-Women, Jessica Drew, Julia Carpenter, and Mattie Franklin, team up with Madam Web to find Charlotte and stop her. Madame Web follows her trail psychically, guiding Mattie and Jessica on foot until they find the villainess and rush into battle. When Mattie despairs, Madame Web tells her, "Concentrate! The powers are still yours, even if they reside now in Charlotte Witter." Thus guided by one who shares her gifts, Mattie reclaims her power from Charlotte and defeats her (Sears, *Spider-Woman* #1). She even gains powers from the others, like Jessica's Venom Blasts and Julia's Psionic webbing. Like Miss Harkness, Madame Web is the insistent voice at the edge of notice, guiding the heroine to succeed.

In *Amazing Spider-Man* #600, Madam Web sits, as she puts it, "in the home of my birth, a shriveled old spider alone in her web … surrounded by the corpses of those who once gave her nourishment." Lost in terrifying new visions, she cries, "A Gauntlet…. Sweet mercy … someone … someone is unraveling the web. They…." Suddenly, Ana Kravinoff, the new Kraven, and her mother attack. Devoted to killing, Ana's family imprisons Madame Web, along with Julia Carpenter, the second Spider-Woman, and Anya Corazón, Spider-Girl. They sit there, maiden, mother, and crone, with Madame Web consoling the other two. Before Madame Web is killed, she turns her power (and blindness) over to Julia "for the good of the web," elevating her from mother to seer and crone. With her new powers, Julia counsels Spider-Man to give up his hate and be a savior, to preserve the web of life. She thus saves the day. Though Madam Web has died, the lifecycle remains intact (Kelly, *Amazing Spider-Man* #637).

Carol Emshwiller's short story "Grandma" explores a Wonder Woman figure in her retirement. Now she wears a kerchief over her brittle hair and has false teeth. "Back in the olden days, Grandma wasn't as shy as she is now. How could she be and do all she did? But now she doesn't want to be a bother. She says she never wanted to be a bother, just help out is all" (220). Now, her granddaughter, the protagonist, helps the woman who raised her. While gawky and awkward, the girl spends her days saving animals, injured junco birds and stranded worms. She's out saving a jackrabbit when her grandmother, with failing vision, flies out looking for her and tragically falls. Though this kills her, the girl continues wearing the costume, channeling the older woman's memory as she does the small tasks of saving animals around her. She thinks, "Who's to say which is more worthwhile, pushing atom bombs far out into space or one of these little things I do? Well, I do know which is more important, but if I were the junco I'd like being rescued" (223). It's a quieter story of small deeds and legacies but a powerful one.

Caryn E. Neumann notes in "Babes and Crones: Women Growing Old in Comics": "Comics have long denied the existence of highly capable, attractive, mature women, which also reflects negative Western societal attitudes about aging women" (119). While there are older men with large roles in comics (Lex Luthor, Perry White, J. Jonah Jameson, Alfred, Professor X), women are basically all young-looking, even venerable queens like Wonder Woman's mother Hippolyte. Superheroines are generally known as "girl" (though they are adults) remaining perpetually in their teens or 20s. For today's writers, youthfulness is also linked with inner beauty. "In other words, heroes and heroines cannot be old and ugly, because they are good people" (Neumann 121). The (very few) powerful crones of comics, past and present, help to break down this stereotype.

Back in the Golden Age, a few superheroines actually found power through growing older. They transformed from nice young ladies into crone faces of rage and power. The beginning of the comic *Spider Widow* explains, "Beautiful Dianne Grayton wages a private war against crime and un–American activities, by transforming herself from a wealthy debutante into the Spider Widow, the most horrible dispenser of justice at all times!" As Widow, she's a wrinkled witch with pointy hat and a troop of spiders. Thus she can face down powerful antagonists without anyone dismissing her as just a girl. Likewise, Fantomah, Mystery Woman of the Jungle (a 1940 character often considered the first superheroine), lives deep in the African jungle, defending her territory from poachers. A beautiful blonde protectress of the jungle, she transformed into a terrifying, skull-faced goddess who judged the guilty with deadly brutality.

Evil Mentor: Birds of Prey (DC Comics, 2004–2011)

The Birds of Prey had a slow-growing origin. After Barbara Gordon was crippled in *The Killing Joke*, she teamed up with Black Canary in a one-off called *Birds of Prey*. The concept succeeded and more followed. The best-known run, which features Gail Simone as writer, added Huntress to the mix (no longer the alt-universe daughter of Batman and Catwoman, but now Helena Bertinelli, sole survivor of a mafia hit between rival gangs). Barbara as Oracle looks over all the world from a fortress, using her amazing memory and research skills to direct the team. Lady Blackhawk, a displaced World War II pilot named Zinda Blake, joins the lineup. Beside her are Dove, a flying fighter who nonetheless inspires peace in others, and her partner, the token male Hawk. There are guest appearances by Big Barda, Hawkgirl, Batgirl, and many other superheroines. Also Batman. The women make up a sisterhood, but find themselves looking for deeper wisdom as well.

Black Canary notes in *Sensei and Student*, "The ironic thing is, unlike most of my costumed peers, I've had no shortage of father figures. I'm waist deep in them. My own father, with all his faults…. The JSA, Batman, to some degree. Even Ollie, although that's a notion best left unexplored." While she has plenty of fathers, she finds herself seeking the feminine in the persona of deadly trainer Lady Shiva. She is the most powerful female warrior, a killing force who also understands the mystical feminine realm of deep perception and intuition. As Canary adds, "In some countries, being killed by her brings eternal honor to your entire surviving family."

Dinah visits Hong Kong and finally wins Shiva's approval—Shiva invites Canary to be her apprentice. "What I could *do* with her skills … what I could accomplish," Canary thinks. On learning more about the savage older woman, Canary declines on grounds of conscience, though Shiva half-jokingly offers to beat that out of her. When Shiva points out that Canary can use the skills as she wishes, the younger woman hesitates.

By the next book, Shiva is mailing her ornate letters ordering her to eat only salad or remove the bright colors from her living space, and Canary obeys. They finally strike a bargain: Each will take the other's place—Shiva will learn nonviolence and Canary will experience a childhood like Shiva's—with Shiva's mother.

When Dinah arrives, the elderly woman gives her a demonic grin and says, "Hello. I am to be your *mother*. This is the moment of your *conception*." What follows is truly brutal, as her new mother nicknames her Tag, meaning swine. She offers no love or mercy, only hardness: "Pretend this jungle is my womb and you are now my daughter in poverty. If you want food, steal it. If you want to keep your virginity, fight to defend it. I will not dress your wounds and I will not sing you lullabies."

Training with the dark mother teaches the heroine about the power of the death-dealer, the crone, as well as the all-powerful goddess, knowledge often held only by the murderous shadow side. As Poison Ivy of the film *Batman & Robin* (1997) notes in her Mother Earth persona, "Men. The most absurd of all God's creatures. We give you life and we can take it back just as easily." Clarissa Pinkola Estés, author of the celebrated *Women Who Run with the Wolves*, explains that the savage old woman in the forest is a valuable mentor for the untrained heroine, as she maintains a strength through grisly experience that the girl lacks:

Not so long ago, women were deeply involved in the rhythms of life and death. They inhaled the pungent odor of iron from the fresh blood of childbirth. They washed the cooling bodies of the dead as well. The psyches of modem women, especially those from industrial and technological cultures, are often deprived of these close-up and hands-on blessed and basic experiences. But there is a way for the novice to fully participate in the sensitive aspects of the life and death cycles [Estés 69].

The witch as antilife often takes the form of a surrogate mother—aunt or other stand-in. "The Magician from Mars" (1940) features Jane Q-X 3, daughter of a Martian and a human, whose exposure to a cathode ray gave her fantastic powers. When orphaned, Jane fell under the care of a callous aunt, who locked her up until she stowed away on a ship for Earth and had exciting galactic adventures. At the climax of her final story, she battles her nemesis the Hood. The handsome Taal steps in front of Jane as the Hood shoots her. He falls. Jane chases the Hood, only to discover "it is not a 'he' but a 'she.' It is Jane's own aunt!" Jane cradles her dying love and vows vengeance.

> Heroes wield their gifts in a more straightforward world, where their powerful swords kill antagonists and defend the helpless. Heroines, however, live in a more treacherous, shifting world, where even their mentor can seek their death. Just as the outdoor world threatens the hero, the interior world of the home offers shocking treachery for the heroine, which she must defeat in order to rule. Only through valor and ingenuity, not swordplay, can the heroine survive this surrounding threat to one day preside over her own household [Frankel, *From Girl to Goddess* 52].

Another story, the origin of X-Men's Firestar, has the girl, Angelica Jones, recruited by the White Queen, Emma Frost, to train at her school, not Charles Xavier's. Frost chortles, "The little fool! She actually worships me—little dreaming that I am secretly training her to become the Hellfire Club's most deadly assassin!" She sends her mutant Empath to toy with Angelica's emotions and gives her a bracelet that produces nightmares, both to turn her against the X-Men. As she comforts the crying girl at night she thinks, "As she slowly loses her grip on what's real, she'll become even more dependent on me!" (DeFalco). The most trusted, closest teacher can turn on the heroine in a way less seen in hero stories. Nonetheless, the cruel mentor has much to impart.

In *Kitty Pryde & Wolverine*, Wolverine drags Kitty into the wilderness and brutally trains her to be stronger. "Stronger the body, stronger the mind and spirit," he tells her. Only in her best shape can she exorcise the demon Ogun from herself. Though his lesson is wise, his methods are savage. When she falls and insists her ankle is twisted he still refuses to help her. She can't go on, Kitty whines. "Then *don't!*" he tells her.

> KITTY: I'll freeze here, Logan, I'll die!
> WOLVERINE: Then get up!
> KITTY: I can't!
> WOLVERINE: You won't. Your choice, girl. Live or die. Struggle or surrender. Maybe it's better this way. Just close your eyes and go to sleep, a quick clean finish rather than a lifetime spent scared stiff that Ogun'll come to claim you.

She accepts his lesson and grows stronger, finally defeating her foe.

In training, Dinah meets the little girl Sin, who touchingly curls up beside her when she's injured and calls her "sister." As generally happens in these stories, the girl represents the main character's innocent helpless side, though she's also a source of perception, noticing things Dinah does not. Sin advises her on whom to watch out for and adds that the villagers are calling her "Witch Bird or Night Canary." Her descent into darkness is beginning.

Soon, warlords prepare to invade the village with tanks. Canary urges Sin and all the innocent villagers to flee, but they refuse. Her foster mother tells her, "That is the problem with owning a sword, Tag. Sooner or later you'll want to unsheathe the blade."

To her horror, Canary realizes, "I can't save them all." At last, she goes into the jungle and obliterates all the warlords with a newly learned savagery. She reminds herself that every injury could save a villager's life and thinks, "I can't think of these men as human. Not and do what I have to do. So that's it. I become what I least wanted to be." As she succumbs to violence, she names herself "the New Shiva. And there is no mercy for you here." She has become the dark force she has trained under.

As she recovers from the battle, her "mother" reveals that she invited the soldiers there for Dinah to destroy as an initiation. "There must always be a Shiva" and she is to succeed the current one. When Canary refuses in horror and declares she's leaving, her mother retorts that if she leaves, Sin will be trained to take her place. She is the corrupter of all the innocents—both Dinah and her new protégé. While her mother chides her for throwing away "a priceless gift," Dinah retorts, "If I have to give up who I am ... then I don't need your gifts that badly." She fights Shiva's mother and defeats her, then adopts Sin and takes her to the U.S. to give her a happy life. Dinah thus becomes a mother at last, though she's determined to be a fun and loving one. In her new home, Sin discovers hopscotch and dolls, while the damaged Black Canary reconnects with her lost innocence after her painful trial.

In End Run, however, Shiva sends the White Canary to kidnap Black Canary or else Sin and her new adoptive family will die. Dinah has a truly horrific task ahead—she must formally challenge Lady Shiva to deadly combat, and with a broken wrist, she's doomed. Dinah notes, "In her own weird way.... Shiva truly cares about me. Wanted me to be her apprentice. I'm sure she agreed for Sin's sake. And for mine."

Lady Shiva says the task gives her no pleasure, but she's coldly determined to go through with it. However, out of love for her teammate, the Huntress challenges Shiva to fight her first. Meanwhile, Black Canary and Lady Blackhawk free Sin and return to end the fight honorably. As a team, the Birds win. Huntress finishes the story realizing how much her sisters love her, while Shiva rewards her for her valor with the name "Iron Owl." She too has turned to savagery and thus become a pupil of the dark mother.

Joss Whedon's comics feature several evil mentors. His young slayer, Melaka Fray, trains with the demonic looking monster Urkonn, who is less than gentle in his methods:

MEL: You hib me wib a girder!
URKONN: How many claws am I holding up?
MEL: You hib my face wib a whole girder!
URKONN: You were meant to duck [Whedon, *Fray*].

True, she has superstrength, but she's only beginning to learn. The true betrayal comes, however, after she finds her child sidekick dead and is spurred to battle the evil lurkers (vampires) and save her community. Later, she realizes the lurkers could not have killed little Loo—only her trusted mentor who longed to provoke her into action.

Whedon's arc on *Runaways* features another cruel mentor. "The more pain you learn to take, the more power you will control," says the Witchbreaker, the tellingly-named ancestress of the witch heroine Nico (*Runaways: Dead End Kids*). She puts her great-granddaughter through a terrifying ritual by teaching Nico how to withstand pain: she will come out of it either more powerful or dead. The Witchbreaker chillingly points out that Nico's pathetic existence isn't worth much, so it's a risk worth taking. Nico, in turn, snarls that she can handle everything the woman can inflict. In fact, she emerges from the ritual able to fly and wielding the Witchbreaker's staff, ready to defend her friends with newer, stronger magic.

Tatiana Caban, a mutant teen on the streets, meets a mysterious woman who takes her and her friends captive in Marjorie Liu's Marvel comic *Nyx*. She says her job is to "break some eggs, as they say. Break some hearts to make them stronger. A little hurt goes a long way." She tries to convince Tatiana that her rarity as a mutant gives her a valuable commodity—one she can either have exploited or exploit herself. The woman adds, "I offer you freedom, Tatiana. A chance to survive on your own terms." She notes that she was like Tatiana once, and now grooms "potential assets." She even hands the girl a gun and dares her to shoot her, insisting she make a choice. After Tatiana shoots (ineffectively), the woman adds, "Remember this, Tatiana Caban: you shot another person in cold blood, to save your life. You pulled the trigger twice. It'll be easier the third time. Eventually, you won't have to think about it." She's training the girl to be a killer like herself. Nonetheless, Tatiana rejects the woman's offer and survives. As she and her friends end the limited run and insist, "We keep surviving," they've taken part of her lesson to heart.

In a final example, the supervillain ruler of Apokolips, Darkseid, grooms villains as his "Hounds," including the imposing Granny Goodness. When Darkseid has Granny train up a dog, then kill it, Granny refuses, sneakily adding that "to have done otherwise would have robbed my lord of a most valuable asset." Darkseid discovers that indeed the dog (ironically named Mercy) will obey him over her mistress and tells Goodness that she has graduated with honors. "You have trained Mercy so well in my name that perhaps you'll do as well training others whose blind obedience I will one day require" (*Jack Kirby's Fourth World Omnibus*). She goes on to become chief of the Female Furies and also teach his elite soldiers, often using brainwashing and torture, and sometimes bringing these techniques to earth orphanages. She is the killer of the innocent, the crone who tortures children with her death powers. Of course, in this story, she is tortured herself and passes this cruelty on to her pupils in an ever-continuing cycle.

Brutal Patriarchy: Spider-Woman (Marvel Comics, 1977)

There's always a girl. Only this one is raised in a lab, manufactured by scientists for a single purpose:

To kill.

Imagine that. Imagine the loneliness of that life, and the coldness. No love. No kindness. No compassion allowed. The girl is stripped of her humanity in order to become a thing that will follow orders. She is conditioned to tolerate pain, and abuse, in all its most terrible forms.

Yet, there is a part of her that remains unbroken—that still thinks, and feels. Even if she does not understand those feelings.

The girl wants to understand, and she wants to be free—if she can figure out what freedom means.

She is X-23 [Liu, "Mutants"].

The poignant story of the young woman grown in a lab echoes through superhero fiction. Her creator is the patriarchy and she is his victim, helpless until she throws off his conditioning and forges her own path, in, of course, a metaphor for overcoming domination and the shaping of women by patriarchal culture.

In her first comic appearance, in *Marvel Spotlight* #32 (February 1977), Spider-Woman, created by Archie Goodwin, Sal Buscema, and Jim Mooney, leaps through the night "on finely spun wings of glistening filament" in a red spandex costume. Suffering from total amnesia, she's come to assassinate Marvel's heroic patriarch Nick Fury. Of course, her lack of identity and purpose makes her a victim of the male writers, lacking the inner quest that makes Spider-Man so endearing.

Overhead, "protected by clouds and anti-radar force screens," a Hydra airship reports in to base that "Agent Arachne has successfully gained entry to the Shield complex." They have named her and now watch from above, emphasizing their total domination. In fact, the name Arachne comes from the original Greek spider but also from a victim of the gods, as jealous Athena changed her into an insect. Inside, Nick Fury is interrogating a prisoner who's is "livin' proof that there's a nest of Hydra vipers around we ain't ever discovered!" Arachne sneaks in through airshafts and along walls until she comes to the Interrogation Room. She bursts through the steel door, then calmly removes her glove and points at the trio of agents. She zaps them with her "venom bolt," though it is "not fatal at this range." Arachne tells Fury he is next. "But the bolt will come when I'm touching you," she says, "bringing death for what you've done ... to the man I love!"

The story then flashes back to Arachne's earliest memories. She was in "a small Alpine village," being pelted with rocks by an angry peasant mob that waves pitchforks and says things like "Witch! Agent of Satan! Flee ... or die!" Clearly ordinary mankind has rejected her, leaving her isolated and friendless. Though she has no memories, she cringes in terror and strikes them with her electric bolts. A limo suddenly drives up, containing the glamorous Count Otto Vermis in a topcoat, cravat, gloves, and fedora. Whisking her to Hydra headquarters he explains sympathetically that Hydra, too, has "been unfairly persecuted, made outlaws by an uncomprehending world we struggle solely to aid and improve." Faced with an organization that's as ostracized as she is, she's convinced and quickly signs up. Commander Vermis treats her with a kind, fatherly affection, and "promises to penetrate that dark barrier clouding her memory."

Though he appears kind, he is the evil father-substitute of fairytale and fiction, preying on the young heroine in his protection.

> The father, as the heroine's choking restraint, represents part of the self that must be overcome. He is a force for tyranny and domination, the opponent in gender warfare, society's demands that the ... maiden surrender all traces of independence and give herself up to be mutilated. He is the predator, maiming the woman's soul along with her body, and presenting an obstacle the heroine must conquer and absorb [Frankel, *From Girl to Goddess* 99].

At this stage, however, Jessica surrenders to his domination. The Hydra scientists put her in a giant metal helmet of a "mind probe." Still, one stunned scientist reports, "No wonder the past has been traumatized from her mind!"

Vermis smiles. "It's perfect, Doctor," he says, "far better than I'd hoped. I can use it all ... mold her into Hydra's deadliest weapon ever!" Her past has given him the perfect leverage. He tells her they can't reverse her amnesia, but they train her to improve her venom blasts and agility, including spiderlike wall-climbing. Her other powers include a pheromone that makes men want her and women fear her, isolating her from her own gender and sabotaging any sense of solidarity.

Hydra gives her training in her powers, a costume, and an identity as Arachne. However, this is all a placeholder of an origin story—a corrupt substitute for real strength. In fact, they are lying to her at every stage, crippling her as much as they empower her. Nonetheless, the red costume and name faintly echo the superhero identity she will one day claim for herself.

She falls for Jared, their "top combat agent." At last, Vermis tells her S.H.I.E.L.D. has captured her true love. "Their director is a fanatic when it comes to Hydra," Vermis tells Arachne, "You know none of us can ever be safe until Nick Fury dies!"

In the present, Arachne and Nick Fury fight. As he runs, Jared grabs him and tells Arachne, "Kill him! Kill him now!" Fury flips Jared and he's the one struck by Arachne's electricity. As Arachne slams Fury against the nearest console, it starts playing back, and she sees Jared holding innocents hostage. She realizes, to her sudden horror, "Everything I've been told has been a lie," and "Hydra has manipulated me … used me." Fury stands to the side caressing his bruised neck. "It's one of their specialties, lady," he tells her.

Dying, Jared confesses that he was ordered to fake affection for her to set up her killing Fury. Arachne vows revenge and sets out for Hydra. She soars in, declaring that "a naïve girl you easily deceived is naïve no longer!" Count Vermis tries to run but Arachne vows to make him reveal "the secret of who I am" before she makes him "pay for all you've done." Hydra may seem menacing at a distance, but Arachne realizes that a single determined warrior can attack them. When she does, the man she had thought was so powerful cringes and flees.

As S.H.I.E.L.D. follows her in, Vermis bargains the truth of her origin for his freedom. As he leaves in a Hydra rocket plane, he says, "Of your true birth I know nothing, but I can tell you much of the moment when the exploding energy was unleashed that shaped you into what you are now." It was the High Evolutionary with his genetic accelerator who created her. This ultimate creator is only one more in the series of powerful men who shaped and remade her body and mind, changing her from human to hybrid. While Spider-Woman stands stunned and weeping, Count Vermis hurls a poison gas pellet at her. Though groggy from the gas Arachne makes "one powerful leap." They fight on the rocket, and she crashes the plane, escaping herself.

Back at the Hydra hideout, S.H.I.E.L.D. has won the day. Colonel Fury lights up a cigar and notes that there is "no sign of that Spider-Dame." He wishes her luck wherever she is—he's afraid she is going to need it.

Deep in the healing forest, Arachne glides down to earth. Her anger has fled, replaced by "bone-deep tiredness." Finally, she knows who she really is. "The only thing I don't know now," she reflects, "is if there's any way I can live or survive with that knowledge." Dejected, she walks into the sunset. This was the character's debut, but not under the name Spider-Woman and not with a clear plan to make her such.

When she shows up in her own comic a year later (Spider-Woman #1, April 1978), she is finally given a name, Jessica Drew. *Spider-Woman* lasted for 50 issues (April 1978–June 1983) with a television cartoon in 1979. However, the first cover's taglines are problematic, reading, "Now in her own book! The superheroine sensation they said couldn't be done! Special origin: All the world against her!" All this stresses the impossibility of making a superheroine comic, thus pitting not only "the world" against her but also readers.

The series continues problematic language around her gender—within the issues she is called a "raven-tressed arachnid adventuress," a "dark angel" or an "alluring arachnid," objectifying her. All men want her and women instantly loathe her because of her pheromone. Team-ups are common in her series. They're a good way to bring in readers, but many of these stories de-emphasize Jessica herself. One critic adds: "Throughout her fifty issue run, Spider-Woman works with Nick Fury, a wizard named Magnus, Jerry Hunt, the Shroud, Spider-Man, Werewolf by Night, and a host of other males. However, besides a quick run in with X-Men such as Storm and a friendship with Lindsay McCabe, Jessica's interactions with admirable females are almost non-existent" (Najafali). In fact, her greatest fights are against females. *Spider-Woman* #16 leaves her in the hospital with a black eye and bruises after her a very physical fight with Nekra.

> There are no instances where the same level of aggression is reached with a male villain and there is an editorial hesitance to have them get really physical with Jessica. This might not be meant to be misogynistic, but it does enforce the idea that female and male heroes are not equal. There's also a spark that is missing from a majority of her fights with males because of this. This overly restrained attitude makes many of her battles contrived and boring. The fights with females are some of the strongest moments of the series' run and should be appreciated; however, there could have been so much more to Spider-Woman if she was allowed to develop on her own without the writers forcing her in to or out of many situations [Najafali].

Her beginning story has her as lost and purposeless as her origin. With no hope of finding a job, as she thinks, she's using her costume to steal cans of tomatoes. After, she walks up to her flat, thinking, "They all sense it. They realize—I'm not all human! And that makes me even more alone than I was before." She can pass for human with curled blonde hair and normal clothes, but she's certain that she creeps people out. Whether this is her own isolation and trauma talking or whether it's true, she's certain she has no place in society.

Stuck in her wounded state, she cannot become a hero. This is a common plight for the heroine after her devastation by the patriarchy. "Because she does not know her feelings, she cannot feel the feelings of others, which is empathy and is the deepest requirement, essential to love and the creation of a better society," explains Gertrud Mueller Nelson in *Here All Dwell Free: Stories to Heal the Wounded Feminine* (43).

In her dreams she reverts to her childhood, to her father's experiments with arachnids. As a young girl, his science damaged her from radiation. To cure her, her father merged her DNA with various spiders, but her mother, horrified at the experimentation, soon died. The scientist who helped her father revealed himself as The High Evolutionary, helping Jessica undergo "uncountable eons of evolution … achieved in mere moments." Jessica awakens, realizing she's "neither human nor spider" but a frightening hybrid. As she concludes, "I no longer belong to anyone. I'm free now. I'm by myself at last. But, heaven help me, it still makes no difference! Now it' s people who shun me … people who run from me." Escaping the control of so many father figures has saved her on the surface, but left her with hideous damage.

Despite her conflict, she begins saving lives and becomes a hero. This of course is a great gesture because she feels set apart from those around her and fears they hate her. Her wounding has left her ill-equipped to deal with people. "To reach out, even inept hands, and begin to accept may be the young Queen's most heroic task—to embrace and accept her cross, her heroic deed," Nelson adds (139).

Spider-Woman's origin story (rebooted in 2009) once more has her father's experiments leading to her condition, damaging her while she's still in the womb thanks to a laser beam with the DNA of different species of spiders. When he discovers she's the spider project he's sought, he begins giving his ten-year-old shots to augment her condition. Here he is a worse villain, not only for his ties to Hydra, but for his deliberate destruction of his daughter. His sacrifice of his daughter suggests tension in their relationship, despite her youth. "When the father is predominantly critical of his daughter or largely unaware, uncaring, or demeaning of her femininity, he sells that blooming possibility to the Devil," comments Nelson (43). The villainy escalates—her mother tries to protect her so her father kills her. Jessica rushes to intervene, and her spider-bite electric power manifests. When the power nearly kills her, General Wyndham of Hydra takes her to their secret base, where she lies unconscious (Bendis, *Spider-Woman: Origin* #1).

As her new story begins, General Wyndham arrives to tell her she's been in a coma for 11 years and is now 21, much as she may feel only a child. In this puberty metaphor of sudden transformation, she is mentally unable to comprehend Hydra's world politics and falls under their control. Insisting, "I'm your friend, Jessica," the General manipulates her cruelly. The rest of the story, from Jared's betrayal to Nick Fury's offer of aid, goes about the same way, but this time her father is even more of an evil mastermind in thrall to Hydra.

Female robots or other constructed women like clones have often been created by the patriarchy, charging them to struggle past their conditioning. There's the new *Lazarus* comics, as well as DC's Platinum or Wolverine's counterpart X-23. Mirage, Miriam Delgado, was originally an orphan from Brazil, kidnapped and loaded with false memories by the Time Trapper. She later becomes a Teen Titan. Nebula, especially in the film *Guardians of the Galaxy*, cannot escape her conditioning to serve her creator Thanos. On *Heroes Reborn*, Hachiro uses his power to bring Katana Girl to cybernetic life so she can protect him. Soseh Mykros and her sister were artificially aged to adulthood by their father and subjected to numerous tests to reveal their powers. Hasmat's power in *Avengers Academy*, unfortunately, comes from the toxic radiation filling her and threatening those closest to her—Norman Osborn only makes it worse. Likewise, Chrysalis, a robot hero created by Dr. Gerard Yves Martet, carries a shell filled with genetically engineered butterflies that carry a deadly virus for a truly poisoned beauty. Their bodies become a metaphor for being recreated by society or the world's rulers, leaving them struggling to adapt.

The marginalized and subhuman heroine is sometimes seen as a race metaphor but also works for gender. It's an alternate path to enlightenment for the gender that's often been seen as a second class type of human or even an artificial construct. "To be feminized means to be made extremely vulnerable; able to be disassembled, reassembled, exploited as a reserve labor force; seen less as workers than as servers ... leading an existence that always borders on being obscene, out of place, and reducible to sex," explains Donna Haraway in "A Cyborg Manifesto" (439). Further, as the cyborg is augmented with technology, she seeks continual self-improvement beyond the conditions of her birth. "Liberation rests on the construction of the consciousness, the imaginative apprehension, of oppression, and so of possibility," Haraway explains (424).

Of course, some fathers are abusers or monsters. Likewise, Raven of *Teen Titans* battles Trigon the Terrible, tyrant ruler of his world ... and her father. When he tortures a child and prepares to kill her, Raven intercedes, using her empathy to take on the child's pain. After, Raven is "drained, lost, helpless, unable to cope with the overwhelming evil her father embodies." He makes her vow to stay with him or he will destroy earth. Helpless in the face of his overbearing power, she feels she has no other option. At last, her friends and her mother arrive to fight beside her, bolstering her resolve (Wolfman, *New Teen Titans* #6).

Most often, the heroine must destroy her creator. In *Guardians of the Galaxy*, Gamora betrays and abandons her adoptive father Thanos, deciding that preserving life in the galaxy outweighs his schemes for power. *Huntress: Year One* shows the young heroine at home. Her father Franco Bertinelli returns and beats his wife Maria for not having his dinner prepared, while eight-year-old Helena hides behind the couch. In fact, her father is the crime boss in charge of Gotham City. During that night's dinner, Helena coldly tells her father that she prayed for his death. At that moment, a masked man enters the house and shoots her family, sparing only her. Helena must wrestle her guilt over seeing the man coming and not warning her father, vicious as he was (Madison).

Occasionally, however, the patriarch learns better, as in the film *X-Men: Days of Future Past*. When Raven points a gun at the manipulative Trask, Charles Xavier appears, but only to plead with her, not force her:

RAVEN DARKHOLME: Get out of my head, Charles!

CHARLES XAVIER: Raven, please do not make us the enemy today.

RAVEN DARKHOLME: Look around you, we already are!

CHARLES XAVIER: Not all of us, Raven. All you've done so far is save the lives of these men. You can show them a better path.

HANK MCCOY: Shut her down, Charles.

CHARLES XAVIER: I've been trying to control you since the day we met, and look where that's got us. Everything that happens now is in your hands. I have faith in you, Raven [*X-Men: Days of Future Past*].

Once in a while, the heroine can flip the patriarchal dynamic and control the domineering force in turn: Wonder Woman actually aids Darkseid to save the world. After, she tells him she didn't just lend him her power but fused part of her soul into his. "There's a piece of me inside you, Darkseid. A piece that believes more than anything in joy and hope and peace" (Jimenez, *Paradise Found*). She hopes that this will transform the great conqueror for the better.

Squirrel Girl takes this a step further, coming to understand world destroyers like Galactus so well that she can work out a compromise. She suddenly realizes that he attacks earth ineffectively each time so humanity will find him an uninhabited world to eat, and she promptly locates one for him—filled with delicious nuts. One critic explains, she "gets all up in the villains' faces. Except when she sees the villains for who they are: wounded, struggling individuals hiding their hurts with rage. Then she decides to help divert their rage rather than beat them to a pulp. She still beats things to a pulp too though (mostly walls!)" (Loree). Through her empathy, she finds ways to let everyone win, even the forces of male power.

Leaving the Father: Aurora West (First Second Comics, 2014–2015)

Teen Wonder Woman notes, "At Super Hero High School, there seemed to be an unusually high number of dead parents. Occupational hazard" (Yee 62). Certainly, being orphaned is common for superheroes of both genders, forcing them to rely on themselves. The heroines of the *Alias* comic and *Dark Angel* are cast adrift on the world after losing their parents to tragedy. Many more heroines grow up with only a father, leaving them skilled in combat but lacking in the deep wisdom of the feminine.

"I'm nine years old when my father dies. He leaves his handprints on my face. His animal shadows in my head. His empty outline on the floor. An echo. Empty. Like me" (Mack). Maya Lopez, Daredevil's love interest, tells of losing her father. She also recalls him bringing her, at age nine, to a reservation. After the Shaman there taught her Indian sign language and told her lots of stories, she resolved to become a storyteller herself. "I hold on to the memory of my childhood," she adds even while telling a story of love, death and betrayal. She also envisions herself cradled in a woman's arms with colorful scarves, flowers, and protective vines. Her father is dead, her mother faded to the point of barely a memory. Thus the Shaman becomes her mentor and she returns to him in times of crisis. He tells her, "If we really want to know ourselves, we must at some point in our lives connect with a higher wisdom that knows all about us. Our weaknesses, our mistakes, our potentials" (Mack).

Anya Corazon, Araña, has a loving father. However, when facing bullies, she finds herself channeling her lost mother who told her, "Now dry your eyes and promise me you'll always be brave" (Avery, *Amazing Fantasy* #1). She wears her mother's locket every day, losing it when she transforms into Spider-Girl. This emphasizes her vulnerability as superheroine and also her desire to embark on her own path, without the burden of the past.

"The woman who fights against her father still has the possibility of leading an instinctive, feminine existence, because she rejects only what is alien to her. But when she fights against the mother she may, at the risk of injury to her instincts, attain to greater consciousness, because in repudiating the mother she repudiates all that is obscure, instinctive, ambiguous, and unconscious in her own nature" (Jung, "Psychological Aspects of the Mother Archetype" 99).

Several heroines find their mothers the true source of inspiration in their lives: their fathers, however powerful, are idols with feet of clay. The show *Birds of Prey* has a telling conversation between Helena, the Huntress, and the woman who will become Harley Quinn. Helena's parents were the absent Batman and murdered Catwoman, leaving her severely scarred.

DR. QUINZEL: Your father is one of the wealthiest men in the country and you move in with a schoolteacher?

HELENA: It wasn't exactly "father knows best." He didn't know he had a kid. Clueless is a radical understatement.

DR. QUINZEL: Sounds like your relationship with your father is somewhat conflicted.

HELENA: What relationship? He didn't raise me, my mom did. I miss her. She … she was funny, crazy and dangerous and … in that one moment, she was gone. That's when everything changed. I changed.

DR. QUINZEL: Into what?

HELENA: Into someone maybe I wasn't meant to be [*Birds of Prey*: "Pilot" 1.1].

Similarly, Aurora West, daughter of Acropolis's greatest hero, Haggard West, has a life defined by her father. She begins as a sidekick in the *Battling Boy* comic, determined to avenge her father's death. The author notes, "Aurora's motivation is revenge. She very much fits into that classic hero role, avenging the death of her parents. She's angry. Battling Boy is serene and she has more anger, and they have a rivalry because he's the hero and she wants to be" (Gilly). It's no accident that she views the superhero world of one of competition, especially between herself and male figures. It's a delightful children's comic, and as the author adds:

> I get asked on tour, "Was it your intention to creating a positive female protagonist, who isn't sexualized or isn't hung up on a guy, or like Wonder Woman, someone who's already an Amazon princess?"
>
> The truth is, the character came about because the story needed it. If Battling Boy was a different character, she'd be a different character. I didn't use a formula to go "this will sell books!" that sort of thing. I just felt like this boy needed a sister figure who is like the Batman to his Superman, you know?

After two appearances as Batling Boy's sidekick in his comics, she gets her own prequel, though here she must fight her way out from her father's shadow.

Aurora grows up with the monster hunter/science detective as the central figure in her life. She notes early on:

> There were three big conversations in Aurora's childhood.
> Age 3. Mother: Your father is a science hero. We fight monsters.
> Age 7. Father: I should tell you the story of how your mom died…
> Age 14. Father: I'm going to train you to fight monsters [Pope, *Rise of Aurora West*].

On page one, her father pushes her to finish her homework … then join him for superhero training. Hunting monsters, her father is her guide and teacher, encouraging her to pull herself up on a pipe, trust her instincts, and back him up. He adds, "Don't call me dad when we're working. I have to be an idea. A force of nature."

Her life reaches a plateau as his sidekick: She flips the switch while he interrogates the monster, or he drops it and she catches. He hauls her around town (while she pleads for her own jetpack, though she's allowed to drive the car). She notes, "I watch Dad fight the monsters and I'm not sure I'm ... *angry* enough." Clearly her transition to the character in Battling Boy is on the horizon. Pope comments, "Haggard is a great man, but with a flaw—she's more of a Hamlet, while Battling Boy is more of a Siddhartha becoming Buddha" (Z. Smith). Each have different quests in the first series as he discovers the pain of human life, a lesson she's always known.

Haggard in turn obsesses over her, saying, "Everything I've done since her birth has been to make the world safe for her. To make her strong enough to survive when I'm gone." Monster fighting fills both their days.

> Many women today, determined to compete in the workplace, "have been content to be men in petticoats and so have lost touch with the feminine principle within themselves." If women have lost touch with the feminine principle, they have lost the power to lead the family and household in their ancient roles of strength. Girls learn that to compete with boys they must never show fear or emotion, never risk being called "hysterical" or "shrewish." Getting "tied down" will end their careers, and so they must choose strength or femininity, never both.
>
> Inside, this ball of frustration churns: Act against one's own nature or seem weak. The girl tries to sort through her complex emotions but nothing in this world of discarded rules and absent standards offers guidance. The feminine principle, buried and pressed into the darkness of her unexplored soul, whispers within her [Frankel, *From Girl to Goddess* 20].

Surrounded on all sides by her father's dominating presence, Aurora finds herself seeking the lost feminine in her life—her dead mother and the mystery of her loss. Other heroines too find themselves solving mysteries of the lost feminine in their lives: In the *Witchblade* series, Sara is the only female cast member. Surrounded by male mentors and a male police force, she protects young women and seeks the history of her female ancestors—wielders of the Witchblade like her. By so doing, she is using her tool of the feminine to guide her to deeper understanding. Hit-Girl, too, grows up as sidekick to the adventurer father, but when she loses him, she seeks the missing part of herself. "Hit Girl's ambitions died with her father. She wanted to be Mindy McCready for a while and so we tracked down the mom who had never stopped searching.... She finally got to do all the things little girls were supposed to do," *Kick Ass* explains.

This quest is hardly unique: Max on *Dark Angel* has rejected her patriarchal creator, but finds herself trying to solve the mystery of her mother. Max assumes the woman was "just another girl looking to get paid" but ex-Manticore staff member Hannah tells her that her mother "wasn't like the others ... she tried to escape because she didn't want to give you up" ("Heat" 102). As Max reveals at episode end, knowing this "changes everything." In fact, "Max's questions about her birth mother in early episodes of Season 1 underline the need for a female (feminist?) protagonist to retrieve her motherlines, her female heritage if she is to challenge hegemonic power" (Jowett).

Talking to her tutor Ms. Grately, her only feminine influence, Aurora recalls her childhood friend Mr. Wurple, who left the night her mother died. The mother, Rosetta West, was apparently killed in an alley by an unknown seven-fingered monster while her father was giving a press conference. As he tells his daughter, it was then that he gave up on inspiring hope in others. "There's nothing in my life now but justice and discipline. Nothing. There isn't space for anything else."

Her father is often a shallow figure and far from the great detective he claims (in a decade of searching he has slaughtered many seven-fingered monsters but never actually found his wife's killer). Despite his reliance on logic, Aurora's father tells her dismissively, "There's only madness and appetite in a monster's motivations." He adds that shooting a fox preying on the family chickens bothered him but killing monsters is "like scraping dog's business off my heel. It's what humans were made to do." However, a female monster captures Aurora and threatens to kill her because Haggard killed *her* offspring. Clearly they have some degree of human feeling. To understand, Aurora will need tools beyond book learning.

Ms. Grately tells her, "You don't have to attack what's attacking you," and sets her on a different path. Aurora begins meditating, and in the quietness, her mother's spirit visits her and brings her a vision of the past. Aurora recalls a childhood trip to Egypt where she broke through a pyramid wall to examine the sarcophagus hidden within. On awakening, she checks her father's files, questing for all that dwells beneath the surface. As she reads his notes, she recalls her imaginary friend originally emanating from the decomposing mummy, a hero who died to save his city from the forces of darkness. The creature emerged, a skinny shadow with an elongated head and warned her, "Don't tell them I'm here." In the present, Aurora clears her mind, learning once more to go deeper. She realizes "Mr. Wurple was real, born of some ancient evil that murdered a great hero and his city." She tells her school friend the truth: "My mom died here … and I think my imaginary friend killed her."

Meditating again, she has another vision of her mother. In it, working on an alphabet puzzle as a small child, she identifies D with the word "dad," center of her universe. In her memory, her imaginary friend appears and confides that like her he is obsessed with his maker or "dad" and on a mission to find him. She names her friend Wurple because he resembles a dark, swirling whirlpool—the sucking pool that is the opposite of her search for consciousness. This, only her angelic mother can bring her.

As Aurora's search continues, she amasses notes, determined to solve the mystery of her mother's death. Her father demands she give it up, so she turns sneaky, hiding her research. This search is a yearning for deeper wisdom, to seek understanding in her superheroine battles rather than simply smashing and grabbing. "Consciousness, in the pride of its youth, may deny its father, but it cannot deny its mother. That would be too unnatural" (Jung, "Conscience, Unconscious, and Individuation" 281). She ends the book seeing her father brought to his knees, begging a demon for his daughter's life. Confronted with his weakness, Aurora takes charge and kills the monster in an instant. She insists she's ready to be a hero in her own right. This encounter with the helpless father is a heroine's journey staple.

> Changed by her adventure, the heroine realizes that her father is not the omnipotent god in whom she had once completely believed. She has her own power now and her own success. In this moment, the heroine realizes that she need not depend on her father, or men at all, to rescue and protect her. She is the heroine, equally as valid as the hero.
>
> Often, this encounter takes place in the middle of the epic quest, before descending into the final conflict with the witch. Though a resting place, it is also a revelation. By returning home, the heroine can see how far she has evolved [Frankel, *From Girl to Goddess* 92].

In the second book, Haggard warns a teenage boy off Aurora only to be told the choice is up to her. His daughter is gaining physical and emotional power in their dynamic. Meanwhile, Haggard is clueless that she's been tracking her mother's killer, and he's determined to keep her a child. "How am I gonna really learn to do this if you're there to save me every time? Especially if I don't need saving," Aurora protests and suggests going independent.

Aurora receives another vision and confides in Ms. Grately. The older woman finally tells her the truth—her mother and father were fighting the demons and her father brought down a building on them, not realizing her mother was caught in the destruction. For Aurora, this is a great revelation—not just the truth of her mother's death, but her father's shortcomings. The Emperor has no clothes. The Wizard is only a man behind a curtain. As she adds in the book, "You grow up. You realize your parents make mistakes. They're human, Fallible" (Pope, *Fall of the House of West*). This is the great changing moment of her life. However, as she adds, "a hero doesn't have that luxury. It's up to the rest of us to lie to them if we have to." She understands that heroes have a responsibility beyond that of ordinary mortals.

In this tradition, the novel *Zeroes* by Scott Westerfeld features a misfit superpowered team including Kelsie, who can ride a crowd's energy and make it surge. Since age ten she would help her father, a con man and petty crook, win at the tables. However, after her father gets caught up in more serious crime, she spends the book trying to save him using her own powers and those of her new friends. While saving him, she transcends her powers, crowdsurfing to a first aid station to get him help. "She'd never felt so much a *part* of anything, so supported and carried.... Now it was obvious—this was where she was meant to be. Her power was strong and it could fix things. It could right wrongs. It was so much bigger than she'd dreamed" (516). In the end, however, she can only sit by his hospital bed and watch him die. She realizes that "Dad was always lost" and will need to rely on her friends as well as her expanding powers (542).

At the time of Mrs. West's death, Ms. Grately discovered the truth but covered up the fact that her father's actions killed her mother because they would break him. With this, Aurora learns a new level of responsibility as protector of her father instead of mere sidekick. Aurora, like Ms. Grately, lies to her father to protect him, but tells Ms. Grately, "You don't ever have to lie to me, okay? I could take it." Her teacher knows this is true. Afterwards, Aurora loses her father and becomes an orphan superhero saving the city. This may be because of her father's legacy, or perhaps despite it.

Finding the Mother: Batgirl (DC Comics: 2005–2006)

Many abandoned heroines seek the ultimate source of identity—the lost mother. *Catwoman: When in Rome* by Jeph Loeb and Tim Sale has Catwoman touring an ancient place of ruins and secrets, seeking her human identity outside Gotham. She investigates dead crime lord Carmine Falcone, whom she suspects may have been her father. Soon after, she meets the blind Louisa Falcolne, who resembles her closely, but the woman denies having a lost daughter. Selina discovers she probably is their child, though there's no proof and she finds herself leaving with little more information than she started with. Still, she departs with the ancestral ring she's stolen—whoever holds it controls the entire Italian crime world. As she decides, she can live without finding everything she wanted, since "it's about who loses the least." Always, this will be her.

> The run is about Selina's search to find her origins. She believes Louisa to be her mother, the person who can unlock the secrets of her past. But this quest also functions as a symbolic searching for the Mother. In literature, gender studies often speaks to the feminist pursuit of a Mother, rather than a Father, in order for female writers and characters to find their voice. In a world dominated by men, and where women are relegated to the fridge to further male's storylines/characterizations, Selina's quest in Rome signals a search for a Mother, a figure who can represent a past and a light through the darkness [Tremblay].

At the grave of her father, she smirks that she has taken her rightful identity by force—the one he chose to deny her. Thus "she is speaking to the ways in which female characters have to fight for their respected positions. Her identity, her

life, is of her own creation and which, this is important, she stole from her possible father" (Tremblay). As a female character in a comic book, she snatches
her place from an existing (and largely defunct) masculine framework.

Back in Gotham, another heroine goes on a similar quest to find her origins. Cassandra Cain had a brutal childhood before becoming Batgirl (one of
several to bear the title). She first appeared in *Batman* #567 (July 1999) and
was created by Kelley Puckett and Damion Scott. Her father, criminal David
Cain, denied her speech, literacy, and human contact, "to adapt the language
center of the brain to interpret physical movement as a language." Thus he
trained her as the world's greatest assassin. She became adept at reading body
language—so adept that she felt her victim's pain and fled her father's training.
However, the pain of her first murder at age eight led her to a life of grief and
atonement. Soon she becomes Oracle's courier, then Batman's apprentice. Batman tells Oracle, "She can read you. Your body. That's why she understands
what you're saying when she doesn't know the words. It's why in combat, she
knows what you're going to do before you do it" (Puckett, *Batgirl: Silent
Knight*). He adds that it took him five minutes to teach her stick fighting. As
she fights criminals and interacts with her friends in a mostly silent, creepy
manner under a featureless mask, she's much like her mentor. Nonetheless, her
strength comes from understanding others at a level below words.

Learning to speak means sacrificing some of her hard-won skills. A
telepath fixes her mind, but with this, her instinctual ability to read people vanishes. Cassandra soon discovers that assassin Lady Shiva can read people like
she once could and asks Shiva to reteach her. Lady Shiva accepts but demands
a duel to the death a year later. Preferring to be "perfect for a year" rather than
"mediocre for a lifetime," Cassandra accepts. A year later, she loses their duel.
After she dies, however, Shiva restarts her heart, helping Cassandra past her
death wish. Cassandra explains later, "I saw how she's like me. Weak where I
am. Hungry to know she's human" (Puckett, *Batgirl: A Knight Alone*). She has
found a teacher like herself.

In *Batgirl: Kicking Assassins* (*Batgirl* #60–64), Batman has given her a
"city of her own" called Blüdhaven, but she's not sure she can handle the responsibility. Cassandra Cain seeks Onyx, another fellow female fighter, to be her
mentor. "Training with her isn't like with Batman or Oracle's, uh, programs.
She's different. She was an assassin once. Like my father. Like Shiva. Like …
me. She understands," Batgirl notes. Unusually for mentor stories, Batgirl is
covered head to toe, complete with mask and cape, while her mentor, bald with
a crop top, appears more vulnerable. Cassandra specifically admires how her
trainer understands her and knows how to turn weakness to strength.

In turn, Onyx insists Cassandra keep her mask on and keep her identity secret. She adds: "Onyx is my name. that is who I am. I never got a chance to be anybody else. Too stupid and too arrogant in my youth to cover my face and protect my name, my life. But you, baby girl, you got a face under that cowl, a name behind that symbol, and if you're smart, you'll get a life too."

Onyx offers the final piece of advice: "You're at your best when it's personal. Let this place, these people matter to you. Otherwise, what the hell are you fighting for?" The heroine's role is to form a community and fight to protect it. Since the hero does less of this, Batman has failed to teach Cassandra the all-important lesson of how to be a true superheroine.

Onyx's lesson drives the next arc's plot. Alfred shows Cassandra her new home, a converted carriage house from the 1880s loaded with all the Bat security. The monitors have her body scans and the computer her face, making her new lair a true extension of herself. A new friend and mentor of a sort is the tea seller on the corner, a girl about Batgirl's age named Brenda. Thugs are hassling her to sell and Batgirl arranges an anonymous donor. Brenda in turn invites Batgirl to a celebratory party and shows her how to take time off her "work," while Batman commends his protégé for taking an interest in improving the community.

Batgirl finally faces not the enemy Deathstroke but his evil daughter the Ravager. She's masked, but her black is broken by blue and yellow, marking them as imperfect reflections. Battling, Batgirl realizes she has the advantage, since "every fight teaches me, every fighter"—her past has prepared her for this dynamic. She wins by understanding the enemy's father-daughter relationship, so much like the one she once had. The girl will look to her father for approval, be distracted, and lose. Then the father will rush the daughter to safety, and Cassandra can win the day.

The mentor appears "in a situation where insight, understanding, good advice, determination, planning, etc. are needed but cannot be mustered on one's own resources" (Jung, "The Phenomenology of the Spirit in Fairytales" 216). The inner voice, manifested as a guide, arrives to fill the gap. While Batgirl is cleaning up the streets, the lost Batgirl Stephanie comes to her in a vision and shows her that her birth—and the murder that took place moments later. Taken from her mother so quickly, Batgirl never saw her, but Stephanie can offer the insight she lacks. After, Stephanie challenges her and tells her "it's do or die time." She hauls herself from the river where she was drowning, her scene of life flashing before her eyes finally complete. Thus Batgirl graduates from male mentors to female ones, physical mentors to spiritual. Still it's not enough without her true mother in her life.

Other heroines go questing the lost mother, though the result is often disappointing. In her own comic, Namora descends into an ocean vent and there has a vision of her mother. It's a seductive meeting, filled with love and forgiveness. Of course, Namora soon accepts it as an illusion. The voice really came from "a titan of legend and myth. A sea god that once had many worshippers." It dreams of recreating a world where it has power and seduces its victims with images of desire. Namora must find the strength to leave her mother behind then kill the beast with her dual bloodline, as her humanity lets her breathe air (Parker, *Namora* #1). Her vision has tempted her with the image of her mother, but this seductive lure masks a monster.

Raven of *New Teen Titans* travels to the Temple Azarath in "a place like no other." There she confronts the bird-crowned mystic Arella. She pleads for help, adding, "Can you let your own daughter die?" but the other woman replies that earth must be destroyed if that is its destiny. "I still love you, Raven, but you should not have come." Arella believes in pacifism and noninterference, while Raven fights to defend life (Wolfman, *New Teen Titans* #4). Like many mother-daughter pairings, they're opposites and set in opposition.

In a more benevolent scene, accompanied by the ghost of her mentor Agatha Harkness, Scarlet Witch follows the Witch's Road into a vortex of energy. There, Wanda meets a woman who calls herself the Scarlet Witch—Wanda's mother Natalya. She tells Wanda, "I know I have to protect you from something. A threat you won't be able to defeat." They battle a monster together and Natalya offers a blessing as she departs. From this experience, Wanda discovers she's the last in a long line of Scarlet Witches, all so-naming themselves as they come into their power (Robinson, *Scarlet Witch: Witch's Road*).

Batgirl: Destruction's Daughter sends Cassandra on a more harrowing arc. Questing to discover whether Lady Shiva is her mother, Cassandra asks her father, beating him up, but leaving him with a clumsy father's day card and a daisy in token of her conflict. She also talks with her old trainer Bronze Tiger, Onyx, and Batman—none are certain of her parentage, though all give her clues. This trip through her past mentors ends when she heads for the source.

She discovers Lady Shiva at last. While Cassandra forced her to be her trainer, now Lady Shiva trains a host of young assassins. Nyssa, daughter of supervillain Ra's al Ghul, taunts them with the concept that Cassandra is her property, as she arranged the girl's birth. Lady Shiva warns Cassandra that she is her creator but also her destroyer, as the name suggests. At the school, the students kneel to Cassandra, calling her the "One Who Is All." This makes her squirm, but Shiva, like her buried inner voice, taunts her, asking, "Does it feel too good?" and reminding her that her adoptive father Batman likes the adoration himself.

In turn Cassandra realizes Lady Shiva wants a student. Meanwhile Nyssa invites her to join and "become everything you were *meant* to be," as she says.

Cassandra can work with the villains to make the world a fairer place without the corrupt system Batman protects. When Cassandra rejects their teachings and escapes, several students—Ox, Tigris, and White Willow—follow her, and she realizes that while she never got an answer about Shiva, she did about herself. Meeting her creator showed her what path she's already chosen as a force for good. "The hero's reconciliation with the mother results in the act of giving birth to the whole self—a reconciliation of self-affirmation with nurturance and self with Other" (Pearson and Pope 199).

Cassandra flees with Ox, Tigris, and White Willow into the forest, Shiva's other students in pursuit, and frames the rest of the story as a fairytale about being lost in the woods where "girls change." They attack, and Cassandra realizes it's all about impressing Shiva once again. As she thinks of Batman's family, she finds herself fighting her father's first pupil, the Mad Dog. Calling her "sister," he launches himself at her. When he escapes her, Shiva counsels Batgirl to track him through remembering his nature and her own. She finds him as he's attacking the last students and sacrifices herself to save them, insisting everyone deserves a chance to change. By defeating her evil brother and agreeing to take mentor Shiva's place, Cassandra accepts becoming a teacher and leader, completing her own small journey, though she is mortally wounded defending others.

Lady Shiva takes Cassandra's body to the Lazarus Pit that can resurrect her. On the way, she tells a story of Cassandra's creation. Batgirl, dying, listens to this tale but murkily confuses her teacher with Stephanie. Both of course represent her mentors, an inner female voice that bolsters the heroine and strengthens her with knowledge of her true powers and origin. In her death-dream, Cassandra discovers the truth. She sees a vision of Sandra Wu-San and her sister Carolyn fighting in a martial arts tournament. Believing that Sandra was holding back for her sister, Cain murdered Carolyn and battled Sandra, showing her how great she could be. He spared her life in exchange for her giving birth to his child and leaving that child for him to raise. She agreed and describes herself as "grateful .... The chance to become someone new. No. Not someone. Something." After Cassandra's birth, Sandra set out to become Lady Shiva, "destruction responsible for creation. Unstoppable but not indestructible." Cassandra dies, but then bursts from the Lazarus Pit, whole once more, to be greeted by Shiva with the words "Come to Mother."

To Jung, meeting the mother is truly transcendent: "An experience of this kind gives the individual a place and a meaning in the life of the generations. So that all unnecessary obstacles are cleared out of the way of the life-stream that is to follow through her At the same time the individual is rescued from her isolation and restored to wholeness" (Jung, "Psychological Aspects of the

Kore" 188). The heroine understands her purpose and potential by meeting the mother she could become.

However, Shiva reveals she's still a killer, and when Cassandra asks if she will ever stop, Shiva responds, "It's why I had you." Cassandra agrees to fight her to the death once more. Upon finding her mother, she realizes that she is meant to be her mother's destroyer, as she protects lives and her mother takes them.

In an evenly matched battle, Cassandra manages to break Shiva's neck, paralyzing her. She tries to place Shiva in the Lazarus Pit, but Shiva pleads with her not to. In response, Cassandra impales Shiva on a hook hanging over the pit, killing her. With a kiss and a "Sorry, mom," she forgives and asks forgiveness from the other woman.

> In fairy tales, the woman typically escapes by rejecting or slaying an actual woman. In real-istic fiction, similarly the hero may begin her journey by rejecting her mother, all conven-tional women, even all women. The important discovery that she eventually makes in the process of her quest is that the Wicked Witch is not an actual woman. She and her ideal-ized opposite, the Chaste Martyr, are patriarchal projections. When the hero realizes that her view of herself and of other women is male-defined, she then rejects and destroys not the woman but the image that society has pressured her and other women into assuming. By destroying that image, she frees not only herself, but the oppressive conventional woman as well [Pearson and Pope 120].

In the fairy tale model here, Cassandra slays the image of woman as death-dealer, the Shiva model the world wanted her to follow. Now she can become a heroine, role model, and teacher as a savior of the innocent.

In a later storyline, Cassandra becomes new leader of the League of Assas-sins, both descending into villainy and following her mother's path. She has not only discovered her mother's heritage within herself and defeated her mother to become the more benign ruler that replaces her—she has also found the heroine's destiny. This is a story of leaving the father's training to take the mother's path—defending the community and becoming leader of a surrogate family. As teacher of the next generation, she can defend and save those who truly need her.

Killer Mother: *Agents of S.H.I.E.L.D.* (TV, 2013–2015)

> The detachment of the growing individual from the authority of the parents is one of the most necessary, but also one of the most painful achievements of evolution. It is absolutely necessary for this detachment to take place, and it may be assumed that all normal grown individuals have accomplished it to a certain extent [Rank 68–69].

In 2010's "Holiday Story," Harley Quinn visits her family for Christmas and her mother screams at her, waving a hot doughnut dipper in her face, "I should throw you *all* out. Force you to fend for yourselves for once! Then maybe you'd all finally *grow up!*" From jail, Harley Quinn's father tries to con her for money. She tells him, "The main reason I became a psychiatrist was so I could understand why you did the things you did to our family." Frequently, the superhero's story exaggerates bad family dynamics, casting the parents or siblings as villains. "In fairytales, the stepmother and wicked witch 'symbolize predatory female sexuality and the adolescent's negative feeling toward the mother.' In other words, the enemy is the part of ourselves we most dislike. We see the negative aspects of our mothers in ourselves and reject them, saying, 'That's as different from me as possible; that quality belongs to the enemy'" (Frankel, *From Girl to Goddess*, 131). Thus the wicked stepmother (a comforting fiction laid over the real mother's dark side) appears in all the fairytales. By her second season, Skye of *Agents of S.H.I.E.L.D.* has her own encounter with a mother far different than she'd expected, dragging her into a horrific civil war.

Season one sees self-named orphan Skye joining the secret alien hunters S.H.I.E.L.D. to seek out her parents—her only knowledge of them comes from a redacted S.H.I.E.L.D. file. Together they have many adventures, though she fails to find her answers. Shot in the stomach, she has a death and rebirth sequence, thanks to GH-325, a mysterious alien serum from the blood of an alien called the Kree. However, her reaction is unusual, suggesting a Kree connection on a deep level.

Her shadow through the first season is Raina, an enemy operative hunting for Skye. While Skye rarely uses hyper femininity to manipulate men (with a shocking pink dress in "The Asset" 103), this is Raina's favorite tool, so much so that she's known as the girl in the flowered dress. The flowers make her appear agreeable and incredibly feminine while the contrasting Skye often wears dark androgynous clothing and trains with warrior woman Melinda May. Raina also uses flattery and temptation. "All I want is what you want—For you to be remembered, to be seen for what you're meant to be. A star," she tells one hero, naming him and setting him on the path to destruction ("The Girl in the Flower Dress" 105). Skye may be the innocent, but Raina is the corrupter.

Halfway through season two, Raina and Skye (fertility and divinity) descend into an ancient Kree city with a lost Obelisk and activate the Terrigen mist. Both are transformed—Skye gains the power of causing earthquakes, and Raina becomes a misshapen beast covered in spines. Both have shed their outer trappings of civilization to become Inhuman. The powerless becomes powerful and the alluring, hideous. To Skye's surprise, her friends admire her: "You managed to be taken hostage by three known murderers, you gunned Ward down. Then were blasted by an alien chemical weapon and walked out unscathed," her teammate Bobbi tells her. "Leper? I think you're a rock star" ("Aftershocks" 211).

Her transformation brings her a new state of consciousness, and with it, the knowledge she's always sought. Just after, Skye meets her father. In fact, Calvin Zabo, the raging Mr. Hyde, is a monster. He's also terribly protective of her, just like Coulson, the team leader and her "good father." On meeting her birth father, Skye gains a new name and identity, though it's her human one, Daisy Johnson, in a reversal on the classic tropes.

Skye goes off to train in the wilderness, armed with a pair of gauntlets to control and suppress her powers, giving her a chance to reassess. The Inhuman teleporter Gordon finds her there and, like Hagrid in *Harry Potter*, plays herald, offering her training among people like herself, the Inhumans. He also asks her the hard questions:

GORDON: What does it feel like, your gift?
SKYE: I don't know. Um .... It's intense. Like 1,000 bees trapped inside of me. And I feel it all the time. It's always there. And I can't stop it.
GORDON: Why would you want to stop it?
SKYE: Because I destroy everything around me.
GORDON: That is simply not true. Every object in this universe gives off a vibration. Did you know that? Nothing rests. Animals, trees, people, even this ratty couch. And you—you have the ability to tap into those vibrations. Don't you see? You can become magnificent. But something's inhibiting you, constraining your energy.
SKYE: Uh, no. No, no. My, um—my friend's a scientist. She made these to protect me.
GORDON: Or do they protect people from you?
SKYE: No, it's not like that. My powers, I—I can't control them. And when I try to, it hurts me.
GORDON: Most gifts come with a price, but you could learn to manage it. I apologize. I'm saying too much. This is probably not the best place to continue our conversation. You don't have the tools and the understanding that you need just yet.
SKYE: To do what?
GORDON: To be who you were always meant to be. Without fear, without pain. We can offer that to you ["One Door Closes" 215].

When she faces danger, she calls out and Gordon whisks her to safety in the secret stronghold of Attilan, in the Himalayas. On the show, their home is called "After Life," suggesting a mystical trip to the otherworld. This is a sanctuary, where the gentle inhabitants glory in their powers rather than fearing them. It also offers Skye a new kind of permanent home.

Soon enough, the leader of After Life, Skye's long-lost mother Jiaying, arrives and offers to tutor her. She tells Skye, before revealing the truth: "I have chosen to be your guide, should you remain with us. All I ask is for a few days. I'll look after you, train you, watch you grow. And if you don't feel a connection between us worth exploring, well…. We never have to see each other again" ("After Life" 216). At last, Skye has found her mother.

Nonetheless, After Life has a dark undercurrent. Soon enough, Skye discovers the monstrous Raina is living in the community. Her father also lives here, locked up for his volatile temper. While her beautiful serene mother rules and tutors her among the soaring mountains, the darker half of their family, the shadow, are hidden away. For Raina is indeed Skye's shadow, her hidden dark side brought to life:

> SKYE: You got what you deserved.
> RAINA: So did you…. We're the same, Skye…. I am on the outside what you are on the inside.
> She throws back her hood, revealing her monstrous face ["After Life" 216].

As the abandoned shadow, Raina feels terribly cheated since Skye got the dazzling powers and a loving family, while Raina is now a monster "unable to bear the light." In the world of After Life, she gradually discovers a new gift— precognition. However, she uses it to control others, as she always has.

> JIAYING: You said Raina's manipulative. But is she dangerous?
> CALVIN ZABO: That depends on how you define "dangerous."
> JIAYING: She convinced Gordon and Skye to go after Lincoln even though they knew it wasn't safe.
> CALVIN ZABO: Daisy's strong. She gets that from you. But if she's not okay, I will personally rip out Raina's little, tainted rat heart! [Chuckles] Or not. W—Whatever you want.
> JIAYING: Who was she when you first met her?
> CALVIN ZABO: She had nothing … no family, no home. Somehow, she convinced this café owner to bring her old pastries … persuaded a tailor to give her leftover fabric so she could make dresses.
> JIAYING: Resourceful.
> CALVIN ZABO: Selfish. Soon, she demanded the warm, fresh pastries, not the stale ones. If they were willing to give her cotton, why not silk? I've never seen her not want something ["Scars" 220].

She's the greedy, demanding side the heroes always reject, now grown powerful as her new family listen to her counsel and give her power. Cal notes that she thrives on chaos, another hallmark of the shadow.

Meanwhile, S.H.I.E.L.D. has developed a weapon that can destroy the Inhumans. They propose a meeting. Since Skye is caught in the middle between her two peoples already, she is made liaison. When she arrives, Jiaying decides to evacuate, but Skye pleads with her: "Please just sit down with him. Coulson … he's a good man. He's … he's the only person who's ever tried to take care of me. And … until now, he's the closest I've had to family. Please, Mom" ("Scars" 220). The struggle between birth mother and surrogate father is beginning.

Skye longs for a safe, healthy pair of families—S.H.I.E.L.D. and Inhumans working together. However, her birth parents want war with her friends, something that's tearing her apart. At this point, Skye must find a new path, rejecting her parents' warmongering as she pursues peace and righteousness. This is a metaphor of course for shaking off the parents' control, especially on finding a new family.

> Social progress is essentially based upon this opposition between the two generations. On the other hand, there exists a class of neurotics whose condition indicates that they have failed to solve this very problem. For the young child, the parents are, in the first place, the sole authority and the source of all faith. To resemble them, i.e., the progenitor of the same sex—to grow up like father or mother—this is the most intense and portentous wish of the child's early years. Progressive intellectual development naturally brings it about that the child gradually becomes acquainted with the category to which the parents belong. Other parents become known to the child, who compares these with his own, and thereby becomes justified in doubting the incomparability and uniqueness with which he had invested them [Rank 69].

Cal insists having their people indexed and tagged is too great a risk and encourages Jiaying to blast their planes from the sky. She resists, noting, "Our daughter wouldn't want that. And my people would never blindly follow me into a war." However, she's determined: "We can't lose our daughter to these people again" ("Scars" 220). Thus it's fear for her child and her people that turns her violent. "Just as the heroine represents life-giving and creative power, the witch figure murders and destroys the new life. Worse yet, she seeks to cast her own shadow over the heroine, blaming her for the destructive deed. And yet, this forces the heroine to face her ordeal: to descend into death but also to acknowledge the child-killing, death-dealing rage within her virginal heart" (Frankel, *From Girl to Goddess* 273).

When Agent Robert Gonzales, the representative from S.H.I.E.L.D., comes, Jiaying kills him, then shoots herself, insisting S.H.I.E.L.D. attacked her and has come to start a war. All her people rally, eager to fight back. Skye, meanwhile, is terribly torn. Seeking counsel, she visits the dark oracle, Raina. Raina once more emphasizes their link, telling her, "It is the thorn that protects the rose. Or, in this case, the Daisy…. My true purpose, my destiny, is to help you become what you're supposed to be" ("SOS Part 1" 221). She adds that Daisy is fated to lead, to become a far better protector than her mother.

Skye leaves and Jiaying slits Raina's throat, before the other woman can reveal what she's done. Metaphorically having killed her conscience, there's nothing to stop Jiaying now except her daughter. In fact, Skye discovers her mother has started the conflict:

SKYE: [Raina] saw who you really are, so you killed her.

JIAYING: Everything I've done, everything I will do is for the protection of our people.

SKYE: You killed Gonzales. [exhales sharply] You want a war.

JIAYING: War was inevitable. I struck first so we would have the advantage.

SKYE: He came to make peace!

JIAYING: Peace? I built this community in the middle of nowhere so we would be left in peace. Yet, S.H.I.E.L.D. found us. No matter where we go or what we do, they will hunt us down. If we are to survive, S.H.I.E.L.D. must be destroyed.

SKYE: What are you planning?

JIAYING: I am planning for our future … your future. Daisy, I won't live forever, and when I'm gone, you must lead these people … protect them as I have done.

SKYE: Protect them? You killed Raina. You are leading them into a war! If they need protection, it is from you!

JIAYING: I'm sorry you feel that way. [knocks her out] Restrain her. Take her with you. When this is done, hopefully she'll understand. And dispose of Raina's body ["SOS Part 1" 221].

Jiaying also sends Cal to surrender himself to S.H.I.E.L.D. Inside their defenses, he transforms into a monster and attacks. The evil parents have revealed their monstrous nature, while the more innocent daughters are incapacitated, unable to stop them. "In a further irony, the Inhumans put power-canceling sleeves on Skye's arms, very similar to the ones which Jemma Simmons had made for Skye—and when Simmons had done it, this was seen as proof that SHIELD were evil and didn't want Skye to master her gifts" (Anders).

Coulson, Skye's "good father," has had several encounters during the show with Skye's "bad father" Cal. Now, he tries to relate to the man beneath the savage Mr. Hyde:

COULSON: What we both want is to protect your daughter. You're a family man.

CAL: Who is sick of you sticking your nose in our business.

COULSON: It was your devotion to them that made you willing to do those terrible things all those years ago, wasn't it?

CAL: Shut up.

COULSON: Nightmarish acts of violence that you didn't want to commit, did you? Your wife made you do it.

CAL: You don't know her! You don't know anything! Say one more word, and I'll…

COULSON: I'm not saying your wife is a monster, Cal. I think you already know she's a monster. What I'm saying is … you're not. I know you've thought so for a long time. But deep down, you're a good man ["SOS Part 2" 222].

It is the story's Lady Macbeth who has transformed him into a murderer, pushed him to make himself a mutant. At last, Cal reveals he once destroyed an entire village so his wife could live off their life energy and heal herself. She is the killer of innocents, no longer a protector.

A similar dark mother is Mystique in *X-Men: Messiah Complex*. Several factions of humans and mutants are fighting over baby Hope, the first mutant born after the devastation of *House of M*. Mystique allies herself with evil and does whatever is necessary, including killing her boss, so she can hold the baby, as she's long plotted. "Everything I've done, it's been to bring us to this moment," she reveals. She touches the baby to Rogue, her comatose daughter, whose presence is now deadly to all those around her. As Gambit, Rogue's lover, protests that Rogue wouldn't let a baby die so she could live, Mystique eagerly sacrifices the child, adding, "Destiny told me I saved her, and if I saved her, maybe she would love me again." Her love for her daughter is all-encompassing, but without the X-Men's heroism, it turns her monstrous. As it turns out, the baby is truly a messiah and survives, purifying Rogue of the poison and even all the souls she's taken. However, when Rogue awakens, she's horrified at what her mother has become. She decides to kill Mystique and absorb her soul, much as she'll never forgive herself for it. Thanks to Rogue's cleansing, Mystique survives, but Rogue has absorbed her memories. She thinks, "Ah don't want to see her again, to be anywhere near her, but—she's in mah head now..." (Brubaker). This psychological complex brought to literal life in the comic is a symptom of many flawed relationships, ones the daughter cannot escape.

Many superhero stories, like other literature, feature the mother daughter conflict, here made literal and often violent as the daughter struggles to find her own path. In *Amazons Attack!* Wonder Woman's mother leads her Amazons in an attack on Washington, D.C., and Diana is caught in the center as the Justice League intervene. Diana must press her mother's blade to her own neck before the other woman relents.

The metaphor has truth to it, as many children feel like all the adults stand against them. This story pattern gives them a chance to work through the pain. In *Heroes*: "Dying of the Light" (306), cheerleader Claire Bennet searches for her birth mother, Meredith. Sandra, her adopted mother, insists on coming. The villain Eric Doyle is threatening Meredith when they find her, and he captures Sandra and Claire, controlling all their movements with his power in a creepy puppet theater. He then forces them to play a demented version of Russian Roulette. First he forces Claire to shoot Meredith, using his power to control Claire's aim of the gun. "You're the hero with the big ol' gun," he taunts her. "What's it gonna be, huh? PTA mom who tucks you in every night? Or cool aunt with flamethrowing action?" Of course, he's acting on Claire's buried anger towards the mothers, giving her the ability to act out her pain. Claire cannot choose, so Doyle forces her to shoot Meredith. When Claire's shot has no cartridge, he has Meredith shoot Claire (emphasizing their hidden conflict and making it literal). However, Claire has healing powers and accepts being shot calmly, only to rise from death and clobber their assailant, rescuing everyone. "Show's over," she says.

In all stories, the innocent Cinderella figure "must face her stepmother and learn how to dominate a household, give orders, acknowledge her own suppressed cruel streak. She needs the shadow's dark vicious strength, and the shadow craves her innocent happiness" (Frankel, *From Girl to Goddess* 134). Thus the daughter trains with the evil mother, absorbing her cruelty and hard choices as well as her power. Skye has learned from Jiaying and now observes her as a captive, knowing the time is coming to proclaim herself the new leader.

> This puts a whole new spin on Skye's identity crisis—instead of being torn between SHIELD, which sees her as a menace, and her "real" family, which loves and accepts her, she's discovered that both sides are capable of being manipulative and kinda evil. And the formative tragedy of Skye's life is no longer about people killing each other to keep her safe, but about her Inhuman mother being, well, inhuman [Anders].

Jiaying activates a distress beacon to lure all the S.H.I.E.L.D. agents to the ship she's captured. She has Terrigen crystals that will destroy or transform all the humans, leaving only her own people behind. On the ship with few allies, Skye tries to convince her Inhuman friends of the truth. At last Cal arrives to confront his wife, telling her, "You need to stop this. This isn't about us or them. This is about our daughter. Think of what you are doing to Daisy." Still, Jiaying will not be dissuaded. She flees with the Terrigen crystals, planning to spread them around the world with a Quinjet, and Skye pursues her, insisting, "I can't let you leave with those crystals."

> SKYE: You started this war.
> JIAYING: This war started decades ago, when S.H.I.E.L.D. was founded to guard the world against people like us. And it will never end. But you and I together ... think of how powerful we could be. We could launch a revolution ... side by side.
> SKYE: I don't want your revolution, because this isn't about protecting me or your people. This is about hate.
> JIAYING: No, you're wrong.
> SKYE: It's consumed you. You can't even tell right from wrong. I can't let you destroy any more lives.
> JIAYING: My daughter. So beautiful. So strong ["SOS Part 2" 222].

With these words, Jiaying actually begins draining her daughter's life energy, using it to extend her own. This older generation preying on the younger is seen in ancient stories like Snow White, in which the mother longs to eat her beautiful daughter's heart and prolong her own time as ruling queen. Jiaying tells her, "I always believed the reason I endured all that torture and pain was for you, that you were my true gift. But you're not. This is," harvesting all she is to feed herself as Skye prays for mercy.

Cal intervenes and kills Jiaying so Skye won't have to, protecting his daughter from the terrible mother. As the season ends, Skye starts gathering a team of Gifted people. As she concludes, "My mother was right about one thing ...

people like me need to be kept a secret, not like the Avengers, out in the open" ("SOS Part 2" 222). By forming her own community, she's following her mother's path, though more benevolently.

Sister Teamwork: *Supergirl* (TV, 2015)

As with the popular, recent *Frozen*, an honest, messy sister relationship lies at the heart of CBS's new *Supergirl*. One fan of the series notes:

> When your family is built through adoption, you rarely see nuanced portrayals of adoptive families in the media. It's all about extremes. Fairy tales and fantasy shows usually resort to the trope of the evil step-parents or the abusive adoptive parents, with the adoptees depicted as mistreated victims. On the other end, modern stories often present the adoptive parents as saviors who rescued abandoned orphans and gave them the perfect life. In reality, neither of these fits our adoptive family. Watching *Supergirl* has normalized our experience, where some parts of adoption are amazing and other parts are really difficult, but what never changes is that we are family, and we love each other [C. Goldman].

When Kara arrives on earth, she's adopted by the Danvers, who already have an older daughter, Alex. "Despite being born on different planets, we both shared one thing: we knew our lives would never be the same again," Kara says, seeing the closest relationship of her life develop. "The strongest bond in the show is with her sister," says Melissa Benoist, her actress. "There's competition. With her adoptive parents, there's [been] comparison" (Keveney). Alex automatically picks out clothes for her sister to wear on a date and reminds her that a normal life isn't bad. She wants to be texted every detail of Kara's evening and acts as a typical big sister … at least on the surface. Episode one has Kara reveal her powers to the world by saving her sister's crashing plane. After, she describes flying as feeling "scared but good scared," like a first kiss and gushes in happiness.

Alex shuts her down and tells her, "Everyone will know about you and you can't take that back…. It's not safe for you to do anything like that ever again!" However, she's reacting out of protectiveness, not fear, and grows supportive in time. As the fan continues:

> During the scenes in *Supergirl* where Alex and Kara explore the painful aspects of their relationship as sisters through adoption, our whole family absorbs every word, every expression, because seeing this dynamic on mainstream television makes our family feel less alone. The fact that both Alex and Kara are kickass, strong, smart, flawed, beautiful women who work hard, cry, laugh, yell, fight, and make mistakes has been an incredible model for all of our girls [C. Goldman].

This constant emotional aid is the real sibling gift, especially for the frightened, selfless superhero.

The TV-MA Netflix show *Marvel's Jessica Jones* likewise shows a loving relationship between superpowered Jessica (Krysten Ritter) and her foster sister Trish (Rachael Taylor). Showrunner Melissa Rosenberg establishes the female friendship as an anchoring element to this series. In their youth, Jessica forces their mother to stop dominating her, and as adults, both young women are the most important figures in each other's lives. While Trish is sweet and supportive, in contrast with Jessica's defensive coldness, they make an excellent partnership covering for each other or providing backup. Taylor comments:

> One thing that I really liked about the portrayal of female friendship in the series is that it's not perfect. They're not just simply perfect friends that talk about boyfriends and their loyalty to each other all the time. When we meet them at the start of the series, there's been a betrayal—or Trish *thinks* there's been a betrayal. Jessica has been in a really bad place and Trish feels that she's abandoned her. So it's an imperfect friendship. It's complex [Huver].

Season one ends with the love interest sidelined and Trish partnering with Jessica. In the final confrontation, the villain threatens her, establishing that Trish is Jessica's dearest love. However, using teamwork, trust, and true affection, the two women take him down.

Likewise, Kate Bishop, the new Hawkeye, squabbles with her sister about how many starving families her wedding dress could feed. Her sister replies that Kate should live for herself, rather than devoting herself to their dead mother's ideals. As she adds, however, "and if it turns out you actually want to spend the rest of your life in soup kitchens and women's shelters, I'll support you because I'm your sister and that's my job. And your job is to tell me whether I look ridiculous in this dress" (Heinberg, *Young Avengers: Family Matters*).

Certainly, some best friends fill a similar role. Most often, they have different qualities than the heroine, providing the caution or intellect while she is the action. This companion acts as a less-developed part of the personality, like a warning from within. She's also a foil, providing contrast between characters that provokes growth in each of them. "The Double is who the hero wants to become—a role model. The hero either admires the Double or is jealous and critical of him…. At their best, Doubles become gurus or guides for the hero. They blaze a trail for the hero to follow or hold space for the hero to blossom on his own" (Schmidt, *45 Master Characters* 189). Though she may not have powers, the superheroine teaches her to be strong in her own way.

> The female hero is neither the traditional helpmate rescuer, who "saves" others by immolating herself, nor is she like the male superhero seen in such works as Frank Herbert's *Dune* and Heinlein's *Stranger in a Strange Land*, who leads while others only follow. She

saves by teaching others that they have the power to be heroic. They do not become her followers, but are coequals in a community of heroes [Pearson and Pope 263].

After revealing herself, Kara is shot with kryptonite and wakes in a creepy lab. To her shock, her sister works there as Agent Danvers of the Department of Extranormal Operations, pledged to study and stop alien threats, possibly including Kara. Alex's double identity also appears to be the reason she's always ordered Kara to keep her abilities secret and not be a hero. "You told me every single day not to be who I really am," Kara tells her miserably.

Director Henshaw reveals that Kara's pod somehow dragged an alien prison to earth and now those aliens are loose—many planning vengeance since Kara's mother locked them up. "I can help you stop them," Kara offers, but they reject her as an undercover agent or useful asset. However, when Kara is fighting one of those aliens, her sister rappels to the rescue. She reveals that she knew the House of El was a specific target. "I'm trying to protect you," she adds.

Kara has a crisis of faith after she fails to stop one of the alien prisoners. In response, her sister bangs on her door and tells her this is who she's meant to be. Alex adds that part of the overprotection was selfish. "Before you came to live with us, I was the star. And then, I mean, how can I compete with you, with someone who could touch the stars? Y'know, I was happy when you decided not to use your powers. Y'know, somehow, you feeling like less, somehow it made me feel like more. And now, the world needs you to fly, Kara." Same-sex siblings tend to be both shadow and ideal self for each other. As Jungian analyst Christine Downing puts it, "She is both what I would most aspire to be but feel I never can be and what I am most proud not to be but fearful of becoming" (111). They maintain a lifelong tension between pride and wistfulness or even jealousy. Though Alex is envious of her sister's powers, she helps Kara become her best self, a hero.

Alex faces her own deep-set insecurity when she asks Director Henshaw if she was recruited only for being Kara's sister, not on her own merits. Henshaw replies, "She's why you got in. You are why you got to stay," an answer that seems to satisfy her. "It is a bit of a tangled web," her actress Chyler Leigh says. Growing up, "Alex is the star of the family, but when Kara comes into the picture, because she's so extraordinary, Alex felt an intense need to train harder, fight harder and study harder so she could feel as special as Kara already was" (Keveney).

Alex takes Kara to headquarters and vouches for her, sending her back into combat with a science-based plan this time. Kara will need to feign helplessness and get cornered (a bit problematic as empowerment metaphors go) then superheat the villain's axe with her heat vision. She succeeds, saving the people of her chosen city.

In *Who Is Wonder Woman*, Donna Troy takes Diana's place. This is complicated by the fact that Donna is an identical copy, raised as Diana's childhood playmate. She was also Diana's protégé, Wonder Girl, before finding her own identity as Troia. In flashback, Donna ponders a life merely imitating her sister, the real chosen one. "If *she* couldn't do it, what chance do *I* have?" she wonders, seeing herself as only a shallower copy. Younger siblings often find themselves struggling to make different pathways, to define themselves as specifically not their sibling. Donna Troy is battling Wonder Woman's classic enemy the Cheetah, when suddenly Wonder Woman appears in her own red and blue. As she raises her arm in a kill stroke, Donna stops her and Diana impales her, insisting, "I'm stronger than you." At this moment, Donna realizes this is an illusion. Doctor Psycho has "got in her head," exploiting her fear that she'll never measure up. Both women, each facing the life choices she rejected, must find ways to accept what they see of themselves in the other person.

A later episode has Kara exposed to red kryptonite and lashing out at her sister:

KARA: I see how you've always been jealous of me! You didn't want me to come out as Supergirl because you didn't want me to own my powers. I can fly. I can catch bullets with my bare hands. And that makes you feel worthless.

ALEX: No. No, I'm proud of you.

KARA: And when you couldn't stop me being Supergirl, you got me to work for you. To retain some control. Those days are so over. I am finally free of you, and I'm ready to soar. Look at that city. They worship me. And those who don't, will.

ALEX: Kara, just listen to yourself.

KARA: Go, cut the big sister act, Alex. We have never been sisters. We don't share blood. And you know what the sad truth is? Without me, you have no life. And that kills you. Deep down, you hate me ["Falling" 116].

After, Alex comforts her and accepts her apology, Nonetheless, she adds, "There's some truth to what you said. We're going to have to work on that." The bond can have jealousy and anger, but it remains intact through everything. Season one ends with Kara bidding Alex a touching goodbye, then flying into space to save the earth. Moments before leaving, she leaves a last moment of light as she tells her sister, "I want you to have a good life. I want you to find love and be happy. I want you to do all the things that being my sister kept you from doing." This goodbye speech to Alex offers camaraderie, love and hope for the future, as well as an understanding of their bond. Before she can suffocate, however, Alex pilots Kara's ship and rescues her, encasing her in the metaphoric womb that protected her as a child. Like *Frozen*, this is a sister story without the need for a Prince Charming.

A problematic sibling relationship appears on *Arrow* as Sara Lance returns from the dead after six years to find her parents split up and her sister a depressed alcoholic. Of course, she disappeared while spending the weekend with her sister's boyfriend, thus complicating their relationship further.

> SARA: How could you not have any questions?
> LAUREL: Because I already know all of the answers to them. How could you still be alive; where have you been all this time? Why didn't you call us? And the answer to all of them is because it's Sara.
> ...
> SARA: Laurel, look, I know you're angry. And you have every right to be. But please don't take this out on dad. If you need someone to blame, blame me.
> LAUREL: Oh, I do blame you, Sara. Every single thing that's gone wrong in our lives is your fault. You got on that stupid boat with my boyfriend. You didn't call us to tell us that you were still alive, even though it probably would have saved mom and dad's marriage. And you brought some crazy assassin into Starling City who nearly killed mom and who poisoned me. You. You stole my whole life away from me. Now get out ["Heir to the Demon" 213].

A few episodes later in "Birds of Prey" (217), Sara, in her guise of the Black Canary, infiltrates the courthouse where the Huntress has taken hostages. She finds her sister in danger and knocks out her assailant. Masked, with her voice disguised, Laurel doesn't know her. Then as Laurel reaches for alcohol, Sara must save her from herself.

> SARA: You don't want to do that.
> LAUREL: Oh, no, trust me. I do.
> SARA: What about your sobriety?
> LAUREL: How do you know about that?
> SARA: The "A" chip on your keychain.
> LAUREL: Do you even know why I'm here today? Turns out I'm decoration. Expendable decoration.
> SARA: What do you mean?
> LAUREL: This whole trial was a sham. I should have seen it. Sara was right. Sara, she's … she's my sister. She said that I wasn't ready to come back, and I just thought she was being overprotective.
> SARA: Well, sisters can be like that. You should meet mine.
> LAUREL: She's gone through a lot. She must have been so strong. I just I wanted to show her, show myself. That I was still strong, too.
> SARA: So show me.

Laurel puts down the bottle. However, as Sara tries to take her from the building, Laurel refuses, insisting on saving the other hostages. As she adds, "I know Helena. She's going to kill all of those people, innocent people. You wanted me to show you I'm strong. This is me being strong. I'm staying. Are you going to help me or not?" The two women act as a team, saving everyone in danger. When Black Canary considers killing the Huntress, Laurel, the moral sister, is the one to stop her. As each counsels the other to stay strong and do the right thing, they emphasize sibling power as a force for good.

Evil Twin: Black Widow (Marvel Comics, 1999–2002)

The shadow "corresponds with the personal unconscious" (Jung "Conscience, Unconscious, and Individuation" 284). It's the buried voice whispering from within, urging the everyday polite self to stop being so "nice" and lash out, have fun, give in to one's urges. "The shadow personifies everything that the subject refuses to acknowledge about himself and yet is always thrusting itself upon him directly or indirectly—for instance, inferior traits of character and other incompatible tendencies" (Jung "Conscience, Unconscious, and Individuation" 285). As such, it reveals qualities the hero can see in other people but not in himself—"such things as egotism, mental laziness, and sloppiness; unreal fantasies, schemes, and plots; carelessness and cowardice; inordinate love of money and possessions—in short all the little sins about which he might have previously [ignored in himself]" (Von Franz, *Individuation* 174). Facing a person who reflects the shadow and embodies all these repressed qualities helps the heroine understand what's missing in her own life.

The evil twin is a superhero staple, with good reason. In children's novels and fairytales, the adolescent heroine battles her inverse, the wicked witch who's adult, powerful, sensual—all the child is not. Superheroines are already powerful, so their most common inverse shares their strength, but channels it into evil. Here are seen Bizarro versions, alt-universe and what-if versions, mutated copies, and, certainly, sisters and classmates.

The Marvel action heroine Black Widow has a chance to grow when she meets her rival Yelena Belova. Dressed in black like her counterpart, she introduces herself as a student of the Red Room, which is still active. As Yelena adds, "You are its greatest legend, Natalia Romanova, even though you are no longer truly Russian." When Black Widow introduces herself, Yelena contradicts her: "You have that wrong, Natalia. It is *you* who will call *me* Black Widow" (Grayson). She is the evil twin seen so often in superhero fiction, the counterpart with the same upbringing, but different choices. Having passed Natasha's test scores, she seeks to usurp Natasha's very identity and legacy. As Yelena insists she still remembers the value of being Russian and has parents at home waiting to be proud of her, she's who the Black Widow used to be. She reflects young, evil Black Widow, desperate to prove herself and take risks as the older Widow is not.

In this way, meeting the shadow forces the questing heroine to face truths about herself that she's repressed—the dark voice buried within has much to teach her. To Jungian scholars, the raging, rejected shadow has valuable qualities: "Envy, lust, sensuality, deceit, and all known vices are the negative, 'dark' aspect of the unconscious, which can manifest itself in two ways. In the positive sense, it appears as a 'spirit of nature,' creatively animating Man, things, and the world…. In the negative sense, the unconscious (that same spirit) manifests itself as a spirit of evil, as a drive to destroy" (Jaffé 316). The new heroine is a challenge to the old and also a remainder of what she's left behind. "I respect and admire you, Romanova, but you are getting older…," says the young woman, seeking to co-opt her predecessor's place.

When Natasha's former boyfriend Daredevil calls, Yelena picks up her phone and answers as the Black Widow. She then co-opts the Widow's mission, tracking a rogue group with a bio-toxin. She's not only competition, but she craves her counterpart's identity. She represents the disguised ignored half, the little girl locked away within, the unused potential of the self. This Widow never had the Avengers take her in and care for her. As she talks to the Widow's boyfriend and lives her life, she gets to feel loved, privileged, accepted, all she's ever longed for. The dark side is seeking love and acceptance from the heroine's friends, as well as an opportunity to strut in daylight, to let the heroine unleash her greedy, selfish side.

The hidden side of the self is enticing, crying out as it does for recognition and sympathy. Of course, loving and accepting the shadow is the true path to moving forward. Marjorie Liu's *Astonishing X-Men: Weaponized* features Karma, a Vietnamese X-Man who must confront her half-sister. D'ao Coy Manh grew up in her father's "other family"—hidden from his proper wife and good daughter as the neglected and unwanted one. In this comic, she returns to take vengeance on Karma, Shan Coy Manh, the "good daughter" who always had everything she wanted. In a glamorous red dress to contrast with Karma's dark clothes, D'ao kidnaps her respected, proper sister and her X-Men friends. Shan has her own mental debate, noting to herself that she's silently allowed all this to happen "because good girls … good little soldiers … we never complain, do we?" She realizes that swallowing the pain as she's always done can make young women like her sister into monsters. In a moment of courage, she embraces the other girl and links with her mentally, telling her, "Look at me, Susan. See my life. Both of us were abandoned. Abused." She promises her sister she's not alone and that she'll never let her go.

The Red Room creates particularly isolated, damaged heroines. The television show *Agent Carter* introduces "Dottie Underwood," who sleeps chained to the bed, something she's grown used to after the horrors of her childhood. In "A Sin to Err" (106), Dottie steals the heroic Peggy Carter's knockout lipstick and kisses her, turning her own weapon on her. The two women use similar strategies—both masters of disguise who are alluringly dismissible. When Dottie's pulled over by a policeman, she giggles, insisting, "I am just the silliest goose," and lulls his suspicions ("Valediction" 108). Though they are enemies, each understands the other's struggle for respect in a man's world. Paralleling each other in business suits, Peggy's blue and white and Dottie's black and red, the women battle in the final episode, physically and aloud. "I used to be so jealous of girls like you. I would've done anything to walk like you, to talk like you. But now I can be anybody I want. Oh I've got a great idea! Maybe I'll be an SSR agent next. Whaddya think of that?" Dottie asks. They stand facing each other and Dottie smirks, "I thought you'd be better." Reveling in her role as the evil mother and killer of the innocent, she hides a poison gas canister in a baby carriage, and then turns a movie theater of people into maddened killers. Peggy, the protector, must stop her at any cost.

As Yelena usurps her "sister's" identity, she's captured by men who believe she's the real Black Widow. As Natasha comes seeking her and then battles her at story's end, she talks to Yelena as she might talk to her younger self: "You learn to be lost all the time, so as to never be able to direct anyone to your employers. Or your heart. Or your vulnerabilities." She speaks miserably at the dispassion that the government forced on her, that still alienates her from friends and loved ones. This mentorship between heroine and villainess is common, a way to emphasize the multifaceted connection between the metaphoric mother-daughter or sisters. By facing this girl who mirrors who she used to be, Natasha struggles to incorporate her lost self into who she has become.

The movie tie-in comic *Marvel's The Avengers: Black Widow Strikes* similarly has a spy trying to assassinate Natasha and announcing she'll supplant the superhero and steal her title if she can beat her. "She wanted to be me, Director Fury. In many ways she was more 'me' than I've ever been," Natasha mourns at the end. When Fury replies that some people aren't worth saving, Natasha points out that people used to say this about her. Though she was forced to kill the other woman, she still mourns (Van Lente).

Touched by the other woman's isolation, Natasha's quest to save the dark side of herself continues: As *Black Widow: Breakdown* begins, Yelena and Natasha switch faces in a S.H.I.E.L.D. operation. Yelena wakes in the Widow's apartment, surrounded by her belongings and her ex-lover Daredevil. To her shock, when she looks in the mirror, Natasha's face is looking back. "She's feeling it now ... she's terrified," says the real Natasha, watching from afar and wearing Yelena's face in turn. Yelena desperately repeats her name to herself, trapped as a pawn in a game she doesn't understand.

Yelena soon receives a mission—to assassinate Yelena. She finds "herself" at the museum and the blonde woman tells her, "You're obsessed with me. You want to be me. You want to kill me." When the blonde woman challenges her, Yelena kills her, or so she thinks. On a subconscious level, Yelena wishes to assassinate this old self and become Natasha—this only brings it to prominence.

Yelena is driven to near madness as the authorities hunt her, insisting she's the Widow. It's finally revealed that Natasha set this up so Yelena could overhear her handler's speech on using Yelena. As he smirks, "She's too naive to have survived, you know that. A child playing an adult's game … easily tricked and far too trusting…. I'd have used her, playing on her patriotism, her pathetic love of Mother Russia. Even if she had taken the money I'd have offered her, I'd have killed her in the end."

Yelena is furious about how Natasha manipulated her and even stole her soul, as she thinks. She tells Natasha, "I understand your arrogance, Natasha Romanoff. I understand you think you are justified in your cruelties." Indeed, Natasha does think that, insisting Yelena had to know how much they're both tools. This time it's the "good" side teaching the "bad" one. Nonetheless, Natasha's harsh expediency only reinforces how thin the line is between them.

Wonder Woman's evil twin Artemis debuts in *Wonder Woman* vol. 2 #90 (1994). With a black halter-top, transparent harem pants, and heavy gold jewelry, she reveals lots of skin and incredibly long alluring hair, in contrast with prim Diana. Artemis is from the Amazon tribe of Bana-Mighdall ("The Temple of Women"), who migrated to Egypt rather than choosing immortality on Paradise Island. There, she grew up hungry and ill-clothed in a painful contrast to Diana's utopian childhood. Soon Hippolyta proclaims Diana has not done enough to promote the Amazons' cause and appoints a new champion—Artemis wins (Messner-Loebs, *Wonder Woman: The Contest*). "The weight of your virtue keeps holding you back, Princess," smirks Artemis, who's less principled. In her new role, she takes all that was Diana's, gloating, "Whine and temporize all you want, sister, it proves my point. You are incapable of real action. Your weakness has cost you your home, your name, and your legend. It has cost you the love of your mother. I have replaced you in everything" (#98). At last, Artemis's rage leads to her defeat in battle in issue #100, and she needs the good sister to defeat their enemy with her wisdom and careful planning. Dying, Artemis tells Diana, "Take back your uniform, Diana. I have dishonored it. My ambition and arrogance nearly got us both killed. You are Wonder Woman" (Messner-Loebs, *Wonder Woman: Challenge of Artemis*). Nonetheless, tangling with her dark side makes Diana harder herself.

All too often, sisters are cast as the dark side and the light. In *Outsiders: Crisis Intervention*, Starfire battles her evil sister Blackfire, who says, "She is very good at getting things handed to her, while I … I have learned to take what I want" (Winick). Likewise, in the *Gotham City Sirens* tale "Sister Zero" Maggie Kyle, a nun, goes to the church, insisting her sister Selina (Catwoman) is "possessed by a demon who has ruined *both* our lives." An angel whispers in her ear, or so she thinks, and tells her, "You have to be a little unhinged to see true evil for what it really is." She tells Selina, "I see you for what you really are … and I love you enough to save you." Driven mad, she resolves to drag her sister out of evil, even if she has to kill her (Bedard). She is certainly Selina's shadow, the side of her who knows her deeds can never be forgiven.

Echoing this symbolism, Power Girl and Harley Quinn have an unlikely team-up in Amanda Conner and Jimmy Palmiotti's *Harley Quinn: Power Outage*. On finding the unconscious and amnesiac Power Girl, Harley rushes to dress them both in matching superhero outfits to gain her loyalty. However, this also emphasizes Harley's secret desire for heroism and acceptance. When Power Girl awakens, Harley convinces her they're teammates and roommates. While the pair adventure, Harley appears the lost voice inside Power Girl, the sublimated voice that defends her, even violently, from lecherous men, yet is always ignored and reviled. They actually form an effective partnership. While Power Girl's plans involve appealing pedantically to people's better natures, Harley encourages her to use her feminine charms and revel in her strength. Soon enough, Power Girl is declaring war while Harley is watching her language— they each prompt the other to try a little goodness … or badness.

Indeed, an encounter with one's evil twin can help one grow stronger. In *Arrow*: "Birds of Prey" (217), the Huntress takes D.A. Laurel Lance hostage, and Laurel reasons with her, connecting with the woman Huntress used to be. As they talk, Laurel finds herself confessing the deep truths of her existence.

HELENA: I said no talking.
LAUREL: We talked that night. You, Oliver, Tommy, and I. At dinner. I remember you telling me your fiancé was killed. I'm so sorry.
HELENA: Does this make us girlfriends?
LAUREL: No. But I know what it's like to lose someone.
HELENA: Ohh. Poor Laurel. Did Tommy dump you?
LAUREL: No. He died. And I couldn't deal with it. So I became a drunk. Every problem I had, I solved with a pill or a drink. My friends and my family, they tried to help me, but I wouldn't let them. You don't have to do this, Helena. It's not too late.
HELENA: Yes, I do. Because once you let the darkness inside, it never comes out.

After her ordeal, Laurel threatens her boss to get her job back. When her boss comments, "I would have thought blackmail was a little dark for you," Laurel responds in Helena's words: "Someone recently told me, once you let the darkness inside, it never comes out." Facing the shadow has toughened her.

◆◆◆4◆◆◆

Male Influences

Friendship: White Tiger (Marvel Comics, 2007)

When former cop and FBI agent Angela del Toro takes over for her uncle, Hector Ayala, the White Tiger, the Marvel superheroes rally around her. Friends, allies, sidekicks, and the support of the larger community are vital for superheroes, who often have crises of faith and need to know they're making a difference.

As she notes, her FBI partner left her his apartment before his murder. "So I get the place, and the neighborhood. And they get me," she thinks in her first panel. She was also fired from the Bureau for standing up for her mentor Matt Murdock. Now he is in jail and refusing to see her ... there's also the lingering animosity of the moment he threw her off a roof and broke her arm. However, Angela bursts into battle, armed only with magic amulets, martial arts training, and a ski mask. The neighborhood is hers, and she plans to defend it. With her uncle's amulets, Angela heals quickly. She grows stronger and faster and only sleeps two hours a night.

While battling the Yakuza, who are selling fake passports, she spies Daredevil, as she thinks. Matt Murdock is in jail and she soon realizes this is someone else, whom she calls "Daredevil 2.0." He in turn tells her she shouldn't "dress like a burglar and play with punks." Though she and real Daredevil are estranged, this substitute version also provides substitute reassurance. She hesitates to get herself a costume, but relents when the new Daredevil sends her to a designer in Hell's Kitchen. Black Widow catches her on the way and warns her to keep her identity secret around the costume maker. She also insists, "I'm not *working*. I'm helping you *shop*. You know, *girl stuff*." This is, of course, girl stuff, but the superhero version of it. Black Widow is sophisticated, independent, capable, and well-established, while Angela is just beginning her journey.

Addressing the practical questions, Angela asks her new female mentor about tightness, sweat, and using the bathroom, which Natasha answers (adding, "Trust me. They look at the outfit. It makes it easier to *hit* them"). While it must be admitted a male-centric comic wouldn't focus so much on the clothing angle, these are logical and pressing questions for the new female hero, adding realism to her actions. Meanwhile Spider-Man shows up to offer his own opinion, and Angela thinks, "*Of course* he's here. I'm surprised the whole *Xavier Academy* isn't here." Having them along offers rookie Angela another moment of community acceptance, this time from the Avengers as she becomes one of Marvel's many costumed heroes.

After, Natasha takes her out for drinks and the superhero version of gossip, about the villains she'll be facing. Tracking her partner's killer to a perfume store, Angela bumps into Emma Frost, who quips about Angela's life but tells her where to find her quarry. To Angela's chagrin, several people have mistaken her for the X-Man, as she and Emma both wear tight white suits. When Angela's injured, Daredevil 2.0 helps her get home, and later he and Spider-Man chat with her over donuts. Spider-Man also suggests she seek help from her family's NYPD contacts. Both men act as the little extra moments of help and advice everyone needs at times.

Angela gets a job working security for James Guererro and his supermodel wife Veronica. Their ten-year-old daughter with an IQ of 198 does their computer research. When she sees White Tiger, she cries, "I want to be White Tiger someday. She looks Latin, I'm half Latin, I have martial arts–" Meanwhile, Veronica encourages Angela to wear something trendy that isn't black, and mentors her in her security guard role. There, she protects NYU students as they go clubbing, though she runs into the bad guys and is forced to battle them. The admiring students call Angela their Shero (a nod to Tamora Pierce's blog on the topic). Angela's adoptive family is growing, from her new fangirl-sidekick to mentor and surrogate mother Veronica. While the *Daily Bugle* claims to be her ally, its description of her as a "hard fightin', gun-totin' hot tamale" with "her white skintight outfit that hugs her curves in all the right places" offends her. Thus she will need to be an example who can guide the public to respect for superheroines. Like the Avengers, and Daredevil himself, she learns to work with her neighborhood and the Marvel Universe's allies and enemies.

Angela's family plays a large role in the story, as she shares information with her brother Rey, who works dispatch for the NYPD. Angela also visits her mother at a get-together of many relatives, only to bump into her adoptive uncle Danny Rand, Iron Fist. She soon realizes that he's the Daredevil 2.0 who's been helping her. She also meets Luke Cage at the gym and he pledges his support. Thus her family becomes a substantial part of her heroism, something common in these stories.

Collaboration with friends, family, or community is common to the female hero—not because she is incapable of succeeding on her own, but because she is more successful when she recognizes, encourages, and utilizes the talents of others. This support system is essential to the evolution of her spirit—which will ultimately make her a better warrior. Additionally, in stories about the female hero, the sidekick—who is traditionally of lesser power than the hero, generally in need of rescue, and often serves the narrative purpose of comic relief—is elevated to the role of hero themselves through collaborative contribution [Stuller, *Ink-Stained Amazons* 92].

Angela's enemies are Sano, who killed her partner, and his henchman Cobra. Cobra bites her and she undergoes a death and rebirth sequence in which she talks with her dead Uncle Hector, the former White Tiger. He tells her she can use the amulets better than he ever could and that he's proud of her. She wakes to find Daredevil 2.0 standing by her. He reveals that she's vanished and been unfindable for three days—like her tiger namesake, she has gained a camouflage power through her ordeal.

Iron Fist and Luke Cage have also intervened for her with her bosses. The Guerreros tells her that they're close to Luke and Danny and realize they and White Tiger have a common cause. They're happy to keep employing her and welcome her outside work, which they can support with their own resources. Angela resents that Danny let them figure out her identity, but he insists they can be trusted. She responds, "It just feels like a major leap of faith—as if I haven't done enough of *those* lately."

He replies, "That's our world, kiddo." Without trusting someone, the superheroes can't function.

Sano shoots her and she falls into the Hudson in another death-and-rebirth sequence. Onlookers call the cops who themselves are quite helpful as they've all watched Angela grow up. Angela explains, "Craig heads the Detective Squad night watch.... My dad's his rabbi in the NYPD, and Craig's Rey's rabbi. All in the family, lucky for me." Craig helps her and reminds her she's one of them so the NYPD will protect her.

White Tiger enters the climactic battle with half the Avengers—Luke Cage, Spider-Man, Black Widow, and Iron Fist. However, she finds a much more unlikely ally who subjects Sano to justice. Sano's father Orii visits Angela and asks her to leave his son alone. She respectfully rejects his request and his bribes. Nonetheless, they part with a polite understanding of each other. Orii ends the war at last by facing his son, who kills him. White Tiger tells him there's only one way to atone for this death according to his warrior code, and Sano agrees and kills himself. Negotiation, not violence, has saved the day.

Angela ends the story gathered with her family, where Hector's widow decides the new White Tiger is a "sign from God" that Hector forgives her. Angela declares that "nobody who wants to hurt my people gets past the White

Tiger." They are a united community—family, Avengers, cops, and the world of New York.

Many other characters gather this sort of public support. Wonder Woman, particularly, began in the 40s with the Holliday girls, a group of college friends who helped her on missions. Leading them was Etta Candy, a short, pudgy college girl who's childlike in her irrepressible desire for sweets, almost a kid sidekick, who nonetheless can help Wonder Woman save the day. Back home, she has her wide community of Amazon sisters.

> Wonder Woman's family of Amazons on Paradise Island, her band of college girls in America, and her efforts to save individual women are all welcome examples of women working together and caring about each other's welfare. The idea of such cooperation may not seem particularly revolutionary to the male reader. Men are routinely depicted as working well together, but women know how rare and therefore exhilarating the idea of sisterhood really is [Steinem 205].

On the 70s television show, Wonder Woman also has the remarkable talent of transforming female enemies into friends by appealing to sisterhood. Paula Von Gunther and "Fausta the Nazi Wonder Woman" are both won over as Wonder Woman pleads for female solidarity against misogynistic Nazis and reveals how badly the men have been treating them all.

> Until his death in 1947, Marston, in collaboration with artist Harry G. Peter, produced a comic in which the hero, while often saving Capt. Trevor, primarily saved helpless women from imminent death and destruction, attempting also to empower women to look after themselves and discover their own physical and economic strengths. Girls are taught that if they "feel [they] can do things, so [they] can do them," and women are exhorted to "get strong and earn your own living" [Emad 959].

When she arrives on earth for her Volume 2 reboot, Wonder Woman is adopted by Professor Julia Kapatelis and her teen daughter Vanessa. In Rucka's Wonder Woman run shortly afterwards, Diana has a close circle of staff at her embassy, including her lawyer Rachel Keast and secretary Alana Dominguez, as well as Ferdinand the minotaur. Peter Garibaldi is press secretary, and she considers his young sons Bobby and Martin family as well.

In a groundbreaking *Wonder Woman* arc, the evil trickster Circe changes the men of earth "into animals or man-beast hybrids" and sends all the super-villainesses to attack in "The Witch and the Warrior." All the DC superheroines converge on the city: JLA, Teen Titans, Birds of Prey, independents. Dozens of named superheroines defend the city, each with unique powers. All ages and races work as teams and partners, defending one another. Oracle supervises from afar, while Wonder Woman, their general, appoints Doctor Light, Power Girl, Troia, Black Canary, Wonder Girl, and Vixen as field leaders (Jimenez,

Paradise Found). It's an army of DC superheroines, all taking their stand against chaos.

Most of all of course are the Justice League or Teen Titans, whose experienced heroes show up to aid the new ones in this and many other comics. The newbies all learn that they're expected to rely on the team rather than going it alone.

Animus Growth: Spider-Gwen (Marvel Comics, 2014)

Writer Jason Latour and artist Robbi Rodriguez introduced a Gwen Stacy with spider powers in *Edge of the Spider-Verse* #2. While she joined in the Spider-Verse event, with all the different alt-universe incarnations of Spider-Man working together, she gained so much fan love that she was given her own series thereafter.

Edge of the Spider-Verse #2, her origin story, shows a great deal about the men in a superheroine's life. Recently infected, Spider-Gwen defends her friend Peter Parker from bullies. She's the aggressive one here, and he represents her nerdy side.

However, he cannot bear life as a sidekick, so he experiments on himself with spider venom and dies in her arms. "I just wanted to be special ... like you," he tells her with his last breath. While J. Jonah Jameson uses Peter as a figurehead for his soapbox appeal that the new Spider-Woman step down, she keeps Peter in her thoughts as a talisman. "I looked into Peter's eyes, Dad. I felt his heart break," she insists later (Latour, *Spider-Gwen* #3). Though regretting she can't tell him how she's always felt, she devotes herself to saving the city in his name, channeling his spirit. Everywhere Gwen goes, she's surrounded by Peter's family, Peter's awards and photos, posters of him spread through the city. Thus he's a constant reminder, pushing itself into her psyche.

Pepper Potts walks in more than another person's shoes when Iron Man builds her her own Iron Man suit. As the superheroine Rescue, Pepper hallucinates a vision of her dead husband Happy, who reassures her. Speaking with him, she decides, "I've been trying to make myself into someone I'm not." She recalls trying to save lives and yet ruining everything. As she sits, she repeats to herself, "*Tony* would have stopped it from happening. I couldn't do it ... inside that gazillion dollar rescue suit I'm still—I'm still just me." Happy reminds her that saving a single life means everything, and she returns to the fight (DeConnick, *Rescue* #1). In this case, wearing Iron Man's suit casts her in his role, and it takes another little voice in her head, a masculine voice, to show her that she can be a different kind of superhero.

Meanwhile, Gwen's father, NYPD Police Chief George Stacy, worries about her goals. He tells her, "The things we love are always worth fighting for," and adds, "But everyone has something they want, what is it the world around you needs? What is it that only you can give?" Gwen is tempted to tell him the truth about herself. Though he is her parent and guide, his advice to her acts like another voice in her head, questioning her actions.

"In the unconscious of every man there is hidden a feminine personality, and in that of every woman a masculine personality," Jung explains, naming these anima and animus ("Conscience, Unconscious, and Individuation" 284). On the heroine's journey, the young woman encounters a best friend or lover who evokes her undeveloped masculine side, training her in its abilities. This animus "evokes masculine traits within her: logic, rationality, intellect. Her conscious side, aware of the world around her, grows, and she can rule and comprehend the exterior world" (Frankel, *From Girl to Goddess* 22).

Many characters exist in partnerships, in pair-ups like Kitty Pryde and Wolverine or Cloak and Dagger, as each offers the traits the other lacks and thus guides their partner to higher wisdom. The former are thought versus action and innocence versus experience, while the latter represent light and optimism empowered by shadowy darkness.

Other characters have male support, from friends and comrades to boyfriends. Sara the Witchblade sees visions of her dead partner, who advises her through the television show to do the right thing. Similarly, Katana's dead husband lives on in her sword, where he continues to advise and protect her. Through her journey, she slowly comes to terms with who her husband really was, even as he continues protecting her out of love (Nocenti, *The New 52: Katana*).

The most primitive animus is a force of brute strength, sometimes a world-destroying tyrant or an abusive relative. In *Spider-Gwen* #1, Daredevil suggests that the monstrous brute Alekss befriend Spider Woman, though he has a vendetta against her father. Challenged by the beast, Gwen beats him easily. "The animus is obstinate, harping on principles, laying down the law, dogmatic, world-reforming, theoretic, word-mongering, argumentative, and domineering" (Jung, "Concerning Rebirth" 124). All this, she gets from him.

As the heroine grows, her animus is replaced by wiser versions: initiative and planning, rule of law, and wisdom, while her enemies follow the same process of growth to challenge her (Von Franz, *Individuation* 206). The Fantastic Four could be said to offer this to Sue Storm—the clobbering Thing, her impulsive, heedless brother, and her wise fiancé.

Emma Frost, in her *X-Men: Origins* comic by Valerie d'Orazio, grows up with a brutal father who hits her and calls her a "simpering buck-toothed patsy."

When the mean girls at school pick on her, she knocks them out with a psionic blast and thus discovers her powers. A second mentor, the contrasting good father, arrives with Charles Xavier, who invites her to mutant school. This is a chance for benevolence and a better teacher, but Emma rejects this. She orders him to leave, and her own father slaps her for eavesdropping. She thinks, "I could burn your mind out, father. Leave you a vegetable. You'd never be able to harass or hurt me again." She leaves before she can become like him, but finds herself a stripper in New York. A new boss recruits her there—Sebastian Shaw, another domineering father but this time with superpowers to match hers. He hits her, but when she tries to kill him with her mind, he applauds her and begins a romantic and supervillain partnership with her. Thus she's seen growing through a father of brute force to one of careful planning, though it's only after joining the X-Men that she learns wisdom.

Initiative is the next stage. In *Black Widow: The Name of the Rose*, the Widow is critically injured, so her friends Wolverine, Bucky, Hawkeye, and Iron Man unite to track down her attacker and clear her name behind the scenes. They act clearly as her animus, the strength that acts on the Widow's behalf when she needs external aid (Liu).

After the *House of M* storyline, in which Wanda destroys all the mutants, she falls into amnesia and loses her powers. Once her heroic sons, like the stronger, more willful part of herself, come remind her who she is, she goes through a stage of rage then one of terrible grief. Wiccan jolts her out of this by telling her that he's been reborn as her son. When the Avengers and X-Men plan to punish her, it's Wiccan, acting as her advocate, who manages to save her once more (Heinberg, *Avengers: The Children's Crusade*). As such, he functions as her guide and guardian, helping her when she despairs.

Spider-Gwen's friends are all female, as she plays in the band The Mary Janes. Thus she needs a male friend, even if she's only remembering a dead one. Of course, Peter's death continues haunting her as cops and angry mobs hunt her as Peter's killer. He was a force of impulse, seeking to become a hero and dying for it as he had no deeper training or thorough planning. At last, well-spoken rock and roll reporter Randy Robertson urges the Mary Janes to let Gwen back into their band, advocating on her behalf when she feels she can't. She decides he's "my current hero."

Soon after, Gwen's father tries to arrest her, and she can only stop him by unmasking and throwing back his own words that "sometimes what we want isn't what the world needs." She shows him that she's been channeling him too, saying: "You're a good cop, Dad. You put on that badge and carry that gun because you know if you don't, someone who shouldn't will. When I put on this mask, I only did it because it freed me from responsibility. I thought I was special. And Peter Parker died because he tried to follow my example. I have to take responsibility for that. To make his death mean something. But I can't do it in a jail cell." She gets through to him by internalizing his lessons and understanding their meaning. He is convinced by her argument, and she flies off into the night (Latour, *Edge of Spiderverse* #2). Of course, he is the animus of rule of law and higher wisdom for the growing heroine. She continues to channel his advice through her own series, noting often that she sounds like him or is following his teachings and passing them along.

Soon enough, Gwen internalizes the entire city as animus. "When I'm here, they want me gone. When I'm gone, they wonder where I am," she notes, irritated by the complaints in the paper. Her enemy this time is the Vulture as well as public opinion—she covers the city with graffiti to challenge him as she learns from her vilification to attack his ego at its source (Latour, *Spider-Gwen* #1). He may be the pompous voice of order, but she can see through him.

When she's knocked out, the pig Spider-Ham appears to be her Jiminy Cricket, as he puts it. He's clearly a substitute for Peter Parker, but without the guilt that Spider-Man would invoke. He advises her on what's important and continues to linger, giving her wisecracking advice. He also pushes her to reunite with the Mary Janes and get a life outside being a superhero (Latour, *Spider-Gwen* #2). "The positive side of the animus can personify an enterprising spirit, courage, truthfulness, and the highest form, spiritual profundity. Through him, a woman can experience the underlying processes of her cultural and personal objective situation and can find her way to an intensified spiritual attitude to life" (Von Franz, *Individuation* 207). Gwen struggles to define herself and rise above the cruelty of the press, but through it all, she has wise advisors to help her climb the steps to her own enlightenment.

The Good Boy: *Dark Angel* (TV, 2000–2002)

In *X2: X-Men United*, Jean Grey insists: "Girls flirt with the dangerous guy, Logan, but they don't take him home. They marry the good guy." The first represents passion, but the second, enduring love. This is often true for superheroines, even after their bad boy flirtations.

In an apocalyptic future, a girl escapes the military complex that's intent on turning her into a supersoldier. Max Guevara (Jessica Alba) runs away to Seattle, a city now a ruin of what it once was, where she works as a bike messenger and struggles to hide the hideous augmentations forced on her by the scientists of Manticore. Through it all, she defends the helpless and searches for news about the other X-5s like herself, other modified children who escaped from Manticore. This is the show *Dark Angel*.

> Like other supergirl protagonists of the late 1990s and early 2000s, Max is constructed as alienated. She strives for a sense of belonging, of being normal, but Max is a supergirl because she is a freak and a freak because she is a supergirl: the two are interdependent and related. The superpower of many female action heroes translates as exceptionalism: the supergirl can never be "normal" because her powers and responsibilities set her apart from other people, and do not allow her to lead a "normal" existence. Instead, like the typical comic book superhero, she often leads a double life. Here Max initially hides her nature as a transgenic from her closest friends and her day- and night-time existences bear little relation to each other [Jowett].

Max slowly assembles and reconnects with the X-5s she grew up with and escaped with, as well as their children. She also builds a chosen family of best friends—her "Sister Girl" Original Cindy and work friends. Protecting them motivates a great deal of her behavior. Unlike supermen, who battle alone, superwomen often expand outward from a best friend to a larger adopted family to the greater community. "Max's love for her family helps her evolve from a pouty, jaded, uber-sultry, and understandably self-protective girl to a courageous leader—a superwoman" (Stuller, *Ink-Stained Amazons* 97–98). She is a loner, stealing from the rich and rejecting romance. Nonetheless, it finds her.

Soon she meets the impassioned Eyes Only (played by Michael Weatherly), a journalist whose anonymous posts with only his eyes showing alert the city to the exploitations of the rich. Though he grew up rich and entitled, he believes in changing the world and spends his wealth in the attempt. He encourages Max to use her gifts the same way, but she insists she'd rather ride her motorcycle than give herself a headache over stuff she can't do anything about. Eyes Only, Logan Cale, retorts, "You accept the way things are … you're an active participant in making them worse."

She can only quip, "Is the social studies class over for today?"

Though she rejects his lessons in the beginning, he's a gentle animus figure, guiding her to care for those beyond her circle of friendship and defend the world.

> For both the questing hero and heroine, the opposite sex brings forth their untapped powers, evoking the man's gentleness and woman's strength. Further, the highly developed animus connects the woman with her spiritual side, making her even more receptive to her own creativity. Thus, the heroine, as well as the hero, obtains the mystical feminine energy that offers endless emotion, sympathy, nature, magic, insight, and perception [Frankel, *From Girl to Goddess* 23].

By episode four of *Dark Angel*, Logan wants Max to protect a key witness in a trial against a brutal exploiter named Sonrisa who had been replacing war veterans' medicine with sugar pills and then selling the real supplies. She refuses, and as a result her friend Theo dies from bad medical treatment, the witness's daughter is kidnapped, and Logan himself is shot. She rushes off to intervene. "Whether Max is driven by guilt or a desire for social justice is up in the air at this point. She saves Logan from a second assassination attempt and rescues the abducted child. She even executes a plan that takes down Sonrisa and his organization" (Stuller, *Ink-Stained Amazons*). Despite her withdrawal, Logan is enticing her into heroism.

Logan hopes Max's involvement means he's cracked her "bioengineered military-issue armor plating [to find her] beating heart" and love for others. Still she resists, telling him she's "not signing up to join the Logan Cale brigade for the defense of widows, small children, and lost animals" (104). Their opposing ideologies and teamwork both seem barriers on a relationship. "The two seem to be in the position made familiar by Mulder and Scully in *The X-Files*— characters who may be romantically or sexually attracted to each other but whose professional relationship is of greater significance" (Jowett). In "Haven" (115) he's still trying to change her:

MAX: You can't right every wrong.
LOGAN: You've got to at least try.
MAX: Whatever. Go talk to your source. This girl's gonna kick back, make S'mores, and relax.
LOGAN: Fine. I'll be back later.
MAX: Don't hurry.
LOGAN: Have fun. Because that *is* the most important thing.
MAX: I'll try. Even though I'll be wracked by guilt since I don't have enough to share with every single person on this planet.

In many stories, the good boy cannot accept the heroine's bad girl side. In the *Catwoman* film, Detective Tom Lone is a cop who enters the story by saving the heroine's life after she chases a cat onto the roof. He compares her drawings to "early Chegall," showing culture as well as an appreciation for her work. He even lectures children on how to "be the good guys" and shoots hoops with them. However, like Logan, he is too good to appreciate her savage, selfish side. When she hints at her Catwoman identity, he adds that "bad isn't something that does it for me." Similarly, Barbara Gordon dates a cop who insists, "Outlaws like Batgirl actually *endanger* the lives of the innocent" (Stewart, *Batgirl of Burnside*). Secret identities always complicate the romance when the good guy is far too good to date a vigilante.

Still, the tough, blocked off superheroine can be startlingly vulnerable when the good boy accepts all of her, even the savage parts. Simon is the most hapless of the superpowered team on the British show *Misfits*. Thus Alisha is shocked when the Superhoodie who's been helping them from a distance reveals himself as an older, much more confidant Simon. His mask has been concealing a different aspect of the same character, one that shows off his long-concealed heroism.

> ALISHA: Since when did you run around, jumping off buildings?
> FUTURE SIMON: Ever since I travelled back from the future.
> ALISHA: Really, did you?
> FUTURE SIMON: Yes.
> ALISHA: Seriously? How does this work? There's two of you.
> FUTURE SIMON: There's the Simon you know, and there's the future Simon. Me.
> ALISHA: You're so different.
> FUTURE SIMON: A lot happens between now and then [203].

The bigger shock is that future Simon can touch her without going mad from her power—she makes men sex-crazed with her touch, so she's been leading a distant life. When she asks why, he simply replies, "Things are different in the future." He appears to come from a better time, when the teens are admired superheroes and he and Alisha are together. "You fall in love with me," he tells her directly, with wide-open vulnerable eyes. Though Alisha is dating the much cooler track star Curtis, she falls for future Simon. She also develops some tenderness for goofy present Simon, as he tells her sympathetically, "Sometimes I think it's difficult for beautiful girls. People don't see past their looks" (203). This man, brimming with empathy, does, however.

Roulette, a character created by Melinda M. Snodgrass for *Wild Cards*, can kill a man while they're having sex. Disturbingly, she does this by channeling the memory of her dead child, born a monster because of the Wild Card virus that created empowered Aces and malformed Jokers. The murderer called the Astronomer convinces her to do jobs for him. However, when she seduces Tachyon, an alien often blamed for bringing the virus to earth, she feels differently. He's more sensitive and solicitous than anyone has been before. "This time it was not an obligation to be bitterly endured. He was an accomplished lover, seeming almost to worship her with his body" (Martin, *Aces High* 163). She allows him to live, convincing herself she's only delaying, but as he cares for her and protects her, she can't bear to kill him. After he discovers the truth, he tries to heal her mind and offers to let her kill him if she feels it will help her. Rather than judging, he tells her, "I have an amazingly elastic and creative conscience" (Martin, *Aces High* 358). He adds that he loves her and will wait, while she can only reply, "I've lived on hate. Now there's nothing. Let me see if I'm capable of anything beyond those two states" (Martin, *Aces High* 359). Nonetheless, her encounter with him has moved her past rage at her child's death into a kind of peace and openness to the next stage. The love of the gentle soul has saved her.

Of course, Max and Logan's affection is also complicated by a third side to the triangle—the bad boy. Alec (Jensen Ackles), is so-called by Max who thinks him a "smart aleck." Designed as Max's mate by Manticore, he's her go-to guy for casual sex, but his help is problematic. He cannot be trusted, and even infects her with a virus on orders from the government.

> The lead males in *Dark Angel*, much like those in *Buffy*, fall into two categories: vulnerable, sensitive men who are never enough for the powerful warrior women of the series (Logan in *Dark Angel* and Riley in *Buffy*), or unreliable "bad boys" who will ultimately cause the heroine more grief than satisfaction (Angel and Spike in *Buffy*, Alec in *Dark Angel*). In this way the writers of the shows make very definite third-wave feminist statements about men. Be wary of them, but do not shun them as your feminist mothers might have done. They are a legitimate mode of sexual expression when they can be tamed, as well as companions when they can be trusted [Ursini and Mainon 230].

With Alec as contrast, Logan is presented as the better choice, even with his too-good idealism, and even at a distance. By the second season a deadly engineered virus prevents them from even touching. They end the season holding hands but only through protective gloves. As the show wasn't renewed for a third, their relationship remains loving but largely unfulfilled. Nonetheless, Logan transforms Max forever through his teaching that she should use her powers for good.

Much literature offers the heroine the dark man who betrays the heroine and the light man who saves and marries her. However, the division is not as clear as good and evil.

> She discovers that the dark man sees her as prey and seeks to prove his masculinity by conquering and ruining her, while the light man wants to marry her and make her a valuable possession. When she demythologizes both men, she sees that they are neither villains nor saviors, but simple, fallible, and somewhat misguided human individuals who can neither save nor damn her [Pearson and Pope 161].

Soldier Martha Washington, in her post-apocalyptic comics by Frank Miller, has a gentler love interest who transforms her through example. While a soldier and revolutionary, Baby's Breath Wasserstein was originally an Apache lawyer trying to save ancestral land poisoned by oil refineries. Further, his name is gentle, with the tiny white blossoms named for babies to the rather Jewish geeky last name in a marginalized mish-mash. A sensitive guy, he takes orders from Martha and she rescues him often—as he complains, "This isn't doing my ego any good at all …." Nonetheless, he's clearly her sidekick. He welcomes her to a hidden utopia of clean land in the midst of a radioactive nightmare, a purified world he wants to share with all cultures. Eventually the loyal and hardened soldier Martha is persuaded to his way of thinking. He remains sensitive and supportive, willing to wait as long as she chooses before they commit.

However, he's taken over by the bad girl, the AI Venus. She smirks that her sexual and intellectual powers far exceed poor Martha's, leaving him willingly in her control. After Martha saves the good boy from the bad girl, however, Wasserstein tells her he thought that in her he'd found an equal. However, now he's realized, "You're better than me, Martha. Stronger. You fought her off. You're better. You have a magnificent destiny, my love—and I'm not a part of it." With this, they separate forever.

Finally, the heroine need not end up with the hero. She is not a Disney princess but rather complete, one-in-herself like the virgin goddesses of old. "The dark and light men in many instances are symbols of the hero's own sense of being divided into two irreconcilable selves—one secular and one spiritual" (Pearson and Pope 161). However, her life need not be this dualistic, if she can grow beyond these models to incorporate all aspects into her life. Echoing Buffy at the end of her own show, Kamala Khan tells her sweet, faithful friend Bruno that she isn't looking for love. She explains, "Being Ms. Marvel—it's filled up my heart and my life in a way that *nothing else* I've done ever has. I'm *not ready* to be anything else, to *anyone* else. I need to give this *everything* I've got" (Wilson, *Last Days*).

Rogue, in her novelization *Going Rogue* by Christine Woodward, falls for a freedom fighter from the future. His name, significantly, is Touch, for emotional availability is his power, even as physical touch between them is forbidden. However, each has a duty to their own time that leave the pair forever severed as he sends her to safety in her own time but stays to fight the good fight. He's kind and tender, responding to her inability to be touched by wrapping her in sheets or blankets and cradling her, or kissing her through a ski mask. She feels increasingly loved, an emotion only matched by his as he invents a way for them to finally be together, briefly, in a dream state. This transforms her, bolstering her into the future. As Rogue thinks, "That time I'd had with Touch—that time out of time—it sure did last me awhile. The kind of happiness brought by loving someone who loves you back, it doesn't just float away" (272).

Shapeshifter Romance: *Batman Returns* (Film, 1992)

Batman Returns popularized the concept of a "bad girl" heroine. Pfeiffer's Catwoman was fundamentally a villainess, but while her motivations were antiheroic, her plight was sympathetic. Deep down she had a soft spot, questioning her actions against Batman as she fell for his true identity of Bruce Wayne. Her alter ego Selina Kyle was battered and abused, but as the sultry Catwoman she took charge, letting no man interfere with her goal—revenge against her male tormentor. Pfeiffer's allure made Catwoman the sexiest screen character of the year. As Catwoman she carried the torch lit by Elektra and helped transform the superheroine: Superwomen could now have looks *that* kill, and the power *to* kill [Misiroglu 537].

However, the heroine has a long arc of transformation. At the start of Tim Burton's *Batman Returns*, Selina Kyle, all in dowdy brown and glasses, stammeringly brings up "a suggestion. Well, really, actually more of just a question...."

Her boss Max Shreck laughingly notes, "I'm afraid we haven't properly house-broken Ms. Kyle. In the plus column, though, she knows how to brew coffee." Miserable, she calls herself a "stupid corndog" as she walks away, berating herself. From the first, she pushes herself to the side, attempting to disappear from view. She already has a wallflower persona shrouding the empowered self she's meant to become.

As a stumbling idiot, she is no match for Batman. Their first meeting is quite telling. Selina, leaning over awkwardly in the street to pick up her glasses, is grabbed by a villain, just as the impressive, imposing Batmobile pulls up. Batman, literally without a word, shoots her assailant, ignoring all her desperate awkward babble asking whether he's "the Batman—or is it just Batman." As she adds, "Your choice. Of course."

Her cat is her shadow, foreshadowing Catwoman, but also contrasting as all she is not. She wears beige, while the cat is a shocking black against the pink apartment. Selina notes that Miss Kitty is "back from more sexual escapades you refuse to share." Selina of course considers herself the responsible one. "But I'm a working girl, gotta pay the rent. Maybe if you were chipping in, 'stead of stepping out...." Unenlightened Selina has fantasies of escape, but nothing more. "When a woman is attempting to avoid the facts of her own devastations, her night dreams will shout warnings to her" such as "flee," or even "go for the kill," explains Estés (54). These are seen in her feline alter-ego.

When she discovers her boss intends to siphon power from the city, he grows intimidating, while she gets even mousier, shrinking away and asking, "How can you be so mean to someone so meaningless?" and adding, "Intimidate me, bully me if it makes you feel big." When she says the fateful "I mean, it's not like you can just kill me," however, he pushes her out the window.

She hits the snow with a jolt: Selina dies on the pavement and Catwoman is born. "When Schreck kills Selina, he kills off the wage-earning, sexually inactive single woman whose only company is her cat; what emerges from the physical and psychic trauma is an antiauthoritarian, sexually alluring, and empowered superheroine" (Landay 4).

Immediately, all the city's cats swarm around her, meowing and licking as if inducting her. Her own cat kisses her mouth in blessing or urgent fairytale awakening, without the prince. Her eyes open in total traumatized shock. She returns home, mechanically feeding the cat (though sharing her milk) and listening to messages. However, when there's an ad that'll have her boss asking her to stay after work, she freaks out. Her shadow takes over as she sprays the pink apartment with black paint, gleefully forces stuffed animals into the garbage disposal, smashes lights, and tears down the good girl persona she's built. No longer will she be sweet and virginal, staying in her unmarried apartment each night. She destroys all the trappings of girlish femininity, whose sentimental teachings have nearly gotten her killed—stuffed animals, dollhouse, kitten nightgown. The cheery "Hello There" sign has a few letters kicked out to read "Hell Here" in a total inversion. "I don't know about you, Miss Kitty, but I feel. So. Much. Yummier," she smirks in her stitched up black vinyl.

She is a victim of the powerful corporate man, and, displaying feminist spirit, goes out hunting muggers. When she finds one, she flirts, "I just love a big strong man who's not afraid to show it, with someone half his size. Be gentle, it's my first time." After rescuing the woman in danger, Catwoman swats her. "You make it so easy, don't you—Always waiting for some Batman to save you." She could be talking to her mousy old self. Now she's grown and exclaims, "I'm Catwoman, hear me roar" as the voice of feminist rage. "Her transformation is from fearful victim to anarchic female trickster; in one fell swoop, male violence (economic and psychological as well as physical) against women results in a vengeful, competent fantasy figure of women's rejection of victimhood, sentimentalism, passionlessness, physical weakness, domesticity, and secretarial drudgery" (Landay 4).

To Max's horror, she shows up at work, businesslike but with her new shadow personality firmly behind the wheel. New Selina wears better makeup and lets her curly hair free. She is much sexier, offering on meeting Bruce to take him to "some grotto or secluded hideaway" and teasing Max that he'll have to buy a new name for her if he wears out her old one. She wears black and gray now and Bruce says, "You don't seem like the type who takes orders from him." She flirts with Bruce, smoothly playing hard to get.

SELINA: Well, that's a ... long story...
BRUCE: Well, I could ... free up some time...
SELINA: I'm listed.
BRUCE: I'm tempted.
SELINA: (backs toward the conference room) I'm working.

Of course, this is followed by their first fateful meeting as night prowlers. Catwoman goes out to blow up Max's store. "After her transformation, after she has crossed over the line and is outside of society, she wants to destroy anything connected with the system of rules that failed her" (Landay 217). When she and Batman meet as costumed heroes, they fight, and then Catwoman crumples.

CATWOMAN: How could you? I'm a woman...
BATMAN: (suddenly taken aback) I'm—sorry, I—
CATWOMAN: As I was saying: I'm a woman, and can't be taken for granted. Life's a bitch—now so am I.

Using her nice girl act as what it is now—a barely concealing persona over her inner badness, Catwoman uses the distraction to attack. She dangles Batman off the side of the building, then after he sprays her with napalm, he leaps up and she is the one caught scrabbling for purchase much like her namesake. He pulls her up—for a moment, they're embracing. She asks him, "Who are you? Who's the man behind the bat? Maybe he can help me find the woman behind the cat." Each senses the other is a reflection and thus contains keys to self-understanding. "Catwoman's relationship with Batman serves to crystalize the split in her personality, as well as the one in the dark knight's own psyche" (Mainnon and Ursini 124). She feels around for his skin, and then digs in her talons. Batman roars and accidentally swats Catwoman off the building, where she lands in a truck of sand, kitty litter as she thinks.

Shapeshifters are common in fictional romance, from vampires and werewolves to masked superheroes. "In the game of love, the hero and heroine each view their partner as a shapeshifter. This 'other half' they must cleave to like themselves has frightening mood swings and unpredictable desires" (Frankel, *From Girl to Goddess* 76). Sometimes the story ends well and sometimes badly, but it's a story of accepting the other's many facets.

One particularly strange hybrid is Andy from Peter David's *Supergirl* #26. As Andrea Martinez lies dying of frostbite, Zed One, also called Andrew Jones, tries to rescue her but they're trapped together. Andrew is crushed that he can't rescue this dying innocent. "Zed One's genetically engineered body broke down, dissolving into its components ... and merged with Andy's frostbitten, tissue-dead form." This new being can switch between male and female ... as well as Supergirl's beloved horse Comet. When Comet changes into Andrew and comes on to Supergirl, both of her own halves (ordinary Linda and the alien Matrix) are stunned. Comet tells Supergirl, "Freud said that when two people make love ... there's always four people involved ... the man and woman in each of us." This story arc obviously emphasizes this aspect of psychology in romance.

In *Runaways*, Karolina falls for Xavin, a Skrull who not only shifts forms, but casually changes from male to female upon hearing Karolina prefers girls. At the same time, Xavin's shapeshifting nature is a bit too bewildering for Karolina, who isn't certain who the real Xavin underneath truly is. When Xavin "girls out" while she and Karolina argue, Karolina realizes delightedly that this is her true form (Whedon, *Runaways: Dead End Kids*).

Lois gets a more disappointing revelation in Gwenda Bond's novel, *Lois Lane: Fallout*. Teen Lois is in high school, defending the downtrodden with help from her online friend SmallvilleGuy. He has never shared his identity with her, worried it would reveal too much, as they met on a website for paranormal phenomena. He aids her through an online gaming program, appearing as a green alien to her surprise. Yet when she battles the gamers themselves, he refuses to help her, adding, "I can't risk getting caught in there. Even as a character." A shocking new side of her friend is thus revealed. He leaves, and she must take on the enemy alone.

Back in the film, Selina and Bruce meet three times after this initial meeting, as themselves at least. On one occasion, she is staring at her reflection, wondering why she's acting this way. At once, Bruce pops up, like a version of her shadow that she can speak with directly. They debate the usefulness of Batman, who of course reflects Catwoman and her place in the world. Bruce tells her she has a dark side, and she notes that he has one too. He asks her to dinner and she agrees.

Later that night they're cuddled on the couch discussing Bruce's issues. She doesn't mind them, adding,   "It's the so-called 'normal' guys who always let you down. Sickos never scare me. At least they're committed." Indeed, she treats the Penguin as a contemptible figure she can manipulate and her boss soon fits the same category. Old Selina dated a nice guy (who breaks up with her on her answering machine so he can "work on himself"). New Catwoman likes the bad boys, and she feels Bruce qualifies, as does Batman. "She recognizes in Bruce a kindred spirit of the night and seeks the companionship that she was denied in her pre–Catwoman existence," explains James F. Iaccino in *Jungian Reflections within the Cinema* (110). However, as she reaches for his scratches and he for her napalm burn, they both back off, afraid of revealing too much. "Their romance is destined to end in disaster for how can such two split personalities establish a lasting bond when their shadow sides keep getting in the way?" (Iaccino 110). They both scramble out of the date with nearly identical reactions as Penguin attacks and their secret identities take over.

Sneaking out, they leave similar sweetly garbled messages with Alfred. Selina however adds the intriguing sentence, "Tell him he makes me feel the way I hope I really am ...." She wants to be the strong, confidant sexual woman as the mousy one is gone forever. But underneath, she is still a rule-breaking bad girl, one that the rigidly-just Batman cannot allow to do murder.

Catwoman and Batman arrive on the scene as adversaries as Catwoman aids the Penguin. They fling chairs at each other and fight very physically.

CATWOMAN: Hey stud: I thought we had something together.
BATMAN: We do.

The Penguin is a darker shadow for both the bat and the cat. He terrorizes the town, framing Batman as he controls Batman's car and makes it appear he pushed the wimpy Ice Princess off the roof. In fact, when he kills the Ice Princess, he's acting out Selina's disdain for helpless females but taking it a step further, to Catwoman's horror. Like Batman, he wants Catwoman.

PENGUIN: Let's consummate our fiendish union!
CATWOMAN: (sneers) I wouldn't touch you to scratch you.
PENGUIN: I oughta have you spayed! You sent out all the signals!

The Penguin is a thwarted bundle of misogynistic energy. Of course, Catwoman certainly uses her seduction as tool when she introduces herself to the Penguin by lying on his bed and cooing at him. "One wonders why Catwoman allies herself with Penguin, as the Penguin represents everything she hates about the world of male privilege, especially when the fowl felon plans to impose more masculine order and control by running for the position of Gotham's mayor" (Iaccino 110). Of course, Batman is the enemy as well, even more a force of order and control, so Catwoman tries to pit one against the other. She notes spitefully, "He napalmed my arm. He knocked me off a building just when I was starting to feel good about myself. I want to play an integral part in his degradation." Male order and male villainy both must be destroyed by the mistress of chaos. If she is playing at empowering the innocent, he is less ambiguous, the hero she could be, if she stopped indulging herself with blowing up her boss's building.

Bruce and Selina attend a costume ball near the film's climax, each in simple black eveningwear. They spend so much time being their fantasies that at the ball they're content to be their less complicated selves. Of course, for this couple, the simple selves are the masks.

SELINA: There's a big, comfy California King over in Bedding. What say we...
BRUCE: (ironic) Y'mean take off our costumes?
SELINA: (sad laugh) Guess I'm sick of wearing masks...
BRUCE: Same here. So why'd you come tonight?
SELINA: You first.
Bruce presses close.
BRUCE: To see you.
SELINA: That's lovely and I really wish I could say the same, but ... I came for Max.
BRUCE: You don't mean ... you and Max?
Selina gives a rather insane laugh that goes on far too long, then pulls out a small
   gun from a holster on her leg.
SELINA: This and Max.

Shocked, Bruce tries to talk her out of it as Selina insists he deserves to die. Though the pair cannot agree, they find themselves quoting lines they had used as their costumed characters, and at the same moment, they realize who the other is.

The great reveal is a singular moment in shapeshifter stories. In *Velveteen vs the Multiverse*, Velveteen dates a true shapeshifter—he's not only a superhero similar to herself (who can animate drawings rather than toys), but he can make shadow copies of himself with his powers, making him the ultimate concealer. When Velma's best friend asks her if she went all the way with him, she doesn't mean sex.

> "Yes, Jackie, you incorrigible snoop, we did it." Velma switched the phone to her other ear, sliding further back on the mattress. "He told me his secret identity, and I told him mine."
>
> "And? Dish, girl! Was it magical? Was it amazing? Did it rock your entire world so hard that you're still a little shaken? I demand details!"
>
> "It was..." Vel hesitated before finally saying, "It was good. I really like him, and I think maybe I can like him even more now that I know who he really is. But it was a little scary, too, and not just because of the whole 'giving up the greatest treasure any superhero has'" [Kindle locations 995–998].

Of course, this plays out as a sexual metaphor for the superheroes, one that is sweet and loving. "If the hero's sexual initiation is not marked by the double standard, the experience is an unqualified source of pleasure and growth" (Pearson and Pope 160). For superheroes, the true relationship threshold is revealing one's hidden self by unmasking.

Laughing and crying manically after the great revelation, Selina will not give up her revenge. As the couple have no idea what to do next, the Penguin solves the dilemma, as shadows generally do, though violence. While the Penguin tries kidnapping babies (foiled by Batman), then attacking with a Penguin army, Catwoman rescues Max from him, though she intends to kill him. Batman intervenes, insisting Max go to jail.

> CATWOMAN: Don't be naive. The law doesn't apply to people like him! Or us.
> BATMAN: Wrong on both counts.
> He tries to grab Max, but Catwoman makes a lunge for Batman's abdomen, sending him reeling. He picks himself up, then, talking in a calming, soothing way:
> BATMAN: Why are you doing this? Let's just take him to the police, then go home together ... Selina, don't you see? We're the same. We're the same. Split right down the center.

Her hair is coming out of her mask and she's half Selina half Catwoman. Bruce pulls off his own mask, continuing to plead with her. At this moment, they are ordinary and superhero at once, shadow and persona. "The unmasked Bruce has high hopes that the split both have lived with can be mended by the other's presence. The still-masked (and symbolically hidden) Selina" refuses (Iaccino 110). She considers then replies: "Bruce, I could live with you in your castle forever. Just like in a fairy tale. I just couldn't live with myself." Old Selina wanted to marry a nice, daylight prince. Bad Catwoman only wants revenge and a life of violence and freedom.

She electrocutes herself and Max in spectacular fashion while an injured Batman looks on in shock. However, her body has vanished. Driving away, Bruce spies her silhouette but finds only her coat. He collects it, emphasizing that he is adopting the spirit of Selina, though the actual woman escapes him.

"Although she falls to her death at the hands (or umbrellas) of each of these enigmatic males the feline figure manages to come back from the grave— reanimated and whole each time. The Catwoman cannot (and will not) be killed, so long as the shadow female voice needs to be heard and asserted in this lopsided male-oriented culture of ours" (Iaccino 110). Batman ends the film well and alive, while Catwoman must keep to the shadows: "Significantly for this discussion of shadow figures of culturally sanctioned femininity, one of the last images we see of Catwoman is her shadow against the alley walls, present but elusive" (Landay 217).

Happy endings are sometimes possible for the reflective pair: the novel *The She-Hulk Diaries* has Jennifer Walters fall for an old flame who's both controlled scientist and popular rock star. He finds her at the book's end, after he has discovered she's also the groupie "Gin" he once loved and the sensational She-Hulk. He tells her, "I did not comprehend how my love could be so diffuse. It was as if I was trapped in a hall of mirrors. Each aspect of you captured my heart, and I was misled into thinking that I loved many women, when it was always you" (Acosta 323). True love appears when the hero or heroine can accept all aspects of the shapeshifter and love each one.

Of course, as with Batman and Catwoman, the mystery and danger don't always come with trust. In the *Spider Widow* comic "The Raven" (1942), Spider Widow (a young heroine in an old woman's mask) helps the masked Raven to save the day. He responds, "Well, darn it! If you'll take your mask off, I'll take mine off, and...." He gives her a huge kiss. However, since each wonders after what the other looks like (as it was dark enough that taking off the masks didn't reveal themselves) their future seems unlikely. They remain safe and anonymous, with only a single moment of passion to remember (Borth).

The heroine often feels a strange pull toward the masked hero who reflects the dark and hidden aspects of herself, shadow to shadow. Gail Simone has Helena Bertinelli (the Huntress) dance with handsome Thomas Blake at a ball, only to discover later that he's Catman. They flirt as they fight, and she tells him to call her when he transforms from villain to hero (*Birds of Prey: Dead of Winter*). In the *Birds of Prey* television episode "Split," Helena also falls for a vigilante while dressed as the Huntress and marvels at how much they have in common. "Indeed, relationships offer strangeness, uncertainty, changing rules.

To many, this lover seems a shapechanger, with personality and desires too changeable to comprehend" (Frankel, *From Girl to Goddess* 79). Thus the shapechanger represents all the mystery and danger of the romance.

The knowledge of shared experience is a powerful draw. Doreen (Squirrel Girl) falls for fellow college student Tomas Lara-Perez, later revealed as the super hero Chipmunk Hunk. Wonder Woman in the JLA cartoons is drawn to Batman, while Simone's Wonder Woman likes perpetual liar/shapechanger Tom Tresser (Nemesis). There's Elektra and Daredevil, Thor and Lady Thor. MCU Black Widow likes Bruce Banner, adding that she's as much of a monster as he is. On *Agents of S.H.I.E.L.D.* Raina says of Ward's feelings for Skye, "We know about Skye's parents. About the darkness that lies inside. I believe in a world where her true nature will reveal itself. And when that day comes, maybe you two could be monsters together" ("Beginning of the End" 122). Black Canary and Green Arrow fall for each other on *Arrow* as perfect partners with secret identities and hidden skills. In "The Fallen" (320), Arrow reflects, "She reminds me so much of me after I came home. When it just seemed, when it seemed impossible to believe in anything even resembling hope." "Velveteen vs. the Old Flame" explains:

> Like most people, superheroes prefer the company of like minds: a community of fellows. Tales of superhero/civilian romance are all well and good for the comic books, but the fact of the matter is pretty simple, if one is willing to set romantic notions aside and really consider the situation. A man who can fly isn't going to marry an investment banker. A woman who can talk to plants isn't going to settle down with a bus driver. Maybe one relationship in a thousand between a powered and a non-powered individual will work out happily. Relationships between superheroes, on the other hand, may be fraught with evil twins, crossover events, worlds in need of saving, and the occasional archenemy at the wedding, but they are, on the whole, permanent things. Psychiatrists theorize that this is due to the difficulty in finding someone whose powers are not only compatible, but tolerable. The human mind is a complicated thing, and the whole truth may never be known.

Bluebeard: Scarlet Witch (Marvel Comics, 1994)

In the comic "Mad Love," Harley prances around in a red nightie singing "I Feel Pretty." As she tries seduction, the Joker shoves her off his desk to the floor. He then yells at her and insults all her jokes as worthless and unfunny. He drags her down to the cellar by her nose and literally kicks her in. She reflects, "Another night I get dolled up, and another night I get the boot...." She realizes she's "hopelessly in love with a murderous, psychopathic clown." Despite his cruelty, she dreams of domesticity—twin children, the Joker old and still in love with her. When she tries to win this happy ending by capturing

Batman for the Joker, however, he's furious at being shown up by his girlfriend. The Joker slaps her and screams, "Batman is mine! You had no right to interfere in my fun!" He shoves her out the window to be dashed to the ground, and the police must call an ambulance. Bandaged in the hospital, she decides, "I finally see that slime for what he really is…" though the Joker's gift of a flower leaves her charmed once more. Clearly this is an abuse story with the victim going back over and over for more (Dini, "Mad Love").

In "Union," the first comic of *Gotham City Sirens Book One*, Catwoman begins the comic explaining, "Two months ago, that psycho Jason Todd put on an armored Batman suit and kicked me through the roof of a parked cat. This was shortly after my heart was ripped out by another lunatic, Hush." Both specifically disguise themselves as Batman, emphasizing the Caped Crusader's ability to destroy her. Afterward, she feels shaky and weakened. Zatanna explains, "Selina was attacked in the most vicious way imaginable. She was made to feel abused and completely vulnerable. That leaves scars no magic can erase." The damage is caused by an alternate Batman, emphasizing the caped crusader's mysteriousness, as well as his power over the heroine.

"Many women have literally lived the Bluebeard tale. They marry while they are yet naive about predators, and they choose someone who is destructive to their lives. They are desperate to 'cure' that person with love," comments Estés (50). Nonetheless, several superheroines find themselves in such a destructive relationship, with the savage male pleading with her to devote her goodness to him and redeem him. This needy, alluring, though also destructive male is a great temptation for the compassionate heroine. She must work through this experience to reject his claim over her and banish him from her psyche: "Today, it is generally understood that the romantic and spiritual man-god—the male ideal worthy of a woman's self-sacrifice and worship, for whom she is expected to set aside herself and her life—simply does not exist" (Pearson and Pope 35).

Dan Abnett and Andy Lanning's short run *Avengers: Scarlet Witch* features such a journey for the heroine. In a far-off dimension, a monstrous creature with a horned skull for a head captures Eleyn, witch-queen of Amzar, and demands her kingdom. Far away, Wanda awakens from a terrible nightmare. If being a queen means sovereignty over oneself, the skull-powered creature is death and entropy, an assault on those borders of the mind.

Realizing there's no one else who can help her, Wanda reaches out to her mentor Agatha Harkness. As Wanda explains in horror, "This time, the monster tore away its mask and its face was mine." After her dark past, Wanda lives in deathly fear that she will have another breakdown and turn against her friends.

Indeed, Agatha tells her, "Listen to me, Wanda. You *are* strong. You must reject all feelings of self-doubt. You must have faith in your own *soundness* of mind." If Wanda is secure in her own mental kingdom, she can vanquish the predator and send him back to the underworld, out of her conscious thoughts.

The next day at Avengers headquarters, horrific pink lizard monsters attack, all hissing, "Witch...." Once again, this is an assault on Wanda's personal stronghold, her own home and place of power. Defeated by the Avengers' iron, the monsters disintegrate, but one says, "The Witch is mine," exactly as in her dream. Agatha brings her to "a private library in the New England village of Unity" which may be able to teach Wanda about her true nature as a nexus being. Before this, Wanda has allowed chaos magic to overwhelm her, all unsuspecting. After her ordeals, she is wiser and prepared to learn about herself. In the library's crypt, however, a mysterious cloaked figure bids her welcome ... then yanks off his cape to reveal the evil Master Pandemonium, the skull-headed man.

The air fills with a maelstrom of shrieking demons. He tells her, "My Wanda! My witch! My love! I have come back for you! I have come back from the brink of hell!" He insists that he clawed his way back to be with her, and she must be his bride forever. Sure in her power, Wanda does not allow him to take her over: "On the impossible edge of nowhere, teetering on the brink between madness and reality, friendless and alone ... one woman feels her body sing with the power and rage that flows through it ... and turns to fight. Her name is Wanda Maximoff."

She runs through a maze of snowy branches, trapped in the Avengers' nightmares, like a morass of guilt and obligation forced on her from outside. At last, Pandemonium saves her, only to chain her to a metal gibbet that neutralizes her magic and physical strength together. In this scene, he has her controlled, pinned down, helpless to his whims.

Representing Wanda's powerful feminine will, Agatha arrives in purple-draped splendor to rescue her student, who, freed, battles her aggressor. The two women together defeat him and chain him to his own gibbet. Wanda wakes in her bed, like Dorothy from *The Wizard of Oz*, only to be told her friends have brought her back from the church where they found her. Wanda smiles, feeling "better than ever before" with the ghosts within her laid to rest as well.

By battling the destroyer, Wanda puts an end to external forces seeking to control her and establishes her autonomy. "Bluebeard is the Animus who's taken over the entire psyche, devourer of the whole self. The heroine must fight back, protecting those emotional parts of herself, such as intuition and autonomy, that the creature most wants to control" (Frankel, *Buffy* 56). The most common source of this metaphor is the evil boyfriend. *Smallville* season eight sees Chloe (herself a superheroine barely aware of her powers) torn between nice boy Jimmy Olson and Davis Bloome, the compelling young man who's secretly the murderous Doomsday. Though she gradually learns of his evil, she finds herself compelled by his darkness. This reflects an internal struggle as the evil Brainiac takes her over and also shows her what it's like to be the bad girl. Chloe's actress Allison Mack explained in an interview with *TV Guide*:

> On the one hand, she's still doing work with Clark and getting married to Jimmy and doing her lovely, good-girl Chloe thing, and on the other hand she's struggling with this "pull" towards Davis and these dark, evil tendencies and a want to destroy things, which is very much Brainiac. She has a massive pull between these two sides of her that she's struggling to suppress until she learns to understand it [Mitovich].

Estés notes that a woman who loses her joys and creative outlets will channel them into dark, disturbing paths like addictions and secrets: "Because a woman feels she cannot in daylight go full-bore at whatever it is she wants, she begins to lead a strange double life, pretending one thing in daylight hours, acting another way when she gets a chance" (237). As Chloe hides the monstrous, unstable Davis in the basement of her home, he becomes her twisted ugly secret. She pretends everything is normal in daylight but spends her nights dumping body parts in trashcans and caring for Davis, murderous Beast to her Beauty. Her best friend Clark protests, "Davis must have done something to her. Chloe would never have lied to me if she weren't trapped…. She'd never choose Davis over her friends" ("Beast" 820). In fact, Chloe is desperate for a selfish life all her own.

Acting on her hidden desires, Doomsday kidnaps her from her wedding to the too-good Jimmy. Beside him, Chloe becomes evil, black-eyed, and bloodstained as she surges with power. "I think she's starting to understand what *she* wants separate and aside from Clark, and she is building her own relationship with herself and her own life, and proactively going after all of that instead of just running around and doing whatever she thinks Clark needs. She's grown into her own woman," Mack explained (Mitovich). While her friends quest to win her back from the force of evil, and eventually succeed, her walk on the dark side feeds the repressed shadow within her that she's never explored.

Avengers: Scarlet Witch is not the only time powerful men manipulate Wanda, who spends her days consumed with guilt and grief over the loss of her sons and her destruction of her fellow heroes, thus leaving her open to manipulation from the outside. Arkon the Magnificent kidnaps the Scarlet Witch in *The Avengers* #76, and, like Doomsday, tries to get her to surrender to her dark side and love him. "But for your world to live, mine must become an *atomic ruin!* How can I love the man who *destroys* all I hold dear … and who keeps me captive here against my will?" asks the Scarlet Witch. He retorts that she will learn to tolerate him over the years, or he can live with her loathing.

Later he offers to save her world and suggests he might learn to be gentle with her guidance. She finds herself a bit tempted. Of course, he is lying, and the male Avengers arrive and rescue her for a happy ending.

Guilt and responsibility are powerful captors for the heroine. Early on, Sue Storm runs into Prince Namor the Sub-Mariner. First he captures her, then he courts her with the ominous words, "You're the loveliest human I've ever seen! If you will be my bride, I might show mercy to the rest of your pitiful race!" When he threatens to unleash undersea monsters, she capitulates, saying sadly, "One life such as mine doesn't matter—but humanity must be spared" (*Fantastic Four* #5).

In *House of M*, the Avengers discover that their alt-world where Magneto rules has been created by his maddened daughter Wanda. As she lay despairing, her brother Pietro persuaded her that she could remake the world to make everyone she'd ever loved happy and so she, her father, her brother, and her children could be a family. "The purpose of all this was that there would be no more fighting," she tells her son. At last she can please all her loved ones. In the midst of Magneto's empire, Wanda realizes he believes mutants should dominate everyone. He's more of a tyrant than she ever realized. Unstable and despairing as she is, she says the fateful phrase "No more mutants." Most of earth's mutants vanish and the world is restored, but at an enormous cost. Her own instability plus her father's need to dominate destroys earth's mutants forever.

Scarlet Witch loses her memory and powers after this. In *Avengers: The Children's Crusade*, she finds herself engaged to Doctor Doom. While the Young Avengers and their older counterparts consider him a villain, he's kind and generous to Wanda, adding that he's fallen in love with her. However, when he lashes out at young Wiccan, Wanda's lost son come to tell her the truth, she is shocked. Freeing Wiccan from Doom's prison, she tells him, "It's all been perfect. Meeting Victor—falling in love—the king proposing to the gypsy girl. It's all been *too* perfect.... Until you showed up and suddenly Victor became someone I didn't recognize."

He is a shapeshifter, not only because of his metal mask. When Wanda channels all her life power, he absorbs it and resembles an angel, with handsome healed face, white tunic, and golden aura as he flies above her. "Victor is here. And I am going to take care of everything," he explains. He proposes again to Wanda, and she tells him, "Yes. If you rid yourself of this power and put it back where it belongs, I will marry you." She senses its ability to corrupt. However, he refuses. Though he promises to use his power to care for the world, the Avengers realize that a benevolent dictator is still a dictator and go to war against him. Even handsome and healthy, he's still a supervillain (Heinberg).

Each time, Wanda is emotionally fragile, so she allows tyrants to guilt her into staying by them, at least for a while. Only when she recovers enough of her sense of self-worth can she banish them from her psyche and her life.

Patsy Walker, Hellcat, has nearly as long a tale of abuse. She begins her heroism when escaping her husband, a Vietnam War veteran. As she explains: "He was so frustrated all the time, with the war winding down and all, he'd come home and smolder all night—or else blow up at me!" When she meets X-Men's Beast, she tells him what she wants most—to be a powerful, liberated superheroine. Eventually, she leaves her husband and goes adventuring with the Avengers. When they find the costume of The Cat, Captain America and the others bestow it on her and she gets a new identity (Englehart, *The Avengers* #144).

As part of the Defenders, Patsy marries her teammate Daimon Hellstrom without realizing the darker implications. When his past as the son of Satan catches up with him, she descends to hell to rescue her husband and bargains with the devil for his soul. In the darkest place of all, he challenges her in turn and asks if her husband would truly sacrifice himself the same way. She insists it doesn't matter and makes the bargain. However, his darksoul floods through him and the satanic impulse takes over the once-good hero. She looks on the face of pure demon power and is driven mad (Nieves, *Hellstorm Prince of Lies* #3). As Warren Ellis takes over, *Hellstorm Prince of Lies* #14 has Patsy narrate as her husband comes home. Driven literally insane, she lies upstairs and chants to herself, "Kisses and horror shows…. I brought you back, Daimon. Brought you back for kisses and got nothing but horror shows. I brought you back…." In his occult cellar, Daimon cheats on his wife, uncaring. As he quests for power, her sanity returns and Patsy cries for hours because she still loves him. "Imagine that. Dragging the only man you've ever really loved back from death … and discovering he wasn't worth the bother." This is every superheroine's greatest fear. She is sacrificed and finally returns from death before she's rid of him.

Later, when her friend Firestar gets cancer, Daimon returns. He bargains that if she spends one night in hell with him, her friend will wake up cancer free. Patsy accepts and he smirks, "Done. Welcome back to hell—where one night lasts forever." He takes her down to her "personal hell"—fighting with her boyfriend for all eternity, where he insists she'll stay until she sleeps with him. Her friends Black Cat, Monica Rambeau and Firestar loyally wish themselves into hell to rescue her. Meanwhile, he has Patsy tied to a chair for an elegant dinner, just so he can berate her about (of all things!) leaving him out of her new book. She escapes only by appealing to his ego and promising him a chapter in which she claims she's not over him (Aguirre-Sacasa, *Marvel Divas*). The battle with Bluebeard is a cat-and-mouse game for autonomy, one the heroine can win through forcefully banishing him or by trickery and subterfuge. Either way, she cannot let him dictate terms for her life.

"To restrain the natural predator of the psyche it is necessary for women to remain in possession of all their instinctual powers," Estés explains, listing among them intuitive healing, tenacious loving, and creativity (44). In Ms. Marvel's third collection, she meets Kamran, a Pakistani boy who's handsome and educated, who loves everything she does, who seems perfect. He even has superpowers and Kamala realizes she's not alone—there's another "nerdy Pakistani-American-slash-Inhuman in the entire universe." She decides, "I think I'm in love," and sneaks out to be with him. She calls him a perfect "golden boy," though he responds, "I'm not that nice." Soon enough, he offers her a ride and whisks her to see his new boss. "You always think you know who the good guys are. Until the guy you have an enormous crush on zaps you with his powers and locks you up in a jail cell in New Attilan," she realizes. When Kamala protests being kidnapped, he replies nastily that she accepted a ride with him by choice and adds, "You put yourself in this situation." When he threatens to hit her, she wallops him with a giant fist. "I gave him power over me. Power over what I do, power over my identity. No more," she decides (*Ms. Marvel: Crushed*).

Government Persecution: *Echo* (Abstract Studios Comics, 2011)

Julie Martin is out photographing the desert. Overhead, Dr. Annie Trotter test-flies a prototype supersuit, then is suddenly shot out of the sky and killed. Suddenly, liquid pellets of her supersuit rain down and form a permanent silver skin over Julie's chest. The innocent bystander has instantly become a super-heroine. In fact, the suit responds to Julie's thoughts and emotions, enacting her will. When she's attacked, the suit responds with electrical force.

What follows is a corporate conspiracy chase as Julie's world shatters. The developers of the battle suit (the Heitzer Nuclear Research Institute or HeNRI) confirm that Julie has absorbed part of their technology worth two and a half billion dollars. They dispatch a young woman known as Ivy Raven to locate Julie and retrieve their technology, though they tell Ivy only that Julie has absorbed radioactive fallout and is a walking nuclear bomb needing treatment.

Julie's suit, a protective force, symbolizes her desperation for security in the face of all this persecution. Back home, her husband is divorcing her and her sister Pam is in a mental hospital after her own husband and children were killed in a car crash. It's no surprise that Julie's armor emerges over her breasts and thus over her heart.

Meanwhile, Annie's boyfriend, park ranger Dillon Murphy, is seeking answers. HeNRI staff tell him Annie has suddenly died—details are classified and there's no body. The U.S. military attack Julie, concerned that she might be a threat, and her suit retaliates with deadly force. Dillon, seeking answers, saves Julie and they go on the run together. An unruly motorcycle gang helps them, emphasizing their status as rebels outside the system.

HeNRI staff recover about a third of the suit, Julie has another third, and the last part is absorbed by Cain, the only other person in the desert. He shouts phrases of Biblical doom and electrocutes those around him with his terrifying metal-encrusted hand. Of course, he is a maddened victim, the evil innocent as Julie is the good one. Ivy later tells her, "You saved a child's life today, while Cain used the same alloy to go on a killing spree. That's the thing about power ... everything depends on who you give it to."

At the same time, Ivy tracks Julie, systematically searching her house. At last, she calls Dillon, insisting she works for National Security and that Julie is covered in nuclear fallout—if the pair surrender, she can "get Julie the help she needs." At last she speaks to Julie directly, telling her she can "stop the army from hunting you down and locking you up for the rest of your life." Thus Julie is asked to choose between evils. Big institution has several roles in the story, as the government is a shadowy threat capable of arresting either Julie or HeNRI. Pam, locked in a mental intuition, has her life controlled by others and is vulnerable to being snatched. In fact, Ivy adds that she's visiting Julie's sister as they speak. She insists, however, that she's not there to threaten, and wants to save Julie from being "terror threat number one."

In fact, Annie was the suit's true inventor, using the Phi ratio found throughout nature to unlock secrets of the universe. She even discovered a new alloy, which she named 618, that had the power to do miracles, though it needed a human body as conductor. When she tested it on herself, it bonded to her as armor. As one of her coworkers describes it, "Annie's thesis changed everything. I can't state that strongly enough. Everything we tried worked. Superstring theory, quantum gravity, the chromodynamics mass gap ... answers came." However, HeNRI kept all the marvelous developments to themselves and chose a single outlet for them—weapons research. When Annie protested, they executed her.

Julie symbolizes the individual, as the suit adapts to enact her will on the world—it heals both her injuries and those of people to whom she feels a connection. It shoots lightning when she feels scared, but not when she's hugged by a loved one. Further, the dead Annie Trotter has bonded with her through the metal, offering her own soul and personality to help Julie like a guardian angel. Together, Julie and her few friends defy the corporation and the government to save the world for other innocents like themselves. The author comments:

> I love conspiracies. I wish one of them was true. But actually, what I think about in a story is a survivor taking the power back.... When I think of *Echo*, I think of a normal woman unfairly saddled with this incredible problem that can change the world. And how fate shows that power ending up in her hands is so much better than it ending up in the hands of a government ... that just one woman going by her heart makes the right decisions. So it was a woman fighting for her own survival, for herself, her identity but also in a much bigger way, things on a much bigger level [Moore, *Toucan Interview* 2].

Soon enough, HeNRI scientists invent a gun that will neutralize the metal—by destroying the person in it and all of Annie's research as well. One horrified scientist protests, "We're not a military contractor! We're the good guys! We play with atomic energy so we can save people—not shoot them!" However, those in charge celebrate the ease with which they can dispose of their problem. At Julie's house, John Foster, creator of the alloy, or so he says, orders Ivy to calm Julie down and send her out. However, Ivy realizes that they want to destroy Annie's alloy and in fact shoot her down, while the alloy might save Ivy's ill daughter.

Ivy changes sides and whisks Pam, Dillon, and Julie to her home. There, Julie discovers she can heal the little girl through empathy, the counter to HeNRI's profit-mongering. She also discovers the force of her power comes from Annie, whose DNA still exists within the metal. Though Julie still longs to get rid of it, Ivy tries to convince her that she needs to keep it, as she's the only one using it for good. On brief encounters, Julie absorbs Cain's share of the metal, until it finally covers her all over, with the Phi emblem on her chest.

It's finally revealed that Dr. Foster of HeNRI plans to use the alloy to power a black hole in an example of total corporate greed. He brags of being brave enough to "play chicken with nature," a moment of hubris that's asking for trouble. This experiment, a moment of military posturing, has the power to destroy the earth, so Julie and her ragtag team sneak in to stop it. In gleaming metal suit from head to toe, Julie talks the soldiers over to her side, generously restoring one to health.

"The female hero isn't genuinely supported in her effort to leave her community and embark on a journey.... When she tries to step out of the roles deemed acceptable for her she meets a societal force that seems overpowering" (Schmidt, *45 Master Characters* 195). As locals attack her where she's weakest—her self-esteem, she must transcend self-doubt to become a hero in truth. Thus the soldiers insist Julie must set aside her power and give it to them. Only by defying them can she become a hero.

At the climax, the story shifts to allegory, explaining how man, looking at light, saw a way to make weapons. By contrast, "the woman looked at the light with new eyes and found perfection." Once again the man made a weapon from this discovery. "When dark matter touched the world, it cracked the sky and the earth groaned as one dying. So the woman smote the darkness with the light that was perfect and the darkness receded. Until the last day, man will chase the light, knowing a woman once caught it. Her mystery endures, her answers long forgotten." Thus with Annie and Julie working together, the world is saved.

Far too many heroines represent the little guy, persecuted by the vast patriarchal evil. *Lazarus* is the story of a few families who have all the power, with a heroine who grows up among the Haves, but befriends the Have-Nots. In *Birds of Prey: Sensei and Student,* Oracle is kidnapped and imprisoned by government goons claiming they have the right under the Patriot Act. She steals a cellphone and enlists the Huntress to come rescue her, though she has no use of her legs. *Birds of Prey: End Run* has the government coming after the team again as Black Canary is accused of murder. Likewise, Marvel's Civil War hinges on government registration, with heroes taking both sides in the conflict. The X-Men often face government persecution. As a summary at the end of *Black Widow: The Name of the Rose* describes Natasha Romanova's life: "The dark side of the Red Room came in the form of a cascade of false memories: parents that were not hers, friends that never existed, a career as a Bolshoi ballerina that never happened, and a patriotic zeal for her homeland (enhanced by brainwashing and pheromone-like chemicals) that was merely a tool for further manipulation" (Liu).

In *A-Force: Warzones!* She-Hulk, Baroness of Arcadia, must mediate Doom's laws of Battleworld to protect the women of her team. She begs the male authority, "Sherriff Strange," for leniency. Nonetheless he tells her, "They are God's laws, and you cannot bend them to protect your friends from their own guilt." To protect her island from Doom's wrath, Ms. America must be sacrificed (Bennett).

Even a school can become the institution. In the novel *Lois Lane: Fallout,* a group of bullies are bound together by an experimental gaming program that links them in a telepathic web. Teen Lois defends a fragile spelling bee champion from their cruelty, only to find they're protected by the school's principal and the gaming company behind him. When her father the general takes the principal's side, Lois must find a way to defeat them all, playing at being apologetic and harmless even as she takes a reporting job and infiltrates their world. With a few misfit journalism students and an online friend from Smallville, she proves that being young and female doesn't mean helpless by a long shot.

The heroine often works obediently for the government before breaking free. In the novel *Soon I Will Be Invincible*, the cyborg Fatale was built by the government, who had been awaiting such a terrible set of injuries (in a situation paralleling the Bionic Woman of television). She thinks, "I was always hoping I'd get to solve mysteries like the FBI agents of television, unravel a story, find a secret conspiracy. But that wasn't what they used me for—most of the time, they threw me on a case just as it was all going to hell. I was shock troops— my job was to soak up bullets for the regular agents and strike terror into the enemy, usually illiterate guerrillas who had never even seen a metahuman, let alone faced one in action" (60–61). The government, having created their cyborg, considers her a tool for their use. It's the heroine's job to defy the vast sucking corporation or government and discover her personal freedom, often forming her own team in defiance of them, though much of her power must come subtly, from stealth.

Shrinking Down: She-Hulk (Marvel Comics, 2005)

> NIGHTCRAWLER: So why not stay disguised all the time? You know ... look like everyone else.
> MYSTIQUE: Because we shouldn't have to [*X2: X-Men United*].

She-Hulk does whatever she wants in Dan Slott's celebrated run. She brings hot supermodel guys home to Avengers Mansion and throws wild parties there. Her Avengers parking pass lets her leave her sportscar wherever she likes. She even ditches the courtroom in the middle of closing arguments to go save the world. Everyone knows she's also Jennifer Walters, but as She-Hulk she has everything. Thus she stays green all the time. Unfortunately, that suddenly comes to a close.

The Avengers decide she's abusing "the cleaning, the pantry, and the free parking," so they kick her out. At the same time, her bosses at the law firm decide her world-saving places undue pressure on juries and fire her. Plus, they add, they want someone serious, and She-Hulk spent the last party photographing her butt on the copier ("It could've been anyone"; "It was a color copier, Jen"). Jen sulks in the bar, feeling low enough that she turns away all the flirtatious guys there and even has a drink with her old nemesis the Blizzard (Slott, *She-Hulk: The Complete Collection*).

She-Hulk in her original run had few female friends, de-emphasizing empowerment of others, and emphasizing her role as sex object. In #10 (December 1989), marketing expert Lexington Loppner describes her as "a nearly impeccable role model for the women of the nineties." He tells her, "You're perceived as intelligent, independent, strong but non-threatening to men, emotionally vulnerable—yet professional enough to manage dual careers, an attorney and an Avenger, no less." However, this "nonthreatening" role might be considered postfeminist. Andi Zeisler, co-founder of *Bitch* magazine, discusses at length in her study *Feminism and Pop Culture*, that the 80s and 90s watched feminist politics grow increasingly complicated in the media. With the 90s, especially, much of popular culture espoused the idea that society was in a "post-feminist" era, in which "feminism was widely considered to be 'done'" (121). For She-Hulk especially there were disturbing moments as she was forced to jump rope naked to boost sales, and a courtroom case revealed her enormous list of sexual partners, slut-shaming her for enjoying sex. One critic protests:

> The thing I love about She-Hulk, and the thing that makes her different from her peers, is that she is unashamedly *female*. While I'm not sure if Stan Lee or David Anthony Kraft had any inkling of this when they wrote her early adventures, She-Hulk empowers female norms the way that the Hulk embodies the male ones. But here's the twist: She-Hulk's feminine traits are her *strength* and not her burden. The Hulk is all about repression and rage, two things that our culture ties to masculinity to a dangerous degree. Yeah, the Hulk plays with male stereotypes (you just know the Hulk would *never* ask for directions), but She-Hulk embraces them [White].

She's pure female empowerment, and shouldn't have to hide it.

Soon the most prestigious law firm, Goodman, Lieber, Kurtzberg, and Holliway, offers her a job. There's only one catch—they want Jennifer Walters, not the She-Hulk. As Holden Holliway explains, "She's a flighty, free-spirited adventurer. I want Jennifer Walters, a sharp attorney with a keen, focused mind."

She hesitates, then decides, "I can stand to be 'her' again. I can step away from the strength, the power, the glamour—all of it." She shrinks down, and then promptly passes out from all the alcohol on an ordinary human metabolism.

She hates being Jennifer, considering her alter-ego "a waif, a target." As she thinks while on the bus, "I used to commute in a $300,000 custom-built sportscar. People on the street would cheer and make catcalls as I drove by. I also used to have feet that could reach the pedals." While modern people often want to reconcile with their shadow and bring it into the light, The Shadow "shears us of our defenses and entails a sacrifice of easy collective understandings and of the hopes and expectations of looking good and safely belonging. It is crude, chaotic, surprising" (Perera 33). As She-Hulk, she gloried in standing out. Now in order to be accepted at work, she's asked to shrink down, cover up, not be so outrageous. It hurts. When she arrives, she has another shock, as the law firm caters particularly to metahumans. Everyone is allowed to be crazy there but her. Many women feel this way about the other gender:

She-Hulk parties. She likes getting dressed up. She likes going to the beach. She likes hooking up with guys. The thing is, in any *bad* form of fiction, She-Hulk would be a gross caricature of a woman, one that we would consider flighty and disposable thanks to her inherently female nature. We live in a culture that subconsciously devalues female traits while lifting up male ones. It was pointed out to me, definitely on Tumblr, that grown men are allowed to freak out about sports like it's nobody's business, while we culturally roll our eyes at literally everything teenage girls freak out about. Girls screaming about One Direction is a waste of time, but men screaming about the Super Bowl is something our country comes together and *celebrates* [White].

Likewise, She-Hulk is surrounded by partiers and meta-humans, but she must act politely ordinary.

Her first case arrives with Danger Man, made superhuman against his will, who wants his old life back. As she protests that no one would prefer a vulnerable life, Mr. Holloway replies, "Being vulnerable means the world can affect you. Touch you. That you can be part of it." Jennifer wins it by proving Danger Man's family has lost him forever—and in exploring the case, she finds herself remembering the old her. She finds herself reading her own comic book, remembering her eager words—"Whatever Jennifer Walters can't handle— the She-Hulk will do." This extends beyond, as this is a comic about being Jennifer, not the sensational She-Hulk at all. However, she still feels being Jennifer is a sacrifice. Each day, she changes back into She-Hulk at home, like kicking off too-tight shoes. As she thinks, the price of her new job is too high. "To live this lie? To go back to this discarded shell? I know who I really am inside."

Restrained Jennifer is welcomed at the superheroic law firm, but her much cooler alter-ego is not. Packer notes, describing Oracle, that this metaphor is common for superheroines. "Feminist critics condemned the roles that female superheroes were consigned to and contended that fictional female superheroes were permitted power only when they were confined to wheelchairs, or otherwise rendered nonthreatening" (219). In *Marvel Her-oes*, Jennifer explains, "To control myself…. I've learned that no matter where I am, I have to lock a part of myself away. Always." The Wasp tells her that locking herself up—inside or outside—is a bad idea, and only by breaking out can they find freedom (Randolph). Hulking out on another occasion, She-Hulk moans, "Parents wanted Jennifer to be perfect. Smart. Study all. Smart all" (Johns, "The Search for She-Hulk"). Becoming savage is a desperate relief, a time when she can cast off responsibility and simply smash things.

However, when she's summoned to dispense justice on distant planets, she uses Jennifer as a tool, training her human side so She-Hulk will be exponentially stronger. Nonetheless, back on earth, she discovers she has become too strong and Reed Richards makes her a suit to dampen her powers, another instance of reducing herself. She begins to enjoy making friends and trying cases as everyday Jennifer, but it's still not enough. Her boyfriend is uncomfortable with her She-Hulk side—a metaphor for a relationship in which the man dislikes his girlfriend for showing strong emotions or a successful career and only wants her to play at nice, helpless girl. "My therapist thinks part of the reason I'm having such a hard time changing into She-Hulk is that my own boyfriend disapproves of this side of me," she tells him. However, she insists he "spend more time with me in this form" and try to accept her (Slott, *She-Hulk: The Complete Collection*).

Talking with a friend, Jennifer describes her wild partying as a way of reveling in being "the She-Hulk that I wanted to be," after the Scarlet Witch enchanted her to kill the Vision and gamma radiation turned her especially savage so she flattened the town of Bone, Idaho. Doc Samson tells her that her transformations are controlled internally—when she's stuck in one form or the other it's because she secretly wishes it—one is all power, and the other, a play at normalcy. As he adds, "For years, you preferred to live out your life as She-Hulk. You even formed mental blocks to prevent yourself from changing back. But recently, you've come into your own as Jen. And I believe this is causing the pendulum to swing back the other way." Jennifer will need to find a balance.

Slott's series ends with Jennifer on trial for trying to alter history and save Hawkeye from death. Many come forward to testify about all the good she's done, but she only wins when her friends describe her unique combination of skills, from lawyer to clever friend to powerhouse. She ends feeling loved for both her halves. Thus she has found a balance indeed, but the number of people who want her to stay human reflects poorly on a world where men and women should be able to equally revel in power.

It's surprising how important readers find it to keep superheroines "nice girls." The Powerpuff Girls must learn to reign in their abilities after they destroy the town playing tag and turn everyone against them. The newspaper announces, "Freaky Bug-Eyed Weirdo Girls Broke Everything," and everyone glares when they pass. As their father tells them: "Well, it's your super powers. I'm not sure how to say this, but.... I don't think you should use them in public anymore ... your powers are very special and unique. And although we have a lot of fun doing unique things around the house, out in Townville, people just don't understand how special you girls are yet. And unfortunately, people often get scared or angry when they don't understand something special or unique." These make painful life lessons for the supergirls and their young viewers.

Even the terribly powerful Wonder Woman shocks the world by killing villain Maxwell Lord to save the world from his control over Superman.

"Footage of her snapping Lord's neck with her bare hands makes national news, causing Wonder Woman to be publicly disgraced, accused of betraying her pacifist convictions, and put on trial for murder. Although she is eventually cleared of all charges, she still surrenders her costume to skulk off into exile for a year" (DiPaolo 167). Batman and Superman reject her and she quests diligently to finally be forgiven. Nonetheless, her "crime" was a defining moment that permanently stained the character. "Wonder Woman is presented as being too violent and too ruthless to be truly heroic, and her honor and purity is somewhat stained by the blood on her hands" (DiPaolo 166).

In an interview with *Entertainment Weekly*, Margaret Stohl, author of *Black Widow: Forever Red* explains:

> If we care about the girls in our lives, we need to empower them to speak up and demand more, demand better. We need to reinforce that they do not have to put up with things that make them feel uncomfortable or sexualized or stereotyped or small. We need to give them, and ourselves, permission to have difficult conversations, to not automatically agree with the teachers and classmates and coworkers and adults in our lives, to not say yes when we mean no. We can choose how we say it, and when, and even who we say it to. But in whatever way we can, we need to say something, no matter what. Cornel West said, "Justice is what love looks like in public," and I think Natasha [Romanov] would get that [Towers, "Margaret Stohl"].

The disturbing trope of women in superhero teams having to give up their powers subtly suggests that only the men should have them. *Thor: The Dark World* features the aether, "an ancient force of infinite destruction," wielded by the Dark Elves and their leader Malekith. In the Dark World, the aether begins to take over Jane Foster, whose eyes flash black as she whispers Malekith's name. This moment could herald a battle with her dark side, leading to enlightenment. But instead, Malekith tears the power away and he and Thor battle, leaving Jane far behind. Thor wins, and Jane reverts to being his human girlfriend on earth. The status quo is restored.

The MCU repeats this trope several times: *Iron Man 3* sees Tony's girlfriend Pepper Potts turn into a superheroine, blazing with the Extremis virus. She has superstrength and can shoot fire, as well as climb from certain death in a fiery pit. She pulverizes the enemy, only to break down with the shocked words "That was really violent!" Accordingly, Tony promises to relieve her of the virus and does. His emphasis on "fixing" her casts him as her benevolent creator and her as his helpless project, soon relieved of the unwanted power. Even when Pepper wears an Iron Man suit, this too is temporary and she loses it, though Iron Patriot keeps his.

The film *Ant-Man* features Hope van Dyne, who knows everything about fighting, controlling ants, and using the supersuit, but must teach it all to the new male recruit instead of becoming a hero herself. In the same way, the Collector's slave girl in *Guardians of the Galaxy* claims ultimate power and burns up. Only male Thanos and half-alien Peter Quill have the strength to wield the Power Gem.

In *X-Men: The Last Stand*, Mystique is "cured" and loses her dazzling powers. Magneto gives down at her, notes regretfully, "She was so beautiful," and abandons her, literally naked and helpless. In the same film, Rogue voluntarily gives up her own powers so she can touch people and live normally. It's revealed that Jean Grey had her powers blocked for decades, because the normally benevolent Xavier feared what she could become. Magneto encourages her to use her powers, but she grows too strong and those very powers kill her.

> The storyline reinforces Jean Grey's unstable emotional and mental state as significantly contributing to the manifestation of her powers. For example, when she gets angry or upset, she accidentally levitates objects in the room. In the final battle of the film, Jean Grey/Phoenix saves all the mutants by stopping needles fired at them containing the mutant vaccine. However, unable to control her powers, Jean Grey/Phoenix begins to systematically destroy the entire island of Alcatraz [Gray 86].

Further, Professor Xavier reminds her that her weakness of character has allowed her powers to run wild, saying: "Look what happened to Scott. You killed the man you love because you couldn't control your power" (*X-Men: The Last Stand*). He has the necessary discipline; she does not.

Monsters vs. Aliens takes the opposite approach. Susan's family rejects her for growing 50 feet tall, and she finds herself on a team of monsters. When she manages to shrink down once more, she rejoins her family, but her fiancé dumps her, fearing that her fame may overshadow his career as a weatherman—he reports the news but she *is* the news. Susan realizes that her time as a monster made her feel happier and more empowered, so she takes back her powers and saves the day, finally dumping the worthless fiancé. As she cries, "Why did I ever think life with Derek would be so great anyway? I mean, look at all I've done without him. Fighting an alien robot? That was me, not him! And it was amazing!" As she adds, pulling herself to her full height, "I'm not gonna short-change myself. Ever again."

Take Back the Night: *Priya's Shakti* (Web Comic, 2014)

> For women, a not-very-subtle symbolic form of maiming (i.e., loss of the self) is the rape. The rape is usually also symbolic in rendering the woman sterile and, therefore, placing her outside the "natural" reproductive role of womanhood, enables her to pursue the more masculine role of avenging warrior. Many of the Greek and Roman goddesses of

vengeance (Nemesis, Ate, the Furies) were represented as either virgins or hags—women who have yet to become part of the "bleeding sisterhood" or have passed beyond their fertile, nurturing years.

The rape-revenge syndrome is such a recurring theme in female action films that everyone knows it by heart. The emotional isolation, the inevitable flashbacks, the bitterness and distrust toward men as she seeks vengeance, if not for herself, then for every other woman who has or will possibly suffer the same fate. If anything, rape is trivialized by how commonly it is rather carelessly used in plots to provide motivation for the woman's sadistic and brutal actions [Ursini and Mainon 163].

The real heroine's journey is not about responding to rape with savagery or sensationalism, but in ending the threat and creating safety, healing, and protection for oneself and others. Going on a rampage against all men, sword in hand, is not the same as building a community of strength and survival.

Seeking this kind of social change, Ram Devineni wrote the comic *Priya's Shakti*. This comic from India features a young woman named Priya who wants to be a teacher. However, her father commands her to stay home and help with the housework. While she's food shopping alone, the men call out to her, noting chillingly that "no one will stop us." This belief was what motivated the comic's creation, to change misperceptions. As the comic's website explains:

Priya's Shakti arose in the aftermath of a highly-publicized gang rape on a bus in New Delhi in December 2012 that outraged India and the world. The project centers on the Goddess Parvati and Priya, a mortal woman devotee and survivor of rape and is rooted in ancient matriarchal traditions that have been displaced in modern representations of Hindu culture. It creates an alternative narrative and voice against GBV [Gender Based Violence] in popular culture through the Hindu mythological canon. Through its message, this project can reach wide audiences in India and around the world—anywhere GBV is an issue.

Certainly, the 2012 Delhi gang rape, which led to the victim's death, was a game-changer—the men's brutality led to days of protests and forced the government to introduce tougher anti-rape laws, including the death penalty for truly severe violence (Pandey). When Devineni, a protestor himself, discussed the incident with a police officer, he was shocked when the officer retorted, "No good girl walks alone at night." Devineni suddenly understood the lesson that the world needed. He adds, "That's where the idea began. I realized that rape and sexual violence in India was a cultural issue, and that it was backed by patriarchy, misogyny and people's perceptions" (Pandey). Usually the victim is the one blamed for being out alone.

"I spoke to some gang-rape survivors and they said they were discouraged by their families and communities to seek justice, they were also threatened by the rapists and their families. Even the police didn't take them seriously," says Devineni (Pandey).

This is what Priya herself discovers. "As Priya grew into a young woman ... her life became much harder. And one day it became much worse," the comic narrates. A cluster of young men find her outside the village and one hurls a stone at her head. Having stalked her, they rape her. Left to limp home after their attack, she wonders, "What will I tell my family?" To her horror, they blame and reject her. Cast out, she runs to the forest where she prays to the goddess Parvati for aid.

The goddess is shocked to learn about the sexual violence that human women face daily. Thus the goddess enters Priya's body and mind, descending to aid her in her quest for justice. Priya searches for answers, but the authorities tell her she brought on the attack, and the gang, even one member she knew from school, ignore her. No one will take her side. When one of the attackers blames her for wearing loose clothes and turns on her a second time, the goddess manifests. Up above, her husband, the god Shiva, senses the attack on his wife. He reacts to humanity's rape culture with fury, cursing men with impotence. The gods, torn by his decision, descend into civil war. As the website adds, "A grand battle begins in the Heavens and on Earth killing millions. Parvati sees the destruction that is being wrought and knows she must take radical action to end the slaughter."

While Shiva gives in to rage, it's Parvati who sees there must be a better way. "He doesn't realize that rape is an act of violence and domination. It cannot truly be opposed with more of the same," she says. Another goddess points out that Shiva's shame at not being able to protect his wife's devotee has made him so wrathful. To turn her husband aside, Parvati invokes her dreaded Kali form. "Transfixed by the great goddess's energy," Shiva backs down.

Then Parvati finds Priya, who has been hiding in the jungle. There, the goddess fills Priya with her spirit, and grants her fearlessness and a magical mantra that she uses to change people's minds. Channeling the strength of all the women who have struggled for a better life, she tells her, "Priya, I have chosen you. You have the courage to persevere and to overcome fear. Take this mantra." She teaches Priya, "Speak without shame and stand beside me. Bring this change we want to see." Repeating these words, Priya mounts the tiger Parvati has sent her and rides through India. As she chants the mantra, she discovers it has the power to change people's minds. Soon a vast crowd is following her, helping her spread the message of equality. "Only when society protects all of its citizens equally will it truly be safe," she insists.

"A superhero is a man or woman with powers that are either massive extensions of human strengths and capabilities, or fundamentally different in kind, which she or he uses to fight for truth, justice, and the protection of the innocent," Roz Kaveney notes (*Superheroes* 4). The goddess power and mantra Priya receives work as a superpower, as does her work in transforming her world. The messiah hero brings change and knowledge to the world. The male is more likely to preach, while the female shows by example, more a Mother Teresa than a Jesus. Some like Priya, however, spread the word and encourage all they meet to join in.

Traditionally, those who maintain the status quo fight the messiah, calling her unholy. However, those open to change can see the message of peace and salvation she preaches. She, meanwhile, devotes her whole life to a single cause and thus changes the lives of thousands. She gives freely of herself, knowing she will receive much more in return. The female messiah in particular knows the suffering women face in a misogynistic world and strives to improve their lives. She recognizes the divinity in others and spreads respect for human life.

Similarly, Deena Mohamed, Egyptian author of the webcomic *Qahera* ("Conqueror" or "Triumphant") explains, "Qahera's mission definitely revolves around changing and improving her environment. She's unlike most super-heroes in that she aims to change the status quo, not uphold it or defend it from supervillains" (Lewis). Mohamed created her superheroine as a response to stereotypes of Muslim women, but to her surprise, it caught on instantly. As she adds, "Naturally, once she was defined as someone who was opposed to both misogyny and Islamophobia, the next step was to really consider what an Egyptian woman with superpowers would do, and that generally means dealing with real-life issues" (Lewis).

In an interview, the author of *Priya's Shakti* revealed he had "basically two goals: one is to challenge those patriarchal views and help create a cultural shift, and the second is to create empathy for rape survivors so that people who have been raped can report it and get justice" (Chatterjee). Devineni adds, "Our target audiences are children starting from 10–12 years to young adults. It's a very critical age in their lives and it's an attempt to start a conversation with them" (Pandey).

Next up for the comic is an augmented reality comic book in which "certain panels will be animated to feature real-life stories and voices of Indian women who have survived sexual assault and faced the ensuing trauma and social stigma. These pieces will be short documentaries, but the women will be animated in order to protect their identities," as the website explains. Thus, it will bring real-life experiences to the forefront.

The "rape and revenge" plot seen in old pulps, as well as modern thrillers like *Girl with the Dragon Tattoo*, is not strictly part of the heroine's journey. Taking back her own power is, but the heroine generally establishes that the patriarchy or Bluebeard cannot deprive her of her personal power—super-heroines are above torture, pettiness, and revenge. When Tigra's students find a video of the Hood assaulting their teacher in *Avengers Academy: Will We Use This in the Real World?* Hazmat, Veil and Striker track him down and torture him. Tigra is furious and expels them all on the spot, insisting, "You broke the law, endangered lives, and engaged in unacceptable behavior" (Gage). Super-heroes should save lives by putting criminals in prison, not beat them up then abandon them to prey on others.

Kate Bishop, Hawkeye's apprentice, is assaulted as a young woman and takes to her bed. "Bad things happen," she explains. "And they will destroy you if you let them. Or you can try to learn from them so that next time you'll be prepared. So that—even if you never feel safe again—you can do your best to make sure that what happened to you never happens to anyone else." She learns to fight and becomes a superhero, even without powers (Heinberg, *Young Avengers: Family Matters*).

Marvel's Jessica Jones explores these themes as Jessica stops her rapist and mind-controller Kilgrave. She does this not for revenge but because he's a truly deadly menace who needs to be ended. Of course, her triumph means that she deprives Kilgrave of his power over her. Mike Colter (Luke Cage) explains: "This is Jessica's story, so this is someone who has done grave harm to her emotionally and physically. It was only fitting that she be the person that dispatches him and figures out how to get rid of her own nemesis. This is about her and it's also about females standing up for themselves and righting a wrong and moving on in life."

In addition to this, Jones is a P.I. which has the old-fashioned noir term of a "dick." Rou-tinely, noir would fixate on short-fused, lonesome men who take the law into their own hands. There are many great noir films, and we romanticize the men who led them (and are supposed to fantasize about the women who hire them). To have Jones hold that "dick" title, and be a strong-willed survivor of sexual assault—but also regularly bypass the kill-able moment of her tormenter in favor of the justice system—is truly a marvel [Formo].

✦✦✦ 5 ✦✦✦

Descent to the Self

Entering the Otherworld: *Daredevil/Echo* (Marvel Comics, 2004)

"My name is Maya Lopez. I'm not sure if I'm still that person. The newspapers called me Echo. That's what I feel like. An echo." With these words, the superheroine defines herself through other's observations, while her "echoing" emphasizes a lack of identity. This is what she most seeks, as shown through the delightfully artistic medium of David Mack's graphic novel *Daredevil/Echo: Vision Quest*—for indeed, it's more artwork than "comic." She tells her story in a scrapbook of "movement and memory. Shapes and colors." Maya is deaf, a perfect warrior who mimics all she sees. Her disability separates her from others, while her gift emphasizes her mirroring, though without a clear self-definition.

"My story doesn't happen in the sound of the notes but in the silence between them. It is the silence between the notes that is important." These words appear on a sheet of music, colored in with an image of her dancing with Matt Murdock (Daredevil). Her description of herself, like her name and like this story, all involve going into the stillness between action adventures to find true meaning. "That is where the magic happens," she concludes.

When her Cheyenne father had troubles, he would go to "the Rez," a Reservation of many tribes, and sometimes he'd take Maya. This was another place of stillness, a retreat from the outside world. She recalls the Chief, a Shaman and storyteller who showed her Indian Sign Language. In this language, understanding comes from the heart, and all tribes can speak to one another.

He tells her of vision quests, explaining, "If we really want to know ourselves, we must at some point in our lives connect with a higher wisdom that knows all about us. Our weaknesses, our mistakes, our potentials. Many Native American tribes do this through our meditation known as a vision quest." This quest is, as he sees it, "the setting aside of a time and place, alone in nature, to connect with the higher power and explore that which is within. Somewhere in that space or times as we are questing, answers come. It's an opportunity to know more about ourselves and our choices in life."

As Maya describes her father's death and her breakup with Matt, she calls these events "parts of a hole. One that I need to fill." The illustration shows the inside of herself, purple-black and gaping. As an echo, she is empty inside. However, she resolves to plant something in that hole and let it grow. Thinking of the old ways, she realizes, "The tribe comes before the individual. There is a harmony. A cycle of actions. Each gesture gives energy to the next." She draws a flock of soaring birds all over her house. Then, following them, she journeys to the Rez then out into the forest.

Hero and heroine both venture into the magical world on their epic quests. "This fateful region of both treasure and danger may be variously represented: as a distant land, a forest, a kingdom underground, beneath the waves, or above the sky, a secret island, lofty mountaintop, or profound dream state; but it is always a place of strangely fluid and polymorphous beings, unimaginable torments, superhuman deeds, and impossible delight" (Campbell 58).

The Otherworld, originally representing the underworld, is a place of hyper-reality, where good and evil have no illusions. Everyone is their enhanced self with magic and superpowers. This is a place where the rules no longer apply. In fantasy, this is an actual magic world like Hogwarts or Oz, entered almost as soon as the hero sets out. Some superheroes do likewise, as the Avengers travel to the flying helicarrier in their first film, or Skye is dragged off to S.H.I.E.L.D. then later to Afterlife, a sanctuary for Inhumans. Yet many superheroes enter the magical realm in the middle of their quest, as a new place offers unconsidered insights. For the hero, this is a chance to discover the lost feminine side of the self. For the heroine, the stark wilderness offers something more—a chance to find herself, free of society's law. "On her quest, the heroine will cross "the crack between worlds," the entrance to a new geography and a new psychological landscape. It is ambiguous in time and space, without familiar referents, a place where a different type of awareness comes to prominence, where deeper archetypal energies can emerge" (Frankel, *From Girl to Goddess* 59). Entering this space suggests leaving the daylight world of traditional rules, of friends and enemies clamoring for attention. It's a place to discover the rhythms of nature and discover the power within.

This Otherworld in fairytales is the deep woods, or in the Pacific Islands, the ocean. Both of these represent the mystical feminine. For the superheroes, it could be any of them, as Magick carries the X-Men into the realm of demons or the Enchantress takes them to Asgard. Namora plunges into the deepest ocean on her quest, while entering the jungle gives Poison Ivy her power. The Golden Age offered Maureen Marine and Wildfire, both adorable little blonde girls nearly killed by drowning in the ocean and burning in a forest fire, respectively. In both cases the nature gods of those elements took pity on the sweet girl and gave her magical gifts—both went on to fight evil using their powers over water and fire (Madrid, *Divas* 144–145). Water offers danger and mystery, though also untamable fertility. It can be a force of destruction, or a haven for the questor.

> The forest, a feminine symbol, represents the dangerous side of the unconscious, its ability to destroy reason. As foliage blocks the masculine-centered sun's rays, it becomes a hidden place, a place of unknown perils and obscurity. This setting forth reflects the adolescent's inner turmoil, as the unconscious intrudes into the everyday world. Since innovative psychologists like Freud and Jung represented myths as part of the masculine cultural unconscious, femininity was constructed as the unconscious of the unconscious, the dark continent of the dark continent [Frankel, *From Girl to Goddess* 59].

The Shaman meets Maya and tells her how her father introduced her to the four directions as a baby and asked the earth to bless her. Now as she ventures out, she returns to all of them. "If you look at an emptiness, your world will become empty. If you look at the blessing, your life will be blessed," he explains.

In fact, the forest is not empty for Maya—it is her feminine place of power. Entering it, the natural world embraces her. "I take a long hard deep breath and I inhale the past. It tastes like earth and sunshine and pine needles and nostalgia," she says. This is not the Innermost Cave or empty desert but a place of beauty and wildness. "It feels good to be home," she decides.

Doom Patrol #72 by Rachel Pollack and Linda Medley has young Dorothy running off into the wilderness. There she meets a strange bird-headed man who calls her Bloodchild because, as he puts it, "other women bleed for babies. You bleed for stories." He praises her for the "old, deep way" of storytelling she offers the wild children there. In fact, her power is to bring her imaginary friends to life, making stories that have power in the real world. Back home on her superhero team, the adult men push her to control her power. But here among the "lost girls," she can glory in it. The forest represents the magic within, something natural to women but unexplored in the hustle of civilization. Once in it, the heroine can learn from her new mentor there and grow. When the girls all raid a store for supplies, she protects them with her gift—she finally has found a place to belong. However, when she discovers Raven, the bird man, has been using her to make her fight her old Doom Patrol friends for his own purposes, she leaves her new community and returns to her true family. As she parts from the wild girls, she glances back sadly and vows to return. Her time in the wilderness has been filled with camaraderie and self-knowledge.

In the 60s, Gerry Conway and Gardner Fox brought back the magician Zatara—all the way from *Action Comics* in 1938—in the person of his daughter Zatanna. As Zatanna quests to rescue her father, Schwartz and Fox spread her journey over multiple comics (collected in the republished *JLA: Zatanna's Search*). Split in half, with part of her in China and part in Ireland, she calls on Hawkman and Hawkgirl to reunite her pieces. Having tracked down her father's magic book, she then asks the Atom to shrink her down so she can track Zatara through the subatomic world. There, the Druid, her father's old nemesis, reveals he sent Zatara "into a world he never knew existed." Off she goes to the lost land of Ys, where her magic is reversed, then the realm of Kharma. For this fearful quest, she assembles the JLA: Batman, The Atom, Green Lantern, Hawkman, and the Elongated Man. Batman, however, realizes they're inside the pages of a book with a candle for the sun. When a bell rings, he knows they're in an artificial world of bell, book and candle—meant to drive out the demon Zatanna is harboring within. Thus the magical realm is like a journey into her deepest self—it reveals her own internal flaw and heals it so she can return to the ordinary world as herself once more.

Setting out on her own spiritual journey, Maya thinks: "I began to understand that the Vision Quest is a way of leaving your old kind of boxed in thinking behind. It is a way of shedding fear and opening yourself up so that you can see the solutions and lessons from nature that are right under your nose. Even though they may not come in the language that you are used to." This is what the magical world offers, a place to battle dragons with magic and discover how to deal with problems outside of normal reality. It represents the unconscious world, the place of dreamspace, of suppressed desires and forgotten memories.

In the forest, a rabbit comes to her, and Echo thinks of *Alice in Wonderland* and a journey to another realm. Then a wild dog comes, emphasizing her inner wildness and conflict. Watching all night, she sees two dogs fighting. After, she spies a questioning owl, suggesting her search for wisdom. She sees herself in the bird, always asking, "Who, who?" as she discovers who she is. Then in a burst of lightning, Wolverine appears. Clearly, he is meant to be her guide ... perhaps even her spirit animal.

After they battle, he tells her his own story—that the two dogs she has seen are a message. In fact, there are two dogs fighting within him, one that echoes his higher self, all "dreams and good intentions. He is full of purpose. And order." The other dog is disrespectful and self-indulgent, filled with only anger. When a Cheyenne chieftain told him this, Wolverine asked which dog would win fights.

The other man answered that "the one that wins is that one I feed the most."

As it turns out, Wolverine learned this traditional Cherokee folktale from Maya's dead father. At this, she understands the power of stories to change lives and influence the world. When she returns from her quest, the chief tells her that her father has visited and given her "the mantle of a storyteller." With her new purpose, she begins performing, sharing her tales with an audience and abandoning her rage. The wisdom and stillness of the forest has filled her, imbuing her with new understanding.

Ana Cortez, Earth Witch, goes on her own journey after her father tells her she's spent too much time surrounded by only men and needs to learn from the women of her family—especially her magical grandmother.

> *I come from a family of witches*, she thought. *I'm not surprised. Perhaps it isn't so bad,* though she didn't feel particularly like God had called her. More like she had walked into the desert without a path to follow.
> Her father wasn't finished: "But the thing you must know about your Grandmother Inez, the most important thing—she's still alive, Ana. If you don't believe me that God has called you, go to her and ask her. Make a pilgrimage. Talk to your grandmother" [Vaughn, "Nuestra Señora"].

Journeying through her ancestral city of Juárez, Mexico, she's shaken by the crowded conditions and violence. However, the young men there direct her to drive far outside of town, following the night sky. She finds herself at a hacienda. "There were flowers, everywhere flowers, climbing roses arcing over pergolas, clematis climbing fences, a dozen different kind of lilies lining the walkway, and never mind what season it was, they were all blooming together." There she's welcomed by her grandmother, *La Señora de la Esperanza*. Her grandmother heals Ana's gunshot wound and counsels her on using her power. She also reveals that she has been waiting for Ana to gently dig a grave for her with her powers so she can rest forever in her garden. Ana stays for her grandmother's natural, peaceful death, then, reassured about her own abilities, finds her way home.

Into the Desert: Vixen (DC Comics, 2011)

The DC African heroine Vixen (Mari Jiwe McCabe) debuted in 1981's *Action Comics* #521. Her powers include borrowing animal powers—elephant strength, cheetah speed, falcon flight—thanks to her ancestral Anansi totem. She was intended to be the first Black female DC superhero to star in her own series, but her line was unfortunately cancelled in 1978. After *Action Comics*, Vixen fought alongside Animal Man, Checkmate, Birds of Prey, and Suicide Squad. When the Justice League moved to Detroit, she quickly joined up. On the team, she was a powerful, clever fighter, always ready with surprising solutions. Critic Deborah Elizabeth Whaley adds, "Vixen transcended the typical trend to make Black characters marginal or sidekicks in comics; she was often the most powerful of female characters" (114). Vixen often appeared on the cartoon *Justice League Unlimited* as well.

On the free online platform CW Seed in August 2015, Vixen (voiced by Megalyn Echikunwoke) joined the *Arrow/Flash/Legends of Tomorrow* CW universe. Season one of *Vixen* with executive producers Greg Berlanti, Marc Guggenheim and Andrew Kreisberg is a brief half hour cartoon with guest appearances by Flash and Arrow. However, in contrast with full, live 22 hour seasons of the other shows, this "season" falls far short. Guggenheim comments on the possibility of a live-action show: "We always say 'never say never,' and if the character resonates with people, that would be wonderful. I would love to be in a position where CW said to us, 'Hey, we want a *Vixen* live-action show.' That'd be wonderful. We'll have to sort of see how things play out" (qtd. in Ferguson). LaToya Ferguson, author of "The Women of Color Heroes We Both Need and Deserve," protests:

> But the implication of Guggenheim's quote is that the CW didn't want a live-action Vixen for fear of the character not resonating with the viewing audience—which is questionable, because the CW took a chance on a niche (to the general public) superhero like the Green Arrow and then, by extension, The Flash. And CBS is now taking a huge chance on "Supergirl," a character whose biggest moment in mainstream pop culture had been a ridiculous movie from the '80s. The question of whether or not "a character resonates with people" is inherent in all of these projects, and yet the one starring an African female superhero is the one that comes out on a secondary platform with a wait-and-see attitude. Yet, on the other hand, if a live-action version does happen, the powers that be have their bases covered with Megalyn Echikunwoke already cast in the role. So why wait?

It's a tiny step, but the heroine has appeared live for a single episode of *Arrow*, played confidently by the same actress. With her understanding of talismans, Vixen brings her magic to aid Arrow in battling wicked Damien Darhk. Arrow quips, "Mari and I had an *animated* encounter last year, and we've stayed in touch ever since" (*Arrow:* "Taken"). The cartoon has been renewed for season two, and will likely appear on television (E. Goldman). Further news of live action appearances has not yet arrived, but she's poised to guest star or join the cast of any or all of the three series or perhaps launch her own show. CW President Mark Pedowitz acknowledged there were more possibilities for the character, remarking, "Hopefully that character can spin itself out or if not, join the *Legends* [*of Tomorrow*]" (E. Goldman).

Television's new heroine is tough and uncompromising. On meeting Flash and Arrow, she tells them, "Show up at my father's house and you're gonna get a really good idea what it's like to be devoured by a lion." She saves herself with no help from them. Her actress, Megalyn Echikunwoke, cheers: "Vixen is a superhero that I have always wanted to exist, but I didn't know she actually existed, so getting to play this and coming on is kind of like jumping on a bullet train. The fans are so excited and they're so rabid for the stories and everyone knows so much more about it than I do, so I am just playing catch-up" (Burlingame).

In the CW Seed cartoon, Mari returns to Detroit, where she reunites with her foster father and tells him she was rejected as a designer because her work "lacks identity"—a critique she knows is true. When she's attacked on the street, she suddenly uses her totem necklace to harness gorilla strength and fights off her assailants. She begins experimenting and discovers the totem will let her channel many other animal powers. Echikunwoke adds:

> I think it's really cool that the world gets this superhero because she's black, she's young, she has an interesting story but she's still very all-American, which isn't unlike my own story, so I can relate to her, and she also inspires me.
> I think what's really cool about her is, to a degree she's kind of a self-made superhero. Her backstory is that she was orphaned: she was born in Africa, she was orphaned and then gets to the United States. Like a lot of Americans, like a lot of children of immigrants or anybody, really, she's trying to find her identity as a young woman. Through this, the discovery of her power and her ability, finds a way to interact with the world that helps her thrive and be the best version of herself.
> Also, I just think that the fact that she's kind of one with the world and that she can communicate with animals, that's a really cool power because it makes her very grounded [Burlingame].

Mari is thus developing her inner power as she researches the origin of the totem. However, a mysterious woman is tracking her and finally takes her captive. Mari wakes in Zambesi Village in M'Changa Province (both fictional places, like the *ashae* spirit of the totem). There, the woman reveals herself as Mari's older sister Kuasa. She is tall and African in appearance with exotic makeup and an elaborate hat as well as the sleek violet gown of a Disney villainess. "My first obligation is to Zambesi," she announces, though she introduces thuggish allies drawn to the totem's power. Apparently, greed has corrupted her. With her jeans, leather jacket, slang, and Pixie cut, Mari looks strikingly American by contrast. Thus this is a war of ideals—tradition versus the modern world as the two women face off far from Mari's home.

Mari runs, but falls unconscious out on the empty plains. This is her wilderness journey, not to the lush forest or magical ocean, but to a place of desolation and emptiness so quiet that she can hear her inner voices, usually drowned out by the bustle of everyday life. This lifeless, stark place is that part of the psyche with "no impact of collective human activities" though it reflects the vast world underneath. To enter there, a woman withdraws "not only from all animus opinions and views of life, but from any kind of impulse to do what life seems to demand of one" (Von Franz, *The Feminine in Fairy Tales* 97).

When someone is wounded at the depth of their soul, "She has first to reach the zero point, and then in complete loneliness find her own spiritual experience," often personified by an angel or other guide (Von Franz, *The Feminine in Fairy Tales* 98–99). The dark savage goddess appears to some questing heroines, showing them their destiny. In a dream state, Mari is visited by the animals and villagers of Zambesi. "You must stop the pretender. The darkness has infected her," a woman's voice tells her. A lion adds, "Embrace your true calling." As they all encourage her not to fear the power within her, she rises dramatically and proclaims, "I will stand with you!"

Mari returns to the village and battles Kuasa and her followers. All the animals of the plains defend her, and Mari decides, "I will embrace my destiny. I will cling fast to my ancestors." She reclaims her totem and accepts her role as superheroine.

Back in Detroit, Mari takes to the streets to capture criminals and defend those in danger. She muses, "My whole life, I thought if I knew where I came from, I'd learn where I was going. What my purpose is. Turns out, I was right." She happily tells her foster father, that she has the "identity" she was seeking. She knows where she belongs and it's the U.S.: "The totem is supposed to help me protect my village. Detroit is my village. It's my home." She adds that she loves him. After, she dons a brown leotard and makes her peace with Flash and Arrow. "I know who I am. I'm Vixen," she decides.

The stillness of the desert doesn't offer inner magic, but silence—there are no distractions separating the heroine from her own abilities. Often it's a quiet place within the Otherworld, a journey within a journey. Marzi, protagonist of *The Strange Adventures of Rangergirl*, ventures into the realm of her own comics to find an oracle and get answers on how to save her boyfriend from the supervillain. She notes that a perilous journey across the desert was a necessary step: "I needed to learn," Marzi says. "Learn how I could shape this place.... Sometimes you have to wander in the desert to learn, Lindsay. And, anyway, things mean more if you have to work for them" (Pratt 317–318). To meet the scorpion oracle, they cross the desert then climb down into a dark pit—the symbolic center of the world—to receive their answers.

During her time with the New Mutants, Karma is taken over by the psychic entity Amahl Farouk. She becomes a crime boss and becomes grossly obese, as Farouk indulges his greed. At last, Karma is freed, but lies around, despairing and suicidal after the violation of her body. The Enchantress kidnaps all the mutants and Karma finds herself alone in the desert. As she thinks, "I am lost. No food. no water. No shelter. No friends. No hope" (Nocenti, *New Mutants Special*). With this, she lies down to die. When she sees a monster attacking a child, however, she takes over the creature's mind and saves the girl, who reminds her of her own little siblings. She decides, "Sin enough to take my own life. But I cannot abandon this innocent. She has placed her trust in me. I must do what I can for her." With no one else to aid them, Karma kills small animals to keep them alive and scavenges clothes from the dead. By the time she reaches the end of the desert, she has transformed into a lean warrior with waist-length hair, still holding the child by the hand. Saving her has helped Karma save herself.

In a similar journey toward agency, Ororo, age 12, wanders deep into the wilderness. "It was summer and she'd been on the road for almost a year. A 12-year-old girl, alone, making her way south from Cairo—across Egypt, the Sudan, and now Ethiopia, some of the harshest, most desolate terrain on earth—drawn by visions and a soul-deep need she didn't understand, but couldn't deny." There she finds T'Challa the young prince of Wakanda being kidnapped for ransom, and she rescues him, soaring through the sky for the first time and swooping down like an angel. They travel together and flirt, then they finally part and Ororo "followed her dreams to the slopes of Mount Kilimanjaro, where she made her home" (Claremont, *Marvel Team Up* #100). Eventually she becomes X-Man Storm. Yet without this adventure she never would have found her hidden powers, or saved the man she would eventually wed.

In "LifeDeath II" by Chris Claremont, a powerless Storm wanders the deserts of Africa (*Uncanny X-Men* #198). "The Elements I shaped to my will have me at their mercy," she realizes, and she wanders aimlessly through rain and pounding sun. The force of the elements remind her of what she's lost as they turn from her servants to her tormentors. Despairing, she crawls into a cave. There she confronts visions of all the X-Men, then finally embraces the poisonous snake she had fled before, thinking, "The snake is as much a part of life and the natural order of things as I." On emerging, she finds the young pregnant runaway Shani and helps her journey home, sheltering them both with her cloak and sharing her story. This lost, devastated woman is like the lost part of herself, vulnerable and friendless. As she helps the young woman birth her child, Ororo has allowed the hidden joy within herself to be born. "Joy bubbles within me like champagne, making me giddy with delight," she thinks. As Ororo learns the village's customs, that they must maintain balance and the old culture must give way before the new, she thinks of the mutants. After, she decides, "I have no powers, my body cannot fly. But I no longer mind, for in my heart and soul—where it truly matters—I soar higher than the stars!" By journeying to a land of simplicity, she has found her peace.

Mari also starred in a short comic book run by G. Willow Wilson and Cafu in 2009. In the collection *Vixen: Return of the Lion*, Whaley admires Wilson for integrating "aspects of feminism and the gender concerns of some African women into the graphic novel." Nonetheless, she believes "the character remains entangled in colonial discourses of US national allegiance and the idea of a primitive, patriarchal Africa." Africa is portrayed as exotic and in some ways accentuated or inaccurate (118). When the mostly-white JLA burst in to intervene, the symbolism becomes problematic.

After Mari discovers her mother's murderer is at large, she returns home to Zambesi to track him down. She faces the warlord Aku Kwesi with her animal powers, all focused through her Anansi totem. However, he defeats her in combat with his own supernatural powers and leaves her gravely wounded. Her powers sputter, suddenly unreliable. With this, her people desert her as well. One of the men of her former village leads her to its edge, telling her, "The land will decide whether you live or die. Goodbye, She-spirit."

In the empty grasslands, this Mari also has visions. By a well, she sees her dead mother, who cautions her that jackals are coming to kill her. However, Mari refuses to die. Her mother tells her, "In the city, you forgot the land that gave you your powers. You must remember now, if you want to survive. Use the land—you need its help." She is no longer a costume or a Metropolis superhero but a woman of Africa alone at night in the middle of the Dagombi Plains. She binds her wounds with bark, sleeps in a tree, chats with a monkey. As she defends herself from jackals with powers of hyena and cobra, she's truly understanding the animals' lives and harnessing the savage within herself. "Living in the forest would mean sinking into one's deepest nature and finding out what it feels like," away from the rules of civilized life (Von Franz, *Fairy Tales* 97).

As Mari sets out again in the morning, she has a vision of her young self playing with her friend. "If the Self appears as a young person in a woman's unconscious productions, it means the newly and consciously discovered Self" (Von Franz, *Fairy Tales* 170). An older woman, like Mari's mother, suggests the deeper self that has always existed far below the strutting Ego, seeking voice. Only in the stillness can the heroine hear it.

The self is too caught up in titles and labels, with perception choked by responsibilities and narrow thinking. Many modern therapists respond with a "controlled regression." This takes the conscious self "into the borderland-underworld levels of the dark goddess—back to ourselves before we had the form we know, back to the magic and archaic levels of consciousness and to the transpersonal passions and rages which both blast and nurture us there" (Perera 56–57). In the daylight world, our conscious self is trapped in old routines—the more mature consciousness needs deeper wisdom, better relationships, more vital tasks. Thus it seeks out the Dark Goddess.

In legend, the Dark Goddess waits in the margins and borderlands, in the empty places of dark forest or silent desert. Like a sharp-edged fairy godmother, she often advices the questing heroine [Frankel, *Buffy* 115].

Mari meets a lion and runs from it, thinking, "I feel so weak. There was a time when a lion wouldn't frighten me—but that was before Anansi, when I still trusted my powers." The lion catches her, fragile as she is. However, it is benign, belonging to the pacifist Brother Tabo. She wakes in his dwelling, the shrine of Saint Amica. This is a place of total peace, where even predators and prey live peacefully side by side. She confides in Tabo about feeling unnecessary among the many JLA superheroes, and adds that they're swallowing her. She has been Vixen so long she has forgotten how to be Mari. Tabo replies, "You feel trapped by your duty to your friends. But do they not also have a duty to you?" He examines the talisman that focuses her powers, realizing that this too is part of Vixen. He asks her to try transforming into something that she feels deep within: "Feel awe, be humbled by your gift, and take joy in it." She channels his advice and soars as a falcon.

Only after she succeeds does he reveal that he's palmed her talisman without her noticing, proving that her power is intrinsic. Free of the Justice League, the burden of her past, and even her totem, she can feel the power of her soul. With a new understanding, Mari channels only earth and sky, not others' expectations, and defeats a lion. She need not keep a desperate control over every aspect of herself, for her powers are a part of her. She returns to the village and faces her mother's killer again. Aku Kwesi appears a terrible force, but it is all illusion, aided by a cocktail of poisons and money from Intergang. She deprives him of his armor, tosses her own talisman aside, and defeats him, inner strength to inner strength. As she forbids the Justice League to interfere and saves Superman from a terrible fate, the most powerful superhero admits that he shouldn't have questioned her, for she truly knows the power of her land. Her journey has renewed her and helped her discover her power.

The *Supergirl* film of 1984 banishes its heroine to the Phantom Zone, just as the show *Smallville* does. Each time, the protagonist must struggle through torments to find her way home, discovering who she is without her powers. Joss Whedon's unmade Wonder Woman film script has a similar plot arc. First, love interest Steve Trevor criticizes Diana for having powers she's never earned, asking: "Has there ever been a day you didn't have everything you wanted? Have you ever been hungry? Been cold? Worked twenty hour days underground for no pay, been spat on, stepped on, shot at...." Moments later, the evil force Strife chains Diana's bracelets, depriving her of her powers, and abandons her in the South American jungle. As well as binding, chains symbolize the links that tie humankind to existence and to one another, a link she's just begun feeling (Cooper 32). In the wilderness, Diana is no longer a pampered princess but a woman with nothing but her own inner strength. There she battles storms, struggles through the jungle, and starves.

Found by the local village, Diana shakes with fever and when asked who she is, she can only respond, "It doesn't matter." However, a small girl comes up to her and repeats her mother's words that she must remember who she is because no one can take that away. As with Mari's vision, this is the voice of the subconscious, both innocence and experience in one. On hearing the voice, Diana struggles from the pit where she's been thrown. Proudly naming herself, she battles the petty druglords terrorizing the South American village, defeating them with only her human strength and ingenuity. At last, she channels her own strength and breaks her chains. In triumph, she returns to the city and defeats Strife.

Hearing the Inner Voices: *Power Girl* (DC Comics, 2009–2010)

Amanda Conner illustrated *Power Girl* #1–12 (written mostly by Justin Gray and Jimmy Palmiotti), a collection adored by many fans. In the story, Power Girl discovers she's really not Superman's cousin. With this revelation, her powers fluctuate. Living with a fake job, a fake persona, an apartment she never visits, she lacks grounding. "I haven't put on anything except the costume in three months. Haven't had a day job in six," she thinks. She soon realizes she needs to track down her real origins.

First, the villain Garn Daanuth arrives and beats her up for his brother's death. "You lie to yourself, Kara. You turn away from everything you are and everything you could be," he snarls. As they battle, he taunts her, "Yes, that's it, child. Show the world that you don't belong here." She pummels him into the ground, only to have the JLA arrive and point out that she's punching the street—the encounter was all in her head. Certainly, Garn Daanuth functions as a threshold guardian, blocking her from embarking on her quest, but his imaginary nature emphasizes that this is an inner battle as Kara struggles to sort out her identity. And as she thinks, after being Superman's cousin, any identity is bound to be a disappointment.

As she sits waiting for Superman on the Daily Planet roof, Jimmy Olson offers her everything she wants in a sympathetic ear and friendship. All at once, the Legion of Super-Heroes arrive from the future to tell her she's one of them—Andromeda, sent back to the past to save the world and now meant to return with them. Of course, Andromeda was a victim and pawn in mythology—an indicator that more is going on. They insist, "You don't belong here,

Power Girl. This world doesn't need you. This world doesn't deserve you." This certainly mirrors the feelings she's having deep within. However, she resists their commands. When they try to stop her from saving a plane, she bursts out, "I don't like people telling me what to do!" and goes ahead with the rescue. While she does, they battle her, tugging at her cape and interfering. After, Superman tells her the people on the plane saw no other superheroes nor Jimmy, only Power Girl flying erratically and fighting with herself. She accepts a hug from Superman but insists she needs to solve everything on her own. Kara also talks with Huntress, who points out that the heroes might like her, only no one seems to know anything about her. Despite her confusion, Power Girl is moving from her fake cousin relationship (Superman) to start making real friends and talking out her problems.

They are interrupted by the Crime Syndicate of America—alt-universe evil versions of the JLA who insist Kara is one of them. As she fights them and Huntress insists no one is there, Superboy and Wonder Girl arrive from the future to tell her she's their daughter. More and more heroes arrive, each with a different origin story—she's from Kandor, the future, the past. These function as wish-fulfillment fantasies, the orphan seeking mythic, larger-than life parents and a great destiny. All of them close in on Kara, hands grasping overwhelmingly. She shoves them all away, but Huntress is the only one there ... or so she thinks. Both women collapse and Kara wakes to see Psycho Pirate, a supervillain covered in masks, bending over her, promising to help.

Psycho Pirate carries her to his lair and tells her, "You need to stop fighting everything. That's all you've ever done." He takes her on a journey of the mind insisting he's the only one who knows the truth—she is from a different reality. After *Crisis on Infinite Earths*, she found herself in the wrong world, one where she never existed. This mad voice, a talking mask, is her bridge to identity as she literally pulls off his mask to discover the real self and figuratively does likewise in her own life. "Now the naive self has knowledge about a killing force loose within the psyche," Estés explains (55). The trick is to fight through his ordeal before it defeats her, blocking off all her pathways to growth.

Evil voices from within can do as much to motivate the heroine as benevolent ones. As Linda Danvers of the 90s struggles to combines her lives as human and Supergirl-Matrix, she has many visions that advise her—Clark Kent and both sets of parents, but mostly Linda's abusive boyfriend—a demon from hell named Buzz. His taunting and fatalism finally challenge her to excel (David, *Supergirl*). Similarly, Jessica Drew, a Hydra agent seeking the truth of her past, hallucinates in *Spider-Woman: Origin*, seeing brutal Otto as her surrogate mother Bova and the ruthless Taskmaster as the werewolf who attacked her parents.

Psycho Pirate explains that all her visions came from Power Girl's mind, but he mined them from her suppressed memories, blocked to protect her. Huntress and Robin from her original world arrive to taunt her, demanding to know why she exists and they don't, voicing her deepest fears as they add that she doesn't deserve to exist. "The way she whines and complains. She's not worth a thing," they smirk.

As Psycho Pirate taunts her and urges her to lose her mind, Kara cries that she already has and punches him, only to find he's not real either, and is no more than a floating mask, continuing to mock her. As she strangles it, it melts away, though insisting she needs to reach inside herself and find a way to matter. As the Predator rampages through the heroine's psyche, he's devoted to "the killing of the creative feminine, the one who has the potential to develop all manner of new and interesting aspects" (Estés 56–57). However, when the heroine stands up to it, she has the power to defeat it. With this, she accepts the truth of her life—she is Kara from another reality, and that's why she's so displaced.

Kara flies away feeling utterly alone, seeking for a place to belong. This catapults her on an outward quest as she makes a life for herself, takes her job seriously and finds a better home. She saves the world and makes a close friend in her protégé Terra. This girl from the underground world, naïve about life on earth, echoes Kara's innocence, the confused alien she used to be. By the end of the comic, she and Terra have shared a profound bonding experience, which helps to ground her. "While the masculine hero may need to do things totally on his own to prove himself to the group, the feminine hero needs to prove herself to herself, then share this knowledge with the group" (Schmidt, *45 Master Characters* 233). She celebrates being female and finding her own path instead of the one defined by men, and shares this knowledge with her new friend. Through the story, she cares for her cat, and Wonder Woman finally tells her the cat wants them to have a real home and stability. It too reflects Kara in her restlessness, and as she settles down on his behalf, she builds a place in the world for herself.

Dosed with hallucinogenic toxins in *Catwoman: When in Rome*, Selina dreams of Batman, who morphs into her own father, the Riddler, Bruce Wayne, and many other men in her life, forcing her to confront her inner conflicts. In her fantasies, he falls in love with her sometimes, and other times, tries to coax her mask off, or slice it off with gruesome surgeries. Batman offers a chance to define herself as a hero, or to cast off the mask and fully reveal herself—all issues she struggles with. Clearly, Catwoman is looking for her own life in a very male-dominated world, but is having difficulty carving it out. "While trying to find her identity and carve out her own space, she must constantly deal with remnants of a world she has temporarily left. In feminist undertakings, we cannot simply create anew, we must deal with the old, as well" (Tremblay). Thus the Bat-villains who haunt Selina echo her pursuit for self, from Two-Face, a literal personality split, to Mr. Freeze, who threatens to lock her inside herself, unmoving and static. She faces each of these and overcomes their lessons. Likewise, Selina tangles with two female characters who represent extremes—one is the Wonder Woman foe Cheetah, who competes with her on thefts, has "taken the cat thing way too far," and threatens, "With you dead, maybe I'll take the name Catwoman." She is more supervillain and more animal than Catwoman herself, representing a possible path. The other is Louisa Falcone, her estranged mother, who represents the lost, sane, human side. With all these mirrors, Selina must choose who she wishes to become (Loeb).

One's imaginary friends can be a crutch or protective force when the heroine is in trouble. *Scarlet Witch: Witch's Road* has the heroine journeying accompanied by the ghost of Agatha Harkness. This spirit of Wanda's dead mentor offers sarcastic observations on the world but also advises Wanda on things outside her experience and perception. Agatha encourages her to go traveling and find the source of unrest in the world, which the pair do together (Robinson).

The short story "Nightingale" by Valerie D'Orazio has Gail Godwin longing to return to her nursing job after a trauma. She recalls seeing a young woman wheeled in, severely injured after being raped, who tried to slash her wrists after. She takes the young woman, Lisa, home to live with her, in order to heal the other woman's trauma and her own. "It was like whatever hysteria gripped this poor woman had then transferred onto Gail from sheer touch alone" (133–134). Soon enough, Gail finds herself seeking vengeance against the rapist, to the point where she buys swords and a razor-beaked costume. After she takes her revenge, she's welcomed back to work as her boss notes how much she's healed. However, as he tells her that her medical bills are covered, she realizes that she was Lisa and always has been. When she gets home, she confronts Lisa, who she realizes isn't real. Lisa replies, "You have a spark in you, Gail—despite all your flaws, all your fears. You have a spark that sets you apart but also gives you a greater responsibility. And that spark is me, Gail" (140). She tells Gail to continue to stick up for herself, and her costume comes alive, facing her, demanding her attention. Wearing it, she continues patrolling the streets as the avenging nurse, Nightingale.

Casting Off Illusions: Donna Troy (DC Comics, 2005)

Donna Troy, Wonder Girl, first appeared in 1980's relaunch of *Teen Titans* by Marv Wolfman and George Pérez "and the series went on to become the most celebrated DC title of that decade" (Lai 190). When the creators at DC saw Wonder Girl was a preexisting character, they added her to the lineup, upgrading her child's tunic to a star-spangled red jumpsuit with golden Amazon bracelets. However, 1950s Wonder Girl was actually young Wonder Woman, instead of a separate character. "When the mistake was eventually discovered, a backstory was hastily constructed for Wonder Girl, and she became Donna Troy, an orphan rescued by Princess Diana and raised on Paradise Island as Diana's sister" (Ryall and Tipton).

New Teen Titans: Who Is Donna Troy? follows the heroine on a quest of discovery. All her life, she had thought she was human, the adopted sister of Wonder Woman whom the superheroine had rescued from a fire. Now Phoebe, Titaness of the moon, arrives to tell her all her history is an illusion (Wolfman, Who Is Donna Troy?). This is often the case for the superhero, as Clark Kent and Donald Blake (Thor) believe they're human, only to discover they're aliens from outer space with great destinies. Power Girl lives in a similar imagined life. As she thinks in Amanda Conner's run, "I believed my own hype for a while. I lived in that wonderful fantasy. Superman's long lost cousin found." As she doubts the truth of her remembered origin story, however, she sets out to find where she really came from.

Casting off the illusion and claiming one's true self is essential for the superheroine. In X-Men: First Class, Mystique disguises herself habitually as a pale-skinned blonde, until Magneto convinces her she's lovely as she is and should stop hiding. Mystique then becomes "a shapeshifter who refuses to live in an acceptable human form and instead maintains her scaly blue skin in defiance of the ruling class" (Mainnon and Ursini 147). Xavin in Runaways is also searching for identity, made more difficult because as a shapechanging teen Skrull, she alternates between male and female. After joining the team, Xavin worries most about being accepted and tries to choose the most socially-acceptable forms, a plan that occasionally backfires.

Donna discovers her own history is just as epic. In actual fact, the Titaness Rhea, mother of the gods, chose young Donna to be one of a dozen New Titans, all with special powers, named for the ancient cities of the world. On the moon of New Chronus, the young heroes Troy, Sparta and the other children were granted superhuman powers and trained in combat, arts, and sciences. "Thought, concept, mind, and body, all trained as one," Donna recalls. She is not a weaker copy of Wonder Woman, not simply an orphan, but has an epic destiny as chosen one.

When the Titan Seeds, as they were called, grew out of childhood, they were sent back to their own homeworlds with false memories, so they could humbly learn the ways of their respective cultures as ordinary people. Once they reached adulthood, they would return to New Chronus to take their rightful places beside the Titans of Myth. This is a classic part of the hero's tale as many are raised in obscurity, ignorant of their true destinies. Now, however, something has gone terribly wrong and the original mythic Titans are in danger. On discovering her true origin, Donna feels a responsibility to fulfill her destiny, despite her self-chosen commitment to the Teen Titans. "My people? Days ago, I never heard of them. Now, everything I am is because of them," she realizes. Donna and the Teen Titans go to New Chronus, in search of the two surviving Titan Seeds.

Unfortunately, one of the Seeds, Sparta of Synriannaq, has become a mad dictator. She is Donna's foster-sister, a dazzling example of another path her life might have taken. Now, it is said, "Hers was the hand that razed her world. Hers were the words that stoked the fires of hatred." She kept her memories, and as they drove her mad, she conquered her own planet, and then declared war on the other Seeds. As she killed each one, she absorbed their powers and grew in strength. Meanwhile, the original Titans weakened.

Donna and her friends, through a great battle, defeat Sparta and restore powers to the real Titans. Rhea takes Sparta to her own home to care for the shattered husk she has become, and tells Donna, "This is the dawn of new creation. Think not of death." As the Titans are reborn stronger than before, they offer Donna heavenly gifts as a reward.

Mnemosyne, the Titan of Memory, gives her a dazzling cloth of starry firmament, Coeus, the pendent of perished Chronus, Hyperion, an armored gauntlet. There are also Phoebe's bracelet and a stone that was once a weight on the scales of justice—now an earring. Finally, Rhea gives her a superhero name in her own right—Troia. Donna Troy ends her story arc by fashioning herself a new costume of starry black with all these godly gifts. She also cuts her hair dramatically short. All this separates her from her old identity as Wonder Woman's sister to create herself anew. These are tokens of her true birthright, but also ones she's earned through her heroism—all a contrast with the Wonder Girl identity she was given as a child. Wrapped in stars, she ties herself to the universe as its mystical preserver.

Many heroines discover they've had hidden powers within their entire lives, or that the world contains superhuman people. All is more complicated than they once believed. Often, this revelation accompanies a call to war as the heroine realizes she can use her powers to save the world. *Birds of Prey* features the young Dinah Lance discovering her own potential:

> BARBARA: There are people in the world, Dinah, a lot of people with abilities beyond what we think of as human. Um, no two metahumans have the same gifts. Don't ask me where their powers come from, no one knows. Natural mutations, biological experiments.

HELENA: There's been some really weird stuff from meteor showers.
BARBARA: The point is, you're one of a long line of people who've had to hide who they are.
DINAH: So I'm like you?
BARBARA: Uh, like Helena, Technically. I'm not metahuman.
DINAH: But you're both heroes, and save people. I wanna join [*Birds of Prey*: "Pilot" 101].

Of course, the quest to cast off illusions may repeat over and over. Years later, Donna is slain by a Superman android. She is then reborn on New Chronus thanks to the Titans of Myth with false memories as the Goddess of the Moon and wife of Coeus (a friend of Sparta). The Teen Titans come, demanding she remember her real self. Caught in her false life, she turns on them. "I am the Goddess of the Moon, Alien," Donna tells Starfire, battling all her friends. "And you are in my way."

In Schmidt's journey stage called the Illusion of the Perfect World, "the Main Character has a false sense of security and is trapped in a negative world that stops her growth. She avoids the reality of her situation by using a coping strategy" (*Story Structure* 86). In contemporary life, this might be an abusive husband, or a false belief that she's respected in her job. In fantasy, this is often an entire artificially constructed world. She's jolted out of this idealism by a great betrayal or realization and is pushed to a fork in the road. Everything she values is stripped away. After this comes an awakening as she quests to regain her power.

When the Titans, turned tyrant, sacrifice Sparta in a war of aggression, Donna begins to remember that these are not her people. "The Titans of Myth claimed they loved me for my soul.... It's unfortunate it took me so long to see ... that it was always the Teen Titans and the Outsiders who were there to *save* my soul," she explains (Jiminez, *The Return of Donna Troy*).

Her protégé Cassie reminds Donna she inspired her to be Wonder Girl and begs her to listen, but Donna refuses. Cassie continues to reason with her as they battle, showing her a picture of the two of them with Wonder Woman— a family—to remind her who she's supposed to be. This is the voice of innocence, echoing from deep within. Donna, the former Wonder Girl, thinks, "In Cassie's eyes, I saw something else. In Cassie's eyes, I saw the power of the Olympian gods—someone who could truly understand me and my vision of the universe." (Jiminez, "The Return of Donna Troy"). For a moment, she's tempted to return.

When their words have no effect, her teammate Raven strips away the illusions and shows Donna the truth of her soul. Finally her friends drag her to the planet's center, a place, like the cellar or the forest, where the subconscious is freed. Here, one can escape the clutter of the ordinary world and in the stillness, hear reality. Donna discovers the terrible weapon the Titans intend to use in their wars. At this, she returns to her friends and swears to fix the damage she's done.

Fighting the Titans, Donna is suddenly swept away as Hyperion takes her to the center of the planet, and there she sees the thousands of alt-universe selves she is, from human Wonder Girl and Troia to Darkstar, Dark Angel, and Harbinger. "I had become the sum total of all of my selves, each of my lives— unique in all of creation, a living connection to every universe that had ever existed," she says. If on earth one sees "through a glass darkly," Donna Troy now discovers all the parts of herself. Campbell's innermost cave, the deepest part of the soul, is a place of total truth with all illusions burned away. There in the subconscious once more, she understands the epic truth of her existence.

She grasps she is the one chosen one meant to open the portal to a new reality and save all the Titans. Donna guides them to a new world thinking, "After everything they did—the invasion, the treachery—it was so odd to realize I still loved them. They were still my parents. That's the weird thing about unconditional love." Nonetheless, she realizes they will conquer the new universe, so she sends them to Tartarus instead.

The war over, Donna returns to her friends. At the end, she notes, "I was no longer a goddess nor a conqueror. I was simply Donna Troy." This is a valuable self-truth as well as Donna chooses the identity she wants, not solely the one the universe has prepared for her. Now completely herself, she claims New Chronus, the world where she grew up, as a home base. The home too represents the self and now she is truly grounded in her identity.

Once her journey is completed, Wonder Woman brings Donna the Harbinger's History of the Universe Orb. "Just as Harbinger recorded the multiverse's history for the Monitor, Dark Angel was to do the same for the Anti-Monitor. Uniquely connected to a thousand universes, I was now to be the keeper of its mysteries and knowledge," Donna realizes. She has grown from innocent to teen superhero to evil goddess to finally benevolent protector. "Show me everything," she tells the orb, claiming omniscience. With her final revelations of what is to come, the comic draws to a close (Jiminez, The Return of Donna Troy).

Healing: Jessica Jones (TV, 2015)

Marvel created the imprint Max—darker, more adult comics in which the sex and swearing could run unchecked. In their first series, Alias, PI Jessica

Jones solves grim crimes as superheroes succumb to drugs and mental illness. Her best friend is Captain Marvel, and she's torn between good boy Scott Lang (Ant-Man) and bad boy Luke Cage. In a world of Marvel goody-goodies, she stands out for her harsh language and cynicism, along with the darker artwork. Her last case drags her back into the superhero past she abandoned as the vile Purple Man escapes prison. She tells Luke Cage how he abused her in a savage rape metaphor:

> The Purple Man did not employ physical sexual abuse as a weapon against Jessica, although he raped other women under his power, ordering Jessica to watch. However, he instructed her to love him, then to beg him for sex, and, as she grimly recounts, "I would beg him to fuck me—I would beg him 'til I cried" (14, no. 25). Jessica's slavery is total: "I lay at his feet. I slept on his floor. I bathed him" (ibid). Despite the horror of this, it is Jessica's description of how this false consciousness feels which may be the most disturbing aspect of this story: "In your head—it doesn't feel any different than when you think it yourself, you see? It's almost soothing. In my mind, I can't tell the difference between what he made me do or say and what I do or say on my own" (16, no. 25). This particular false consciousness is chemically induced, but this could easily be a description of the patriarchially imposed ideological false consciousness, with Killgrave as its smirking representative [Kaveney 68].

Like Donna Troy, she lived a lie, controlled by the patriarchal force until she managed to fight off his influence. By facing this terrible past, Jessica finally achieves healing and recaptures the villain. This is also a story of self-definition. "*Alias* as a title for the series as a whole indicates that it is a book about all the people Jessica has been—daughter, orphan, mother, lover, sister, hero, drunk, slut, detective, and moral agent; it is a title linked to our discovery of who Jessica actually is" (Kaveney 68).

Marvel's Jessica Jones (2015), one of the first superheroine television shows since the 70s, debuted to rave reviews from critics and the public, along with a Critics' Choice Award for star Krysten Ritter's performance. The Netflix show closely adapts the comics' Purple Man storyline, looking at rape and domestic abuse through the superhero metaphor. Of course, book and show are recommended for mature audiences only. Both are emotionally valid and stirring, as the heroine recovers from her trauma by confronting it. Rachael Taylor (playing Jessica's foster-sister Trish Walker) explains:

> What makes it so unique is that it really is an allegory for many different types of abuse, whether it be sexual abuse, physical abuse, or psychological abuse. That's what makes this such an incredibly bold show. It's such a sharp, potent topic that we really should have discussions about more openly and more often. To do it within the framework of the superhero world and the comic book world is so incredibly brave and unique [Radish].

Jessica begins her show as a cynical private investigator tracking cheating spouses and serving violent lowlifes with subpoenas. She notes, "People do bad shit. I just avoid getting involved with them in the first place. That works for me. Most of the time" (101). She insists she has control. As she lives her ordinary life, however, it's clear something's wrong. Flashbacks intrude—a man's voice saying "You want to do it. You know you do." A hand stroking her hair. As the camera blurs and spins, emphasizing her confusion, she recites street names to ground herself in the present.

In fact, creative camera angles up drains and in mirrors stress her dissociation. Flashbacks are often tinted, emphasizing a removal from normal perception. Mike Colter, who plays Luke Cage, explains how the show really digs into this type of suffering. He says, "It's very difficult to understand PTSD. In that regard, it opened doors to be relatable to so many people. It's about being damaged, and then trying to figure out how to go on with your life" (Radish).

Suddenly a case intrudes that shatters Jessica's equilibrium. The Shlottmans from Omaha are tracking their missing daughter Hope. As Jessica traces the lingerie she's been buying and the restaurant she visited, Jessica realizes her terrible past has resurfaced. Terrified, she scrabbles for money to buy a ticket to Hong Kong, shaking down every contact, then out of desperation seeking her successful foster sister she's avoided for six months.

When she goes to Trish, their conversation reveals that it's been a year, that Jessica had thought her tormentor was dead, that she went to therapy for PTSD.

> The trauma Jessica endured from Kilgrave goes far beyond rape. As she explains, he "violated every cell in my body and every thought in my goddamn head," even making her kill for him. Though most survivors aren't struggling with the weight of murder, how Jessica flagellates herself over what happened is powerfully resonant. She isolates herself from everyone, convinced that she is hopelessly broken and only burdens those around her. And that—the shame, the self-loathing, the self-doubt—is often the trauma hardest for survivors to overcome ["How Jessica Jones"].

As the story slowly reveals, superpowered Kilgrave (the Marvel comics character, though with normal pigmentation and a birth name of Kevin Thompson) used mind control to force Jessica to do his every bidding—to smile for him, to have sex with him, to be perfect and docile. His constant insistence that she smile is a metaphor not only for rape but for covering the abuse with makeup and excuses, for insisting everything is fine. "The mundanity of control he exercises over Jones, over nearly every woman who crosses his path, is what makes him so evil, even more menacing than the typical villain. Kilgrave is every woman's worst nightmare: he is a rapist, an unrepentant stalker, a man who, at any moment, can exercise his power and does" (Edwards).

Now learning that Kilgrave has returned from apparent death throws Jessica into a panic. Despite her pain, Trish encourages her foster-sister to intervene. She tells Jessica, "I know one thing, you are far better equipped to deal with that animal than some innocent girl from Omaha. You're still the person who tried to do something."

Jessica rejects this argument. "Tried and failed. That's what started this. I was never the hero that you wanted me to be" (101). Trish gives her the money to run, but a conscience-torn Jessica goes to Kilgrave's hotel and saves Hope. When the girl's revealed as mind-controlled, Jessica carries her out by force, much as she would have wanted someone to do for her. After, her conversation with the girl shows a great deal of empathy.

JESSICA: His control, whatever it is, it wears off. But it takes time and distance, so we're both getting out of here.
HOPE: [sniffling] He made me do things that ... I didn't want to do, but I wanted to. [sniffles]
JESSICA: What street did you live on as a kid? What was the name? Picture the sign.
HOPE: Harrison. Harrison Street.
JESSICA: And the next block over?
HOPE: Florence.
JESSICA: [sighs] Listen to me. None of it is your fault.
HOPE: You don't know.
JESSICA: I know. Okay? I know. I want you to say it. "None of it is my fault." Say it back to me.
HOPE: It's not my ... [sniffles] [sighs] It's.... It's not my fault.
JESSICA: Good. That was good [101].

This is all a trap—Hope suddenly shoots both her parents and, in a message from Kilgrave, tells Jessica to smile. In horror, Jessica runs from the taxi to get herself on a plane. Then she hesitates. She repeats the line she said at the episode beginning about cheating spouses: "Knowing it's real means you gotta make a decision.... One, keep denying it. Or two ... do something about it." She turns away from the taxi and sets out to take down Kilgrave. As Trish said, she's the best one to succeed.

Episode three is about the many ways to deal with trauma. Jessica discovers Trish now lives with video surveillance, a steel-reinforced door, bulletproof windows, and a safe room. Jessica tellingly asks if Trish's mother is back (though certainly, the existence of the Purple Man is another concern). Trish replies that she doesn't need Jessica to protect her now that she's learning Krav Maga. "No one touches me anymore unless I want them to. I let you fight my battles for too long" (103). Jessica has to smile at seeing her sister's empowerment.

It's that play between the power of men and the strength of Jones (and her female compatriots) that drives the show. Strength here is explored in all of its complexities, both physical and psychological, in a manner that's unusual for the superhero genre, typically underpinned by the idea that both control and strength are the domains of men. *Jessica Jones* is an unraveling of the stereotypes that form the genre. Control and strength here play with and against one another; their possession is survival. Though Jones has strength, control has been seized from her by Kilgrave, thus undermining her power. It's the reconstituting of both that fundamentally drives the narrative [Edwards].

With help from Trish and the lawyer Jeri Hogarth, Hope fights back by speaking out about her experience and publicly revealing what Kilgrave can do. Jessica, who's spent the past year hiding from what happened and trying not to face it, tries to stop her.

TRISH: We're doing a live remote with Hope from the prison.
JESSICA: No.
TRISH: Jess, you asked me to defend her.
JESSICA: Yeah, not to drag her out in public with her guts hanging out.
TRISH: Hey, it's me. I'm on her side. I'll go easy.
JESSICA: Trish, he'll be listening. He wouldn't miss it. Probably not. He'll be listening to her and thinking about me.
TRISH: He's already thinking about you. Hope wants to fight back and I want to help her [103].

In fact, Trish is right—ignoring Kilgrave won't keep Jessica off his radar—he's already stalking her. Trish takes the fearless, direct approach, challenging Kilgrave on the air to Jessica's horror: "So yes, I think he's out there, this sick, perverted man.... He is preying on the hopeless so he can feel powerful, probably terrified of his own weakness, which suggests impotence.... Probably suggests some serious Oedipal issues..." (103).

He sends someone to kill her, but she's not frightened off. However, Jessica persuades her to save her own life and pacify him by apologizing on air. Afterwards, Trish is disgusted with herself:

TRISH: I need a shower.
JESSICA: Saying the words doesn't make it true. Remember acting? It's how you won that award.
TRISH: My mom blew half the jury to get me that award. It might not have been about my acting.
JESSICA: Fine, but Kilgrave knows you're afraid of him, and that's all he cares about. [104].

Trish pushes Jessica to take a stand, while Hope often slumps in despair, and the lawyer considers practicalities and plea bargains. All reflect aspects of the heroine herself, urging her down different paths. Jessica's love interest Luke Cage is more steady and supportive. With a straightforward view of the world, he's the only one to react without judgment when Jessica tries to buy drugs to knock out Kilgrave in the third episode. "Luke has never bought into most of the stock but unneeded aspects of superheroing—the costume, the mask, the secret identity—and he has always been 'hero for hire'—a mercenary. He is not Captain America, nor does he pretend to be; he is not the embodiment of an ideal, just a working stiff with powers" (Kaveney 84). His actor, Mike Colter, adds:

> The way that I was able to see how Luke dealt with Jessica, he's a supporter. He could have intervened with Kilgrave, but that was something she had to deal with for herself. He couldn't come to her rescue because that wouldn't change the horror of what she'd been through. In that regard, it defined who he was and how he looked at her, as a person who's a complete individual that can do things for herself, but if she needed him, he was there for her [Radish].

Since he hides nothing and pretends nothing, Jessica trusts him, though he's a teller of unwelcome truths. In episode six he apologizes to her for dismissing her warning about Kilgrave and adds a simple "Maybe I can make it right." However, Jessica's confession that under Kilgrave's power she killed Luke's wife shatters him.

After this, with her neighbor Reuben's murder as well, she feels so consumed by guilt and shame that she tries to throw herself in prison. It's a trap for Kilgrave, but also a means of penance. Even though Jessica wasn't responsible, she can't bear the condemnation of those around her. Later, she surrenders to Kilgrave to stop him from killing. When he enjoys saving the day but tells her, "I can't do it without you," she actually considers staying with him forever to teach him how to use his powers for good. She's willing to give her own life in service to others, all in return for acts she was forced to commit.

As a hero, Jessica considers herself far too responsible for everything. When Kilgrave responds to her death threats by insisting he has hostages, he adds, "There would've been a rash of suicides across the neighborhood, and who would've been to blame?" When she says it wouldn't be her, he retorts, "You keep telling yourself that. Maybe you'll actually believe it someday" (110).

Nonetheless, it's clear that Kilgrave genuinely has no moral understanding—using people as puppets all his life has left him unable to differentiate. As often happens in comics, his fantastical powers leave him saying the same things uttered by many in real life: He asks her, "Which part of staying in five-star hotels, eating in all the best places, doing whatever the hell you wanted, is rape?" and insists he had no way of knowing she didn't consent.

> When confronted by Jessica about raping her, Kilgrave complains, "I never know if someone is doing what they want or what I tell them to do." He is full of excuses for Jessica's supposed misconception about the nature of their relationship, ducking responsibility at every turn. Yet the one thing he never considers is simply stepping back and listening to what she has to say. Instead, he steamrolls over Jessica's version of events, insisting that she enjoyed her time under his control because he took her to fancy hotels and nice restaurants.
> The fact that Kilgrave is seemingly unclear about whether Jessica did or didn't consent

doesn't make him any more sympathetic. It makes him more terrifying, because the notion of a man abusing women without full comprehension of his actions is not fantastical. It's bleakly real. And while Kilgrave may not grasp the nature of consent, the show makes it excruciatingly clear that none of Kilgrave's victims consented to what he made them do and what he did to them. Despite this, many of his victims struggle with guilt over having their agency unwillingly taken away—none more so than Jessica ["How Jessica Jones"].

Other arguments follow, as Kilgrave insists his parents abused him and that it's not fair for Jessica to blame him for her own drinking problem (108). Abusive boyfriends have said all of this, and Jessica, like many women, struggles through the morass of arguments. He has taken her agency, but he leaves his victims fearing that some part of them was willing. "Given the low percent of rape that is actually reported, and the extremely-high percent of PTSD from victims, this a perfect parallel for what a rapist actually does: exert power over someone's body and mind" (Formo).

Nonetheless, Jessica insists on keeping Kilgrave alive so he can take responsibility for his crimes—the murder of Hope's parents, but everyone else's loved ones as well. "For Jones—and any survivor—her physical torment won't go away simply by killing her abuser. But making sure that he can never commit it again and that he is properly punished—judicially—makes his horrors known, and could likely benefit more survivors, because such a public display could get more survivors to come forward" (Formo).

> The show also highlights the need for the police, the legal system and other members of society to believe and support victims, rather than blame them. Because sadly, the fact that Hope (Erin Moriarty) is the one who winds up in jail after being raped and abused by Kilgrave rings true. Every year, victims are arrested after reporting their own rape. Women are repeatedly written off as "crazy" and unreliable narrators of their own story, particularly when their rapists are wealthy, attractive white men, such as Kilgrave.
>
> That's why the small, but crucial decision to have Jessica fight not for vengeance against Kilgrave, but to force the world to believe his victims is so important. The tendency to blame victims for their own assaults is why so few rapes go unreported (68 percent) and unprosecuted. And even if they do make it to court, they rarely result in any jail time (2 percent), creating a cycle that revictimizes rape survivors and shelters the attackers. This sad truth is what eventually drives Jessica to realize there is no possibility for justice within the established legal system, and why she is ultimately forced to resort to more guerilla tactics ["How Jessica Jones"].

Jessica tries following the rules (loosely at least) and recording Kilgrave's abilities so she can exonerate Hope. Nonetheless, Kilgrave escapes and takes Hope prisoner. He realizes all Jessica has done is for the other girl. Jessica longs to restore Hope's life, or as much of it as she can, since this will show herself that she too can heal from what Kilgrave did. He smirks, "She'll never kill me. Despite her calloused, hard-bitten, and, frankly, poorly styled facade, despite her several problems, she still hopes that, at her core, she might just be a hero. But only if she can save you. The ultimate innocent victim" (110). In response, Hope kills herself so Jessica will kill Kilgrave and end the threat. With Hope dead (literally and symbolically), Jessica crumples in despair. Kilgrave vanishes, and resurfaces at last to taunt Jessica with the death of her boyfriend, as he says. Jessica rushes to Luke moments before his bar explodes with him in it. Luke is safe, but his mind is taken over and he turns on Jessica. Though she pleads for him to stop, she's forced to shoot him. After, she insists that the responsibility is Kilgrave's not hers—she's finally moving past taking the blame for everything he does. "I did have a choice and I chose to survive," she asserts to Nurse Temple, who herself understands heroism. Nonetheless, Cage's wounding takes a heavy emotional toll as she's opened herself up to feeling. She thinks: "Pain is always a surprise. I try to avoid landmines. Avoid caring. I can even see it coming. But until it hits, you have no idea what pain is" (113).

Of course, Kilgrave contacts Jessica and pushes her to blame herself: "Should have known you'd save your own skin, boyfriend be damned. Selfish as ever. Clearly, it's not better to have loved and lost." He's the voice of negativity and blame, the self-hate spiral, even as he takes no responsibility for any of his own acts. Part of Jessica is striving to find love and connection, but her own doubt keeps sucking her down.

Jessica tracks Kilgrave down again, only to discover that Hogarth's experiments have made him stronger. She confronts Hogarth, who's become another of Kilgrave's victims, while her girlfriend Pam was forced to kill to defend her. In another response to trauma, the former shark of a lawyer is ready to give up. Hogarth tells her, "I don't know what else I can do to pay for my mistakes. I have bled for them, I have lost everything that I care about. Pam is facing murder charges, and she won't see me, and my partners are forcing me out."

In a reversal from her earlier isolation, Jessica responds that she should fight for her place rather than giving this up too. She gives Hogarth an assignment defending another of Kilgrave's victims and adds, "And this does not make us square. But doing something ... good ... it helps with the self-loathing. Trust me." The source of Jessica's determined heroism is revealed.

In her final showdown, she walks into Kilgrave's trap, prepared to be put under his control again. She gives him everything—following his orders, telling him she's not a hero, and finally letting him take her sister. Facing her worst fears and being strong enough to endure them indicates how she's grown from the first episode, where even a glimpse of Kilgrave throws her into a panic. Subjecting herself to these horrors convinces Kilgrave she's under his control, allowing her to trick him. When she turns passive, he joyfully rushes to her and says: "Oh, God, it's true, isn't it? You would let me take your beloved sister.

My God. It's finally over. You're mine now. No more fighting. No more of these ugly displays. You'll be with me now. Look, after a while ... however long it takes ... I know ... I know you will feel what I feel. Let's start with a smile." She smiles for him, his favorite command, then, throwing the word back at him, she breaks his neck.

> In the end, Jessica does defeat Kilgrave, snapping his neck and preventing him from ever abusing someone again. However, *Jessica Jones* does not present this as a happy ending. All the issues that plagued Jessica throughout the season do not magically go away after killing Kilgrave. The world still does not believe his victims, despite the mounting number of those who've come forward. Kilgrave's death has not erased Jessica's PTSD, nor has it helped her recognize her own self-worth, a feat that is now probably made harder by the rising body count for which she blames herself ["How Jessica Jones"].

She has further to go to be comfortable with herself—there is no instant fix here. Nonetheless, she has found some peace and stability with the threat removed. Through her journey she has taken back power from Kilgrave, though she will still have to live with herself. Her actress, Krysten Ritter, adds: "For Jessica, that final victorious, triumphant moment when she kills Kilgrave, I found that very conflicting, in terms of her head space. He's the reason why she got up, every day. He's the reason why she went out in the world. It really gave her a purpose. And I don't think that the past trauma just goes away with his death. So, her head space is really complex" (Radish). Nonetheless, there's a hopeful ending as she's destroyed her demon at last.

Empathy: Batwoman (DC Comics, 2013–2014)

The first Batwoman was invented in 1956 to convince Batman's readers that Robin wasn't the only person in his life. With a purse full of exploding makeup, Kathy Kane had subtle, girly powers ... though she spent quite a lot of time being rescued. Her greatest goal was to trap Batman into marriage, and her niece, Bat-Girl (Betty Kane), treated Robin much the same. By chasing after the heroes or fainting into their arms between their many kidnappings, they proved constant nuisances. Undoubtedly, both male characters breathed a sigh of relief when the two women vanished without explanation in the comic's overhaul of 1964. Other Batgirls followed, but decades passed before another Batwoman.

In 2006, Batwoman returns, transformed from Kathy Kane to Kate, and now much tougher. Her cousin Bette is also reimagined, as superheroine Flamebird of Teen Titans. Modern Kate is fiercely independent and decidedly doesn't work for (or date) Batman. A Jew and a lesbian, drummed out of the army under Don't Ask, Don't Tell, Batwoman showcases several minorities. In an interview, Greg Rucka tells the anthology *Chicks Dig Comics:*

> I was given Kate—she was gay when she started. And God bless DC Comics for that. I mean, there are many things you can perhaps lay a torch at that building for, but DC said from the start that they were bringing Batwoman back, and she was going to be gay. She's going to be gay. We're not going to say maybe she's gay, we're not going to do a Very Special Episode of Batwoman where she comes out. She's queer from the start, and she's perfectly fine with it. Any other trauma in her life notwithstanding, she is not at all troubled by her orientation.
>
> At the time, I was writing the Renee-and-Charlie storyline in 52, and the story dealt with Kate, so I ended up with the character as a result. And I'm very glad and proud, I hasten to add, of what [editor] Michael Siglain and [artist] J.H. Williams III and I did with the character. When all is said and done, there will be a short list of my works for which I will be remembered, and I hope *Batwoman: Elegy* will be one of them. I'm very proud of that one.

In *Batwoman: Elegy*, Kate faces a violent criminal who calls herself Alice and speaks only in quotes from the Lewis Carroll novels. The women are polarized—Alice dresses in dead white, with matching makeup and blonde ringlets, more doll than girl. Batwoman wears dramatic adult black and red. One cover juxtaposes them, with Batwoman in the lavish white cult robe with exotic embroidery and winged skull. Batwoman is a loner; Alice works for a cult. In fact, Alice's cult, the Religion of Crime, has been tracking Kate, who's determined to know why they care so much about her. On her first encounter with them, they tried to carve out Kate's heart, a metaphor that will soon manifest symbolically. When Alice kidnaps Kate's father and plans to destroy Gotham by spreading a deadly airborne chemical from a hijacked airplane, Batwoman stops her. When Alice tumbles from the plane, Kate catches her hand. Alice then shocks her by saying that Batwoman has "our father's eyes," revealing that she is in fact Kate's twin sister Beth, believed dead. Alice stabs Batwoman, who drops her.

Now in *The New 52* by H. Williams III and W. Haden Blackman, Batwoman is rebuilding her shattered world through friends, partners and lovers who resemble herself as she quests for her sister once more and puts the pieces of her life back in order. Carol P. Christ explains "If the negative side of women's development is that they have weaker egos than men, the positive side is that identification, sympathy, and mystical experiences are easier for them to achieve" (qtd. in Schmidt, *45 Master Characters* 193). This is the heroine's emotional quest.

Kate cannot forgive her father for concealing that her sister survived and must deal with all that happened. This Kate began living with the closest relationship possible—a twin who represents half of herself. As Kate explains,

"She's in my head, telling me when it's enough … when I've fought enough, bled enough, punished someone enough…" (*Batwoman: World's Finest*).

As with many heroines, Kate receives her call when little ones are endangered. A ghost many think is La Llorona, the wailing woman, kidnaps a dozen children. The grieving parents go to the police every day, and Batwoman vows to retrieve the children. Across town, her love interest, Captain Maggie Sawyer, fears she can't make the same promise, but vows she'll never stop looking. Already, the two women are a matched set.

Agent Cameron Chase of the Department of Extranormal Operations is sent by Director Bones to take down Batwoman. Batman tells Kate, "She's not driven by duty but by hate," making her another traumatized young woman determined to fight in the world of superheroes. First she approaches Maggie, suspecting that she's truly Batwoman. Then she approaches Kate's father, who remarks that while he regrets his daughter's choices, Cameron's father must feel the same. Once more the two young women are linked. Director Bones and Cameron finally discover Kate's identity and ask her to work for them taking down the kidnapper. When they threaten her father, Kate gives in (*Batwoman: Hydrology*).

Back home, Bette pushes Kate to reconcile with her father, while Kate tells Bette she must get rid of her silly costume and get "a uniform" as Kate has. The pair know each other so well that everything is already understood—Bette can become another Kate, fighting beside her.

Batwoman falls into the water and meets La Llorona who calls her "a sad little girl alone in your sorrow" and forces her to face her loss, turning her into her drowned sister until she can fight her way out of the delusion. Staggering home, Kate fires her cousin, calling her "just a privileged tennis player. You're not even fighting *for* anything" (*Batwoman: Hydrology*). If Kate is a seasoned soldier, she sees her cousin as only a pale imitation of herself and rejects her for being soft. Thus driven, Bette suits up as her cousin suits down. Confronting a vicious hook-handed criminal, she's nearly killed. She lies in a coma for some time, and only wakes when her uncle offers to train her as he once trained Kate. Even during her recovery, she soldiers on, comparing herself to her tougher cousin.

Kate confronts La Llorona. If Bette is her innocence that she's lost, the Llorona is her constant, seeping guilt. As the other woman's ghost tries to literally drown her with images of the dead, Kate battles through it, insisting, "You have no power over me, I didn't choose for my sister to become that … maniac but I refuse to feel guilty for it anymore." She persuades La Llorona to save the kidnapped children, and the ghost tells her Medusa is responsible before fading away (*Batwoman: Hydrology*).

Next the DEO send her to capture a Medusa agent named Sune and take her from police custody. This damaged young woman, sister to a powerful criminal, is yet another poignant reflection of Kate. The DEO even send the pair on missions together, on which the two action women debate morality, like Kate's inner voice prodding her. Sune also makes a romantic move on Kate, provoking her to consider her relationships before reaffirming her bond to Maggie. She shares her photos and life story with Maggie and Maggie responds with a photo of Jamie, her daughter, another blonde innocent like Kate's sister.

Meanwhile, Bette struggles on the edge of death and her uncle tells her about his two daughters. He confesses that Beth was so sweet, "in Beth I saw nothing of me." Kate however was tough, protective, stubborn, and stoic—exactly like himself. Thus another reflection appears.

The organization Medusa swears allegiance to the Mother of All Monsters, the goddess Ceto, so Kate recruits a god to track her down—Wonder Woman. The pair descend into the Greek underworld together, both superheroines. Together they debate the hard questions of trust and morality, even while each secretly envies the other's courage and certainty. Before she descends, Kate leaves a message for her father offering some amount of reconciliation. All the team-ups have forced her to examine her soul and discover no one is blameless. Meanwhile Maggie stops the parents from taking things into their own hands with the calm certainty of a superhero. As Kate and Diana battle the Greek monsters, their unity of purpose is reflected in Flamebird, healed and a superheroine once more.

After, Ceto stands alone on a beach, naked, wishing she could start over. Understanding her plight, Diana and Kate aid her in this, then Kate destroys her secret recording of the Underworld. In return, Diana promises to aid her any time. Triumphantly, Batwoman gathers the kidnapped children and leads them to Maggie, kissing her, revealing her identity, and joyously proposing marriage. The split within herself has been healed by the journey.

With the third volume, this arc concludes, but the next takes a more personal stab at the heroine. The DEO have Alice and offer to release her … in return for Batman's secret identity. Batman arrives, and Kate notes, "Figures … when Gotham is under siege from *Medusa*, you're nowhere to be found. But the minute I take down one of *your* villains, here you are…" (*Batwoman: This Blood Is Thick*). She looks on Batman as more rival than inspiration, noting, "When I first put on the uniform, I was in awe of him. But then I tried to *work* with him…. He doesn't share. He doesn't play nice with others. He doesn't respect me. He's a *control freak*. Don't even say it" (*Batwoman: This Blood Is Thick*). She thus realizes they're two of a kind.

In a subplot, DEO Agent Cameron Chase meets with her own sister, Terry. She explains, "I think I'm about to do something horrible." Based on this statement, her sister does what she's clearly been summoned for and tries to talk her out of it. Terry tells her that battling and locking up superheroes won't get her real closure with her father. As Cameron talks things over with her sister and lashes out against her father, she parallels Kate once again. Bones meanwhile is revealed as being obsessed with his own family as his father always preferred his sisters to him. He even believes Jacob Kane is his father and Kate is his sister, though his file reveals this is not the case. Likewise, Agent Cameron Chase easily succumbs to paranoia and prejudice "due to her own family history with 'extranormals'" (*Batwoman: Webs*). All of these mirrors for Batwoman try to bring her conflicts into prominence.

Meanwhile, to share her lover's trauma, Kate injects herself with the same fear toxin that Maggie once suffered through, adding, "I love you. I hope this will show you how much" (*Batwoman: This Blood Is Thick*). Kate wakes up with her lover and realizes how powerless she felt and how great a betrayal it was to leave when the other woman needed her. They reconcile and are closer than ever.

Kate, trapped in a world of impossible choices, tries Batman's classic move of "I have to do this alone," only to be shut-down from a surprising source. Kate's stepmother Catherine vows support of the young superheroes, noting, "She's a Kane. It's in her Goddamn blood! But it's in mine too." The two parents, along with Bette and Maggie, stage an intervention, confronting Kate when she comes home and convincing her to work *with* them to save her sister and Batman together. As Schmidt explains, the heroine "accepts others as they are and embraces the female aspect of supporting one another. She begins to see the oneness that we all share together" (*45 Master Characters* 233). Her entire family unites with Batman and his people to spring a trap on Bones. At last, Alice is saved (*Batwoman: Webs*).

Batman and Batwoman set out on patrol together, now in accord and united as never before. They have defeated their own family issues through trust and reliance on others, though the paranoid agents of the DEO have not. By facing all these reflections of herself and treating them all with understanding, listening to their problems and solving them, Kate Kane manages to fix herself piece by piece. She lets go of her guilt and embraces love, finally rescuing her sister and bringing in Alice to fight beside her. With friends, family, and lover all united in her life, her psyche is fully mended.

Facing the Shadow

Descent into Death: *Pretty Deadly* (Image Comics, 2013–2014)

> He raised Her a Reaper of Vengeance,
> A hunter of men who have sinned
> If you done been wronged,
> Say Her name
> Sing this song
>
> Sound the bell's knell
> That calls Her from hell…
> Ginny rides for you on the wind, my child…
> Death rides on the Wind!
> —The Ballad of Deathface Ginny

Pretty Deadly begins with this ballad, emphasizing its fairytale roots. It's a comic set in the Weird West, written by Kelly Sue DeConnick and drawn by Emma Ríos, with more than a touch of magical realism. Its complex plot and dream surrealism has many comparing it to *Sandman.* "The book is absorbing us while breathing on its own," said Ríos. "Sometimes I feel we are hidden behind a rock, gasping, watching the characters do their things" (Parreno).

The blind man, Fox, and a little girl with mismatched eyes and a vulture cloak, Sissy, go from town to town, telling the Ballad of Deathface Ginny, the Daughter of Death. Deathface Ginny was a girl born with skull markings on her face, born between the woman Beauty and her lover, Death itself. When Beauty's living husband went down to the realm of death and saw the child, he demanded the right to raise her as her closest living relative. Death offered mercy, but only if the husband would slay a "beast." It was a crying baby, and the man couldn't do it.

Over and over Fox and Sissy tell this ballad, emphasizing that those in danger can call on her for aid … or vengeance. But when Sissy steals a binder from a man and Fox burns it, it unleashes Deathface Ginny in the flesh. She's come for her destined revenge on her stepfather, the blind old man who once killed her mother. Other characters include pale-haired Big Alice and her gang, Death's bounty hunters. When Ginny stops to defend children crying out for her help, Big Alice tells her, "Your daddy sent me. Says it's time to come home." The pair fight, and Ginny slays Alice, sending along a message to her father, Death, that she refuses. The boys' mother, Sarah, can see the dead, emphasizing her mystic power over the other realm. She tries to counsel Ginny, explaining that human beings are like the scorpions of the desert. "You don't see them, don't think about them at all 'cept as the occasional nuisance when one of 'em manages to bite. But they watch us like their lives depend on our whims ... 'cause they do." She adds that Ginny's intended victim Fox is a good man.

Death symbolism fills the story. Not only is the frame story that of a dead rabbit telling all to a butterfly (a traditional symbol of the soul and rebirth), but when Big Alice dies, her body turns into a herd of butterflies. Dying does not release her, however, as Death sends butterfly-Alice back once more to bring him a special child. DeConnick notes that the Western, according to Leone, is an otherworldy space: "The important thing is to make a different world, to make a world that is not now. A real world, a genuine world, but one that allows myth to live. The myth is everything" (Parreno). This myth of course is that of the unending lifecycle.

There is more going on, as Sissy burns the note without reading the knowledge that has always been kept from her. Thus a summons to the realm of Death is also a summons to dip into her subconscious and discover the hidden truths of her life.

In ancient times, "the most powerful and thus frightening aspects of female divinity were relegated to the caves, to the dark corners of the world as chthonic goddesses, contrasted with those ruling from Olympus." The patriarchy was supreme, and dark Hecate and the Furies were rejected. "However, it is an even greater need to seek it to discover it, to learn its vital lessons. Those who suppress their dark side are vulnerable to its impulses and desires, yet unable to accept them" (Frankel, *From Girl to Goddess* 129). Thus Sissy is summoned to explore her other half, the less-innocent world of knowledge.

This is an initiation, leaving one's ordinary world as a child to return with powerful, dangerous gifts—the ultimate test for the superheroine. "Initiation usually requires a 'decent into hell' to overcome the dark side of nature before resurrection and illumination and the ascent into heaven" (Cooper 88). This also works when the hero descends into danger and darkness, or faces death and is transformed.

Arnaudo describes the epic hero's mythic descent into the underworld as "another theme that recurs in superhero comics more than in any other contemporary genre" (124–125). In *Wonder Woman: Land of the Dead*, Wonder Woman, Wonder Girl, and Ferdinand the minotaur journey to the Underworld to free Hermes. There, both women must confront all the ghosts of those they've failed and especially those they've killed. In this land of stark reality, Cassie discovers the truth of her parentage and Diana saves the god Hermes, earning divine rewards in consequence.

When Doctor Strange wonders why some superheroes return from death, he enlists Dead Girl to guide him into hell—a role played by Dante's Beatrice and many other spiritual guides for the central hero. She recruits Mockingjay, Moira MacTaggert, and Gwen Stacy from the Dead Girls' Book Club to help him find the Pitiful One. However, when Doctor Strange is suddenly returned to life, Dead Girl must lead the quest on her own through her own traditional realm—that of the underworld. She succeeds and brings Strange the Eau de Profundis, though with her errand complete, she must return to death (Milligan).

When Fox and Sissy are separated in a flash flood, Sarah and Ginny find Fox at the same time. Ginny and Fox fight, with Fox telling her he's content to die but he needs her to look after Sissy. He adds that revenge won't make Ginny happy. When Ginny assumes Sissy is his child, Fox denies it and adds, "Her father was violence and her mother was grief and she was meant to live and know love … so that when she took your daddy's place she'd feel the weight of that duty." She spares him.

Upon finding them, Sissy realizes that she was the "monster" Fox pulled from the river. He tells her, "No, Sissy. You're my heart made flesh, all bumping around on dry land. You saved me … and now you're gonna save the world." Together they all descend into the realm of death to meet their fates. The Underworld "is a well-known symbol of the unconscious with its unknown possibilities" (Von Franz, *Individuation* 170). Sissy has been living under an illusion and only the realm of Death itself can reveal her destiny, the latent power awaiting activation. This is a vital part of mythic journeys, one the authors have tapped perfectly.

Continuing her own journey, Ginny demands passage from the Shield Maids who guard the gates. They call her "the one who made us two," and it's revealed that Death, with his heart broken, has let the deadly realm fall into despair and decay. They refuse to let her pass. "Then may I?" Sissy asks startlingly. As she adds with vulnerable sweetness, "I don't look like much, I know. Dirty little beggar girl. Truth is, I'm shaking in my shoes. I don't…. I don't want to die. I don't want to face a monster. *Really* don't want to *be* one."

However, she adds that she's never had a home or a purpose and it "seems like this way offers both."

Calling her "the ascendant who wears the vulture crown," they lay down their weapons and open the gate. The split guards, one of gentle day and one of horrific night, are healed and rejoined. In death's domain, the underworld resembles a Western town prepared for a duel, with monstrous crows and terrible fires. Ginny reveals that Fox died in the flood and that she locked her childhood sin away, sending the key to Sissy. If Death manages to get hold of Sissy, there will be no more death, no more new life. Ginny battles death and dies, but Sissy sings her ballad and Beauty arrives to slay Death and offer Fox forgiveness. Sissy becomes the new master of Death's Doman and restores the Soul of the World, freeing it from Ginny's hiding place.

The realm of death tears us apart, breaks us down, but only to allow us to incorporate new energies, new powers. Death is the natural order of things, part of the cycle of life. Estés writes, "This is our meditation practice as women, calling back the dead and dismembered aspects of ourselves, calling back the dead and dismembered aspects of life itself. The one who re-creates from that which has died is always a double-sided archetype. The Creation Mother is always the Death Mother and vice versa" (33).

> These stories all emphasize the connection between birth and death. Within the Great Goddess both concepts link, showing the deep understanding ancient people had for the duality of life. The heroine completes her journey by mastering this knowledge, incorporating the death-energies of the underworld into herself and acknowledging their glory. Only thus can she merge with the cycle of life, growing gracefully into mother and wisewoman without fearing death. For it is not an ending but a regenerative spiral. As one life ends, another begins, and on, and on [Frankel, *From Girl to Goddess* 172].

Of course, death need not happen to the protagonist—fridgings are effective because the death of the girlfriend enacts change on the hero without actually killing him. The hero "may either be a mere witness of the divine drama or take part in it or be moved by it" (Jung, "Concerning Rebirth" 117). Thus the heroine may literally die and return, or she may experience the death of a friend or loved one, or even death of some aspect of herself. From here, she rises out of literal death or perhaps depression or hopelessness to find a new state of being.

After Elektra loses her father in her first appearance (*Daredevil* #168), she tells Matt, "I used to love the world. Now I can't let it touch me. Ever again." She turns from political science major to bounty hunter (Miller, *Daredevil Visionaries Vol. 2*). In the same way, Chloe faces death on *Smallville* (actually, Lois's death at the end of season six) and uses her superpowers for the first time to revive her cousin, though the effort sinks her into a near-death state.

Chloe has several deaths, from her apparent death in the safehouse of season three's finale to her possession by Brainiac in the season seven finale. "I passed out, and when I woke up, I was different," Chloe explains. She wields enormous power, hacking every computer at once, black-eyed and able to enact all her wishes. While the Brainiac encounter is the most dramatic, each time, these bring her new abilities and insights.

Dying to Save the World: Kitty Pryde (Marvel Comics, 2004–2008)

Youthful and klutzy yet a genius, Kitty Pryde has always been a boundary-breaker, a girl power teen of the 80s and 90s. X-Men writer Nick Lowe notes: "She is the most everyman X-Man. She is how 90% of people see themselves, I imagine: Earnest, positive, funny, imperfect, smart, good-looking but not ridiculously good-looking" (Morse). Joss Whedon, who partially based his Buffy the Vampire Slayer on her, later wrote an X-Men run, in which he featured his favorite spunky X-girl saving the world—through her "harmless-looking" power of disappearing.

As the story begins, Kitty returns to the newly rebuilt school as a teacher. There she confronts her past, both as flashbacks and in the person of the new teacher, Emma Frost.

Kitty shows up late, and Emma remarks, "This, children, is Kitty Pryde, who apparently feels the need to make a grand entrance."

Kitty retorts, "I'm sorry. I was busy remembering to put all my clothes on" (Whedon, *X-Men: Gifted*). Kitty has always hated Emma, since the first X-Men villain she ever encountered was the White Queen. "Whenever I think about evil, whenever I think about the concept of evil, yours is the face that I see," she says.

Leader Scott Summers (Cyclops) tries to play peacemaker, but it's clear he thinks Kitty is far weaker than Emma, his lover. Seeking a spokesperson for public relations, Scott tells Kitty, "You're not a fighter. Your power isn't aggressive, it's protective. That's good to show. And people *like* you." Emma, who can control minds and transform into diamond, condescendingly calls her "sweet" and their "own poster child." Kitty has a long way to go.

In the first volume, Kitty enters an alien stronghold on earth. There, in a sphere of strange alien metal, she discovers her beloved Peter Rasputin (Colossus) has returned from the dead. This is a true devastation for the vulnerable heroine. "You have to know that if you're a clone or a robot or yeah a ghost or an alternate universe thingie, I can deal … but if you are some shapeshifter or illusionist who's just watching me twist, I will kill you, I will kill you with an axe," Kitty tells him. Disoriented and reduced to nothing but rage, Peter has difficulty returning to his old self. Kitty cradles and reassures Peter, but their relationship takes a long road back to healing. Both struggle through the series to transcend their issues and regain all they've lost (Whedon, *X-Men: Gifted*).

After several adventures, Agent Brand of the government's extraterrestrial branch, S.W.O.R.D., drags the team to the Breakworld, a planet that has a missile pointing at Earth. As Agent Brand says, "The Breakworld believes we as a species need to be put down" (*X-Men: Dangerous*). This is their Otherworld, a place of terror and violence. The team crash on the planet and are split up—Kitty and Peter find themselves sheltered by the few compassionate citizens. Their leader Aghanne offers a night's safety, a moment, as he describes it, to hear the silence and discover a third path for themselves other than killing or being killed. This respite before the great battle is seen in most stories before the all-important descent. In fact, Kitty and Peter take advantage of the pause to make love. As she puts it: "Everything is so fragile. There's so much conflict, so much pain ... you keep waiting for the dust to settle and then you realize this is it; the dust is your life going on. If happy comes along—that weird, unbearable delight that's actual happy—I think you have to grab it while you can. You take what you can get, 'cause it's here, and then ... gone" (Whedon, *X-Men: Unstoppable*).

In the morning, Kitty investigates the missile and discovers it's a tremendous bullet of alien metal—the same metal that blocked her entry and strangely attempted to bond with her before. If she is life, the metal is death, imprisoning Colossus and then threatening to destroy the Earth. It's also a protective barrier, a womb in which things can vanish and then emerge more powerfully. She enters it, but doing so costs all her strength. "I'm in the cage I freed Peter from," she realizes, coming full circle. As Breakworld fires the bullet at the Earth, Kitty is trapped onboard.

Back on Earth, all the superheroes, from Thor and Iron Man to the Fantastic Four, are trapped in a magical stupor. "The most powerful seem to be the most powerfully hit." As they each fantasize they've stopped the bullet with their brute strength, all they can actually do is stand and drool. Earth will be destroyed, with Earth's mightiest heroes all rendered helpless. All the greatest brute force can do nothing.

Rather than battling her destiny, Kitty embraces it, allowing herself to bond deeper with the bullet. Emma Frost links with her and demands she save herself. Kitty replies that the alien metal has become part of her—there's no fighting to escape. Instead, she finds herself communicating with it, fusing deeper and deeper. In their mental link, opposing shadows Emma and Kitty accept and understand each other in a way they never have before.

EMMA: Kitty.... I ... I can put you somewhere else. I can make you less afraid.
KITTY: Nah. Nah, I'm gonna see this through. Peter should know ... well, he should already know, so don't worry about it.
EMMA: This was never meant to ... not you.
KITTY: Yeah, I was supposed to take you out, as I recall. Disappointed Ms. Frost?
EMMA: Astonished, Ms. Pryde [Whedon, *X-Men: Unstoppable*].

"Give me strength!" Kitty cries. Using all her will, she doesn't fight the bullet but surrenders and merges deeper. Thus she turns the entire bullet insubstantial and it passes safely through the earth. Kitty, the smallest X-Man, uses her quiet power and saves everyone. The story ends with the bullet careening into space, Kitty still permanently fused with it. "Everyone has the potential to be the hero. The Feminine Journey is available to all, not just the rich, strong, and admired" (Schmidt, *Story Structure* 84).

In later comics, Magneto restores her, though she has been rendered insubstantial and requires more intervention to return to herself. All this emphasizes the rocky road to return from death. In *The Birth of Generation Hope*, she drifts in her phased form, "stuck between here and there." Her body lingers in the in-between state until she can remember how to pull herself out of it. This is the painful path back to wholeness. Nonetheless, her descent has helped her grow. "The woman, no less than the man, has her initial trials of strength that lead to a final sacrifice for the sake of experiencing the new birth. This sacrifice enables a woman to free herself from the entanglement of personal relations and fits her for a more conscious role as an individual in her own right" (Henderson 126). X-Men writer Kieron Gillen notes that after this journey, Kitty's moved on from Colossus. He adds, "I think that comes from the bullet experience which focuses in on what she actually wants now that she has life left" (Morse). Through her journey, Kitty has evolved from girl to woman, but now with a new vision for her life.

Other heroines too literally give their lives and receive great power, becoming one with the universe as well as saving their loved ones. Jean Grey dies to save everyone in *X2: X-Men United*. Her power has been growing, as she explains, growing to the point where she feels she can do anything. This signals an imminent death and rebirth as she withdraws from the world to absorb her new status. When her friends are trapped, their plane unable to take off and a flood coming, she lifts the entire plane, saving them all but sacrificing herself ... or so it appears. When she returns, it's as the powerfully dangerous Phoenix.

Avengers: The Enemy Within follows Captain Marvel and Spider Woman as they seek a solution to Carol's brain tumor that threatens, as she thinks, "My memory, my sense of identity … everything that makes me *me*." The evil Yon-Rogg, the adversary who led to her creation, plans to destroy New York. He will spare Carol because there's a piece of him in her head. "As it grew, your strength became my strength," he adds. When she realizes he's powering his plot with her energy, she flies off, though using her powers may cause a hemorrhage. In space she passes out and loses much of her memory, though she also saves the city. After, the mayor presents Captain Marvel with a new home in the Statue of Liberty's crown (DeConnick).

As the first year of *DC Bombshells* concludes, a terrible titan rises from the seas. A force of blackness and lightning, his ambition far outstrips that of the Nazis. He turns on London to create "an Eden of darkness and stillness and peace." He announces, "Among the dead, all things find a home. In death, all things are made whole … and nothing is ever lost again." The Supergirls, Kara and Kortni, realize the threat it poses to everyone. However, stopping it will cost "a life" (Bennett, *DC Bombshells* #35). Supergirl realizes that whenever enemies threaten her mortal sister, Stargirl, she does whatever they demand. As such, she's a liability to the team. "This is right…. I will do what I must to protect the ones I love," she decides. However, Stargirl clobbers her with her magical staff. Soaring up to meet the enemy, she thinks, "I'm flying. Truly flying. This is what I'd always wanted. I always thought I couldn't compete. Too human. Too weak. Ha." She decides this is a chance to write her own story and tell her own ending. "I am a new story. I am a story for mothers to tell their little girls. We must decide for ourselves what we would create, what we would change, and what we would leave behind. What you leave will be the thing that most defines you. What you save will be the thing that saves you." By flying into the creature, she destroys it and all its servants. Though it's a terrible sadness, death leads to new life—in the midst of all these horrors, the story follows a baby being born in London. Finally, Wonder Woman vows Stargirl will live forever in the stars as the constellation of "The Little Sister," riding her magical staff (Bennett, *DC Bombshells* #36).

Shadow Transformation: Dark Phoenix (Marvel Comics, 1975)

The change of character brought about by the uprush of collective forces is amazing. A gentle and reasonable being can be transformed into a maniac or a savage beast. One is always inclined to lay the blame on external circumstances, but nothing could explode in us if it had not been there. As a matter of fact, we are constantly living on the edge of a volcano, and there is, so far as we know, no way of protecting ourselves from a possible outburst that will destroy everybody within reach [Jung, "Psychology and Religion"].

One of the most famous shadow descents of the superheroines is the Dark Phoenix saga, written by Chris Claremont in 1975, and followed by another journey down the Dark Phoenix road in the 2000s and in the film *X-Men: The Last Stand*. Many other X-Men went dark, especially the women. After losing her children, Scarlet Witch lashed out at her team, and finally destroyed almost all the mutants in the House of M storyline. Storm too turned evil, and Kitty Pryde was taken over by a demon, as was Illyria Rasputin. Glowing red and yellow like a sun, Binary fights in outer space, a figure of colossal power. Yet she notes, "All I've done since is what I did before—as Carol Danvers—fight, kill, survive. There's no joy in me anymore, only grief. And Hate. The Brood helped make me what I am. It's a mistake they'll live to regret" (Claremont, *Uncanny X-Men* #166). "It seemed to be a requirement that the women who wore an "X" on their costumes would eventually take a dip in the crazy pool at least once. Power intoxicated these women and made them cruel, maniacal menaces who cast aside loyalties to friends and lovers. Even when possessed by an evil entity, the implication was that a suppressed part of the heroine's soul was reveling in the rush of deviltry" (Madrid, *Supergirls* 231). When Elektra and Natasha face off in *Black Widow: The Name of the Rose*, Elektra demands, "You and I both know that any of us can be turned. How many times has it already happened? One of us, going bad" (Liu).

Nonetheless, these moments of darkness are a necessary part of growth. "The darkness which clings to every personality is the door into the unconscious and the gateway of dreams, from which those two twilight figures, the shadow and the anima, step into our nightly visions, or, remaining invisible, take possession of our ego-consciousness" (Jung, "Concerning Rebirth" 123). Pretending one has no dark side leads to shallowness and stagnation, whereas facing one's dark side and learning from it leads to transformation.

Beginning in Claremont's *Uncanny X-Men* #133, Jean Grey is manipulated by Jason Wyngarde (Mastermind)—she finds herself in a fantasy of living several centuries before, loving the villain Sebastian Shaw, and wedding him. Her transformation is complete when she dresses identically to Shaw's henchman the White Queen, though reversed in black with blazing red hair. As the Black Queen, she gets a taste of unlimited power, untampered by morality or conscience. Thus Jean is lured to the dark side, but also frightened enough to escape into another identity. She has recently established a permanent bond with Scott, something also enticing and terrifying. All this has made her easy prey for the fantasy of becoming someone else. Of course, there's also the knowledge that her willpower has been stolen away—she's been stripped of free choice, forced to love Shaw, in a metaphor that's truly disturbing. Thus the rage she's always bottled up unleashes as the Phoenix force defends her and takes revenge.

This Phoenix, an immoral, indestructible manifestation of the primal force of the universe, has recently become part of her. Scott Summers, their prisoner, realizes that Jean has been having "dramatic upsurges in her power as Phoenix. That frightened her—and me too—and yet, it fascinated her as well." This is the power of female rage, blossoming in the daylight heroine for the first time. Lloyd Rose in her Dark Phoenix essay for *Chicks Dig Comics* explains:

> Dark Phoenix attacks, torments, hates. She barely stops herself from harming her family, and when she takes on her former friends the X-Men, she's out for blood. This isn't lust, it's scorched-earth rage. We're looking at Hell-hath-no-fury, and it's no longer a cute put-down. It's the fury of the raped woman, the violence of rape turned outward—savage, merciless, beyond reason, all the male clichés about "crazy women" in full scalding flow [Rose].

Sebastian Shaw usurped her will, made her a puppet, toyed with her. Now the darkness within her is gathering and striking back. It is a force of wish-fulfillment that augments superhero powers. However, this rush of dark energy and rage is overwhelming. As Jean's friend Moira MacTaggert notes, "As Phoenix, Jean realizes her ultimate potential as a psi. She possessed the power of a god, but only the experience and awareness of a young woman. She couldn't cope with that totality of power—I doubt anyone on earth could."

Though her friends rescue her and carry her off, Jean can no longer suppress the energy within. Her song of power builds and finally releases. Her green jumpsuit transforms to red and gold, fiery colors as Dark Phoenix. Even the light around her shifts from yellows and golds to sickly mauve and deep purple-black like a bruise. Thus she becomes death incarnate, glowing and savage.

She blazes into glory and her friends think, "Jean's enjoying this! Using her power is turning her on—acting like the ultimate physical/emotional stimulant!" She's reveling in the new energy, casting off her good girl shape to be the glorious bad girl. Storm realizes this is indeed the dark side: "I sense pain, great sadness, and an awful, all-consuming lust," she thinks. These are all emotions ordinary people, especially nice girls, repress, emotions they consider unproductive or bad. However, they can only be pushed down for so long before they explode into the psyche, overwhelming Jean's normal personality. Total chaos arrives. "The phrase 'female empowerment' fits Phoenix like a ballet shoe fits a panther. She was way beyond that, a goddess of destruction unleashing days of wrath," comments Rose.

Jean flies off into the sky. She has the power to do whatever she wishes without consequences or repercussions, and to lash out at a world that has victimized her. She destroys a star ... and with it five billion gentle people living on one of its planets. Thus the Shi'ar declare war. Their queen is a force of order in the universe, even as the Dark Phoenix is chaos. She's sick of being selfless, of giving everything, including her life. Now she wants to take and take, as she feels like the universe owes her. Having devoted herself to fighting for good for so long, part of her longs to fight for evil—and now it has its chance. Jung notes:

> The individual who wishes to have an answer to the problem of evil, as it is posed today, has need, first and foremost of *self-knowledge*, that is, the utmost possible knowledge of his own wholeness. He must know relentlessly how much good he can do, and what crimes he is capable of, and must beware of regarding the one as real and the other as illusion. Both are elements within his nature, and both are bound to come to light in him, should he wish—as he ought—to live without self-deception or self-delusion [330].

Jean has lived so long denying her dark side, ignoring the screaming rage of the Phoenix within. Now she has no experience mollifying it, and can only ride the wave of fury.

In John Byrne's *Fantastic Four* #280 (1985), there's an elaborate shadow descent as Sue Storm is depressed after a miscarriage and has no way to process her grief. Suddenly, the team discover a wave of cruelty spreading through the city. She-Hulk, a figure of strength and rationality, finds herself facing Malice, Mistress of Hate, a figure in a spiked mask and costume of jagged black and white cutouts with a sharp-edged red cape. "It is just as the Master said! I have been wasting my powers, frittering them away on childish things. Now Malice will rule!" she laughs. Wielding cunning forcefields, Malice traps She-Hulk with rockslides and calls her a clumsy beast. This, one assumes, is an insult nice-mannered Sue would never make, but one that bursts from acerbic Malice.

Reed Richards appears but tells Malice he is not really "the man you most hate in the world" but a face-switching copy of him. He is truly Doctor Unger, the Hate Monger, and his greatest triumph is creating Malice out of Sue Storm (*Fantastic Four* #280). When the real Reed arrives and exclaims, "A woman?" Malice retorts, "Don't you mean just a woman, Reed Richards? Someone to be ignored at worst, patronized at best? Someone to be stifled, frustrated at every turn? Capable of bearing children but never responsibility. Certainly not someone capable of doing this!" As she strikes out, her dark side is speaking the truth about her life. Finally, the men realize who she is. However, as her brother Johnny protests that they love and respect her, she strikes him with a forcefield.

At last, Sue can rage and scream, punish the men who always take her for granted. However, this proves the key to reaching her. Reed provokes her with cruel, sexist comments about how useless and self-indulgent she is and the power taking her over burns out. As he explains, "I had to force you to truly despise me, if only for an instant, to unbalance the effect, reverse it." Nonetheless, she has voiced the disturbing truths of her life. Only by agreeing and allowing her to fight through them, can Reed allow her to defeat her demons and return to herself.

Jean too faces family and friends, showing them the furious, savage side of herself she's always kept hidden. She returns to her childhood home to discover her mother and sister now fear her. The place is foreign to her, because she is now a different person. As they contrast her two sides, they tell her: "Jean Grey is a gentle, loving woman who cared so much for those she loved that she defied death itself to save them. Phoenix is a destroyer of worlds who cares only for herself." Her family rejects this needy, suffering dark side, even as a small Jean part of her thinks, "Dad, No! Please" in horror. Seeking to intervene in her wave of terror, the X-Men battle her but Scott tells her he loves her and that the Jean side of her still loves them. "Your existence, your very creation, springs from love, from the noblest emotions a human can attain. And now, you want to deny that? To deny yourself?"

She confusedly replies, "Yes! No. I ... hunger, Scott—for a joy, a rapture, beyond all comprehension. That need is a part of me too. It ... consumes me." The buried shadow is primitive, uncontrolled emotion—it's rage and fear but also excitement and creativity. Her damaged will has spent too long running from the dark force of power within her—a force more valuable than she had ever realized. However, once she gives in to rage, she's unable to contain it. "The conscious personality here has come in touch with a charge of unconscious energy which it is unable to handle and must now suffer ... while learning how to come to terms with this power of the dark and emerge, at last, to a new way of life," Joseph Campbell explains (146).

At last, Jean fights her way back, only to have the Shi'ar queen demand her death and the X-Men rally to defend her. In the fighting, the Phoenix takes over once again. As her friends refuse to give up on her, Jean insists that the two halves of herself need each other to survive—Phoenix is her lifeforce, and Jean, her will. She fears that Dark Phoenix will thus always threaten to take her over and hurt her friends. Thus she declares this is her decision to make, even as she hears the seductive voice of the Phoenix and as she admits, "Part of me welcomes it." She sacrifices herself and, exploding an energy cannon, blazes into nothing to stop the dark power and save everyone. She surrenders to the darkness and goes down into the underworld, though she will eventually return, her two sides aligned at last.

In Bodine Amerikah's 1988 Australian comic *Niteside and the Rock*, the goddess Lilith offers Astria Blaque and her boyfriend Rickard superpowers to use for the good of humanity. As Niteside, Astria controls dark cosmic energy which she can use to shoot potent black energy bolts, to fly and to heal herself. However, the dark energy becomes an addiction and in the future year 2028 her powers overwhelm her. She finally destroys the solar system and then the sun in a burst of apocalyptic carnage (*International Catalog*). Her dark side, once fed, is just too powerful.

With a happier conclusion, Raven's evil father Trigon sends a group of souls that he's controlling to possess Raven. She turns demonic and battles her mother Arella. However, her mother refuses to give up. She insists, "Azar cleansed our souls. She penetrated the darkness and pointed us toward the light. Azar herself may be gone, but what she was survives. And neither Trigon's evil nor the power of a corrupted Azarath can withstand her everlasting truth." She holds on, and, though all three are sacrificed, Raven's spirit is cleansed. Further, all the trapped souls of Azarath are released to freedom in a vast pink vortex of peace (Wolfman, *New Titans* #84).

Embracing the Self: Wonder Woman (DC Comics, 2011)

Often with women, love is stressed again and again—making it necessary to wonder about this particular emotion, or ethic, consistently being linked to the source of a female hero's strength. Does love constitute a reimagining of heroism? It's certainly a different motivation from that of a quest for a prize, be it grail, fleece, dragon, or damsel. It is also a break from the "Lone Wolf" model of heroism, which is rooted in traditional uber-masculinity and isolationism. Does the suggestion of love as strength, or as gift, embrace innately female characteristics? Does it infuse what is "naturally" powerful about women into a liberating archetype? Or does it reinforce stereotypes about how women should behave as self-sacrificing nurturers? The assumption that love is inherent in women, but not in men, is a sticky, even sexist concept, and the idea that a female superhero's greatest gift is her nurturing temperament or her ability to love selflessly certainly has the potential to reinforce stereotypical feminine ideals. But there's evidence that love in the superwoman does in fact present a reimagining of heroism [Stuller, *Ink-Stained Amazons* 87–88].

The hero usually battles and defeats the all-powerful supervillain, though compassionate Luke Skywalker and Harry Potter urge the villain to repent and choose goodness in the end. Heroines sometimes overthrow the villainess, but are even more likely to redeem her through empathy and kindness.

For issue #600, J. Michael Straczynski wrote the arc *Wonder Woman: Odyssey*, later collected in two volumes. After the Final Crisis rebooting, he was free to reimagine the character with a new beginning, so he did, making her alt-world and, perhaps most controversially, in pants.

"She's been locked into pretty much the exact same outfit since her debut in 1941," Straczynski wrote. "If you're going to make a statement about bringing Wonder Woman into the 21st century, you need to be bold and you need to make it visual. I wanted to toughen her up, and give her a modern sensibility." He added, "What woman only wears only one outfit for 60-plus years?" [qtd. in Gustines].

The reimagined American teen lives in the rough city, listening to loud music and (with cloudy morality) extorting a pawn shop owner so she can feed the needy and help an abused wife leave town. An orphan, she forms a community of misfits, though her inward journey outweighs the outer one. She begins fighting assailants on the street but afterward she confronts long rows of hooded figures. They try to keep her inside to ensure her survival, while she's determined to fight crime. Angrily telling them "you made me afraid," she ignores their warnings. They may be seen as voices of caution or cowardice from deep within, insisting on safety. Finally, they try to dissuade her from seeing the Oracle, but when she insists, they back down, as phantasms of the mind always do.

The Oracle tells Diana of her past—men invaded Paradise Island and Hippolyta sacrificed herself to send Diana away but swore her daughter would bring revenge. Now Diana tries to safeguard the other Amazons who escaped the slaughter, though they're distant and hidden, much like her knowledge of her past and destiny.

She finds a temple of lost Amazons in Turkey. They give her a shield with an imprint of her mother's face; with it her mother is symbolically watching over and guarding her. In the temple she confronts Aphrodite, who warns her she cannot intervene. Diana cannot find rescue outside herself, only from within. Aphrodite tells her her duty is "to learn to bear a queen's burden of life and death and not let it destroy you. And in so doing … save as many as you can" (part 1). However, Philippus, the shield-bearer, is killed.

On the battlefield, the Keres, harpies, come to collect the dead. When they discover Diana can see them, they decide, "Take her soul, for she does not deserve it." This is Diana's survivor guilt, after seeing a sweet young Amazon die for her. Though she fights, she's overwhelmed. They drag her down to Tartarus and threaten to tear her apart. "Instead of passing outward, beyond the confines of the visible world, the hero goes inward, to be born again" (Campbell 91).

"Fascination, bewitchment, 'loss of soul' possession, etc. are obviously phenomena of the dissociation and suppression of consciousness caused by unconscious contents. Even civilized man is not yet entirely free of the darkness of primeval times" (Jung, "Conscience, Unconscious, and Individuation" 281). Ancient mythology and ritual has people losing their souls and shamans facilitating rituals to force the soul's return. Only through acknowledging what lies hidden in the self, facing and accepting it, can the heroine move on.

In the underworld, Charon saves her and reveals that almost two decades before, Hades vanished and all the souls were left stranded in torment. Diana escapes the underworld and returns to her friends with a new quest. For the others' freedom, she bravely surrenders herself to the Dark Man who killed her mother. Once a mass murderer, he swore himself to the forces of darkness that needed him as their vicious tool. He notes that he will kill her with her mother's lasso. "Her lost daughter, maddened by grief, consumed by the need for revenge, caught in the same loop that killed her mother ... reaching across the grave to trap you as she was trapped. A circle without an end ... except in death" (part 1). Indeed, the loop of violence and revenge keeps cycling, becoming far more than metaphor.

Diana binds them both in a magical fire, accepting the cycle of revenge and even embracing it. In this moment, the inner voice of protection, her mother Hippolyta, appears. She takes on Diana's battle and urges Diana to release the vengeance and hatred. This Diana does. As the source of inner wisdom, Hippolyta's last words of warning follow her—that the Dark Man was in service to the deadly Morrigan.

The Morrigan, ancient goddess of death and destruction, is the true enemy. She is a three-part goddess made of Greek Enyo, Celtic Anann, and Roman Bellona. "They feed on the horror of war, grow fat on the blood of the innocent dead" (part 1). In fact, the Morrigan's true mission is to corrupt Diana by sending monsters to torment her. She says, "She is in the full flower of vengeance now, her hatred for her enemies smothering the innocence at her core. With each new atrocity we heap upon her, she inches one step closer to us."

It is she who has remade Diana into this alternate version, isolated from her certainty and destiny. The incarnation of truth and justice has lost her friends and family, the clarity of her mission. Nonetheless hints linger, in memories of past lives, in dolls and drawings she sees of classic Wonder Woman. The Morrigan's monsters—a resurrected Cheetah, Giganta and Artemis—nearly kill Diana and leave her dying in an alley. However, she dreams. A vision of Dr. Psycho (like the monsters, another staple villain from classic *Wonder Woman*) tells Diana: "You have been cut off from your source. You feel it now, don't you? The immoral force aligned against you has eroded your heritage, left you cornered in this one bleak, feeble present. So it can eliminate *hope* from existence once and for all" (part 2). After stranding her, the Morrigan has slaughtered her allies and friends one by one to make her despair.

Dr. Psycho tells her of alternate lives when she was an African chieftain, a blind leader, pirate's daughter and more. Surrounded by visions of past selves, Diana hears the words "create yourself" but "repeated in some unearthly harmony." She swims and flies through the ocean and wind, realizing they're part of herself. When she reaches the Olympian Temple, still surrounded by copies of herself, she declares, "I choose this" (part 1). Only after does she wake.

She awakens in the hospital with a nurse named Diana Prince caring for her. Symbolically she has dragged her own self back from death. Clotho, the Fate, sends her a starry blue blanket, giving her direction. When Diana goes to see her, Clotho tells her she was always meant to be the embodiment of an ideal, thus her struggle between vengeance and mercy has a greater meaning for all the world. When her enemy destroyed her, Clotho wove her a second life beneath the first—this one.

Jung notes, "When a summit of life is reached, when the bud unfolds and from the lesser the greater emerges, then as Nietzsche says, 'One Becomes Two' and the greater figure, which one always was but remained invisible, appears to the lesser personality with the force of a revelation" (Jung, "Concerning Rebirth," 121). Having journeyed deep into her unconscious in the dream and seizing a heroic destiny, she is ready to reclaim her Wonder Woman side at last.

Other heroines also face themselves—the shadowy voices from within or dark copies of who they might have been. Each time, facing this alternate self with courage and not shying away from the hard questions helps the heroine to grow. In "The She-Hulk Story that's a Riff on *A Christmas Carol*," Jennifer is visited by the ghosts of her past, present, and future to explore her choices. Her present-day self interrogates her on the witness stand. "Isn't it true that you're unable to see all the good you've done? That you can only focus on your shortcomings?" She-Hulk punches her interrogator and insists her life has value. Her past ghost is a monster and future ghost is evil, emphasizing her shadows—dark possibilities that exist within (David).

In *Batgirl of Burnside*, Barbara and the cop she's dating start receiving calls from "Barbara Gordon," who threatens to spill all her secrets. Barbara begins to worry she's hallucinating. However, a chance comment from Black Canary reminds her that her algorithm containing her brain scan was stolen. The computer her says, "My anger became more acute, I was only a ghost—she still wore my body. She could feel and touch what I could not. I needed to take it *back*." This disabled, disembodied force echoes wheelchair Barbara, watching Batgirls grow and train but feeling unable to join them. Barbara beats the algorithm by facing it and reminding it that she used to be angry but now she's made friends and grown past all the darkness. She then uses computer logic to tell the algorithm it is the criminal here and must destroy itself. Fully understanding and accepting her adversary gives her the tools to banish it (Stewart).

In her own epic, Diana forgives the Keres and they are freed from their torment of others. She then befriends her three traditional enemies, showing them who they are with the lasso of truth. By loving all these metaphorical parts of herself, she frees them and makes them a strengthening part of her core self, wielding them rather than fighting against them.

However, there is more going on. "The Morrigan are *toys*," Clotho reveals. "A greater evil manipulates them and *despises* you. The spirit of *vengeance*, of unreasoning *punishment*, seeks to scour the earth of all life" (part 2). Only Diana can challenge her. Though scattered and torn from her past, she remains earth's last possible champion. This enemy is Nemesis, who draws strength from despair as Diana does from hope. She appears, however, as Wonder Woman herself, in traditional garb. Facing her, Diana thinks, "This is the woman I was meant to be. This is my other self, my *true* self" (part 2).

Nemesis surrounds them with the ghosts of Diana's family and friends who hang around her like shadows of guilt. "You don't even know who you are," Wonder Woman taunts Diana. "To bring my retribution to man's world, I must scour it of its valor" (part 2). She is "justice unalloyed with pity." In medusalike armor, she kills alt-world Superman, taunting him for being weak and letting tyrants like herself take over. She glories in the fury and "the purest anger I've ever felt in my heart," as she says. Brandishing a murderous skull-decorated sword, she is far stronger than Diana. However, Diana sees this other self is "dark" and "lonely."

"The witch stands for a *matrenatura* or the original 'matriarchal' state of the unconscious, indicating a psychic constitution in which the unconscious is opposed only by a feeble and still-dependent consciousness" (Jung, "The Phenomenology of the Spirit in Fairytales" 233). It's a powerful force, but one of decay and evil, that destroys innocence because it can. It's Medea or Snow White's stepmother, preying on children and trying to halt the lifecycle before she herself ages into obscurity. Queen Gedren, who orders the heroine raped and her family slaughtered in the film *Red Sonja*. In this tradition, the villain of *The Strange Adventures of Rangergirl* is the Outlaw—an ancient god embodying the spirit of savagery in the Old West. He savagely kills bystanders just to bring chaos and tells Marzi, "I'll flatten your house. All the houses. Return everything to dirt and dust and nothing" (Pratt 228).

"Now is the Hour of the Harrowing when we shall feed on nations! Their rich treasures will be ours. Ideas, resources, fashions, technologies. We will slake our thirst on the juices of their accomplishments," the witch queen of *Seven Soldiers of Victory* cries. Still, she does not see her ravaging as evil, adding, "Humankind has ever preyed upon the earth, and we are only the last link in that chain—we super-survivor organisms" (*Seven Soldiers* 4). Her morality is murky as she notes, "In your bright world, there is black, and yes there is white, we've seen it. But here, in the red smoke, there are only subtle shades, deceptive appearances. Words that slither."

On Wonder Woman's 1987 reboot, she battles Decay—the force of destruction itself (Peréz, *Gods and Mortals*). Supergirl faces a similar creature in her own volume two return: When researcher Daniel Pendergast observes modern society as "decay," he turns into a hulking creature and begins to melt and consume matter (Kupperberg). In both tales, the superheroines, life incarnate, stop the terror and restore life's balance.

Nemesis controls Wonder Woman now, all but the small human sliver who has grown and fought for humanity through this story arc. This Wonder Woman has been the one to kill Diana's loved ones, to make her crave vengeance and destruction. Diana, however, protests that making her mortal made her care for the people of earth. Love is her one strength. As Schmidt defines the Moment of Truth stage of the heroine's journey, "She has found her strength and goes for her goal with gusto. She has awakened and sees the whole world differently. She faces her worst fear and still remains compassionate and complete" (*Story Structure* 88). Filled with compassion even for the dark murderer she could have become, Diana describes the fulfillment she's found on earth—then takes the thread of her own life Clotho gave her and binds herself to the other Diana. In this moment, she accepts the rage of her buried shadow side and incorporates it into herself. Individuation means becoming an individual "a separate indivisible unity or 'whole'" (Jung "Conscience, Unconscious, and Individuation" 275). This is the hero or heroine's true mythic quest.

Campbell describes facing this shadow as "destruction of the world that we have built and in which we live, and of ourselves within it; but then a wonderful reconstruction, of the bolder, cleaner, more spacious, and fully human life" (8). Now reintegrated, the new Wonder Woman pummels Nemesis, insisting, "The trials you thought would *weaken* me have only made me stronger!" Nemesis tries to make the new Diana her champion, with her armor and snake helmet spreading over her, but Diana breaks the skull sword. "This is not a reality I will accept. And this is not the woman I choose to be," she declares. She wakes on Themyscira, her mother, friends, and original identity restored. Nonetheless, she tells her mother this journey through alternate forms of herself has shown her that new realities always come and replace the old ones and that another shift is coming. Her mother reminds her that she remains Wonder Woman, true to herself through every incarnation. "Whereas the masculine hero "gets the girl" or an external reward in the end, the feminine hero gets something internal, a reward of spirit that continues on. Just because she has attained her goal and changed her life doesn't mean society has hanged right along with her. There will still be tyrants, ogres, racists and sexists in the world; she's just more equipped to deal with those obstacles now" (Schmidt, *Story Structure Architect* 240). It's not quite right to say the woman doesn't get a treasure because she is the treasure. More accurately, the damsel she rescues is the innocent side of the self, represented sometimes by a child or friend. In either case, her true reward is reconciliation with the stronger darker part of herself and its reintegration. "The treasure the hero claims at the completion of the journey is herself. Discovering herself—her whole and authentic self— she finds that her entire world is transformed. She partakes of the eternal, enjoys a new sense of trust in her perceptions about the world, and thus rejoices over her journey to the underworld" (Pearson and Pope 223).

Return to Life: Danger Girl (IDW Comics, 2014)

> The underworld ... is the realm of the unconscious, of magic, of desires made manifest with a wish, and, yes, of death. This is the woman's traditional sphere of power—the world of emotion and spirit. Yet too long a stay will transform princess to death-crone, Kore to Persephone. Thus the heroine must finally ascend, richer for her underworld knowledge, and yet committed to the world of life [Frankel, *Girl to Goddess* 176].

Resurrection may be literal or metaphorical—a change in "the general conditions of existence" (Jung, "Concerning Rebirth" 114). Yet when the heroine has visited the realm of death or even been touched by it, she must tear herself from its insidious temptation and return. *Danger Girl: Mayday* by Andy Hartnell and John Royle illuminates this struggle clearly.

Off the coast of Hammer Island, weapons smugglers pull the unconscious Danger Girl from the water and the crew promptly take cyanide in terror. The curious April Mayday wonders who she is, but on seeing the power she has over the men, is eager to revive her. April represents the helpful voice within, the innocent savior and best friend when the heroine needs aid.

Danger Girl wakes in terror, trapped in the violence of the past that nearly killed her. Panicking, she snatches a sword and smashes her way through the ice, crying, "Why is this happening to me? Where am I?" Of course, her memory is gone.

The return to life is traumatic, and memory loss is common in fiction, emphasizing a burden of the past that is too great for the heroine to bear. Later, Danger Girl has mostly recovered on an island of only women in Bhutan, South Asia, where she gazes up at the stars and wonders. This is a safe haven, a sheltered place to prepare for what comes next. As one of the women explains, "Any visions from her past are haunting ... cryptic. She can remember nothing."

Her rescuer, however, has researched and discovered her identity, determined to restore Danger Girl to herself. April, a self-described "borderline obsessive fan" tells her she was a skilled assassin for a covert agency. However, Danger Girl turned on her team, betraying them to work for the evil organization called the Hammer to help bring about the Fourth Reich. At last, she was killed, or so it appeared. Upon learning this, Danger Girl protests: "If what you say is true—that I was a traitor—well then … you never should have revived me. *I deserved to die*." She's still clinging to the underworld, uncertain how to live again or whether she wants to.

As she faces the darkest, most horrific aspects of her past, April speaks as her inner voice of hope and reassurance. In fact, April retorts that her new friend deserves a second chance, and that Hammer manipulated her into joining them. "What I'm offering *now* is a shot at *redemption*," April concludes.

If the traumatized heroine accepts the invitation, she can rejoin her old world and find a new role in it through trusting others. She is a different person now, with new lessons to impart. "When she removes the masks and shares her heroic vision through her actions and words, the hero is usually successful at finding or creating a sense of community with other people. Confident in herself, she is able to share her new understanding both of herself and of her world around her" (Pearson and Pope 243).

Nonetheless, Danger Girl returns to the island's priestess and protests, "Whoever they thought I was … whatever kind of *warrior* they were hoping to resurrect…. *I'm not her anymore*." She wishes to remain nameless among the sisters, but the priestess tells her she must move forward and heal her mind, whatever the pain this will cost. She fights through a vision of Abbey Chase, the "good girl" who looks startlingly like her and recruited her to the team, then killed her when Danger Girl betrayed them all. The dark, raging side of her personality cannot yet incorporate the pleasant daylight self she's left behind.

To spark her memory, April recreates her uniform and weapons. As Danger Girl tries them on in a splash page, April tells her, "Your name is Natalia Kassle. And you're the most dangerous woman who ever lived. Twice." Here she returns the other woman's identity to her and thus leads her back to life in the outside world.

On the spot, April recruits her to stop a Russian agent who's stolen canisters of deadly gas. Reluctantly, Danger Girl goes. On her new, ill-fitting team, Natalia feels disconcerted, uninformed, when the others fail to tell her of a nearby train and possible escape route for the villain. In turn, her new team are startled by her violence, berating her for killing the enemy.

A similar level of violence and rage fills Sara Lance on *Arrow*. The episode

"League of Assassins" (205) follows Sara's journey. First she's a frivolous delin-quent, yachting and falling into bed with her sister's boyfriend, lying to her dad that she's at college. She tumbles into the water in a storm and nearly drowns, only to awaken and see a canary beside her. After this near-death, she's rescued by the creepy Dr. Ivo, whose gang of slavers takes her onto his ship. Eventually, she becomes one of them. On returning home, she protects her father and sister but refuses to see them, certain they won't forgive her for becoming a killer. She adds: "There were things that I did; things that I had to do to survive. Things that there's no forgiveness for." Green Arrow can only tell her, "Well, that's the thing about forgiveness—you can't get it until you ask for it." In season three, she dies more literally, returning in season four as a sav-age animal. Her sister has brought her back through the Lazarus Pit, but her family fear that her soul is gone forever. She slowly learns to talk again, but to their horror, she's addicted to killing and finds herself drawn to death. While the heroines of children's fantasy come back moody or withdrawn, superheroes often become mass murderers, as Dark Phoenix does, and have a harder, more adult road to redemption.

This extreme disassociation is common as the old way of life no longer fits the experienced character. On her own return from death, Hellcat returns to her small town origin only to find that it's been turned into a theme park. Now it's a destination resort for people who want to experience small town America straight from the source. The "Patsy Walker Experience" there is like a fictional movie of her life, reminding her who she can never be again. As she tours the place and sees the recreated soda shop and merry-go-round, it all reminds her how much she's grown beyond it. These feelings are exacerbated when she walks around, but feels a strange sense of foreboding, even panic. As it turns out, she's right to feel disconnected, as all her old friends are possessed by demons. Salem's Seven attack, and Hellcat is relieved to have enemies she can actually pummel. She finally decides to stay in her hometown, enroll at Centerville U and "try to pick up the threads of my old life," as she thinks (Bus-iek, *Avengers Annual* 2000).

Natalia, too, faces her former partner, a black-haired girl with a dragon tattoo, and admits that dying has left her "feeling a bit ... disturbed." To her shock, April and her team have been using her to steal the deadly explosives and Danger Girl's equilibrium is shattered once more. Fighting April and deter-mined to destroy both of them, Danger Girl sets off an explosion on the train, and they both find themselves clinging by their fingers. "You wanted to find out who you are? *Now's your chance,*" April smirks.

"I know who I am! I'm the person who's going to kill you!" Danger Girl retorts. All is lost in confusion, save her passion.

When April reveals that sweet, youthful Abbey Chase is still on the train, bound and trapped, she adds that Danger Girl doesn't have time to deal with them both and that "It's what you do *now* that will *define who you are.*" Her choice is clear: revenge or an innocent life. But more particularly, Abbey is her conscience, the side of her that pledged to be a Danger Girl and strive for justice ... and killed Natalia when she lost her way. Saving her means saving this lingering aspect of herself, lost but not unattainable. Danger Girl saves Abbey in secret and sets out to track down all the criminals of the Hammer Empire, correcting her past mistakes. Finally, Danger Girl ends the series in a tight black skin-baring outfit in contrast with Abbey's white t-shirt and jeans. Though she's still haunted by darkness, she has her mission of redemption.

Just as most superheroines have a death descent, they find the road back difficult. DC's One Year Later storyline emphasizes this rocky road for many characters. Green Lantern's daughter Jade's return to life is accompanied by chaos. She falls to earth in a fragment of the all-powerful Starheart and adds, "When I came back to life ... that shook the bulk of the Starheart that was still out there in space" (Robinson, *JLA: Dark Things*). Now all the world's magic and elemental powers are chaotic and unnatural—she will need to bring a balance with the help of the JLA. The chaos without is a metaphor for turmoil within as all the universe matches the heroine's pain.

Twice in her life, after a family car crash where she lost her parents, then after getting beat up by the Avengers while under the Purple Man's influence, Jessica Jones falls into a coma. Each time she awakens stronger, harder, with a new identity and new priorities (Bendis, *Alias*). The new her is no longer sweet superhero Jewel, but as a PI, she still saves lives.

In an even more dramatic shock, Psylocke returns from death ... only to see her body lying on a slab. "That's my former body on that table .... I should feel something .... I should have some connection," she thinks. This moment echoes the traditional disassociation of trying to rejoin one's old life. Psylocke has memories but as she thinks, "I can't match myself up with who that other person is, the person I was before the insanity began." She finds herself craving death, or at least "something to fight. Something to hurt." However, upon defeating an old enemy, Matsu'o Tsurayaba, she spares him. When he begs for death, she discovers Wolverine has been dismantling him piece by piece. She fights her friend and ally, then finally surrenders to him, embracing death as a pathway to hope and forgiveness. Wolverine stands down, but tells her, "Someday the two of us are gonna have a talk about this death wish you've developed." He walks away, letting her kill Matsu'o Tsurayaba with honor and finally put the feud to rest. Death and surrender bring healing. By learning mercy from the beginning, she manages to incorporate part of her old kind, daylight self into the pain-filled darkness. At last, Psylocke decides, "Now I know who I am," and refuses to let anyone take her mind from her again (Yost, *Psylocke*).

In fact, the road back is possible. It simply requires small efforts, practice and torment. On *Powers*, Zora (Logan Browning) is the newest hottest super-heroine, with the ability to manipulate light. In the final episode of season one, she faces down the worst super-criminal of the city and is badly injured. Detective Christian Walker, the main character, comes to see her in the hospital. He agrees that she screwed up. "You went in there alone, when you knew you shouldn't, because you had something to prove.... So now what? Now you own it. People will still respect you if you own it. You're still you. Don't walk away from that." As she lies there, she begins to channel light, feebly at first, and smiles as it grows.

Wolverine offers a similar rough mentorship of Jubilee, after the young heroine becomes a vampire. As she hurls herself around her cell in rage, Wolverine convinces the X-Men to release her and hauls her off to the gloom of Siberia. There he rejects her self-pity and drags her out to the wilderness to test her abilities. When she smashes his motorcycle and makes him walk back, he doesn't hold a grudge, though he does destroy the barstool she's on with a swish of his claws. In danger of death at the story's climax, Jubilee decorporealizes, emphasizing that with her new powers, she's discovered extraordinary new abilities ... she just needed trust and friendship to help her get there.

Finishing the Battle: "Call Her Savage" (Short Story, 2010)

Marjorie M. Liu's short story "Call Her Savage" is distinctive for its protagonist: not only a woman, but a half–Cherokee and far older than most superheroines. It is set in an alternate history where a Chinese Empire has colonized North America—the world has mysterious crystals created by ancient crystal skulls that power their technology ... and occasionally citizens.

Marshal Namid MacNamara, a living legend, bears the burden of her own renown as everyone tells ghost stories of her exploits and gazes at her with widened eyes. Some time back, she retreated to the mountains to retire in peace ... until once more she was summoned back to battle. "The crew would talk. Best to make a good impression, what little was left," she thinks as they haul her gasping from the sea to a submarine that will take her from New China (our United States) to China in a war against the British. Though the boys of the crew stare in awe, she thinks, "She did not feel fearsome. Just wet, and cold, and tired. A woman old enough to be their mother, black silvered braids dripping seawater against skin the color of sun-dried walnuts" (309). Her entire appearance, from her shining badge to the revolver on her hip, is meant to please her worshipful audience. Her true power, in fact, comes from within as she takes up the responsibility of war once again. Liu defines a strong heroine saying, "It has nothing to do with physical strength, that's for sure. Muscles are fleeting. Bodies give out. But integrity, honor? The confidence to be oneself, to follow one's heart? The compassionate drive to help others, even at great risk? That's strength" (Bernal). "The hero may have to be brought back from his supernatural adventure by assistance from without. That is to say, the world may have to come and get him. For the bliss of the deep abode is not lightly abandoned in favor of the self-scattering of the wakened state.... Society is jealous of those who remain away from it, and will come knocking at the door" (Campbell 207). Namid MacNamara was happy to pass on the responsibility to others, but in Campbellian style, is dragged back. Captain Shao escorts her to her mission and tells her, "They all said you were dead.... No one could imagine another reason for you to abandon your responsibilities. Not when you had so much power. Not when someone like you was needed in the rebuilding" (316).

She responds with the words "I was a killer" and "My time was over" (316–317). A new era goes on now, one that doesn't need her. However, as she goes ashore, she hears voices of the past whispering, "We will die if you cannot turn them back. All of us, our freedom, lost. Shut your heart to the blood, shut your ears to the screams. You were born to no other purpose. You are exceptional only in death" (323). She keeps walking. All of society, past and present, is placing their hopes on her, a crushing weight that she had left behind, only to re-assume. Liu adds that "the archetype of the superhero will always stay the same: a person for whom great power comes great responsibility" (Bernal).

Of course, the power of death can fill the heroine with true strength as well as wisdom. In battle, Donna Troy learns she is the team's best hope. As a Blue Lantern tells them, "One of you has endured so much, more than any of us. And that person has been changed from everything they've gone through. Death. Resurrection. The death of loved ones." He adds that the energy of her soul has grown brighter from her trials. When she enters the battle, she fights with this new energy. After, she insists this combat has "burned up all of my own darkness," leaving her clean and healed (Robinson, *The Rise of Eclipso*).

When she finds the traitorous empress, her husband dead, Namid leaves her flailing in the ocean. After all she has experienced, all the carnage she has faced, she is judge, jury, and executioner in truth. The death crone, a force of terror and judgment for those ordinary people who revere her. Upon sending the boy soldiers of Captain Shao's ship to safety, she battles the Juggernauts, people augmented through the crystal skulls as she is. They are, to her, "monsters made: rapists and murderers, freed from prisons to be fed to the skull engineers and their experiments" (326). By pitting herself against these destroyers, she safeguards the lives of the young soldiers.

"The female journey includes the relation between the individual and the group. The hero goes through her own awakening and comes out willing to accept help from others. She can't be betrayed again because she has her own strength and self-realization that can't be taken away from her" (Schmidt, 45 *Master Characters* 232). Namid, as soldier and matriarch, puts her trust in the team even as she battles to defend them. Preserver of the next generation is one of the roles given to the mature woman who has faced death, especially the crone, more of a grandmother and guide than a literal mother. Saving the young people is an end in itself, though it can also be a path to greater wisdom.

In the *Heroes* episode "Cold Snap" (320), the mystery hero known as Rebel frees Tracy Strauss from her prison. After making a bargain for her own life, she leads her captors to him, only to discover he is her young nephew, Micah Sanders. On finding she's betrayed him, he's horrified. As they run, he reminds her of youthful idealism, challenging her to be more like the public political face she presents to the world. As he represents her innocence, she fights to safeguard this metaphorical part of herself. When they're cornered, Tracy tells Micah to set off the sprinkler system. He escapes, while she freezes everyone with her abilities as mystical choral music echoes. She too is frozen, then her assailant Danko shoots her and she shatters. Nonetheless, she returns from death in a later episode more powerful, with the ability to manipulate and transform into water. Now virtually invincible, she hunts and kills the agents who once imprisoned her.

Often this symbolizes the more powerful woman, strong with the universe and deep magic, saving the younger, weaker male hero. Conan the Barbarian's movie girlfriend Valeria (Sandahl Bergman) dies but becomes a mighty Valkyrie. As he fights in a losing battle, she returns to fight beside him, nodding to her earlier promise, "If I were dead and you were still fighting for life, I'd come back from the darkness. Back from the pit of hell to fight at your side."

The old woman as supreme warrior has largely vanished from storytelling.

Once, the whole Goddess reflected this entire spectrum: kindly and terrible, as the awesome Mother Earth. However, the conquering patriarchy split her into her three aspects. Although patriarchal cultures could find a place for the virgin and mother energies, they could find no such use for the old woman. The young virgin could represent stored energy, and she maintained some sacredness for that reason. The mother transmitted energy, gave it to others. The old woman, however, only had knowledge; this could be threatening, and was increasingly trivialized, as well as actually truncated in its development by the discriminating patriarchy. Thus the crone was frequently divorced from the pantheon. Just as Athena, Artemis, Demeter, and Hera were respected goddesses, the Furies and their mistress Hecate were relegated to the underworld, demonized, discarded [Frankel, *From Girl to Goddess* 174].

Nonetheless, she appears in some myths as the bloodthirsty lion goddess Sekhmet of Egypt, as Scáthach, ancient trainer of the Irish warrior Cuchulain. Other young heroes seek the ancient crone, as Monster Slayer of the Navajo entreats Spider Woman's guidance or Oedipus faces the Delphic Oracle and the Sphinx. Kali is the death-destroyer goddess, but her ravages lead to growth and new life at the end of things.

In this tradition, Namid hides the young soldiers in the mountains. She is the warrior; thus she must battle the monsters to protect their youthful idealism, and symbolically her own. At last she is shot and falls, to awaken disarmed by a fire. There she finds Maude, once her greatest friend and Captain Shao's sister. "But the years had not been kind. Everything had dulled. Golden skin looked like stone. Her hair was gray" (328). Maude reveals that while Namid was exposed to the crystals before birth, Maude chose it deliberately because "I was only human and wanted what you had." (328). She betrayed them all and led the enemy to them, then spent ten years awaiting Namid's revenge. "Why didn't you ever come looking?" she asks. "I expected it. I expected you at every corner, with your hands at my throat." However Namid had spent the years avoiding the final confrontation. "Namid had hated the redcoats, but she had been unprepared to hate a friend" (329). Returning to the fight has forced her to take on this final battle, the one she's most dreaded, the ultimate test. She kills Maud and ends it, then Captain Shao appears. As he notes, "I understand now why you left" (330), the two head off to one final battle. She promises him that one more time, she can be what their people need.

The heroine often retreats to a paradise or idyll—safety in the woods, comfort in the home of a friend. However, this is only a temporary respite or delay in all that her duty demands. Eventually she must take up her neglected quest. In this case, Maude is Namid's dark shadow, the subversion of herself created out of jealousy, the one it is her responsibility to defeat. The boy soldiers cannot face the death crone's dark magic—only another death crone can do it. As Liu describes characters who face their personal demons:

I like them because they never give up. It's not in their natures to just sit down and take the world as it is—even if that's what they want, more than anything else. Tired, battered, but never broken—these characters, even in their darkest moments, find the strength to take one more step. Just one. And it's that step, and the courage and grit behind it that lets them overcome all the terrible obstacles in their lives. Namid, in "Call Her Savage"—as well as Maxine Kiss, whose story continues in my latest book, *A Wild Light*—are both particularly determined to fight against the odds, not just to save their own lives, but to save those they love [Bernal].

Finding Balance: Supergirl (DC Comics, 1996)

The sweet Supergirl got an extreme makeover in 1996 thanks to Peter David and Gary Frank. In *Supergirl* volume four #1, the Matrix, an alt-world artificial copy of Supergirl, finds a dying woman named Linda Danvers and merges with her. "I was empty and ... and I needed to learn," says a dazed Matrix in Linda's body. Before their joining, Matrix was incomplete. She explains, "I've had human sensibilities layered onto me ... like a brightly painted statue. But that's ... all I am. For I have looked into my eyes. And I've finally realized.... I've never seen anything looking back." Matrix was an unpopular character as she was a lifeless construct, conning Supergirl's family and friends into sympathy. Now, at last, Matrix had gotten a life ... though it was someone else's.

However, Linda herself is a tormented character. Brought up to be the perfect good girl, she ran away from her controlling parents policeman Fred Danvers and his wife Sylvia and found herself naïve girlfriend to a charming murderer. Buzz Aldrin (no relation) tells her religion is hypocrisy that's created to keep people down and lures her to his den of vices, an evil place that the good girl finds terribly tempting. "And so begins Linda's initiation into a darker world. A world which grows darker still as the years pass, as new secrets were revealed. Gradually, the macabre becomes commonplace." She becomes accomplice to his killing, until he finally murders her in turn, slashing her with his dagger to release a demon into the world.

Supergirl-Matrix flies to the rescue and battles the cultists, fusing with the dying Linda. Suddenly the lost, subjugated human girl gains extraordinary powers and a new mission of redemption, while the disconnected Matrix has a human life. They remain two people with two sets of memories, trapped in a single body. As they alternate sharing it, one is taller and blonde while the other is shorter and brunette. This total disassociation between the two halves emphasizes the superheroine's trauma at her return from death, terribly changed: Each half has new abilities she is unable to process.

They are each tormented by glimpses of past memory as well as the demon Chakat, trapped outside the world and still trying to enter. Matrix is also haunted from within as she realizes, "Linda was no victim. Not at first. She was ... she was part of it. An accomplice, a willing witness. She was *evil.*" This is the survivor guilt and doubt of life post-ordeal, wondering if she deserves to exist and struggling to reconcile the inner darkness. Supergirl has visions of Buzz taunting her, plotting to corrupt saintly Supergirl as he corrupted Linda. Battling these forces, Supergirl challenges and defeats Chakat, musing to herself, "What we see on our world is merely the tip of an iceberg ... barely hinting at a war that crosses realities." Enlightenment is dawning and Supergirl hopes that Linda was possibly chosen to be saved for a higher purpose. If this is true, Supergirl can be her savior.

During a terrible eclipse, Buzz unleashes the talisman called the Heart of Darkness. The people of Leesburg, maddened into doing monstrous acts, call on Supergirl to be their savior. She thinks, "They want answers I cannot give them ... miracles I cannot perform." Her powers are unreliable as she's redefined herself mentally and the powers haven't caught up. Gorilla Grodd, wielding the Heart of Darkness, challenges her. At last, Supergirl falls under the spell and turns bestial and violent. He tells her, "I am within you. I give you the strength for hatred, and the resolution to take that which is denied you." At the same time she's trying to reconcile merging with Linda Danvers, struggling to accept the darkness she now knows lies within. Though he calls her "a human female in a Supergirl suit," she's starting to adjust.

Summoning her courage, she denies the darkness within humanity, calling him "just a thing" and "a museum piece with attitude." At that moment, the sun comes out. As Grodd roars, "None can defeat the beast," Supergirl's blast dislodges a giant icicle, which impales Grodd. "I didn't intend it ... but perhaps someone else *did,*" she thinks. As she pledges service to a higher power, it comes to her aid. She is slowly turning from construct and victim into superhero and beyond that ... into goddess.

Through her journey, she is urged on by Linda's mother, the Reverend's assistant and a devout believer, while Ma Kent, a skeptic, provides a counterpoint. In her new calling, Supergirl/Linda becomes a messenger for higher truths. She visits a televangelist eager to exploit the masses as she struggles with memories of the cult and tries to make him a laughingstock. She also speaks with the boy Wally, always watching her from a distance, who appears to be the embodiment of God. She tells the blob monster Chemo it can't aspire to a better life, but feels terribly guilty when her lie makes it depart in anguish— she has saved human lives but at the cost of a higher truth. This conflict is part of the superhero's life especially, deciding how to help the greatest number of people but mourning the sacrifices that result. Estés explains, "Because of this dual nature, or double-tasking, the great work before us is to learn to understand what around and about us and what within us must live, and what must die.

Our work is to apprehend the timing of both; to allow what must die to die, and what must live to live" (33).

Supergirl is still conflicted, thinking, "I had thought to redeem a life gone wrong ... bring light to a darkened soul and benefit us both. But perhaps that's *arrogant*. As if I'm so perfect that making Linda more like me automatically brings her soul closer to heaven. Instead ... we might both be dragged, kicking and screaming, in the other direction."

As the first collection concludes, Linda's mother sets her daughter up on a blind date ... with Buzz. At dinner (with Linda's parents joining them, constraining Linda from crushing Buzz to death as she wishes), Buzz suggests that he is sent by the devil while Supergirl is an angel, born to combat him. As he adds, "Whereas the demon, believe it or not, had a streak of *good* he fought to overcome ... so did the glowing angel require a streak of *evil*." Each is multifaceted, Supergirl with the murderer's accomplice Linda inside her, and Buzz with a sliver of human decency remaining.

Buzz sends the demon Tempus Fugit to appear to kill the Danvers parents, and Supergirl battles him, despairing and considering the world a "cosmic joke." From deep within, however, Linda tells Supergirl, "You're the most human creature I've ever met." At last, guided by her human side, Supergirl understands and refuses to kill him in revenge. She thus resists corruption, and Buzz's controllers from the underworld reclaim him. Nobly, she even tries to save him, but he vanishes into the pit.

Though her two sides are approaching concord, Supergirl is still confused about her purpose. The boy Wally tells her at last that the Matrix's original sacrifice for Linda has made her an earth-born angel, in this case, the angel of fire. "An earth-born angel is believed to be created under very specific circumstances, when one person selflessly sacrifices himself or herself for the purpose of saving one who is, in every way, beyond hope" (David, *Supergirl* #26). This total generosity leads to great enlightenment.

In the crisis known as Day of Judgment, with hell literally freezing over, Supergirl meets Zauriel, a "real" angel. He tells her that with practice, she will be able to detect the presence of God (David, *Supergirl* #38). Though he doubts her strength, she fights past all the chiding male voices in her head and manifests fiery bat wings, burning with power. With a flaming sword, but also the shining star spirit of human belief (and even the power of movies!) she defeats the demon. After, Zauriel tells her that as an earth-born angel, rather than one from the heavens, she is drawn from shechina (the female aspect of God) in the earth. Supergirl/Linda is thus a part of God, not simply his creation. However, no human can contain the power of an earth-born forever, for the incredible power begins to corrupt them. The bat wings are an early indicator (David, *Supergirl* #38).

As Supergirl continues her adventures, she faces many shadows, from present and past angels to terrible demons. Linda and Supergirl are torn apart and Linda, with half her powers remaining, quests for her lost angel side in a perfect metaphor for the quest to enlightenment.

At last in *Many Happy Returns* (*Supergirl* #75–80), the conclusion of Peter David's run, Linda, the new Supergirl, discovers a rocketship containing young Kara Zor-El from the Pre-Crisis timeline. As she thinks: "This is insane. This is simply *not* happening. A girl doesn't just show up wearing a Supergirl costume and announce she's from Krypton. Superman's the only survivor of Krypton! I know that! Everybody knows that! And God, she's so peppy and innocent she makes Mary Marvel look like Hannibal Lecter!" Linda eventually becomes the other girl's mentor and comes to care for her. When Kara must be sent back to fulfill her destiny and die in the Crisis, Linda goes in her place, demonstrating she understands the meaning of true nobility after her time as Supergirl. There, Pre-Crisis Superman admits he loves her, and they wed and have a daughter, Ariella. This is marriage of hearts and minds, producing the magical child, symbolic of perfect bliss, magic, and balance.

♦♦♦ 7 ♦♦♦

Motherhood
and Enlightenment

Becoming Supermom: Invisible Woman (Marvel Comics, 1968–1973)

Sue Storm was the first of the Silver Age Superheroes, as Stan Lee invented *The Fantastic Four*, followed by *Thor, The Incredible Hulk, Spider-Man, X-Men,* and *The Avengers*. Three of these are male heroes with supportive girlfriends and three are team comics that each began with one woman and a small group of men. As Lee specifically planned, Sue was not Lois Lane, the ignorant love interest fooled by a pair of glasses, but a superhero in her own right and equal to Reed Richards. Or at least this was the intent. Her superpowers and effectiveness on the team told a rather different story:

"As is the case with the other fantastics, her particular superpower is an extension of her salient premutation qualities. Sue Storm was a distinctly—almost pathologically—shy and retiring girl" (Robinson 88–89). Her invisibility power is less than intimidating as is her typical title of "Invisible Girl," which makes her sound like a wallflower at a middle school dance. She is so shy in her first appearances, that invited to a government dinner in their honor, Sue whimpers, "Oh, Reed, I—I'm afraid to go! I'm not used to meeting all those important people! I'm liable to get so flustered that before I know it, I might vanish in front of their eyes? If that ever happened, I'd simply die of embarrassment!" (Lee, *Fantastic Four* #7).

On the cover of *Fantastic Four* #1, she's seen struggling in a monster's fist, unlike her more dynamic male teammates. As Sue Storm serves coffee, jokes about the clothing bills she's run up, attends a fashion show, and faints dead away, Trina Robbins observes: "Unlike the insecurities and self-doubts that afflicted male heroes, and which encouraged the reader's identification and evoked admiration when the heroes overcame them, Sue Storm's … flaws were almost a caricature of Victorian notions of the feminine, an invisible woman who faints when she tries to exert herself" (*The Great Women Superheroes* 114).

Stuller comments that she "perfectly illustrates the tensions inherent in cultural responses to the second wave of feminism. She was a contradiction— a superwoman whose power is the ability to be unseen" (*Ink-Stained Amazons* 33). She drifts through the comics as their least effective member. In "A Visit with the Fantastic Four," Reed and his friends engage in a spirited defense of Sue and her place on the team, refuting fans' complaints that she contributes very little. However, dwelling on how she inspires them as Lincoln's mother did Lincoln hardly makes a superheroic case.

Brown describes superhero moms as most often giving up their children for career, giving up superheroing, putting the child at risk because the heroics keep going, or becoming a monstrous figure altogether through abandoning or neglecting the child ("Supermoms" 189). "Supermoms are more likely to be portrayed as falling short as mothers and/or restricting their husbands from fulfilling their heroic needs. Outside of comics examples like Elasti-Girl from the animated film *The Incredibles* and Stephanie Powell, the work-a-holic mother from the television programme *No Ordinary Family*, are characters who illustrate negative depictions of would be supermoms" (Brown, "Supermoms" 189).

Talia al Ghul trains Damien, her son by Batman, to be a deadly assassin, but finally puts a bounty on his head and gets him killed by her own agent (whom she cloned from Damien!). X-Man Rahne abandons her frightening son as does Mystique. Black Widow has a stillborn child in *The Name of the Rose* and is sterile in the films. The Kryptonian Ursa abuses and tortures her son while in the Phantom Zone, before Lois and Clark save and adopt him. Lady Shiva, Catwoman, and Black Canary also fulfill these tropes. Good moms who stay with superheroing and raise the babies include Jessica Jones, Spider-Woman, and Sue Storm, but these are rare exceptions.

If the superheroines are to remain perpetual "girls" like Batgirl and Supergirl or virgins like Wonder Woman, they can't grow into the next stage of life. In token of this, many stories avoid showing pregnancy, preferring to have the heroines keep their tight spandex.

Children may pop from alternate universes (it happened to Power Girl) or the heroine may have a superfast pregnancy (it happened to the Invisible Woman) or they may be alluded to only in flashbacks (it happened to the Black Widow). In a recent storyline the entire DC Universe skipped ahead a full year so that Catwoman suddenly had a baby but the series managed to avoid illustrating her as anything but her usual flawlessly fit and sexy feline fatale [Brown, "Supermoms" 189].

Sue is one of the few to fall pregnant, however briefly, in Lee and Kirby's *Fantastic Four Annual* #6 (1968). Her pregnancy threatens her life thanks to "a manifestation of cosmic impulses" from her original accident. Her men charge into the Negative Zone to defeat Annihilus (the supreme tyrant force) and find anything that will save Sue's life. When Annihilus proclaims, "Here in my hands I hold the most precious item in all the world. My life-giving life-prolonging cosmic control rod! And not man nor beast shall ever wrest it from me," he sets the conflict in motion.

Reed realizes this is the device Sue needs, while Annihilus proposes to destroy them all, only for his own amusement. Their battle with aggressive superpowers (over a Freudian rod of power) forms most of the plot while Sue labors behind closed doors. After they succeed, the monster roars, "My cosmic control rod is gone!! They have stolen my most precious possession. Without it, immortality can never be mine! Without it, I will die, like any lesser being." His patriarchal power has been stolen to give to Sue—though this experiment deprives her of her own power, cementing her new role of traditional wife and mother.

The team return to the normal universe to spend several panels in the waiting room. Upon hearing Sue has had a healthy son, the men go in and see baby Franklin while Sue can barely manage a word. Sue has achieved motherhood, though the more active plot goes straight to the men of the team.

Though she loves her son Franklin, motherhood is not completely a happy ending for Sue. "In spite of (or perhaps because of) her superpowers, Sue suffers multiple pregnancy problems that include miscarriages and stillbirths and premature births and fetal anomalies (such as mutant births) and postpartum depression" (Packer 170). Having powers is thus shown to damage her, emphasizing problematically that powers are truly meant for the story's men.

> In the heroine's journey, this struggle to emerge from death alive with a healthy child is reflected in individual quests, questing in the Otherworld for a stolen child, or, as a less traumatic substitute, a stolen sibling. For mother goddesses, the stolen child is echoed in the mother's own lost fertility: the land turns barren or animals refuse to mate. Only with the restoration of the mother's status can spring return [Frankel, *From Girl to Goddess* 249].

Superheroes, already rescuers, spend a great deal of time saving sidekicks, friends, youthful bystanders, and other stand-ins for their own children. When they have biological children of their own, this is the most terrifying threat of all, one worse than their own safety.

Sue's newfound motherhood offers her a specifically feminine plot arc— the mama bear who defends her helpless child against all threats. In *Fantastic Four* #130 (1973), Sue enters the fortress of the Sandman to retrieve her kidnapped child. Discovered, she cries, "Since there's no longer any use in my remaining invisible, I'll end this charade and fight force directly with force!" She reappears, child in her arms. She adds, "But I warn you—if you harm one hair on my baby's head...." She uses a mental blast to disintegrate the Sandman, emphasizing the power of her will against more powerful-seeming but actually crumbling enemies.

Despite her new strength, Reed rescues Sue and tells her to keep out of the fighting, adding, "I won't let the mother of my child...." After the battle, he yells at her for being "a woman who can't put first things first" to spend all her time with the baby instead of going off saving the world as he does. She in turn is insulted that she's no longer his battle partner and equal. She leaves, taking their son, "Until you can treat me as an equal," as he retorts, "Good! At least that way, our son will get a little attention!" The 70s were a complex time as women left for the workplace but still struggled with the question of who would raise the children. Sue fights beside the other heroes and also rescues her child, but is chastised for doing so in a superhero world not completely ready to welcome women.

"Because the birth of the self is analogous to physical childbirth, the female hero often experiences the birth of a child and the emergence of her heroic nature as complementary events" (Pearson and Pope 198). As a mother, Sue finds her powers expanding as she finds creative new uses for them. She gains more authority and begins choosing paths for herself. In fact, "her role and powers increased with time and become most interesting in the period from 1968 on" (Robinson 89). This helps because she has so much more to accomplish now.

The term "supermom" emphasizes how many skills the mother needs—doctor, teacher, chef, crafter, chauffer, and much more. Today, while being the full-time caregiver for multiple children, many women also balance a career. Superheroing becomes a metaphor for this as the literal needs of the world clash with the cries of the child, who also needs full time attention.

Ruth Diaz's novel *The Superheroes Union: Dynama* starts with TJ Gutierrez (Dynama) saving the world, only to get a call that her daughter has the flu and needs to be picked up from school. With her supervillain husband escaped from prison, the single mom can't cope and hires a nanny named Annmarie (herself the powerless child of superheroes). Annmarie grows to love the children as well as their mother (with whom she begins a steamy relationship based in love and comfort as well as romance). At the novel's climax, she faces down the children's father, telling him that an accident of genetics doesn't mean he can kidnap the children he's never met. "She was sick to death of so-called parents who weren't worth the name traumatizing their kids and claiming they had some kind of divine right." As she adds, "I've only known them for four days, and they're more my kids than they are yours." When he levitates their car then suddenly loses control, Annmarie's power activates, creating a gleaming forcefield around the children she's so determined to protect. Thus her love gives her mama bear powers of her own. She ends the story telling TJ, "You're not alone anymore, hon. You don't have to stop being super just because you're also Mama.... Go be Dynama. Go save the world."

In *X-Men: The End*, Rogue and Emma Frost each have their children stolen. Emma, injured, asks Rogue to take her powers and use them to rescue the children.

EMMA: Be *my* hero, Rogue
ROGUE: You sure?
EMMA: Must I beg?
ROGUE: My power isn't selective, Emma. Ah borrow your abilities *and* your psyche. Your memories. Your secrets.
EMMA: For *your* children, Anna, would you do *less*? [Claremont].

Rogue charges in, glowing with the power of both mothers, and saves the children.

Elastigirl in *The Incredibles* is a true Supermom, separating her squabbling children with elastic arms. When their plane is crashing, she snatches them both and bundles them in her own body. As they tumble toward the ocean, she transforms herself into a parachute. She then transforms herself into a boat, instructing her speedster son to kick and provide the motor. She's endlessly resilient and versatile as she leads her children on a rescue mission to save their father. Sue must demonstrate the same abilities as she blends superpowers with daily life.

Sue has a second child, Valeria, though her origin is filled with surprises. Created by Chris Claremont for *Fantastic Four* #15 (1999), she emphasizes a new way of thinking. Valeria von Doom suddenly materializes in the Fantastic Four's headquarters, professing to be from the future, the daughter of Doctor Doom and Sue. As she aids them on missions, she reveals alternate paths Sue's life might have taken. When the timelines are unwoven and rewoven, Sue falls pregnant with Valeria. However, in a new twist, the cosmic rays make the delivery dangerous, and only Victor von Doom himself can help (*Fantastic Four* #54). Sue allows Von Doom to aid her and then name the child, acknowledging that evil has a power in the world as much as goodness. In fact, Valeria is the next to go on a shadow descent in place of her mother, as she becomes Von Doom's confidante, and in a time of crisis, sides with him over her mother.

In this way, the magical daughter can be a catalyst, provoking the heroine with knowledge of unseen opportunities. The daughter is a smaller copy, one that cannot be easily disassociated from the mother. Having a child often signals the completion of the journey, though it can also be a start. Fairytales end with marriage and children. Superhero comics mirror this, with special issues celebrating weddings. Other times, the start of a series like Spider-Woman 2016 can have the heroine falling pregnant and giving birth, embarking on a new lifestage with its challenges. Motherhood means a new state of being with new challenges but also mental and spiritual rewards. "While to a woman the birth of the divine son signifies a renewal and deification of her animus-spirit aspect, the birth of the divine daughter represents a still more central process, relevant to the woman's self and wholeness" (Frankel, *From Girl to Goddess* 249).

Sometimes the mothers identify too closely with the daughters. In *Grace Randolph's Supurbia*, a parody that sees the superheroes aging and settling down, Batu, one of the Daughters of Bright Moon, marries an anthropologist. She names her daughter Sarangerel, meaning "moonlight" in Mongolian, and trains her constantly, though her powers refuse to surface. Her son, she ignores and tells he must go to his father for training. "He is male and will not be gifted with the powers of my tribe," she decides dismissively. When he reveals himself as super, she calls him an "abomination," rejecting him brutally.

Sue's children each develop superpowers of their own, requiring a special kind of parenting. "For a mother to happily raise a child who is slightly or largely different in psyche and soul needs from that of the mainstream culture, she must have a start on some heroic qualities herself" to stand up for her child and for what she believes (Estés 176).

In one later comic, Sue Storm reveals her fears of motherhood, magnified by her superheroism: "Will the kid be normal? Will the kid survive being the kid of two superheroes? Will I make it through the delivery? Will a supervillain kidnap my child to get revenge on me for stopping a bank robbery ten years ago? Will my damaged DNA codes create a mutation in my child that his biology can't support?" (Bendis, *The Pulse* #11). She adds that she most fears screwing them up, but not because of any superpowers.

While children seem like a vulnerability in superhero fiction, constantly kidnapped and used as leverage, they can be a source of great strength or even a weapon. In Mary Anne Mohanraj's "Sanctuary," Kavitha and Michael have the magical child Isai, a shapechanger who can grow to a Garuda form with eagle head and massive 12-foot wings. While half-Black, half Korean Michael is ordinary, Kavitha has her own South Asian powers of the kundalini, the serpent energies of the inner chakra. Dancing, she channels this power into beautiful energy shapes like golden flowers. "The energy poured out in a bright shimmering blaze, surrounding her. Surrounding *Natya*—that's who she was now, the living embodiment of an ancient dance. Thousands of years of art, funneling down to this one moment" (Mohanraj 367). When her child is kidnapped, she plans to go in and hurl her kundalini spheres onto everyone, enclosing them all in harmless bubbles to await the police. She's a pacifist, noncombatant dancer after all.

> It was a great plan, and it went right out the window the moment she burst into McGurk's and saw the guns lifting up, raising to the ceiling, taking aim at her little girl.
> Her peaceful intentions shattered. She flung one arm out and a blazing crimson wave of force sprang out with it, throwing three men against a wall, knocking them out. Maybe she hurt some of them, maybe killed some of them. Natya couldn't care less [Mohanraj 376–377].

She battles the thugs and protects her daughter "in a cascade of coruscating fields of light" with forcefields, energy blasts, and a set of golden stairs (Mohanraj 379). In turn, the child defends the mother: She takes her Garuda form, larger than her parents have ever seen as she "shrieked her rage and hurled herself up into the sky. Chasing the birds that had hurt her mommy" (Mohanraj 379). Thus she acts as an extension of her mother to protect her.

"As the mother cares for the infant, she comes to understand the nature of the body, with its vulnerabilities and desires, and thus reaches a greater understanding of the self. As she nurtures, she learns" (Frankel, *From Girl to Goddess* 249–250). *Spider-Woman* has a baby through artificial insemination in 2015, changing the stories of evil alien pregnancies and reclaiming agency. She delivers in an alien space hospital, then when Skrull rebels attack, seeking a young prince, Spider Woman insists that her doctor close her up so she can go save the day. Though in tremendous pain, she leaps into action—supermom indeed. Back home on earth, as a montage panel sees her feeding, cleaning, and comforting her baby, she begins to despair at the amount she must do. Nonetheless, she resolves to keep both of her worlds going. "Motherhood isn't just something that happened to me. It's a decision I made," she explains, and adds that to be her best self, she must keep being Spider-Woman (Hopeless, *Spider-Woman* #5). "What better day to save than one that ends with holding a baby," she concludes (Hopeless, *Spider-Woman* #4).

In *Spider-Woman* #8, the heroine fields a call about where her baby's summer pajamas are, all while fighting a tentacle creature. Issue #5 sees her attacked by Razorback while walking her baby in a stroller. She pummels Razorback in fury, yelling, "There's a baby right here, you #$!* moron! My baby!" She adds between punches, "And if you think your stupid getaway is more important than the life of my child then you're about to think again," then demands an apology. She also realizes that she can't return to heroism and risk her life without worrying about orphaning her baby. She adds to Captain Marvel, "Tell me it's not selfish to do what we do when there's a baby at home who needs his mother." She adds, "It's like someone ripped off a callus. Now I have to feel everyone. All the time." She finally resolves to return to her investigative work, as even a half hour of it made her feel like herself again. "I decided to raise that child by myself ... and if I want to do that, and do it right.... I need to be me. Spider-Woman is who I am" (Hopeless). This way she can be a role model to her child, as others mentored her.

Evil Child: Ms. Marvel (Marvel Comics, 1980–1981)

Avengers #200 begins with Ms. Marvel in labor—with a mysterious full term pregnancy that's only lasted three days! She gives birth painlessly in Avengers Tower. When the Wasp gushes over the baby and calls her lucky, Carol bursts out, "I've been used! That isn't my baby. I don't even know who the father is" (Shooter). From the beginning, Marcus has already taken over Carol's entire body in the most intimate way possible, feeding off her from within the womb. Carol spends the story with her body used against her will, and then hiding in her room in a depressed state, then unconscious. As such she's a passive pawn in the story of Marcus versus the Avengers.

As the child grows at an accelerated rate, Carol refuses to have anything to do with him. Soon little Marcus resembles a five-year-old but speaks like a professor and requests electronics to tinker with. Though Carol expects to hate her son, when she finally goes to see him, she discovers he's already an adult and feels "an unexplainable and undeniable attraction." She finds she can't walk out of the room, so desperate are her feelings for him. He soon admits he forced these feelings on her through a machine, much like a date rape drug. When she won't agree to leave earth with him forever, he knocks her out with an energy pulse, adding, "Forgive me, my love."

When confronted by the team, Marcus reveals the story of his existence: "I wasn't really going to kill them. I only wanted them to kill me.... I couldn't bear the thought of going back, of living like I have ever since my father left.... Ever since the last days of Immortus...." This master of time and ruler of limbo found a wife from earth who was dying in a shipwreck and wooed her "through a combination of gratitude and the subtle manipulation of my father's ingenious machines." He raised Marcus in a pocket of Limbo, but after he and his bride were pulled from the pocket, Marcus resolved to be reborn on earth and decided Ms. Marvel would be "the perfect vessel." He took her to his land, where he courted her with figures from history as well as "a subtle boost from Immortus's machines." He impregnated her with himself then wiped her memory and sent her home. Now he longs for her to join him in Limbo.

Of course, this storyline's metaphor is brutal. As critic Carol A. Strickland reacts:

> Here Ms. Marvel had been kidnapped, held for "weeks," according to the narrative provided by Marcus himself, and not been won over even though Marcus had done the A-B-C of stereotypical male-mindset romance: given her nice clothes, serenaded her with history's best musicians. Why, I bet he even gave her candy and flowers. At no time is love or respect—not even "like"—mentioned. But apparently she hadn't been won over because he says, "with a boost from Immortus' [mind] machines" (which he had access to), Ms. Marvel finally became his (and we may think of this being the truly possessive use of the word). At which point he impregnated her using non-technical techniques without her knowledge of what he was truly doing. Okay, class, anyone see anything wrong with this?

As the comic continues, it gets even worse. Overwhelmed by her artificial feelings for him (confusingly, both maternal and romantic ones), Ms. Marvel resolves to go with Marcus as she feels "closer to [him] than I've felt to anyone in a long, long time." She accompanies him into space, with the Avengers hoping blandly and unconvincingly "that she lives happily ever after." This plot twist was used as a sudden exit for the character.

In the issue, Jim Shooter and his male staff "slaughtered Marvel's symbol of modern women, Ms. Marvel. They presented her as a victim of rape who enjoyed the process, and even wound up swooning over her rapist and joining him of her 'free' will" (Strickland). At the time and after, this pat departure combined with an incestuous, sudden love story, bothered many readers and Marvel uncomfortably sidelined the character afterwards. As Strickland adds: "It should not just be the women who raise the roof over such a story. It should be everyone. Isn't everyone entitled to respect as a human being? Shouldn't they be against something that so self-consciously seeks to destroy that respect and degrade women in general by destroying the symbol of womankind?"

The evil child fantasy is a fundamental fear of the pregnant heroine, uncertain what will be born. When the alien swarm known as the Brood attack, they turn the X-Men into incubators. Kitty Pryde notes: "We've all been murdered! We all carry queen embryos inside us! When they hatch, we'll turn into sleezoids!" (Claremont, *Uncanny X-Men* #166). This monstrous pregnancy that will kill the host (male or female), is a deep-seated example of body-horror. Following this, in *Astonishing X-Men: Torn*, Kitty has a child with Colossus in a telepathically controlled hallucination. Though she loves the baby and defends it with all her powers, it's actually the monstrous remains of evil child Cassandra Nova, who is manipulating her. Kitty too is used for her body and devastated after.

A truly creepy fantasy is the literally evil child—the vampire or undead baby come to haunt the grieving mother. In *Blackest Night: Black Lantern Corps,*

Donna Troy's dead baby and husband Terry return and attack her. "Maybe you will be a better mother this time around," Terry tells her as she cries with horror, though she manages to defeat them. This is her deepest misery, dragged from the depth of her guilt and anguish for her to face as the baby bites her, infecting her and turning her into another Black Lantern. Saturn Girl of the Legion of Super-Heroes has twins, one good, and one who's stolen by Darkseid and transformed into the mindless monster Validus to destroy his parents (Levitz). In her own comic, the swordswoman Katana's enemy resembles a little girl. However, her ally Sickle tells her, "Don't think of her as human. She's centuries old. She's killed thousands. Legend has it that Mona Shard stopped growing of her own free will. She knew it gave her an *edge* to look like a child" (Nocenti, *The New 52: Katana*). The heroine must then struggle to kill the tiny warrior.

On *Agents of S.H.I.E.L.D.*, warrior Melinda May is transformed forever after a moment of past trauma, revisited in the episode "Melinda" (217). She's sent in to rescue a team of agents, and through it all, struggles to protect the little girl taken hostage. In a painful twist, she discovers the villainess holding them hostage is not Eva Belyakov, but her 12-year-old daughter Katya. Her mother has turned her Inhuman ahead of schedule, and the girl has become a monster, feeding on the pain of others. "Let them go. We can fix you. We can help," Melinda pleads, but the creepy child replies, "Give me your pain. I need a new mother. I'll take your pain." Melinda is forced to shoot her. Afterward, S.H.I.E.L.D. rewards her, but Melinda is deeply traumatized, and retires from field duty, divorcing her husband soon after.

Certainly, Ms. Marvel's tale of evil-child-as-adult-rapist is especially disturbing. However, the heroine returns from space some time later. In Claremont's *Avengers Annual* #10 (1981), Spider-Woman Jessica Drew grabs her as she falls from the Golden Gate Bridge, unconscious. In the hospital, she's revealed to be Carol Danvers, but with amnesia after the trauma of her return. Spider-Woman calls Professor Xavier, who scans Danvers and confirms, "Her conscious mind has been completely erased." He discovers Rogue was the one to attack her, and as part of this plot, Rogue keeps Ms. Marvel's powers. Now Carol has lost everything—memories and superpowers as well as her sexual autonomy.

With their fight finally over, the Avengers reunite with Carol at Professor X's school. "Hi Carol, how are you doing?" Beast asks neutrally.

She replies, "I'll never regain all my memories," and adds that Professor X has helped her a great deal. Nonetheless, there is no quick fix here—only permanent damage.

As Hawkeye asks about Marcus, she replies distantly that he's dead. Iron Man offers consolation, but Carol lashes out at him furiously. When she weeps,

Thor, another clumsily well-meaning teammate, tells her: "Be not ashamed of thy womanly tears, Carol. Thou hast lost the one thou didst love."

She screams "NO!!" as she slaps Thor in the face. "I didn't love Marcus! I *never* loved Marcus! Don't any of you realize what happened months ago, what Marcus *did* to me?" She explains that she never left of her own free will, adding:

> He was a sad, pathetic creature—possessing the abilities of a god, the body of a man, the emotional maturity of a child. In Limbo, his every wish was granted. He saw me, desired me. He used me as a means to escape from Limbo to Earth and when that plan failed, he took me back with him. You saw it happen, Hawkeye—you, Iron Man and Thor. You heard his story. Marcus said that Immortus' devices could bend me to his will, but he didn't want me that way. He set out to win my love and finally, as he told you 'with a subtle boost from Immortus' machines' he succeeded. But for all his brilliance, Marcus was careless. He made a fatal error in his calculations. When I … 'gave birth' … to him, his body shifted fractionally out of sync with the rhythm of life in Limbo. Where before, time passes normally for him, it now passed at a fantastically accelerated rate. In days after our return, he aged years. By the time he realized what was happening, he was too old and senile to deal with it. Within a week he was dust. Free of his mind-control, I learned enough of Immortus' secrets to allow me to transport myself home. The rest you know.

Scarlet Witch asks why she didn't return to Avengers Mansion, and Carol explains how furious she was.

> There I was, pregnant by an unknown source, running through a nine-month term literally overnight—confused, terrified, shaken to the core of my being as a hero, a person, a woman. I turned to you for help, and I got jokes. The Wasp thought it was great, and the Beast offered to play teddy bear. Your concerns were for the baby, not for how it came to be—nor of the cost to me of that conception. You took everything Marcus said at face value. You didn't question, you didn't doubt. You simply let me go with a wave and a bouncy Bon Voyage. That was your mistake for which I paid the price. My mistake was trusting you. After a trauma like mine, it's easy to wallow in bitterness and self-pity. But both grief and … guilt … have to be faced, dealt with, exorcised. There's more … there *has* to be more … to being heroes than simply defeating villains. You have a role, a purpose far greater than yourselves. You have to set examples, lead the way. You represent what we *should* be, what we dream of becoming, not what we are. You screwed up, Avengers. That's human. What is also human is the ability to learn from those mistakes. To grow. To mature. If you do that … even a little … then perhaps what I went through will have a positive meaning. It's your choice.

Carol then asserts that she will continue to pick up the pieces of her life and survive.

This is a more emotionally real reaction than Carol happily moving in with the overgrown child who impregnated her and made him love her against her will. Here, Claremont seeks to heal the jarring unlikeliness of Ms. Marvel's speedy exit and provide a more emotionally valid chance for her to lash out, expressing her own rage and that of her readers.

After trauma such as this, a time of recovery is needed. With her super-powers gone, Carol joins the X-Men as their ace pilot and intelligence operative. Later she turns to alcoholism to cope with her lingering despair and lack of control. Eventually she recovers and continues as one of the Avengers.

Unfortunately the disturbing pregnancies with the heroine as helpless victim, often of incest, occur across comic book storylines. Donna Troy, Raven, X-Men's Haven, and especially Power Girl join this lineup. The goddess's pregnancy generally symbolizes divine completion. Some superhero stories, however, discard feminine power and leave the heroine only a womb to be used as the superheroes and monsters desire.

Losing the Child: Scarlet Witch (Marvel Comics, 1986–2012)

After wedding the Vision, Scarlet Witch decides to settle down and have a normal family—including children. Thus she uses her magical and ability-altering powers to absorb the energy of the Salem's Seven (a battle in which she'd lost mentor Miss Harkness) and infuse it with her and her husband's essences. In *Vision and the Scarlet Witch* vol. 2, #12 (1986), Scarlet Witch gives birth to twin boys, Tommy and William (named for some of the Vision's influences). The loving relatives, from the Avengers to Quicksilver and even Magneto come together. All seems perfect.

However, Wanda feels a symbolic disassociation, which (as with all comics) manifests itself through events. "Birth and death are indelibly linked. Birthing represents a separation between mother and child, a severing of the bond that has spent nine months growing. After birth, they will exist as two organisms, separate in their skins" (Frankel, *Girl to Goddess* 37). After this, Wanda's world begins to fall away piece by piece. The Vision is dismantled and replaced with an emotionless version (obviously symbolizing the husband's sudden alienation). Several successive governesses tell Wanda her babies are disappearing and she ignores all their efforts to convince her. She's kidnapped by Immortus, adding to her stress. She begins to feel she can't handle any of this—not the marriage, and especially, not the children.

Miss Harkness returns from apparent death (as she points out, witches are too powerful to be stopped by such matters). It is Miss Harkness who makes Wanda face the truth that the twins are not normal and that "when you're not thinking about them, they disappear" (Byrne, *Avengers West Coast* #51). Scarlet Witch is in denial, but Miss Harkness pushes her, reminding her, "In the danger-fraught life you lead as an Avenger, there are many times when your concentration must turn wholly to the task of survival." As a multifaceted person with a career and outside life, she must separate herself from her children at times. Now the universe is responding by making them disappear utterly.

The evil Master Pandemonium suddenly takes the children. "Imagine, if you can, my joy upon discovering Thomas and William are pieces of my stolen soul!" Mephisto chortles, and uses Scarlet Witch's strength, now invested in her children, against her (Byrne, *Avengers West Coast* #52). The questing heroine must learn that too much pity will destroy her. Back on Earth, Agatha Harkness explains to several supporting characters that the Scarlet Witch had "children" through wish fulfillment—they are one step above being illusions.

While Witch is too blinded by love and worry to understand what is happening, Miss Harkness acts as her higher reasoning. She also sends the Human Torch to their aid. After the team win their battle, Mephisto reveals that the children have returned to his own essence. When the Avengers return to earth with an unconscious Wanda, Agatha erases all memories of the children from Wanda's mind to help her deal with a grief too all-encompassing to handle (Byrne, *Avengers West Coast* #52). Once again, the mentor is sheltering the heroine, helping her branch out in other ways instead of losing herself wholly in motherhood. Miss Harkness is training Wanda in becoming the Destroyer and independent crone as well as the all-nurturing, all-sacrificing mother.

Sparking the events of *Avengers Disassembled*, Scarlet Witch remembers her children and goes on a fury-filled rampage in *Avengers* #500. Taken over by her chaos magic, her friends do likewise. The Vision and She-Hulk go mad and attack their friends. Tony Stark has a violent outburst at the UN and is forced to resign as secretary of defense. Avengers Mansion explodes, killing Ant-Man, Scott Lang. The Kree invade. As it turns out, this is all caused by Scarlet Witch projecting her pain outward and catching them in it.

The Avengers find Scarlet Witch living in a dream world with illusions of her husband and sons. When they break through it, she goes mad, and fights them until Stephen Strange shuts her down and Magneto carries her off. After, Sergeant Fury discovers Miss Harkness's decomposing body. It's quite likely Miss Harkness really did die at the stake, and since then has been an illusion of Scarlet Witch's projection, helping guide her to the truth (Bendis, *Avengers* #503). Unfortunately, Miss Harkness's hard truths and steadying influence are not enough to save Wanda from descending into despair.

Partnering with Doctor Doom, she channels all the Nexus energy into herself to restore her children. "It possessed Wanda and transformed her into an entity with the reality-shaping ability of a god" (Heinberg, *Avengers: The Children's Crusade*). With this power, she goes on to destroy the world's mutants in the House of M storyline. In the mythic tradition, her sons' loss makes her an unstoppable force of sorrow. Unfortunately, her comic arc portrays her as an emotional agent of chaos unable to control her own powers, tying this to her motherhood. Thus it suggests women are unfit to be superheroes.

> That her maternal desires are portrayed as selfish, destructive, psychotic, delusional, and ultimately villainous, is indicative of the genre's conflicting message about femininity—not just in terms of sexuality but more specifically regarding issues of maternity. The depiction of maternity in recent superhero comics reveals and reinforces cultural fears about female bodies as unstable and uncontrollable agents of abjection [Brown, "Supermoms" 185].

In *Young Avengers*, her sons are reborn and begin questing for their mother. Tommy and Billy have contrasting powers—Billy has the Witch's and Tommy, his uncle Quicksilver's (Heinberg, *Young Avengers: Family Matters*). In *Avengers: The Children's Crusade*, Scarlet Witch meets the boys at last when Billy (Wiccan) storms Doctor Doom's castle to rescue her (Heinberg). After a great battle between the Avengers and Doom's forces, Quicksilver and Magneto both try to claim Wanda. However, she tells them, "I've only ever been Pietro's twin, Magneto's daughter, the Vision's wife. It's time for me to take responsibility for myself and be there for my children." Once more, she leaves the bonds of family to reassess and reprioritize, though she goes to the children that were sacrificed long before.

Sue Storm, too, must face the temporary loss of her child, also through the grandmother-mentor Miss Harkness. The magically-powered nanny becomes Annihilus's puppet: She kidnaps Franklin and his mother and brings him to the Negative Zone in *Fantastic Four* #141. Annihilus plans to free Franklin "from the bonds of his humanity" to restore his power. Reed staggers upon seeing his newly empowered son, thinking, "Galaxies ... endless stars.... The universe spread at his feet. They're like toys to him. A child's toys." When they get home, Franklin's eyes are glowing and "his energies are building to critical mass!" If they don't stop he'll explode in a blast of psychic force strong enough to kill everything on earth. Using the weapon he created from the Negative Zone, Reed shuts down Franklin's mind, to Sue's horror. "He was your son, Reed. If you've never loved me ... you should have loved him," she cries. She leaves him, breaking off ties with his sanctimonious decision-making.

At the wedding of Crystal and Quicksilver, a time of symbolic union and healing, their child is restored. In *Fantastic Four* #150, Ultron attacks. A comatose Franklin's immensely powerful brain is wakened by the psychic assault and he strikes back at Ultron. Their son is healed, the parents hug and cry. All is well again.

The psychology here is mythic and complex. Reed is revealed as the Bluebeard of the story, shutting off their child like flicking a switch. However, the child himself is quite symbolic. The holy marriage produces the Divine Child, an archetype with indescribable power. (As time goes on, Franklin reveals mutant powers of reality-warping, telepathy, precognition, and more.) Since Franklin also has "the ability to create life"—Robinson notes, "Sue Richards, Invisible Woman and Superwoman, is also, at least sometimes, the mother of God!" (113).

After giving birth, the mother finds her needs and identity subsumed into those of her child. Thus, the child will sap the mother's life simply through his existence. If Sue or Wanda is the Mother of God, she will have to witness her child's sacrifice, just like Mary.

> The mother has become too identified with the son. His accomplishments are her pride, his needs are hers, to such a point that she cannot separate them into two entities. At the heart, this is egoism—she cannot say no to him because she cannot say no to herself. Her inability to accept that she cannot fix others' lives is the true inability to accept unmendable flaws in herself.
>
> While this seems natural, the child must learn limits and learn to separate himself from the mother if he wishes to grow to independence. The mother, too, must surrender the child to move beyond the stage where she sacrifices too much, helplessly mothering all around her. The mother defines herself by her child's perception of her—she fears being too harsh with him, or spoiling him, or being less than perfect. With each perceived error, she sees herself reflected in the baby's eyes as lacking the goddess-like perfection that baby expects from her. This substitute for her true childself is actually stifling her—she defines herself by her child's values, not her own [Frankel, *From Girl to Goddess* 251–252].

This time without her child and husband allows the heroine to reassess priorities and remember life as a single superhero, to rediscover herself as more than mother and wife. The death of the child gives the heroine a chance to be independent and also reveals what she's capable of without the ties of motherhood. Bereft of her twin sons in the comics, the Scarlet Witch gains the power to drag her brother back from death. In *Avengers: Age of Ultron*, when her brother (a substitute child) dies before her, she turns into a powerhouse of fury.

For another example, at the season one finale of *Witchblade*, Sara sees the wicked patriarch kill her partner and her young sidekick. Earlier in the episode, Ian Nottingham, cloned from her grandmother and thus a close relative, sacrifices himself to save her. Sara witnesses these deaths, and then slays Ian's evil replacement, as she has nothing left to lose. Channeling all her inborn power, she reverses time, unraveling their deaths and the entire year, back to her partner's death in the first episode. Only the sacrifice of her friends allows her to accomplish this.

In *Angela: Asgard's Assassin: Priceless*, Angela saves a baby and has him raised with knowledge of his debt to her. However, when she calls in the debt and he refuses her, she kills him and appoints another to take his place as king. She leaves sadly, cradling her adopted child, all too aware that debts must always be paid to balance the universe. This is the true consequence of the heroine's quest.

Death Crone: Claire Voyant (Timely Comics, 1940–1942)

After facing her own death and losing her loved ones, the heroine may become a shadow of herself, or even an antihero of horror. *Mystic Comics* #4 (1940) introduces Claire Voyant as "the strangest, most terrifying character in action picture magazines—the Black Widow. You've heard of the black widow spider—that evil creature whose bite spells doom. Now start the adventures of another black widow—a human tool of Satan whose very touch means death." She only appeared five times from Timely Comics (Marvel's first incarnation), all written by George Kapitan.

She's first introduced as "Madame Claire Voyant—spirit medium," leading séances. Her job as a bridge between life and death is already part of her character before her superpowered awakening. Voyant announces to the mother, brother and sister who are employing her, "I promise to make your husband appear at nine o'clock—but you must remain quiet." James, the brother, skeptically tells his sister, "I think she's a fake."

At the stroke of nine, a red glow fills the room and Claire transforms into her alter-ego. Gone is her slinky green dress. Her new black leotard incorporates a black widow spider on the front, giving her her name decades before Natasha Romanoff. Her blonde hair blows back. With dark shadows around her eyes, her face bones stand out until her face resembles a skull and she appears the ultimate bad girl, sexy and vicious.

The Widow Wagler insults her, telling Claire, "I came here for a séance, not for a lesson in witchcraft!" Claire starts to retort, but "a strange power takes hold of her—the power of evil!" Satan appears before her (nude, which was daring for Golden Age art) and whispers to her. Under his influence, Claire places his curse on the family. As the Waglers drive home, their car accordingly skids and crashes. The mother and sister die, while James vows revenge with Satan egging him on in turn. James shoots Claire, and she vows revenge as she dies. Satan has engineered this Faustian descent into brutality for both of them, emphasizing how all mortals are pawns in his hands—while this may be a revenge drama, it also emphasizes the hopelessness of the human condition.

Claire tumbles down to hell, where Satan cries, "By the almighty evil I command you to change into the Black Widow!" As she rises dramatically from the flames, he tells her, "You are endowed with supreme power!" The fire swells around her, giving her the power to kill with a single touch. For her first task, he adds, she should "go above and avenge your death in the name of Satan!"

As James grieves his family, the Black Widow appears surrounded by flame. "I warned you I'd be back. I must avenge my death—now!" Pale, James cringes away from her. With the power of the underworld at her back, Claire's rage and death magic make her truly terrifying. "As the Black Widow's hand touches James' brow, a flame blazes forth and—James falls—dead!" The police find his corpse lying there, branded with a black widow spider.

She reports back to Satan and he tells her, "On the upper world are mortal creatures whose hearts are blackened with wickedness and corruption. You, the Black Widow, will bring their souls to me!" Thus she turns from a selfish, evil character (who in fact curses three people to death for insulting her) to an agent of justice and messenger of death. Certainly, they all take their place as Satan's playthings in the story, but through Claire's obedient service, she becomes a powerful force of hell. She is the unrelenting judge, who sees the wickedness or goodness in men's souls and responds with deadly sentencing. She continues as the superheroine and death-dealer Black Widow, empowered by her dark side as much as by her light.

As heroines turn from life-giving mother to sacrificer, they may descend even further and become the crone, a murderer in service to the underworld. Claire is an antihero, a willing servant of Satan. Unremorseful about killing her victims, she mercilessly sends their souls to Hell for eternal torment. She acts from anger at the evildoers, an unusual motivation for a Golden Age heroine. Her costume is tight, with sexually accentuated lines. At the same time, her thin, skull-like face links her with death. Since she prolongs her life by killing the unworthy, there's more than a trace of vampire about her.

Around the world, old women were the shepherds of the soul through life's passages—birth, illness, and death—moments where human limits present themselves. By bringing justice to those who have escaped death, the Black Widow enacts the duty of the mythic crone.

> The Crone is primarily in relationship with All-That-Is (where Virgin is primarily with Self, and Mother is with Other). Achieving the status of Crone means moving back into the great sentience out of which all arises, thus she sees into the elements behind form.... In an altered state of consciousness, with her ego weakened, she can directly connect with the deep unconscious [Frankel, *From Girl to Goddess* 293].

Claire serves the underworld, which gives her deep wisdom and perception. A single glance at a person shows her the evils of their heart. With this, she pronounces sentence. "The crones are mentors or soothsayers, prophesying the triumphs of kings and the downfall of kingdoms" (Frankel, *From Girl to*

Goddess 275). They hold within the forgotten lore of the world, the ways of magic. They are also tricksters, solving riddles and using disguises or even shapechanging to accomplish their aims.

The 40s, an experimental time for the genre, had several crone-heroes, though later decades had almost none. Mother Hubbard appeared in *Scoop Comics* #1–3 (1941–1942). In the first of these, she "commands the power of ancient witchcraft to battle the evils of the present day" in a classic witch costume. Nazi collaborators trap her in an iron maiden, but she uses her magic to rust it open. She then saves the inventor Professor Boggs and his son from torture, preserving the innocent and slaying the wicked. As she explains, "For long, witchcraft has been the power of evil … but I have determined to use it for good … as you are about to see!" (Madden).

A more nuanced heroine, the Spider Widow, has two forms, sweet maiden and "grandmother of terror." The beginning of *Spider Widow* explains, "Beautiful Dianne Grayton wages a private war against crime and un–American activities, by transforming herself from a wealthy debutante into the Spider Widow, the most horrible dispenser of justice at all times!" (Borth). By day she's a pretty girl, but to be a superhero, she wears the mask of an old woman. In this form, she can defy criminals, terrifying men with the fear of the grave and not letting them discount her. Her shapechanging emphasizes women's flexibility—gentle maidens one moment, but always with the death power and anger of the crone dwelling deep within if they choose to unleash it.

In similar fashion, Fantomah, Mystery Woman of the Jungle, (a 1940 character often considered the first superheroine) lives deep in the African jungle, defending it from poachers and criminals. "Fantomah, described as 'the most remarkable woman ever known,' was a beautiful blonde protectress of the jungle. When evil struck, she transformed into a terrifying, skull-faced goddess who judged the guilty with lethal force" (Madrid, *Supergirls* 4). She exemplifies the beautiful and terrible sides of the birth-and-death goddess, transforming from damsel to angel of destruction when meting out terrible justice (Madrid, *Divas* 142).

Claire Voyant had more adventures as her own instrument of vengeance. For her next appearance, the comic "Garvey Lang," Satan orders her to drag the train robber of that name down to hell. She arrives in the midst of his heist and influences one of Garvey's men to try to take control. Garvey shoots him. When Black Widow spooks another of Garvey's men, he shoots that one as well. Any attempts to shoot the Black Widow have no effect, and she simply continues coming, inexorable. She has come full circle, growing from Satan's victim to Satan himself. Finally, Black Widow appears at Garvey's masquerade party gorgeously dressed in something of a nod to Poe's "Masque of the Red Death."

She charms him, so he asks her to doff her mask and kiss him. She reveals a terrifying face, with skulls in place of her pupils, and gives him the death touch.

Her next assignment is munitions salesmen Lewis and Sykes who are selling to Axis and Allied forces alike. Claire disguises herself as a woman seeking a secretarial job, and Lewis interviews her. Alone in the room with him, she sheds her disguise and kills him. Sykes comes in but the Black Widow, like an invulnerable force of vengeance, withstands the corrosive chemical he throws at her. It bounces back and kills him. Her final panel has the Widow gazing directly at the viewer and saying, "I'm not on Earth now, but as soon as I learn of evil which must be met with quick punishment, I shall travel the great distance and return to your people to treat them to—death!"

In *USA* #5, she destroys Murder, Unlimited, owned by contract killer Karl Koodamore. He's placed one of his men in the play "The Duel with Death," in which his man (playing Death) will kill the target with an electrified sword. The minion slays his target, and the Black Widow kills him with her widow's touch, then slays all his other minions. When she finally catches Koodamore, she forces his car off a cliff. The message is clear—he can counterfeit death, but she is the reality.

In her fifth and last Golden Age appearance, she is sent to harvest the soul of Ogor, a charlatan faith healer. When she confronts him, he dies of heart failure. Before returning to hell, however, she uses her powers to regenerate the amputated leg of a young boy Ogor promised to heal. This moment shows her becoming a superheroine in truth, not just a force of deadly justice and entropy. Though her missions of vengeance she has surpassed her missions of cruelty and finally come to save the helpless. Her kindness also emphasizes her knowledge of the body, a common skill of the wisewoman. With her perception, she can bring life as well as death.

In 1994 and 2005, Claire cameoed in the retro miniseries *Marvels*, fighting beside Cap and Bucky against the Nazis. The Black Widow returned in 2008's *The Twelve* by J. Michael Straczynski with art by Chris Weston. This is a story of 12 Golden Age superheroes placed in suspended animation by the Nazis, then released into modern times. The Phantom Reporter, Richard, narrates the story as he falls in love with the mysterious messenger of death.

This time, her origin is rewritten to make her much nobler—when her sister is murdered by an untouchable mobster, Claire stands over her grave and wishes for the power to enact vengeance. Satan comes, and Claire signs over her soul. Her origin still is based in retribution, but this time she's less petty.

As an eternal, unaging goddess, she is less fazed by the new world then the others. She rises above the petty squabbles among the other superheroes, concentrating only on her divine mission. In fact, she promises Satan nothing's changed. "I am your instrument of vengeance. I belong to you and to no one else." Flying through the city at night, she uses her death touch on those who have escaped justice, sometimes tearing them apart with her bare hands. "You will be ageless ... beautiful ... terrifying," Satan promises. She is more an angel of death than a living person. As the Phantom Reporter watches her through the window, her eyes glow red and she appears a vampire in truth. He confronts Claire at last, asking what she's become. She responds, "I strike only against the wicked, Richard. Only against those who deserve death." She turns her face of frightening rage on him and he shrinks back as the devil stares from behind her. "If I wished you harm, I would not have to be invulnerable to bullets. You would simply never have the chance to pull the trigger," she thunders.

She is a figure of terror, as men run from her gaze. Thus she echoes the mythic Medusa, once a beautiful maiden but later a snake-faced hag whose gaze is so terrible it changes men to stone. With gnashing teeth and protruding tongue, Medusa's head on doors and statues functioned as a curse, warning men to keep away. At the same time, Medusa the mythic character exists in the underworld, pregnant but unable to give birth, eternally a victim of the gods. Only at the story's end, when Perseus decapitates her and carries off her head, can she deliver the unborn Pegasus and thus rejoin the cycles of life.

In this model, Claire exists but cannot grow. She rejects the reporter's romantic interest to fulfill her destiny, determined to be Satan's as long as he demands her service. However, when her tasks are done, she returns and they fall in love. The pair end the story finding peace as private investigators—the embodiment of fire and shadow.

As the young women at the army base flee because they find her creepy, Claire befriends others at a goth club, who realize she has true knowledge of what they're playing at. Thus she tutors girls in the mysteries of death. Clearly, she has a touch of grandmother-mentor to her, as well an unearthly wisdom.

> In the war of mother-daughter, the crone has wisely retired, understanding the cycle of life, but in many ways transcending it: Her next stage is ascension to the spirit realm as a divine protector. She carries her disciples through the harvest and respite of life, the dark moon of the self, and ushers them through the death passage transition. The funerary priestess of the soul, she extinguishes the old cycle, and, as midwife, births the new [Frankel, *From Girl to Goddess* 275].

Mistress of Dark and Light: Storm and Illyana (Marvel Comics, 1983–1984)

When Marvel launched the all-new *X-Men* in 1975, among its cast of mutants was Storm, an ethereally beautiful African woman with long white hair. Storm was a survivor, an orphan who once supported herself with thievery. This weather manipulator became one of the X-Men's most popular members, and remains a favorite in the 2000s, particularly through actress Halle Berry's portrayal of the character in the live-action films *X-Men* (2000) and *X2: X-Men United* (2003) [Misiroglu 534].

Storm became famous, as did the Russian hero Colossus (Peter Rasputin). Less well known is Peter's sister, Illyana, who has her own terribly mystical journey.

On her 14th birthday, safely among the X-Men, Illyana remembers her life in Limbo. She was born only eight years previously, but in fact, she spent half of her life in a demonic Limbo, where she was consort to a devil. Now a flashback adventure details her life there. When the X-Men fled the realm, the evil sorcerer Belasco managed to snatch little Illyana from them. The older, alternate Storm who dwelt in Limbo tried to intervene, but couldn't prevent Belasco from binding Illyana's soul to evil and conjuring a bloodstone from her. As Belasco proclaimed, "Illyana will be the perfect vessel through which his masters, the Elder Gods, will gain control of Earth, and then the entire universe!" (Claremont, *X-Men–Magik*).

Ororo sets out on a quest to save Illyana, noting, "How like a child though—insatiably curious, blissfully unafraid, totally trusting of the world and everything in it." Outwardly, the girl is perfectly innocent. Astrally entering Illyana's soul, Ororo finds a dark castle, and Illyana cries, "This is *my* domain, Storm. You enter at your own risk." A cloak of green tendrils springs from her shoulders, suggesting corruption or poison. Storm will have none of it: "Monster, I deny you as I denied your maker! I was born a mutant long before I turned to magic, and the elements of nature are still mine to command!" She calls up a great wind and wakes in the real world, realizing that Belasco is too entwined with the girl—freeing her will free him as well. "But I may be able to teach her to combat it," she concludes. Ororo begins training Illyana in her private garden. "I was grown up and nasty. That wasn't really me, was it?" the girl asks. Ororo cannot answer. The hidden Illyana is her shadow side, one that horrifies Ororo. At the same time, the shadow is the place of buried power and wisdom. Denying it to be a nice girl will cut off Illyana from the superheroine she could be.

In her garden, Ororo dresses all in white like a sage, and the girl in the red of growing maturity and life, blonde hair gleaming. Unfortunately, the color also links her to the sorcerer who dresses the same way. They sit under Ororo's primal tree, her "oasis of life amidst the desolation of limbo—an acorn to nurture and grow." Guiding the girl to lean back, Ororo has her feel the birdsong and the coursing of her own body, then leads her into her astral form. There, she tells Illyana about respecting the natural world and not imposing their wills on it. This is the gentle, kind path, one of passivity and control.

Meanwhile, their half-feline friend Cat (an alternate Kitty Pryde transformed by the demon) comes to Illyana and tells her, "I offer you a way home. There are risks—the road is fraught with peril, you may well perish in the attempt—but at least you'll die clean, free of any sorcerous corruption." If Ororo is Illyana's spiritual protector, Cat is the friend who offers hidden abilities dormant in the young heroine.

Outside Ororo's sanctum, in the tunnels that make up most of Limbo, Illyana and Cat face Peter's corpse: Illyana's brother cannot protect her here. In the savage wilderness, Cat kills a two-headed sabertooth for dinner, embracing her wild instincts. Seeing Cat's feral features when the other heroine takes off her mask, Illyana is frightened. However, Cat not only glories in her savagery but makes Illyana a fur body suit to wear, initiating her into the savage side. Cat forces her to fight and train, though they're interrupted by Ororo, who begs them to return so she can heal Illyana. One is a mentor, the other a fierce sister, and both have valuable skills to offer the young heroine. However, to learn the power of her inner shadow, Illyana will need a different trainer.

Illyana is stretched between good mentor and evil one, in a common pattern of the journey. The heroine has no experience with darkness, no understanding of how to face death, how to be savage as she discovers her sensual, powerful side. In this story, Ororo teaches her to respect life, but not how to kill to protect her people or rule a realm. This she can only learn from Belasco.

When she sees Belasco change Cat into a more animalistic form, Illyana finds herself tempted by the power, as Ororo wouldn't let her play with living things. The good mentor is protecting her innocence, but also keeping her trapped, like Rapunzel in her tower. Illyana, however, is ready for a new stage of growth. Illyana apprentices with Belasco, reveling in her dark side, though her acts of cruelty horrify her on occasion. Learning from his evil, her mutant gift—teleportation—surfaces. Belasco gives her a knife, and Illyana willingly cuts herself and so conjures the second bloodstone.

She schemes to overthrow the demon, but an astral form of Ororo protests that giving in to corruption, even as a hoax, is too dangerous. Illyana sees a vision of young Storm's battle with Belasco and discovers that by killing him while he was helpless, Storm permanently corrupted her soul. Thus, she is bound to him forever. Even the best person in the demon realm has a dark side, and Storm has responded by fleeing from her savagery, trying to keep Illyana pure and good. Illyana must find the balance—the path that is neither too brutal nor too kind.

Cat attacks Storm and Illyana sorrowfully kills her friend. A dying Ororo tells her she must continue the fight and find the key to victory within her own heart and soul. Belasco, however, orders Illyana to conjure the third bloodstone and then sacrifice Ororo's living soul to the Dark Ones. Illyana begins the ritual, but mercifully kills Storm, thus preserving her soul from the darkness. This savage act is something the innocent Illyana could not have done, though darker, experienced Illyana can. Ororo's death empowers her, making her one with the lightning, which she turns on Belasco.

Belasco forces the third bloodstone from Illyana and banishes her to the wilderness. Crouching in the garden, Illyana tries again and again to create an acorn from her soul to break free from Belasco's hold and prove she still has goodness within. At last, she realizes that Ororo formed her own tree from her belief in life, while Illyana only craves vengeance. Channeling Ororo's peace, Illyana uses the last remainder of the oak's lifeforce to create a sword from a part of her own soul. This Soulsword, born of pain and fury, is the embodiment of her will. As a traditional token of the heroine, it is formed from life, but its sword shape emphasizes that Illyana is a killer as well as a healer.

With this, Illyana teleports into Belasco's citadel to challenge him. "Remember me?" she asks with a triumphant grin. As they battle, Illyana slowly recalls that young Ororo's duel with Belasco went the same way. The inner voice of her shadow urges her to kill him and Illyana, understanding her task here, refuses. Belasco is shocked that she is rejecting his place as the Dark Ones' standard bearer with her childish act of mercy, but she stands firm. Having learned savagery and mercy, she can wield both as tools according to her will.

Standing before her old teacher, she finds herself mixed—mutant and sorceress, clutching a mottled sword of her self. She is now mistress of Limbo, where she could stay, and try to heal the place into wholeness like Ororo's garden. Or she could go to face the X-Men and return to her childhood there. She chooses earth and arrives seven years older, though for the X-Men, no time has passed.

The maiden descends into death's realm and learns there, though many heroines become the ruler of death itself, like mythic Persephone and Inanna, embracing the dark world and mastering all its lessons. Angela, Asgard's Assassin, soon becomes Angela, Queen of Hel. Her lover is trapped in the underworld, and, as reflected in ancient tales, Angela goes down to find her. However, the laws of Hel will not let Angela retrieve her. Sera tells her, "You cannot defy Hel. But you can conquer it."

Of course, the daylight heroine is not yet strong enough. As one of Hel's minions complains, "The little wingless brat. You grew up a pet and plaything of the Queen, dandled and fondled and cooed over in her court. All because of your treacherous Mother, who snatched you from the death you deserved and brought an infant Asgardian into the Angels' realm. You come? You, who have never suffered? You?" To rule the dark realm, Angela must come to understand the darkness within herself. The first trial is fear—she slays the monster that represents it, crying that losing Sera was her worst fear, one she's already faced. Angela tries rescuing the imprisoned angels but they consider Angela a traitor and one challenges her to single combat. Thus she has solved the second trial—chaos—and shown mercy. Third, she faces the dark self she would have been without Sera. Having mastered the darkest of emotions—fear, chaos, and the shadow, Angela has incorporated all she needs to become queen of Hel. Though Hel fights with monsters and memories, Angela seizes her mask-crown and frees Sera and all the angels. Then she notes, "I do not want or need this anymore," and relinquishes the crown. Taking Hel's teen daughter Leah, they all leave for freedom in New York (Bennett). Angela has mastered worlds of dark and light and thus chooses who she wants to become.

As Magik, Illyana joins the New Mutants and trains in the use of her powers. To her disappointment, she had been more powerful in Limbo. Like Dorothy Gale or the Narnia children, she is now ordinary once again, with only memories of her magical adventures. Nonetheless, she maintains her rulership of Limbo, winning Belasco's servants and wielding the Soulsword.

> Heroes in fantasy and myth enjoy a magical, symbiotic relationship with the culture. They slay a dragon and return to the kingdom, which is rejuvenated or transformed as a result of their deed. In realistic literature, the kingdom is not necessarily miraculously transformed but the hero is usually rewarded with love and community on a smaller scale. She may find community with the natural world or with the spiritual world, with women, with men, or with both, and she always feels at home and comfortable with herself. The hero's life contrasts with that of the fairy-tale damsel in distress who waits for a prince to transform her world; unlike the passive damsel, the hero actively affects the outcome of her story and creates or chooses her new family [Pearson and Pope 226].

Illyana is more than an X-Man now; she is a sorceress and mistress of Limbo, able to channel demons to aid her on earth at need. When she summons her Soulsword, an eldritch armor covers her body, starting with her left arm. The sword is "the ultimate expression of Illyana's might," defending her and enacting her will on the world (Claremont, *New Mutants* #36). Each time she uses it, the armor grows larger, suggesting her increasing invulnerability. Thus she maintains life in both worlds.

In *New Mutants* #30, she's described as "a fifteen-year-old mutant with the face of an angel and at least part of the soul of a devil incarnate" (Claremont). Both sides are part of her now. "I'm a demon sorceress," she tells her friends frankly. "A part of my fundamental self—my soul—is evil." It can rise to the surface, as she tells them, "with the same unthinking ease you draw a breath." She has mastered the power, but it remains within.

In *New Mutants* #36, Illyana's best friend Kitty Pryde is captured. A demon from Limbo proposes to kill her and make a fourth bloodstone. Illyana fears taking back her powers and becoming evil. But as she adds, "If I let her die, though, how can I call myself 'good'?" (Claremont). She erupts into a horned demon, dressed all in red with a belt of spikes and her "eldritch armor." This is the power of the shadow, one Illyana can now conjure from within as she accepts the angry strength always dwelling beneath the surface. Thus she saves her friend, but pleads with Kitty not to hate her. Kitty, a true friend, accepts Illyana's dark and light.

> The heroine completes her journey by mastering this knowledge, incorporating the death-energies of the underworld into herself and acknowledging their glory. Only thus can she merge with the cycle of life, growing gracefully into mother and wisewoman without fearing death. For it is not an ending but a regenerative spiral. As one life ends, another begins, and on, and on [Frankel, *From Girl to Goddess* 172].

Apotheosis: Promethea (America's Best Comics, 2001–2005)

The spiritual side of the quest is often ignored in favor of the physical, from stabbing one's dark side to saving the world from apocalypse. Nonetheless, the mystical component remains, and is vital to the heroine's quest. In a galactic war, Wonder Woman convinces all the Amazons to lend their energy to Darkseid. "Diana asks them to pray, to bring all their spiritual focus to bear. To set aside all other emotions and center on that intense core of belief within them, to look inward towards the one energy that constantly nourishes them and renews them, and gives them the power and reason to live." They offer up this force and the world is saved (Jimenez, *Paradise Found*).

Promethea by Alan Moore offers a summoning born of pure inspiration. University student Sophie Bangs avidly studies the legends of mystic warrior woman Promethea. She notes that the earliest mention appears in the poem "A Faerie Romance" by Charlton Sennet in 1780 (he appeared to be inspired by his lovely housemaid rather than his wife). In the poem, Promethea falls for a "mortal shepherd lad with mooncalf eyes" though the real poet dies young and depressed after seducing the housemaid. Sophie notes that there have been many other versions: Margaret Taylor Case (1900–1920), author of *Little Margie in Misty Magic Land*, wrote Promethea into her comic book as a helpful spirit. After this, she was a character of Grace Brannagh's, a pulp magazine cover illustrator in the 20s and 30s. For gay comic artist Bill Woolcott from 1939–1969, Promethea was a "science-hero" a bit like 60s Wonder Woman. Barbara

Shelley inspired her husband, comic book writer Steven Shelley, to write his own version.

Researching this character's movement through the mediums, Sophie goes to visit Barbara Shelley. The woman warns her, "You don't wanna go looking for folklore. And you *especially* don't want *folklore* to come looking for *you*" (Book One).

Under attack by villains, Sophie runs for her life, then is rescued by an Egyptian woman—Promethea herself! She explains to Sophie that in the fifth century she was a real child. The god Thoth-Hermes came to her after her father's death and offered to guide her into the Immateria, a magical elseworld that dreams and stories come from where she would "live eternally, as stories do" (Book One). Promethea adds: "Promethea became a living story, growing up in the realm that all dreams and stories come from. Sometimes, she'd wander into the imagination of mortals. Charlton Sennet, the poet. Margaret Case, the cartoonist. And Grace Brannagh, the illustrator. Comics artist William Woolcott and writer Steve Shelley. They *channeled* Promethea!" (Book One).

Some became her and others projected her onto their lovers so that Promethea took them over. Other people through history saw her as a guardian angel on the battlefield or stood up in church, filled with her spirit. The journey has gone on and on without pause, echoing the heroine's journey more than the hero's. "Many women writers feel their stories are episodic, continuing like a circle rather than ending in a straight linear line. Some say the female story model doesn't have an ending at all" (Schmidt, *45 Master Characters* 239).

Suddenly, Sophie realizes she's really speaking to Barbara Shelley, Promethea's latest avatar. She has come to tell Sophie she will be the next Promethea. Following the ancient tradition, she tells Sophie to write a poem or story about the character, using her inspiration and imagination to draw down the superheroine. She even gives Sophie a pen as her token to start her on her quest. Sophie writes a poem, defining the heroine in a new way and thus forming her much as all writers do. She finally incarnates into the superheroine to save Barbara, proclaiming, "I bring you fire!" (Book One).

As Promethea/Sophie takes Barbara to a hospital, the older woman says, "Baby.... I know just how this feels. What's in your head right now, everything, every moment's like stained glass. It's ... it's all right *now*, and full of this heroic *fire* as if all of *existence* was alight...." This of course is an excellent description of poetic inspiration, the force that now fills Sophie. Sophie reads *The Book of Promethea* and explains that the book conjures "this ideal lover ... a heroine of infinity" with "a simplicity that defies description" (Book One).

Sophie finds her friend Stacia and explains that she's been "fused somehow" with "living story." As she adds, "But I don't know how to shut the storybook. Not before I get to the part with the wolf" (Book One). The world of pure inspiration is much like Oz, Wonderland, Narnia. Entering it fills one with a glowing rush of power, makes fingers dance on the keyboard and creates an entire world. It feels like flying (which Promethea can do), feels like beauty and art and magic all at once. The trick is to understand how to pull back after and return to oneself.

Stacia, endlessly practical, suggests acting like her old self and finally lovingly describes her friend, from the promiscuous mother to the lack of social life. At last, Sophie returns. As Sophie quests, Promethea's past avatars look on from the Immateria and offer commentary and judgment, like the little voices in one's head. In the real world, Sophie reads their books and discovers their stories. Stacia, too, acts as a helpful voice, encouraging and helping her to change perspective.

Sophie finally enters the Immateria. It's a land where the sun has a face, of sunsets and pink waterfalls and tiny winged tigers running through the flowers. Adding to the metaphor, she meets the harpielike Pandeliriums, which Promethea describes as "just distractions. Gibberish, fluttering thoughts to lead the mind astray. You have to be stern with them" (Book One). Promethea adds that imagination is a place, a shared world: humans walk through worlds of matter and mind at once, and following a thought means treading the paths of Immateria. She adds that ideas are as common as flowers there, but the artists, scientists, and philosophers go into the deeper jungle seeking rarer blooms.

Here, Promethea tells Sophie her destiny: Promethea tempts people into Immateria, but if too many people follow, they would all leave their bodies to explore the mental realm in something she calls "The Rapture" or "end of the world." Sophie is the guide who will bring this about. As Rebecca Salek explains in her essay, "Spirituality in Comics": "Promethea is both a creature of the spirit world, and a childlike explorer within it. As she explores, Promethea draws on the knowledge and research of the spirit world by her current mortal vessel, Sophie. However, Promethea and Sophie both continuously discover that knowledge provides only the bare clues needed to survive, not the wherewithal to thrive or conquer a particular challenge" (Salek).

Promethea's avatars tutor her there—Margaret in compassion as she acted as a battlefield angel of World War I. Grace teaches her the way of the sword—reason and discrimination. Sophie also battles Marto Neptura, the out of control writer force that was the pen name of many pulp era Promethea writers, and slays him with reductionism from her studies. The series comments on the nature of superhero comics and fantasy, as many writers have named their characters Human Torch or Miss America. With Promethea, Moore addresses the changing nature of the medium. This journey is also an allegory as Sophie (meaning wisdom) pursues inspiration. Moore explains, "There are 1000 comic books on the shelves that don't contain a philosophy lecture and one that does. Isn't there room for that one?" (E. Campbell).

"Myth opens the world to the dimension of mystery, to the realization of the mystery that underlies all forms" (Campbell and Moyers 38). In the next books, Sophie enters the magical world to ascend spiritually. First, Bill guides her there to teach her physical magic. When she sees an image of a woman embracing a snake, Bill tells her, "The snake is the spiraling DNA. It represents all earthly life. The moon woman is all dream and fantasy" (Book Two). Thus flesh and imagination dance together. Sophie follows the path of the Sumerian goddess Inanna, stripping away "her pride, her dignity, her identity ... and all the clothing that represents those things" to face the dark goddess who dwells beneath it all (Book Two). Next, Bill encourages her to train with Jack Faust, who teaches her about sex magic and the sacred marriage. This is, as Jack explains, the grail quest for the feminine ideal, a journey up the body's chakras toward enlightenment. He explains to her that gender is fluid—magicians are male "because they are that which seeks to penetrate the mystery" (Book Two). Women of course are magic, and the mystery itself. As she journeys, she finds her real self and transforms from goddess Promethea into human Sophia with much more to learn.

Next, Sophie decides to cross into the underworld and rescue Barbara, whose body died fighting the villains. She entrusts her best friend Stacia with Promethea, telling her to defend the earth. Once again, Stacia fulfills the best friend's role, allowing Sophie to be in two places at once, doing two jobs. She finds Barbara and drags her out in a storm of emotion made literal. Before Sophie can move on, she must face her demons—turbulence, anger, self-blame. This she does by accepting them, owning them, even physically swallowing them down.

> The strongest theme in *Promethea* ... deals with spirituality and the spirit world, particularly about the human connection between imagination (the Immateria) and all of the worlds beyond this one. Regardless of what belief system you hold dear, our ability to imagine a world beyond this one is the primary thing that sets humans apart from all other creatures we have thus far encountered. In the first three trade paperback editions of Promethea, the reader is treated to a ride through Promethea's own past and imaginative mythology, the symbolism of the Tarot and the Hebrew numbered spheres and alphabetical pathways of the Kabbalah [Salek].

Sephirot, mythology, tarot, astrology, and kabbalah blend, each as a way of understanding spiritual ascent. Sophie meets the universe itself, "where matter meets imagination" (Book Three). There, she climbs steadily, seeking the highest self or soul. Continuing to climb, Sophie meets Promethea's real human father, then her own. From the power of the father she ascends to the feminine. Her guide there is Aleister Crowley, now female as "Here, magicians become the magic itself" (Book Four). She reaches the highest female sphere—the Sephirot Binah, understanding. She is every goddess and also Sophia, "wisdom's female face." Thus Sophie the questor finds herself. She reaches the apex—heavenly light, godforce, and total sensitivity to the world. She finally completes her quest and sees Barbara reach heaven, then Sophie goes home and tells her mother the truth of her father's death.

In the outer world, Sophie learns to change reality by writing poems. However, her friend has embraced Promethea's power and refuses to give her up. An allegorical myth follows, about Promethea incarnating in two girls, one in Constantinople, the other the storyteller Scheherazade. Even as the two avatars met and battled, they realized that they were two halves of the same self and reconciled as they died. Stacia, possessed by Grace, battles Sophie, but they finally accept they're channeling the same energy.

Escaping from the FBI in the real world, Sophie reluctantly takes on Promethea's mantle to carry out one final task; bringing about the end of the world. "Now everything is revealed," she explains. Many people go into fits of what looks like religious visions. Of course, perception of the material world as the only one is really what's shattering, as people see the world beyond, which is just as real. She tells her disciples, "We are all sparks of ecstatic, blazing consciousness. And we are rare. And we are precious. And we are all one thing. And all conceivable places are in truth one place" (Book Five). The rapture comes, and Promethea explains to everyone on earth, individually, that man and woman are divine in an existence beyond physical matter that never ends.

> In creating Promethea, Moore seems to be dancing around the idea that if God created man in his own image, couldn't man create (and re-create) God in his own human image? Of course, Moore has pointed out repeatedly in Promethea that attempting to frame the entirety of the beyond in human terms is sheer folly. Human understanding is mortal and therefore limited in scope, and to define consciousness beyond our own humanity as male or female is a very base-level hubris. Promethea's mantra seems to be, "unlearn what you have learned" [Salek].

After a near-death experience, "colors seem sharper, family and friends are more important, and time is more precious. The nearness of death makes life more real" (Vogler 164). Thus having achieved goddesshood, Promethea brings it and its inherent lessons to everyone.

She tells them to stay awake in the new world, though any may change their lives once reality is restored. Sophie and her boyfriend realize the world didn't end "with a bang" or "a whimper. It ends with 'Hey, yeah, I get it.'" The

Promethea spirit has moved on and left them a couple in love with only themselves. The Promethea soul rests, her task completed.

Thus the series encourages people to reach beyond the superficial, consumerist lifestyle and look deeper. "For the viewer, Promethea is not quite a spiritual carnival ride or an existential video game—it is, in its own way, a textbook or a map. You'll find that you get out of it just what you put into it. Some things have to be believed to be seen clearly" (Salek). Of course, the title Promethea implies the feminine version or inversion of the mythological Prometheus. She brings, not material fire, but understanding. "Life is cyclical, regenerating in an unending spiral of faith and acceptance. With each generation comes new talents and knowledge, new streams branching from life's churning river" (Frankel, *From Girl to Goddess* 294).

In a similar tale, Ann Tenna is a celebretante in New York who dishes up dirt on celebrities in Marisa Acocella Marchetto's *Ann Tenna, A Novel*. However, a brain injury then lightning strike hurls her into a series of comas. There, she faces her shadow in the persona of SuperAnn, who insists she's Ann's "superconscious … superconnected to the universal mind." They are identical, though SuperAnn flies and has glittering megalashes. She explains that they were born as one, but Ann has been devolving from a higher life. Now is her moment to get back on track. Ann is skeptical and rejects her superconscious, who in turn goes to seek "God the mother herself." This divine being decries "corporate greed, religious wrath, government lies" and a long list of other sins, then cradles the babylike SuperAnn and reminds her she was sent to be a messenger—and still has a message to deliver. She appears on the Times Square jumbotron of Ann's mind and disconnects her from everything, sending her to a black void of stick figures. There, Ann Tenna curls up, despairing. There is only one thing she can say to save both of them—"I love and forgive myself … and you too." She says it and reintegrates and finally awakens. Now with superpowers, she hovers in a sparkling chair, beaming a "special message" around the world.

> Having affirmed a commitment to the discovery of the true self in exiting from the garden, and having discovered that she has within her both male and female attributes, the female hero discovers and affirms the full humanity obscured by traditional sex roles. She learns to be autonomous and to achieve without exploiting or dominating others; and she learns nurturance that is not accompanied by a denial of the self. With the achievement of this unified vision, the hero is prepared to return to the kingdom and to enjoy a new relationship with the world [Pearson and Pope 219].

Wisdom, naturally enough, is a token of the feminine side as are subtle spiritual gifts rather than physical ones. Led by the newly created goddess, artistic inspiration itself, they can remake themselves and find new truth.

Of course, this sort of galactic power can lead to physical salvation as well as spiritual. Singularity, introduced in *A-Force: Warzones!* has the power to shelter all her new friends within her nebulous body. On her self-sacrificing death, She-Hulk tells Nico, "She was herself, and what we taught her. What we made her. And what she made us." She rises into the sky but continues to exist, protecting all of the island within herself (Bennett). In the X-Men comics, the Acanti soul is held prisoner by the Brood Queen in *Uncanny X-Men* #166. Binary "becomes an eldrich creature of light and fire, a living star—her celestial radiance reflected and amplified by the crystal cavern—until finally she's generated enough power to release the Acanti soul." It flees to freedom, "Leaving in its wake a song of longing and joy and eternal love" (Claremont, *Uncanny X-Men* #166). In a similar tale, Jean Grey dies saving New York City, and possibly the world. Upon her death, she finally transcends the flaws of the Phoenix Force by becoming immortal. As a White Phoenix of the Crown, she now helps to shape reality benevolently.

Guiding the Next Generation: *Birds of Prey* (TV, 2002–2003)

In 2002, *Birds of Prey* reached television, though only for a single season. The show is unique for its all-female team, in contrast with the token female of the original Avengers or Justice Society. It's a story of adoption, as two women take in a runaway teen, only to discover she has her own talents and wisdom to contribute. Unlike with a male hierarchy, the three become a circle of friendship and strength, relinquishing leadership to each other as needed.

The story begins with the Joker shooting Barbara Gordon, crippling her and stripping her of her Batgirl identity. His mysterious goon murders Catwoman, leaving her teenage daughter Helena sobbing in the street. Across America, the child Dinah Lance wakes in terror, dreaming of both events. Instantly, she is linked to the two superheroines. As Alfred narrates in the voiceover, "Dinah knew her visions would become her future."

Seven years later, Dinah runs away to Gotham, as she's certain these visions represent her destiny. When a man dies in front of her, she has a vision of his being attacked with terrifying visions. With this, she's received her call to adventure, as she's the only one whose powers can sense what truly happened. On the other side of town, Barbara and Helena are investigating the same murders. Though their outside lives are complicated by their night jobs, they consider superheroing a calling:

HELENA: Doesn't it ever bother you? We spend all our time trying to save this
   city—

BARBARA: Shh.
HELENA: —fighting crimelords and supervillains, for what? Lousy hours? Non-
existent pay? No recognition and traffic tickets?
BARBARA: That's the downside of having a secret identity—the secrecy.
...
BARBARA: Could you maybe focus here for just one second?
HELENA: I am focused. Focusing on why we do it—why we even bother.
BARBARA: We do it because it's who we are [101].

Superheroism is their calling but it's becoming hopeless and dismal. Soon
enough, Dinah is attacked in an alleyway, and the mysterious savior Huntress
comes to her rescue. "I'm the Huntress—and you're the prey," she tells the
attacker.

After, Dinah tries to tell Helena she saw her in a dream, but Helena dis-
misses her. Grasping her arm, Dinah has visions of the heroines' clock tower
and the access code to enter. With her powers tying in so neatly, it appears
Dinah truly is destined to work with the other women—her visions have guided
her to find them in Gotham, then guided her to their very doorstep. Dinah
breaks in, discovering their secret identities from basically the first moment.
While Helena and Barbara have had nearly a decade to build a trusting partnership, all at once, their third team member has forced herself on them. They
don't realize that she has known them for the same seven years they've known
each other.

DINAH: I wanna join.
BARBARA: No.
DINAH: Why not?
HELENA: Sorry, we don't have an opening for Junior Supergirl.
BARBARA: You can't stay here. You have to go home.
DINAH: Do you honestly think I'd get on a bus and come to a city where I didn't
know a soul, no money, no job, if I had a place to go back to. I mean, I came to
New Gotham looking for something and I didn't even know what it was, and now
I do...

Barbara finds herself sympathizing and tells Helena, "It's just one night.
One. I remember another girl with no place to go who fell asleep on that couch."
She raised Helena, and now embraces Dinah as their team's newest recruit and
surrogate child. In the morning, however, Barbara rethinks her decision and
says, "This is no place for a kid. What would she do anyway?"

On cue, Dinah pipes up, "Are you investigating this? Because I was there
when he died, and it wasn't a suicide." Despite Barbara's resistance, Dinah is
claiming a place.

The fourth member of the Birds' team is Alfred, who brings them food
and supplies as well as advice. Wayne Enterprises offers the funding, but the

Batman vanished when Catwoman died, and hasn't come back to Gotham. All three women have been abandoned, Barbara losing her mentor, and Helena, both parents. Dinah is in similar straits. Thus all of them, including Alfred, find themselves seeking a surrogate family. Barbara, who was once mentored by Batman and Alfred, understands how much the younger women need her and is eager to mentor them as she was once trained.

The team members provide contrasting abilities: Alfred has the world-wisdom and experience after a lifetime with Batman. As Oracle, Barbara is the computer genius and eyes in the sky. At the same time, she's the team mom, insisting Dinah attend the school where she teaches. Helena has not yet completed her journey and is still resisting the bonds of community. Thus she's the aggressive, untrusting loner, as well as the team muscle. A mentor and trainer for Dinah, she teaches combat and aloof independence as Barbara teaches love and family. Dinah is the sensitive child, a reader of minds and emotions. Her perky attitude contributes, representing the youthful idealism and wonder they've lost. She also can watch Helena's back close up:

HELENA: Check the Dockyards. It's the only lead we have.
DINAH: I can go to the Dockyards.
Both Helena and Barbara ignore her, however.
BARBARA: You can't be in two places at once.
HELENA: Okay. So you take the dockyards and I'll guard Ketterly.
DINAH: I could go to the Dockyards.
Once again, they ignore her.
BARBARA: You know I don't like you going out in the field without backup.
HELENA: You mean without looking over my shoulder.
DINAH: (Yells) Let me go to the damn Dockyards!
They turn and stare at her outburst. She shrugs and tucks a fold of hair behind her ear.

While Helena chats with Ketterly, an old family friend, Dinah investigates and discovers he's the murderer. Suddenly, he uses his powers of despair on Helena. The Huntress, who has always feared losing all her loved ones, tries to stab herself in the chest. Just then, Dinah runs in. Ketterly slams a fireplace poker into Dinah's stomach and calls her "Just another little girl." However, Barbara arrives and hurls a birdarang at him. On defeating him, she discovers Ketterly has trapped Helena in a prison of the mind. "It doesn't matter what you do to me here—part of me stays with her in there. Where I've taken her, no one can follow," he gloats.

Only youthful Dinah can follow Huntress using her own gifts. She puts her hand on the other two women's and plunges into Huntress's mind. Seeing Helena at the site of her mother's death, Dinah says, "She won't hear me. Not here. But maybe she'll hear you." They need the voice of maturity not idealism.

Standing in her Batgirl costume, Barbara appears in Helena's mind and comforts her there, reminding her what it means to be a hero. She adds, "You haven't failed me. I chose this life, and—and all of the risks that came with it. You don't have to protect me, Helena, do you understand? We have to protect each other. I can't do this without you."

This telepathic rescue emphasizes intimacy as it's within the memory of Helena's and Barbara's trauma. It also symbolizes a spiritual partnership: Joining with others in a family, marriage, or team helps to complete the self—the differing personalities offer new slivers of completion. Even Helena's vulnerability and rescue are a moment of mentorship for young Dinah. "The hero lets someone else lend her a hand, give her a boost, and in turn that person will be exposed to the benefits of going on an inner journey. Her journey affects and guides others, so this isn't a handout she's receiving but an example she's giving" (Schmidt, *45 Master Characters* 233). Even in dire peril, Helena can guide the girl to her own empowerment as savior.

Ketterly attacks them in Helena's mind, and Helena fights back. He taunts her, "Why bother, Helena? Even if you kill me, you'll still be alone. You'll always be alone."

She retorts, "Maybe. But it's my screwed-up life and I'll decide when it's over!" She kills him and the three women clasp hands, emerging together into the real world, still touching. Since Dinah has saved both their lives, with an intuition and power they lack, Barbara and Helena find themselves offering her a place with them. She's their student, but in other ways, their teacher.

> BARBARA: There are going to be some ground rules.
> DINAH: I'll do it.
> BARBARA: I haven't even said what they are.
> DINAH: I don't care. I mean, as long as I can stay.
> ...
> BARBARA: As long as you go to school. And work on developing your skills, both mental and physical ... then you can stay!
> DINAH: Cool!

Thus the first episode ends. The trio form a family, with Barbara as loving mom, passing on the lessons from her Batgirl days as she raises the next generation of heroes.

Throughout the show, Barbara struggles with her loss of the Batgirl identity, as she invents a suit to help her walk, but still cannot perform acrobatic feats, only a slow shuffle. Alfred must gently point out that her Batgirl suit "no longer fits" and, like him, she must aid the new heroes instead of being one in the field. Finally, Barbara accepts their raising of Dinah as a calling. She tells Huntress: "Helena, think about how we learned. How we all learned. Dick

Grayson, Tim Drake, Jason Todd, even you. It's more than a tradition, it's a legacy. Take in those like us, mentor and train them. Never turn away someone with the hunger to become what we are. That's what your father would have done" (102). This is the path to superheroism. Thus the heroine "may pick someone to make the journey and continue the cycle, sharing her experience with others. She is the support for the next wave of journeyers" (Schmidt, 45 *Master Characters* 239).

Meanwhile, guarded Helena hesitates to share her life with everyone, from her cop love interest to her psychiatrist (who's actually Harley Quinn!). However, the episode "Three Birds and a Baby" (104) has the trio finding a genetically engineered baby who grows up in a day. When he finds he's programmed to be a soldier, only the metahuman Helena can connect with him.

HELENA: Guy, you're a hunter, just like me. You killed a man. Even though it was an accident, you cannot do that.
GUY: Why not? He was bad.
HELENA: Good point. I ask myself that same question all the time. We have to try not to hurt people.
GUY: Even bad people?
HELENA: I know it's hard. Sometimes I wanna hurt people too. A lot of the time, actually. But we can't. Because we're strong. We have to be responsible with our power. Because that's what being strong's all about [104].

She explores these issues in herself while consoling her foster son. She also finds herself passing on her lessons: "When I was a kid, Barbara never gave up on me. I won't give up on him," she decides. She cannot save Guy, but she turns him from the path of violence and gives him as happy a childhood as she can. As Doctor Quinzel remarks sarcastically, "She overrode millions of dollars in bioengineering research and surgical procedures by becoming his friend. Don't be insane." In fact, this is exactly what happened. Throughout their story, learning to trust each other and bring up Dinah are central as the heroines grow into a team.

Barbara continues her mentoring role far into the future. Scott Peterson and Annie Wu's *Batman Beyond Unlimited* #18 features a team-up between a grey-haired Commissioner Barbara Gordon and a new 15-year-old Batgirl. While the commissioner can hold her own and take down "a dozen guys," she holds back and tests her counterpart. This story not only focuses on this passing of the torch, but it stays with the commissioner's perspective as she tries legal routes to clean up her city but understands all too well what could inspire a teen to choose more direct action. At last, she admits she respects the young Batgirl's determination to protect the poor areas of the city and gives her blessing ... though she also tracks the teenage Nissa down at her school. It should be noted that the women of this story are drawn practically, with the commissioner in short hair and a long beige coat. Batgirl skips teen Barbara's impractical flowing hair and high heels for a simple streamlined black suit. Foregoing the cheesecake poses as well, the two women are shown with a respect and straightforwardness often only granted to male superheroes.

Other heroines grow from central figures in their stories to guardians of the next generation. Teen Calista Secor (Olesya Rulin) spends the series *Powers* wishing for special abilities. She intends to use them on her abusive father for hurting her mother and goes to incredible, life-risking lengths to acquire them. In the final episode, the supervillain claims that he's been stealing powers through a type of sharing to create "a legacy. A family that could outlast me. I never meant to eat them. They were just so ripe." He befriends Calista and, dying, gives her his enormous power. As she adds, she will use her new strength to help other struggling teens. She tells the protagonist she's going to the club called the Kidz house. "It's empty. I thought if I was there, I might help anyone that was lost."

Kitty Pryde goes from student to teacher in Whedon's *Astonishing X-Men* run, comforting the students traumatized by a suicide. In fact, Kitty's care for the young superheroes parallels her own pregnancy. Though it takes place only in a vision, Kitty uses the lessons from mentoring to become a true momma bear, defending her special child Michael with everything she has when the other X-Men turn against her. "Mommy's here," she thinks, plunging into a case of impenetrable metal to retrieve him (Whedon, *Astonishing X-Men: Torn*).

Later, when Wolverine splits from Scott Summers to return to the old academy, she goes with him. X-Men writer Jason Aaron notes: "I think that like Wolverine, she just wants things to be better for the next generation of mutants than they were for her. That's why she came with him to open a new school. She wants there to be a generation of mutants that can grow up to be doctors and lawyers or whatever they want. Not just another line of soldiers. She realizes that way will never win the war or change the world" [Morse]. Other, gentler X-Men like Blindfold, Armor, Rogue, Rachel Summers, Beast, and Iceman go too. Storm only stays to be Scott's conscience. Even fierce Emma Frost, Scott's lover, tells him, "I love children. I'm a teacher." She sorrowfully reminds him that at the their so-called Utopia, they train, but they don't truly guide the children anymore (Aaron, *X-Men: Schism*).

At last, in *X-Men: The End*, Kitty Pryde runs for mayor, and finally becomes president, changing minds through her benevolent example. Of course, her run for office is plagued by prejudice as men deface her posters, hurl bricks, and finally murder one of her student volunteers. Through it all, even the death of a beloved friend, she manages to keep her poise and inspire those around her. She insists, "Life is a *gift*. Every breath, every step we take, is an expression of *hope*—that we can build on today to make a better and brighter *tomorrow*" (Claremont). This is her goal and the ultimate mission of the superheroines.

Conclusion

Many more series are in the works with Freeform's teen television show *Cloak and Dagger* and new seasons of *Agents of S.H.I.E.L.D.* and *Supergirl*. The Wonder Woman film is coming 2017 and Captain Marvel in 2019. Today, most superhero films and shows bring in the hero's journey as each season arc pits the hero against a relative or other shadow adversary.

How does one construct a good superheroine film? Famously, the superheroine films already produced are all problematic. Stuller notes, "Weak scripts, hurried effects, and one-dimensional characters plagued features such as *Lara Croft: Tomb Raider* (2001) and *Catwoman* (2004)" (*Ink-Stained Amazons* 82). *Elektra*'s terribly slow, dreamlike filming with slower flashbacks lacks the action expected in a superhero film. Catwoman's plot is shallow, with far more emphasis on how she looks in her suit. The pathos, madness, and hope of redemption of the character in *Batman Returns* is gone. Likewise, Susan J. Douglas in *Enlightened Sexism* describes Lara Croft as "able to leap tall buildings in a single bound and sporting breasts the size of watermelons" (94). This, one assumes, is the main reason to watch. Of course, the bad writing on these films has convinced many producers that any future films of this sort are doomed. One critic notes:

> If Wonder Woman's role in *Dawn of Justice* is well-received, it might make actress Gal Gadot popular enough to spin off into her own star vehicle. Director Sam Balcomb thinks one film could end the stigma against superheroines: "All it will take is one blockbuster hit, and the floodgates will open. I can't wait for that day." On the other hand, it might only take a failed Wonder Woman movie to convince studios of what they already believe now: that audiences would rather see a talking raccoon than a female star [Weinman].

In contrast with Batman and the Avengers, or the beloved Buffy and Xena television shows, superheroines in film rarely crack jokes at all. On *The Avengers*, Black Widow is the "straight man," like ultra-serious Storm in the *X-Men* trilogy and Gamora in *Guardians of the Galaxy*. Unless they're falling in love with the hero, none of them ever seem to be having a good time. In her own film, Cat-woman calls herself "fun-deficient." Many strong women like Hit-Girl end up lacking a personality and being only a living weapon. Wonder Woman in the *Justice League* cartoon movies is hard and uncompromising, without a fun, friendly, or vulnerable side. In 2016's *Batman vs Superman: Dawn of Justice*, she glows with divine light and traps Doomsday in her gleaming lasso, but seems more distant goddess than woman (admittedly Superman has a similar characterization). Phil Jimenez, Wonder Woman's artist and writer from 2001, notes:

> Without the sex, gender and love stuff in *Wonder Woman*, you're left with, essentially Xena-lite or the DC version of Lady Sif; a generic warrior maiden who doesn't represent all that much except strength through war, honor through violence, victory by the blade of a sword. Obviously, this imagery is powerful to some and incredibly effective in its way. It says a lot about how we feel about violence, war and its value. The shift also suggests something about what we think about sex, our comfort level with sex and sexual power, and a general, cultural sexism that suggests most things feminine are weak, and the way to really prove one's value (literally and figuratively) is shedding the feminine (especially if its sexual, but not sexualized) and embracing the masculine [Illidge].

Token girls in team-up films have severe problems beyond this. Even tough Black Widow runs from the Hulk and interrogates Loki by fake crying. Rogue needs rescuing in the first *X-Men* and loses her powers in the third. Mystique walks around naked, Emma Frost nearly so. Harley Quinn dresses in sequined panties and an increasingly wet t-shirt, eagerly volunteering for the Joker to abuse her again. The Enchantress and Amanda Waller spend the same film trying to control all the world and miserably failing (with the former in a bikini and chains). Likewise, Marvel also has a trope of women gaining too much power and needing to be deprived of it—not just Dark Phoenix, but girlfriends Pepper Potts (*Iron Man 3*) and Jane Foster (*Thor: The Dark World*).

Of course, sometimes the women of film are too militant, attacking men because they have something to prove in a way that's a bad example for children as well as shockingly violent. In the Justice League *Wonder Woman* cartoon movie (2009), Wonder Woman criticizes the "advanced brainwashing" that makes women like secretary Etta Candy assume they need to ask men for help. At the same time, when Diana sees little boys picking on a little girl, she teaches her to swordfight with a stick and sends her to attack them. Empowering, yes, but love interest Steve Trevor makes a valid point that Diana's teaching the girl to "disembowel her playmates" and solve her problems with violence. Wonder Woman slaps Steve every time he makes a move on her, until she suddenly changes her mind at film's end. The Amazons behave similarly, calling fellow Amazons traitors for falling in love. All in all, the film becomes far more gender battle than path to cooperation.

Other films were lighter and more girly ... but arguably *too* girly. Stuller notes, "The tongue-in-cheek (and ultra girlie) *Charlie's Angels* (2000), produced by Drew Barrymore, consciously foregrounded style over substance" (*Ink-Stained Amazons* 82). Every time the Angels must go undercover, they play geishas, strippers, and other scantily-dressed sex dolls. These young women use "their barely clothed bodies to entrap the villains, thereby adding back into the warrior woman scripts the message that true killer power comes from hyperfemininity" (Douglas 93). The *Buffy the Vampire Slayer* film of 1992, like *Charlie's Angels*, has the heroine possessed of useful, butt-kicking skills but obsessed with fashion and fun more than world-saving. Uma Thurman as Jenny Johnson/G-Girl in *My Super Ex-Girlfriend* (2006) is another joke; she's manipulative and only uses her powers selfishly. The Powerpuff Girls are goodhearted, but as kindergartners they are ridiculously naïve and in need of a babysitter. These are all ploys to make a superpowered woman less threatening—these are only goofy, frivolous "girls" after all, and none need to be taken seriously. By contrast, Spider-Man has somewhat ridiculous powers, but the films all emphasize his realistic qualities—a geeky ignored teen coping with enormous adult responsibility and meeting the challenge with courage. While in high school, he even gets a name with "man" in it.

It seems terrible to say, but one can be too first wave feminist ("It's wonderful that I'm serving as secretary to real heroes because I'm tough too," Peggy Carter suggests in *Captain America: The First Avenger*), too second wave ("All men must die," the Amazons suggest in the *Wonder Woman* cartoon movie), or too third wave (It's okay for Charlie's Angels to win the day by stripping because they *like* stripping). All in all, many comic books have achieved great epic heights, presenting superheroines who undergo the journey with depth and pathos ... we're still just waiting for a film to do the same. With a new era of superheroines upon us, one hopes empowerment in films will follow.

Glossary

Adaptation—The art of transferring a work from one medium to another.

Agent Carter—2015–2016 television miniseries starring Peggy Carter and the SSR just before S.H.I.E.L.D. is formed in the Marvel Cinematic Universe.

Agents of S.H.I.E.L.D.—A television show (2013–) in the Marvel Cinematic Universe (MCU) featuring Agent Coulson's team working behind the scenes.

Alternate Universe, Alt-Universe—Genre that changes elements of the source work, such as having Superman raised on Krypton or adopted by different parents on earth.

Anima—A man's inner female.

Animus—A woman's inner male.

Auteur—The author brand (such as the vision of MCU producer Kevin Feige), not necessarily the same as the actual writer.

Canon—Material designated "official" or "sanctioned by the author" contrasted with other authors' contributions to a franchise (The *Star Wars* movies, for instance, are considered canon; the spin-off novels and comics are not). The comic books and films have separate, often contradictory details, as do movies by other adaptors.

Cartooning—The simplification of shapes, an exaggerated style popular in early comic books. More modern comics have a more naturalist rendering style, with more realistic coloring.

Comic book—A short collection of comic pages published in a magazine format, often serialized.

Cosplay—Short for "costume play." Wearing costumes and occasionally acting them out.

Crosscutting—Alternation within one sequence of scenes taking place in different locales.

CW—The CW Television Network is the home of the shared universe DC television shows *Arrow/Flash/Legends of Tomorrow*, while its online CW Seed produces the cartoon *Vixen* in the same universe. All of these follow the CW's successful *Smallville*. *Supergirl* and *Gotham*, while DC television shows airing concurrently, are produced by different networks.

Dark Angel—Post-apocalyptic television show featuring the genetically enhanced savior Max Guevarra. 2000–2002.

Dark Horse—Third most popular comics company in the U.S., publisher of *Buffy*, *Hellboy*, *ApocalyptiGirl*, and other franchises.

Dark Lord—The destructive tyrant as Patriarch, classic Shadow and antagonist for the male hero.

DC Comics—Publisher of Wonder Woman, Superman, Batman, Justice League, and many other comics. They have had several universe reboots including Infinite Crisis and The New 52. There is also an extensive film franchise.

Deconstruction Age—Mid–1980s–1990s. Comics from this time, like *Watchmen* and *Dark Knight Returns* questioned the nature of the superheroes themselves. Frank Miller's *Daredevil* is among them.

Foil—A character who brings out traits in another through contrast—often showing the hero a path not taken or opposing belief system. Similar to shadow.

Girl Power—A 90s trope of empowering young, vacuous, or otherwise harmless looking young women—Buffy or the Powerpuff Girls. A story may be empowering without incorporating the heroine's journey, or vice versa.

Golden Age—Comics produced between 1938 and the late 1940s. The original Wonder Woman, Human Torch, and Captain America date back to this time. These heroes were generally uncomplicated, altruistically fighting the forces of pure evil. Many major conventions of the genre were established in the 40s, as earlier comics had mainly been adventures or thrillers.

Good Mother—Endless source of love and caring, vulnerable angelic side of the self.

Graphic novel—Technically a novel-length bound book made of comic panels, one intended from the start to be a large story. Since today most comic books are collected as trade paperbacks, the distinction has blurred a great deal.

Gutter—The white space between comic panels.

Hero/Heroine/Chosen One—The rule-breaker who changes the world while growing to adulthood and enlightenment, representing the Self.

Independent Comics—All comics not DC or Marvel (Dark Horse is borderline). Some have clear branding styles, like FirstSecond's children's comics. Others, free from major branding, have the freedom to experiment, producing *Pretty Deadly* and *Womanthology* or reprinting the Golden Age classics.

Layout—The formal arrangement of panels within the space of the page. Styles include Simple Story Layout (grid-shaped, panels arranged in tiers); Complex Story Layout (panels have irregular shapes to place more emphasis on the formal unity of page); and Poster Layout (panel borders are discarded, presenting the entire page as a single image).

Marvel—The publisher of *The Avengers*, *X-Men*, *Spider-Man*, and many other franchises. Stan Lee is likely its most famous creator, who invented all of these during the Silver Age.

Marvel Cinematic Universe (MCU)—This refers only to the shared movie and television universe of *Iron Man, Thor, The Avengers, Agent Carter, Agents of S.H.I.E.L.D., Jessica Jones*, etc., excluding the more extensive comics.

Marvelverse—Anything that takes place in the fictional world of Marvel Comics, including *The Avengers, X-Men, Fantastic Four*, and *Spider-Man*. Guest appearances between series are common.

Mentor—Trains the hero or heroine in qualities needed for adulthood.

Novels and short stories—These rarely follow superheroes, with the exception of a few series such as *Wild Cards*. Nonetheless, superhero prose is growing post–2010, thanks to the massive interest in superheroes. Many are self-published with original characters who span race and gender. Other more mainstream ones include film tie-ins along with *The She-Hulk Diaries* or *DC's Super Hero Girls*.

Ordinary World/Conscious World—Everyday life, the "normal world" of work and polite behavior.

Other/Outsider—The outcast or monster rejected by society.

Patriarchy—The force of authority and conformity, the restrictive father.

Persona—One's superficial self presented to others.

Self—The total personality, encompassing many archetypes, including those undiscovered.

Shadow/Alter-Ego—One's dark side: everything a person buries and refuses to acknowledge in herself.

Silver Age—Comics produced in 1956 through the 1970s. Stan Lee's inventions of *The Hulk, Thor, Iron Man, The Avengers, Fantastic Four, The X-Men*, and *Spider-Man*, finishing with *Daredevil*, number among these. These superheroes were more conflicted and had to balance jobs and messy family relationships with their heroism. DC's *Justice League* was created at this time as well.

Speech bubble/balloon—The cartoon bubble containing the dialogue in comics.

Splash Page—A single-panel page. Often the title page or a page that depicts a crucial story moment out of narrative continuity.

Superhero—An individual with superhuman powers who fights to protect the innocent.

Trade Paperbacks—Five or six comic books are usually reprinted in this format for mass distribution to libraries and bookstores. More durable than comic books.

Transmedia—Works that appear across multiple medias, such as comics, online games, and video.

20th Century Fox—Producers of some Marvel movies—*X-Men, Fantastic Four, Spider-Man, Elektra, My Super Ex-Girlfriend*.

Twenty-first century comics—These have a tendency towards dystopia and self-reference, aware as they are of the decades that preceded them. *Echo* or *Power Girl: Power Trip* can be counted among these, along with the MCU world.

Unconscious World/Magical World—The realm of dreams and fantasies below awareness. Often symbolized by the underworld or the magical realm.

Works Cited

Comics and Graphic Novels

Aaron, Jason, et al. *X-Men: Schism.* New York: Marvel Worldwide, 2012.

Abnett, Dan, and Andy Lanning. *Scarlet Witch* #1–4. 1994. *Avengers: Scarlet Witch.* New York: Marvel Worldwide, 2015.

Aguirre-Sacasa, Roberto, and Tonci Zonjic. *Marvel Divas.* New York: Marvel Worldwide, 2010.

Avery, Fiona, and Mark Brooks. *Amazing Fantasy* #1. New York: Marvel Comics, 2004.

Badower, Jason, and Caitlin Kittredge. *Sensation Comics Featuring Wonder Woman* #16. New York: DC Comics, 2015.

Barr, Mike W., and Diogenes Neves. *Suicide Squad: Most Wanted Deadshot and Katana* #1–2. New York: DC Comics, 2016.

Bedard, Tony, and Peter Nguyen. "Sister Zero." 2010. *Gotham City Sirens Book One.* New York: DC Comics, 2014.

Bendis, Brian Michael, and Olivier Coipel. *House of M* #7. New York: Marvel, 2005. Marvel Unlimited. Marvel.com.

Bendis, Brian Michael, and Mike Deodato. *New Avengers* #15. New York: Marvel Worldwide, 2011. Marvel Unlimited. Marvel.com.

Bendis, Brian Michael, and David Finch. *Avengers* #503. New York: Marvel, 2004. Marvel Unlimited. Marvel.com.

Bendis, Brian Michael, and Michael Gaydos. *Alias Ultimate Collection Book 2 (Alias #16–28).* New York: Max Comics, 2010.

_____. *The Pulse* #11. New York: Marvel, 2005. Marvel Unlimited. Marvel.com.

Bendis, Brian Michael, Brian Reed, and Jonathan Luna. *Spider-Woman: Origin* #1–4. New York: Marvel, 2005. Marvel Unlimited. Marvel.com.

Bennett, Marguerite, and Mirka Andolfo. *DC Bombshells* #25–27. New York: DC Comics, 2016.

Bennett, Marguerite, and Laura Braga. *DC Bombshells* #35–36. New York: DC Comics, 2016.

Bennett, Marguerite, Ming Doyle, Laura Braga, and Marguerite Sauvage. *DC Bombshells: Enlisted.* New York: DC Comics, 2016.

Bennett, Marguerite, Kim Jacinto, and Stephanie Hans. *Angela: Queen of Hel.* New York: Marvel Worldwide, 2016.

Bennett, Marguerite, G. Willow Wilson, and Jorge Molina. *A-Force: Warzones!* New York: Marvel, 2015.

Binder, Otto, and Jim Mooney. *Action Comics* #253–254, #265. 1959–1960. *Showcase Presents: Supergirl 1.* New York: DC, 2007.

Binder, Otto, and Al Plastino *Action Comics* #252. 1959. *Showcase Presents: Supergirl 1.* New York: DC, 2007.

Borth, Frank M. "The Spider Widow." *Feature Comics* #58. 1942. *Divas, Dames & Daredevils.* Ed. Mike Madrid. Minneapolis: Exterminating Angel Press, 2013. 90–94.

_____. "The Spider Widow and the Raven." *Feature Comics* #60. 1942. *Pure Excitement Comics.* Ed. Bill Nolan. http://pfeonline.tripod.com/20three1.html.

Brennan, Michael. *Electric Girl* vol. 1. San Francisco: AiT/PlanetLar, 2000.

Brubaker, Ed, et al. *X-Men: Messiah Complex.* New York: Marvel, 2008.

Buscema, John, and Jim Steranko. *Fantastic Four* #130. New York: Marvel, 1973. Marvel Unlimited. Marvel.com.

Busiek, Kurt, and George Peréz. *Avengers* vol. 3, #4. New York: Marvel, 1998. Marvel Unlimited. Marvel.com.

Busiek, Kurt, and Norm Breyfogle. *Avengers Annual 2000.* New York: Marvel, 2000.

Byrne, John. *Avengers West Coast* #51–52. New York: Marvel, 1989. Marvel Unlimited. Marvel.com.

_____. *Fantastic Four* #280, #284. New York: Marvel, 1985. Marvel Unlimited. Marvel.com.

_____. *Wonder Woman: Second Genesis. (Wonder Woman* #101–105). New York: DC Comics, 1997.

Byrne, John, and Graham Nolan. *Spider-Woman* vol. 3, #9. New York: Marvel, 2000.

Cain, Chelsea, and Kate Niemczyk. *Mockingbird* vol. 1: *I Can Explain.* New York: Marvel Worldwide, 2016.

Claremont, Chris, and John Byrne. *The Dark Phoenix Saga (Uncanny X-Men* #129–137). New York: Marvel Entertainment, 2006.

_____. *Marvel Team Up* #100. 1980. *X-Men: Worlds Apart.* New York: Marvel Entertainment, 2009.

Claremont, Chris, and Sean Chen. *X-Men: The End.* 2004–2006. New York: Marvel, 2009.

Claremont, Chris, and Clayton Henry. *Uncanny X-Men Annual* #1. New York: Marvel, 2006. Marvel Unlimited. Marvel.com.

Claremont, Chris, and Jim Lee. *Uncanny X-Men* #256. New York: Marvel, 1989. Marvel Unlimited. Marvel.com.

Claremont, Chris, and Allen Milgrom. *Kitty Pryde and Wolverine.* 1984–1985. New York: Marvel, 2008.

Claremont, Chris, and Bill Sienkiewicz. *New Mutants* #30. New York: Marvel, 1985. Marvel Unlimited. Marvel.com.

Claremont, Chris, and Paul Smith. *Uncanny X-Men* #166. New York: Marvel, 1983. Marvel Unlimited. Marvel.com.

Claremont, Chris, and Mary Wilshire. *New Mutants* #36. New York: Marvel, 1986. Marvel Unlimited. Marvel.com.

Claremont, Chris, and Barry Windsor-Smith. *Uncanny X-Men* #198. New York: Marvel, 1985. Marvel Unlimited. Marvel.com.

Claremont, Chris, et. al. *X-Men—Magik: Storm & Illyana.* 1983–1984. New York: Marvel, 2013.

Claremont, Chris, et al. *Essential Ms. Marvel. Vol. 1. (Ms. Marvel* #1–23 and *Avengers Annual* #10). 1978. New York: Marvel, 2007.

Conner, Amanda, et. al. *Power Girl: Power Trip (JSA: Classified* #1–4 and *Power Girl* #1–12). 2005 and 2009–2010. New York: DC Comics, 2014.

_____. *Harley Quinn: Power Outage.* New York: DC Comics, 2015.

Conway, Gerry, and Rich Buckler. *Fantastic Four* #149–150. New York: Marvel, 1974. Marvel Unlimited. Marvel.com.

Conway, Gerry, Carla Conway and John Buscema. *Ms. Marvel* #1–2. 1977. *Essential Ms. Marvel. Vol. 1.* New York: Marvel, 2007.

Conway, Gerry, and Gardner Fox. *JLA: Zatanna's Search.* 1964–1967. New York: DC, 2004.

Conway, Gerry, and Joe Sinnott. *Fantastic Four* #141. New York: Marvel, 1973. Marvel Unlimited. Marvel.com.

Cook, Katie. "Penelope Parker." *Spider-Verse* #1. New York: Marvel Worldwide, 2014. Marvel Unlimited. Marvel.com.

Cornell, Paul, Elena Casagrande, and Jenny Frison. *Spitfire* #1. New York: Marvel, 2010. Marvel Unlimited. Marvel.com.

David, Peter, and Ed Benes. *Supergirl: Many Happy Returns*. New York: DC Comics, 2002.

David, Peter, Gary Frank, and Terry Dodson. *Supergirl*. (*Showcase '96* #12, *Supergirl* #1–9). 1996–1997. New York: DC Comics, 1998.

David, Peter, and Leonard Kirk. *Supergirl* #26–28. New York: DC Comics, 1998–1999.

David, Peter, Shawn Moll, and Val Semeiks. *She-Hulk: Jaded Vol. 6*. New York: Marvel Worldwide, 2008.

David, Peter, and Jonyboy Meyers. "The She-Hulk Story that's a Riff on Christmas Carol." New York: Marvel, 2011. Marvel Unlimited. Marvel.com.

De Campi, Alex, and Neil Googe. "Venus Rising." *Sensation Comics Featuring Wonder Woman Vol. 2*. New York: DC, 2015.

De Liz, Renae. "Untitled." Hickman 18–22.

DeConnick, Kelly Sue, and Scott Hepburn. *Avengers: The Enemy Within*. New York: Marvel Worldwide, 2013.

DeConnick, Kelly Sue, and Andrea Mutti. *Rescue* #1. New York: Marvel, 2010. Marvel Unlimited. Marvel.com.

DeConnick, Kelly Sue, and Emma Rios. *Pretty Deadly* vol. 1. Berkeley: Image Comics, 2014.

DeConnick, Kelly Sue, and Dexter Soy. *Captain Marvel* #1. 2012. *Guardians of the Galaxy: Guardians Dissassembled*. New York: Marvel Worldwide, 2014.

DeFalco, Tom, and Ron Frenz. *Amazing Spider-Girl* #1. New York: Marvel, 2006. Marvel Unlimited. Marvel.com.

DeFalco, Tom, and Mary Wilshire. *X-Men Firestar*. New York: Marvel, 2006.

Denson, Abby, and Emma Vieceli. "Ad Vice." *Girl Comics* #2. New York: Marvel, 2010. Marvel Unlimited. Marvel.com.

Devineni, Ram. *Priya's Shakti*. New York: Rattapallax, 2014. http://www.priyashakti.com.

Dingle, Adrian. *Nelvana of Northern Lights*. 1941. San Diego: IDW, 2014.

Dini, Paul, and David Lopez. "Holiday Story." 2010. *Gotham City Sirens Book One*. New York: DC Comics, 2014.

Dini, Paul, and Guillem March. "Union" 2009. *Gotham City Sirens Book One*. New York: DC Comics, 2014.

Dini, Paul, and Bruce Timm. "Mad Love." 1994. *The Batman Adventures: Dangerous Dames and Demons*. New York: DC Comics, 2003. 126–190.

Ditko, Steve, and Will Murray. *Marvel Super-Heroes* vol. 3, #8. New York: Marvel, 1991.

D'Orazio, Valerie, and Karl Moline. *X-Men Origins: Emma Frost*. New York: Marvel, 2010. Marvel Unlimited. Marvel.com.

Dorfman, Leo, and Kurt Schaffenberger. *Superman's Girl Friend Lois Lane* #70–71. 1966. *Catwoman: Nine Lives of a Feline Fatale*. Ed. Jasmine Jones. New York: DC, 2004. 37–69.

Ellis, Warren, and Peter Gross. *Hellstorm Prince of Lies* #14. New York: Marvel, 1994.

Englehart, Steve, and Sal Buscema. *Avengers* #128. New York: Marvel, 1974. Marvel Unlimited. Marvel.com.

Englehart, Steve, and George Peréz. *The Avengers* #144. New York: Marvel, 1976. Marvel Unlimited. Marvel.com.

Fite, Linda, et al. *The Cat* #1. 1972. *Marvel Firsts: The 1970s*. New York: Marvel, 2012. 302–323.

Fortuner, Lisa, and Cathy Leamy. "Meanwhile! On Tethys, Orbiting Saturn..." Hickman 198–201.

Fraction, Matt, et al. *The Birth of Generation Hope* (*Uncanny X-Men* #526–529). New York: Marvel, 2010.

Furth, Robin, and Agnes Gabowski. "Clockwork Nightmare." *Girl Comics* #1. New York: Marvel, 2010. Marvel Unlimited. Marvel.com.

Gabrych, Anderson, et. al. *Batgirl: Destruction's Daughter* (*Batgirl* #65–73). New York: DC Comics, 2006.

Gage, Christos, and Mike McKone, et. al. *Avengers Academy: Permanent Record*. New York: Marvel, 2011.

_____. *Avengers Academy Vol. 2: Will We Use This in the Real World?* New York: Marvel, 2011.
Gaines, Max, Gardner Fox, and Sheldon Moldoff. *The Happy Houlihans* #1. New York: E.C. Comics, 1947.
Garza, Ale, Pop Mhan, and Jesse Delperdang. *Batgirl: Kicking Assassins (Batgirl #60–64)*. New York: DC Comics, 2005.
Gillen, Kieron, and Phil Jimenez. *Angela: Asgard's Assassin: Priceless.* New York: Marvel Worldwide, 2015.
Gillen, Kieron, and Jamie McKelvie. *Young Avengers: Style >Substance.* New York: Marvel Worldwide, 2013.
Giunta, John, and Michael Mirando. "The Magician from Mars." *Amazing Man* #11. 1940. *Divas, Dames & Daredevils.* Ed. Mike Madrid. Minneapolis: Exterminating Angel Press, 2013. 220–226
Glass, Adam, et al. *Suicide Squad Vol. 1: Kicked in the Teeth.* New York: DC Comics, 2012.
Goodwin, Archie, and Marie Severin. "Spider-Woman #1." New York: Marvel, 1971. Marvel Unlimited. Marvel.com.
Goodwin, Archie, Sal Buscema, and Jim Mooney. *Marvel Spotlight* #32. New York: Marvel, 1977. Marvel Unlimited. Marvel.com.
Grayson, Devin, and Scott Hampton. *Black Widow: Breakdown.* New York: Marvel, 2001.
Grayson, Devin, and J. G. Jones. *Black Widow* vol. 1. New York: Marvel, 1999.
Hamilton, Edmond, and Sheldon Moldoff. *Detective Comics* #233. New York: DC Comics, 1956.
Harras, Bob, and Steve Epting. *Avengers* #369. New York: Marvel, 1993. Marvel Unlimited. Marvel.com.
Hartnell, Andy, and John Royle. *Danger Girl: Mayday.* San Diego: IDW, 2014.
Heinberg, Allan. *Who Is Wonder Woman? (Wonder Woman* vol. 3, #1–4, Annual #1). New York: DC, 2007.
Heinberg, Allan, and Jim Cheung. *Avengers: The Children's Crusade.* New York: Marvel, 2012.
Heinberg, Allan, Andrea Diuito, and Jim Cheung. *Young Avengers: Family Matters (Young Avengers #7–12)*. New York: DC, 2006.
Hembeck, Fred, and Richard Howell. *Vision and Scarlet Witch* vol. 2, #3. New York: Marvel, 1985. Marvel Unlimited. Marvel.com.
Hickman, Jessica, et al., eds. *Womanthology: Heroic.* San Diego: IDW, 2012.
Hopeless, Dennis, and Javier Rodriguez. *Spider-Woman* #4–5. New York: Marvel Worldwide, 2016. Marvel Unlimited. Marvel.com.
Immonen, Kathryn, and Colleen Coover. "Good to Be Lucky." *Girl Comics* #2 New York: Marvel, 2010. Marvel Unlimited. Marvel.com.
Immonen, Kathryn, and Phil Noto. *Wolverine and Jubilee: Curse of the Mutants.* New York: Marvel Worldwide, 2011.
Jiminez, Phil, Chuck Kim, and José Luis García-López. "DC Special: The Return of Donna Troy." *Teen Titans, Outsiders: The Death and Return of Donna Troy.* New York: DC, 2006.
Jiminez, Phil, et. al. *Wonder Woman: Paradise Found (Wonder Woman* vol. 2, #171–177). New York: DC Comics, 2003.
Johns, Geoff ,and Scott Kolins. "The Search for She-Hulk." 2003–2004. *Avengers: The Complete Collection by Geoff Jones, Vol. 2 (Avengers #64–76)*. New York: Marvel Worldwide, 2013.
Johnson, Mike, and Mahmud Asrar. *The New 52: Supergirl Vol. 3: Sanctuary.* New York: DC Comics, 2014.
Jones, Casey, and Jason Reeves. *All Fall Down.* Burnaby, BC: Arcana Comics, 2011.
Kanigher, Robert, and Ross Andru. *Wonder Woman* #153. *Showcase Presents: Wonder Woman Vol. 3 (Wonder Woman #138–156)*. 1963–1965. New York: DC Comics, 2009.
Kapitan, George, and Stan Drake. *Mystic Comics* #7. New York: Timely Comics, 1941.
Kapitan, George, and Harry Sahle. *Mystic Comics* #4–5. New York: Timely Comics, 1940–1941.
Kapitan, George, and Mike Sekowsky. *All Select Comics* #1. New York: Timely Comics, 1943.
_____. *USA Comics* #5. New York: Timely Comics, 1942.

Kelly, Joe, and Max Fiumara. "Violent Visions." *Amazing Spider-Man* vol. 2, #600. New York: Marvel, 2009. Marvel Unlimited. Marvel.com.

Kelly, Joe, Michael Lark, and Stefano Gaudiano. *Amazing Spider-Man* vol. 2, #637. New York: Marvel, 2010. Marvel Unlimited. Marvel.com.

Kirby, Jack. *Fantastic Four* #94. New York: Marvel, 1970. Marvel Unlimited. Marvel.com.

_____. *Jack Kirby's Fourth World Omnibus, Volume 1*. New York: DC Comics, 2007.

Knisley, Lucy. "Growing Pains." *I Am an Avenger* #4. New York: Marvel, 2010. Marvel Unlimited. Marvel.com.

Kupperberg, Paul, and Carmine Infantino. *The Daring New Adventures of Supergirl* #1. New York: DC Comics, 1982.

Latour, Jason, and Robbi Rodriguez. *Edge of the Spider-Verse* #2. New York: Marvel Worldwide, 2014.

_____. *Spider-Gwen* #1–3. New York: Marvel Worldwide, 2015. Marvel Unlimited. Marvel.com.

Lee, Stan, and John Buscema. *Savage She-Hulk* #1. New York: Marvel, 1980. Marvel Unlimited. Marvel.com.

Lee, Stan, and Jack Kirby. *Avengers* #1. *Essential Avengers* vol. 1. New York: Marvel Worldwide, 2009.

_____. *Fantastic Four Annual* #6. New York: Marvel, 1979.

_____. *Fantastic Four* #1–7. *Essential Fantastic Four Vol. 1* (*Fantastic Four* #1–20). New York: Marvel, 2005.

Leth, Kate, and Brittney Williams. *Patsy Walker a.k.a. Hellcat* #1. New York: Marvel Worldwide, 2015. Marvel Unlimited. Marvel.com.

Levitz, Paul, and Keith Giffen. *Legion of Super-Heroes: The Great Darkness Saga*. 1982–1984. New York: DC Comics, 1989.

Liu, Marjorie, and Daniel Acuña. *Black Widow: The Name of the Rose*. New York: Marvel, 2011.

Liu, Marjorie, Kalman Andrasofszky, and Sara Pichelli. *Nyx: No Way Home* #5–6. New York: Marvel, 2008.

Liu, Marjorie, and Mike Perkins. *Astonishing X-Men: Weaponized*. New York: Marvel, 2013.

Loeb, Jeph and Tim Sale. *Catwoman: When in Rome*. New York: DC Comics, 2004.

Mack, David. *Daredevil/Echo: Vision Quest*. 2004. New York: Marvel, 2010.

Mackie, Howard, and John Byrne. *Amazing Spider-Man* vol. 2, #6. New York: Marvel, 1999. Marvel Unlimited. Marvel.com.

Madden, Bill. *Scoop Comics* #1. Chesler/Dynamic, 1941.

Madison, Ivory, and Cliff Richards. *Huntress: Year One*. New York: DC Comics, 2008.

Marston, William Moulton, and Harry G. Peter. *All Star Comics* #8. 1941. *The Wonder Woman Chronicles Vol. 1*. New York: DC Comics, 2010.

_____. *Sensation Comics* #7. 1942. *The Wonder Woman Chronicles Vol. 1*. New York: DC Comics, 2010.

_____. *Wonder Woman* #1. 1942. *The Wonder Woman Chronicles Vol. 1*. New York: DC Comics, 2010.

_____. *Wonder Woman* #13. 1945. *The Wonder Woman Archives Vol. 6*. New York: DC Comics, 2010.

MacLean, Andrew. *ApocalyptiGirl: An Aria for the End Times*. Milwaukie, OR: Dark Horse 2015.

Marchetto, Marisa Acocella. *Ann Tenna, A Novel*. New York: Alfred A Knopf, 2015.

Marz, Ron et al. *Magdalena* vol. 1. Berkeley: Image Comics, 2011.

McCourt, Mariah, and C.K. Russell. "Becoming." Hickman 238–241.

Messner-Loebs, William, and Mike Deodato. *Wonder Woman: The Contest* (*Wonder Woman* vol. 2, #0, 90–93). New York: DC Comics, 1995.

_____. *Wonder Woman: Challenge of Artemis* (*Wonder Woman* vol. 2, #94–100). New York: DC Comics, 1995.

Miller, Frank, and Dave Gibbons. *The Life and Times of Martha Washington in the Twenty-first Century*. 1994–1997. Milwaukie, OR: Dark Horse Comics, 2010.

Miller, Frank, and Bill Sienkiewicz. *Elektra: Assassin*. New York: Marvel, 2003.

Milligan, Peter, and Nick Dragotta. *X-Statix Presents: Dead Girl*. New York: Marvel, 2006.

Mills, Tarpé. *Miss Fury: Sensational Sundays 1944–1949*. Ed. Trina Robbins; Des. Lorraine Turner. San Diego: IDW Publishing, 2011.

Moore, Alan, and J.H.Williams III. *Promethea Collected Edition* Books 1–5. La Jolla: America's Best Comics 2000–2005.

Moore, Terry. *Echo: The Complete Edition*. 2008–2011. Houston: Abstract Studios, 2011.

Morrison, Grant, et al. *Seven Soldiers of Victory* vol. 4. New York: DC, 2006–2007.

Nicieza, Fabian, and Paco Medina. *I (HEART) Marvel* #3. New York: Marvel, 2006. Marvel Unlimited. Marvel.com.

Nieves, Rafael, and Michael Bair. *Hellstorm Prince of Lies* #3. New York: Marvel, 1993.

Nocenti, Ann, and Bret Blevins. *New Mutants Special* #1. New York: Marvel, 1985.

Nocenti, Ann, Alex Sanchez, and Cliff Richards. *The New 52: Katana. Vol. 1: Soultaker*. New York: DC, 2014.

Parker, Jeff and Sara Pichelli. *Namora* #1. New York: Marvel, 2010. Marvel Unlimited. Marvel.com.

Pérez, George. *Wonder Woman: Gods and Mortals (Wonder Woman* vol. 2, #1–7). New York: DC Comics, 1987.

Pfeifer, Will. *Amazons Attack*. New York: DC, 2008.

Pierce, Tamora, and Timothy Liebe et al. *White Tiger*. New York: Marvel Publishing, 2007.

Pollack, Rachel, and Linda Medley. *Doom Patrol* #72. New York: Vertigo, 1993.

Pope, Paul, J. T. Petty, and David Rubín. *The Fall of the House of West*. New York: First Second, 2015.

_____. *The Rise of Aurora West*. New York: First Second, 2014.

Puckett, Kelley, Scott Peterson, Robert Campanella, and Damion Scott. *Batgirl: Silent Knight*. 2001. New York: DC Comics, 2016.

Puckett, Kelley, and Damion Scott. *Batgirl: A Knight Alone*. New York: DC Comics, 2001.

Randolph, Grace, and Russell Dauterman. *Grace Randolph's Supurbia*. Los Angeles: Boom Entertainment Inc., 2012.

Randolph, Grace, and Craig Rousseau. *Marvel Her-oes*. New York: Marvel, 2010.

Reed, Brian, and Roberto De La Torre. *Giant-Size Ms. Marvel* #1. New York: Marvel, 2006. Marvel Unlimited. Marvel.com.

_____. *Ms. Marvel* vol. 2, #1. New York: Marvel, 2006. Marvel Unlimited. Marvel.com.

Robbins, Trina, and Anne Timmons. *Go Girl!* Milwauke, OR: Dark Horse, 2002.

Robinson, James, et al. *JLA: The Dark Things*. New York: DC, 2014.

_____. *JLA: The Rise of Eclipso*. New York: DC, 2012.

_____. *Scarlet Witch: Witch's Road*. New York: Marvel Worldwide, 2016.

Rodi, Rob, and Dante Bastianoni. *Rogue: Going Rogue*. 2004. New York: Marvel, 2005.

Rucka, Greg, and Michael Lark. *Lazarus One*. Berkeley: Image Comics, 2013.

Rucka, Greg, and Jesus Saiz. *The OMAC Project*. New York: DC, 2005.

Rucka, Greg, and J.H. Williams. *Batwoman: Elegy. (Detective Comics* #854–860). New York: DC, 2010.

Rucka, Greg, et al. *Wonder Woman: Land of the Dead (Wonder Woman* #214–217). New York: DC, 2005.

Sears, Bart, Randy Elliott, and Raymond Kryssing. *Spider-Woman* vol. 3, #1. New York: Marvel, 1999.

Shooter, Jim, David Michelinie, and Sal Buscema. *Avengers* #173. New York: Marvel, 1978. Marvel Unlimited. Marvel.com.

Shooter, Jim, and George Pérez. *Avengers* #200. New York: Marvel, 1980. Marvel Unlimited. Marvel.com.

Siegel, Jerry, and Jim Mooney. *Action Comics* #285. 1962. *Showcase Presents: Supergirl 2*. New York: DC, 2007.

Simone, Gail, and Walter Geovani. *Red Sonja Vol. 1. Queen of Plagues (Red Sonja* vol. 2, #1–6). Mt. Laurel, NJ: Dynamite Entertainment, 2014.

Simone, Gail, and Neil Googe. *Welcome to Tranquility* vol. 2 (*Welcome to Tranquility* #7–12). New York: WildStorm, 2008.

Simone, Gail, et al. *Birds of Prey: Dead of Winter* (*Birds of Prey* #104–108). New York: DC, 2007.

_____. *Birds of Prey: End Run* (*Birds of Prey* #1–6). New York: DC, 2011.

_____. *Birds of Prey: Perfect Pitch* (*Birds of Prey* #86–90, 92–95). New York: DC, 2007.

_____. *Birds of Prey: Sensei and Student* (*Birds of Prey* #62–68). New York: DC, 2004.

Simonson, Louise, June Brigman, et al. *Power Pack Classic. Vol. 1* (*Power Pack* #1–10). 1984–1985. New York: Marvel, 2009.

Simonson, Walter, and John Buscema. *Avengers* #291–294. New York: Marvel, 1988. Marvel Unlimited. Marvel.com.

Slott, Dan, and Giuseppe Camuncoli. *Amazing Spider-Man* #8. New York: Marvel, 2014. Marvel Unlimited. Marvel.com.

Slott, Dan, et al. *She-Hulk: The Complete Collection. Vol. 1* (#1–12 and #1–5). New York: Marvel Worldwide, 2005.

Soule, Charles, and Javier Pulido. *She-Hulk, Volume 1: Law and Disorder.* New York: Marvel Worldwide, 2014.

Stewart, Cameron, Brenden Fletcher, and Babs Tarr. *Batgirl Vol. 1: Batgirl of Burnside* (*Batgirl* #35–40). New York: DC, 2015.

Straczynski, J. Michael, and Chris Weston. *The Twelve: The Complete Series.* New York: Marvel, 2014.

Straczynski, J. Michael, et al. *Wonder Woman: Odyssey Volume 1.* New York: DC, 2011.

_____. *Wonder Woman: Odyssey Volume 2.* New York: DC, 2011.

Thomas, Roy ,and John Buscema. *The Avengers* #76. New York: Marvel, 1970. Marvel Unlimited. Marvel.com.

_____. *The Avengers* #83. New York: Marvel, 1970. Marvel Unlimited. Marvel.com.

Thomas, Roy, Gil Kane, and John Buscema. *Captain Marvel* #18. New York: Marvel, 1969. Marvel Unlimited. Marvel.com.

Thomas, Roy, and Paul Ryan. *Avengers West Coast* #62. New York: Marvel, 1990. Marvel Unlimited 2009.

Thompson, Kelly, and Stephanie Hans. "SuperLess Hero." Hickman 9–11.

Vasquez, Deborah Kuetzpalin. "Citlali, La Chicana Superhero." *La Voz de Esperanza* (Feb. 2002): 8–9.

Vaughan, Brian K., and Adrian Alphona. *Runaways: Pride & Joy* (*Runaways* vol. 1, #1–6). 2004. New York: Marvel, 2009.

_____. *Runaways: Teenage Wasteland* (*Runaways* #7–12) 2004. New York: Marvel, 2009.

_____. *Runaways: The Good Die Young* (*Runaways* #13–18). 2005. New York: Marvel, 2009.

_____. *Runaways: Escape to New York.* (*Runaways* vol. 2, #7–12). 2006. New York: Marvel, 2009.

Whedon, Joss, and John Cassaday. *Astonishing X-Men: Dangerous.* New York: Marvel, 2007.

_____. *Astonishing X-Men: Gifted.* New York: Marvel, 2006.

_____. *Astonishing X-Men: Torn.* New York: Marvel, 2007.

_____. *Astonishing X-Men: Unstoppable.* New York: Marvel, 2008.

Whedon, Joss, Karl Moline, and Andy Owens. *Fray.* Milwaukie, OR: Dark Horse Books, 2003.

Whedon, Joss, and Michael Ryan. *Runaways: Dead End Kids.* (*Runaways* vol. 2, #25–30), 2007–2008. New York: Marvel Entertainment, 2009.

Wilcox, J. Harrison, and Ryan Stegman. *She Hulks: Hunt for the Intelligencia* (*She-Hulks* #1–4). New York: Marvel Entertainment, 2011.

Williams, H., III, and W. Haden Blackman. *Batwoman, Vol. 1: Hydrology* (*Batwoman* #1–5). New York: DC, 2012.

_____. *Batwoman, Vol. 2: To Drown the World* (*Batwoman* #6–11). New York: DC, 2013.

_____. *Batwoman, Vol. 3: World's Finest* (*Batwoman* #0, #12–17). New York: DC, 2013.

_____. *Batwoman, Vol. 4: This Blood Is Thick* (*Batwoman* #18–24). New York: DC, 2014.

_____. *Batwoman, Vol. 5: Webs* (*Batwoman* #25–34). New York: DC, 2014.

Wilson, G. Willow, and Adriean Alphona. *Ms. Marvel: No Normal*. New York: Marvel Entertainment, 2014.

Wilson, G. Willow, and Cafu. *Vixen: Return of the Lion*. New York: DC, 2009.

Wilson, G. Willow, Jacob Wyatt, and Adriean Alphona. *Ms. Marvel: Crushed*. New York: Marvel Entertainment, 2015.

_____. *Ms. Marvel: Generation Why*. New York: Marvel Entertainment, 2015.

_____. *Ms. Marvel: Last Days*. New York: Marvel Entertainment, 2015.

Winick, Judd, et al. *Outsiders: Looking for Trouble* (*Outsiders* #1–7). New York: DC, 2004.

_____. *Outsiders: Crisis Intervention* (*Outsiders* #29–33). New York: DC, 2006.

Wohl, David, Christina Z, and Michael Turner. *Witchblade Origins Volume 1: Genesis*. Los Angeles: Top Cow Productions/Image Comics, 2008.

Wolfman, Marv, and Tom Grummett. *New Titans* #84. New York: DC, 1992.

Wolfman, Marv, and Carmine Infantino. *Spider-Woman* #1. New York: Marvel Comics, 1978.

Wolfman, Marv, and George Pérez. *The New Teen Titans* #3–6. 1981. *The New Teen Titans 1*. New York: DC, 2014. 76–179.

_____. "Clash of the Titans." *New Teen Titans 2*. New York: DC, 2015. 87–114.

_____. *New Teen Titans: Who Is Donna Troy?* (*New Teen Titans* #38, *Tales of the New Teen Titans* #50, *New Titans* #50–55). New York: DC, 2005.

Yost, Chris, and Harvey Tolibad. *Psylocke*. New York: Marvel Entertainment, 2010.

Prose

Acosta, Marta. *The She-Hulk Diaries*. New York: Hyperion, 2013.

Bond, Gwenda. *Lois Lane: Fallout*. North Mankato, MN: Switch Press, 2015.

Carroll, Michael. *Super Human*. New York: Philomel Books, 2010.

Claremont, Chris. *X-Men: The Last Stand* (novelization). New York: Random House, 2006.

Diaz, Ruth. *The Superheroes Union: Dynama*. Toronto: Carina Press, 2012. Kindle Edition.

D'Orozio, Valerie. "Nightingale." *Chicks in Capes*. Ed. Lori Gentile and Karen O'Brien; illus. Emily Stone. Calumet City, IL: Moonstone Press, 2011. 131–142.

Emshwiller, Carol. "Grandma." *Super Stories of Heroes and Villains*. Ed. Claude Lalumière. San Francisco: Tachyon Publications, 2013. 220–225.

Grossman, Austin. *Soon I Will Be Invincible*. New York: Random House, 2007.

Hirahara, Naomi. "Tat Master." *The Darker Mask*. Ed. Gary Phillips and Christopher Chambers. New York: Tor, 2008. 143–158.

Liu, Marjorie M. "Call Her Savage." *Masked*. Ed. Lou Anders. New York: Gallery Books, 2010. 305–330.

Martin, George R.R., Melinda M. Snodgrass, et. al. *Wild Cards Volume 2 Aces High*. New York: Bantam, 1987.

_____. *Wild Cards Volume 3: Jokers Wild*. New York: Bantam, 1987.

_____. *Wild Cards Volume 11: Dealer's Choice*. New York: Bantam, 1992.

_____. *Wild Cards Volume 15: Black Trump*. New York: Baen, 1995.

_____. *Wild Cards Volume 19: Busted Flush*. New York: Tor, 2008.

_____. *Wild Cards Volume 20: Suicide Kings*. New York: Tor, 2009.

McGuire, Seanan "Velveteen vs. The Isley Crayfish Festival," "Velveteen vs. The Coffee Freaks," "Velveteen vs. the Old Flame," "Velveteen vs. The Junior Super-Patriots," "Velveteen vs. The Blind Date." *Velveteen vs. The Junior Super-Patriots*. ISFiC Press, 2012.

_____. *Velveteen vs. The Multiverse*. ISFiC Press, 2014.

Mohanraj, Mary Anne. "Sanctuary." *Fort Freak. A Wild Cards Mosaic Novel*. Ed. George R.R. Martin. New York: Tor, 2011. 125–138, 359–383.

Nocenti, Ann. "Switchback." *The Darker Mask*. Ed. Gary Phillips and Christopher Chambers. New York: Tor, 2008. 219–244.

Pratt, Tim. *The Strange Adventures of Rangergirl*. New York: Random House, 2005.

Spector, Caroline. "Lies My Mother Told Me." *Dangerous Women*. Ed. George R. R. Martin and Gardner Dozois. New York: Tor, 2013. 647–699.

Stohl, Margaret. *Black Widow: Forever Red*. New York: Disney Publishing, 2015.

Vaughn, Carrie. *After the Golden Age*. New York: Tor, 2011.

_____. "Nuestra Señora de la Esperanza." Torwww, 2014. http://www.tor.com/2014/10/15/nuestra-senora-de-la-esperanza-carrie-vaughn.

Williams, Walter Jon. "Prompt. Professional. Pop!" Torwww, 2014. http://www.tor.com/2014/11/21/prompt-professional-pop.

Westerfeld, Scott. *Zeroes*. New York: Simon Pulse, 2015.

Woodward, Christine. *Going Rogue*. New York: Hyperion, 2013.

Film

The Avengers. Dir. Joss Whedon. Perf. Scarlet Johannsen, Robert Downey Jr., Chris Hemsfield. Paramount Pictures, 2012. DVD.

Batman & Robin. Dir. Joel Schumacher. 1997. Warner Home Video, 2009. DVD.

Batman Returns. Dir. Tim Burton. 1992. Warner Home Video, 2009.

Batman vs Superman: Dawn of Justice. Dir. Zack Snyder. Warner Bros, 2016.

Buffy the Vampire Slayer. 1992. DVD. 20th Century Fox, 2001.

Catwoman. Dir. Pitof. Warner Home Video, 2005.

Conan the Barbarian. Dir. John Milius. 1982. Universal Studios, 2000. DVD.

Guardians of the Galaxy. Dir. James Gunn. Disney Studios, 2014.

The Incredibles. Dir. Brad Bird. Walt Disney Home Entertainment, 2004. DVD.

Iron Man 3. Dir. Shane Black. Disney Studios, 2013. DVD.

Monsters vs Aliens. Dir. Conrad Vernon and Rob Letterman. Paramount, 2009. DVD.

My Super Ex-Girlfriend. Dir. Ivan Reitman. 20th Century Fox, 2006. DVD.

Mystery Men. Dir. Kinka Usher. Universal Pictures, 1999. DVD.

The Powerpuff Girls: The Movie. Warner Home Video, 2002.

Red Sonja. Dir. Richard Fleischer. 1985. Warner Home Video, 2004. DVD.

Sky High. Dir. Mike Mitchell. Walt Disney Home Entertainment, 2005.

Supergirl. Dir. Jeannot Szwarc. 1984. Warner Home Video, 2010. DVD.

Thor: The Dark World. Dir. Alan Taylor. Disney Studios, 2013. DVD.

Whedon, Joss. "Wonder Woman." *Scribd* 7 Aug. 2006. http://www.scribd.com/doc/236441030/Wonder-Woman-by-Joss-Whedon.

Wonder Woman 2009 (Two-Disc Special Edition). Warner Home Video, 2009. DVD.

X-Men. Dir. Bryan Singer. Perf. Patrick Stewart, Hugh Jackman, Ian McKellan, Halle Berry, and Famke Jannsen. 20th Century Fox, 2000. DVD.

X-Men: First Class. Dir. Matthew Vaughn. 20th Century Fox, 2011. DVD.

X-Men: The Last Stand. Dir. Brett Ratner. Perf. Hugh Jackman, Halle Berry, Ian McKellan, and Famke Jannsen. 20th Century Fox, 2006. DVD.

X2: X-Men United. Dir. Bryan Singer. Perf. Patrick Stewart, Hugh Jackman, Ian McKellan, Halle Berry, and Famke Jannsen. 20th Century Fox, 2003. DVD.

Television

Agent Carter Season One. ABC. 2015. Television.

Agents of S.H.I.E.L.D. Season One. ABC. 2013–2014. Television.

Agents of S.H.I.E.L.D. Season Two. ABC. 2014–2015. Television.

Arrow Season Two. The CW Television Network. 2013–2014. Television.

Arrow Season Three. The CW Television Network. 2014–2015. Television.

Arrow Season Four. The CW Television Network. 2015–2016. Television.

The Bionic Woman: Season One. 1976. Universal Studios, 2010. DVD.

Birds of Prey: The Complete Series (2002–2003). Warner Home Video, 2008. DVD.

Buffy the Vampire Slayer: The Complete Third Season. The WB Television Network. 1998–1999. DVD. 20th Century Fox, 2006.

Buffy the Vampire Slayer: The Complete Fourth Season. 1999–2000. The WB Television Network. DVD. 20th Century Fox, 2003.

Buffy the Vampire Slayer: The Complete Seventh Season. UPN. 2002–2003. DVD. 20th Century Fox, 2008.

Dark Angel: The Complete First Season. 2000–2001. 20th Century Fox, 2007.

Dark Angel: The Complete Second Season. 2001–2002. 20th Century Fox, 2009.

Glee: "Dynamic Duets." 2012. Writ and Dir. Ian Brennan. *Glee Season Four.* DVD. 20th Century Fox, 2013.

Heroes: "Cold Snap." 2009. Writ. Bryan Fuller. Dir. Greg Yaitanes. *HHeroes Season Three.* DVD. Universal Studios, 2009.

Lois and Clark: "Ultra Woman." Writ. Gene O'Neill and Norren Tobin. Dir. Mike Vejar. 1995.

Marvel's Jessica Jones. Netflix. 2015. Web.

Misfits: "Episode Three." 2010. *Misfits: Season 2.* DVD. BBC Home Entertainment, 2013.

Powers: Season One. Playstation Network. 2015.

The Secrets of Isis—The Complete Series. 1975–1977. Bci / Eclipse, 2007.

Smallville: Season Six. 2006–2007. Warner Home Video, 2008. DVD.

Smallville: Season Seven. 2007–2008. Warner Home Video, 2008. DVD.

Smallville: Season Eight. 2008–2009. Warner Home Video, 2009. DVD.

Smallville: "Prophecy." Writ. Bryan Miller and Anne Cofell Saunders. Dir. Michael Rohl. *Smallville: Season Ten.* 2010–2011. Warner Home Video, 2011. DVD.

Supergirl Season One. CBS. 2015–2016. Television.

Teen Titans: "The End: Parts 1–3." 2005. *Teen Titans: The Complete Fourth Season.* DVD. Warner Home Video, 2007.

Vixen Season One. CW Seed, 2015. http://www.cwseed.com/shows/vixen/vixen-season-1.

Witchblade: The Complete Series. 2001–2001. Warner Home Video, 2008. DVD.

Wonder Woman pilot. Adrianne Palicki. NBC. 2011.

Wonder Woman: The Complete First Season. Warner Home Video, 2004. DVD.

Secondary Sources

Anders, Charlie Jane. "So THAT Was the Point of Skye's Story on *Agents Of SHIELD.*" *Io9,* 13 May 2015. http://io9.gizmodo.com.

Arnaudo, Marco. *The Myth of the Superhero.* Trans. Jamie Richards. Baltimore: Johns Hopkins University Press, 2013.

Beard, Jim. "Tuesday Q&A: Squirrel Girl: Ryan North and Erica Henderson Launch One of Marvel's Most Beloved Characters into her First Ongoing Series!" *Marvel.com* 7 Oct. 2014. http://marvel.com/news/comics/23414/tuesday_qa_squirrel_girl.

_____. "WonderCon 2012: Captain Marvel." Marvelwww 17 March 2012. http://marvel.com/news/comics/18290/wondercon_2012_captain_marvel

Beatty, Scott. "Granny Goodness." *The DC Comics Encyclopedia.* Ed. Alastair Dougall. New York: Dorling Kindersley, 2008.

Beaudet, Denyse. "The Monster." Downing 219–225.

Bernal, Gina. "Marjorie M. Liu Talks 'Call Me Savage,' Female Comic-Con Geeks, and Paranormal Romance." *Speakeasy. The Wall Street Journal.* 21 July 2010. http://blogs.wsj.com/speakeasy.

Brew, Simon. "*Avengers 2,* and a Black Widow Solo Film." *Den of Geek* 13 Feb. 2014. http://www.denofgeek.us/movies/avengers.

Brown, Jeffrey A. *Dangerous Curves: Action Heroines, Gender, Fetishism, and Popular Culture.* Tuscaloosa: University of Mississippi, 2011.

_____. "Supermoms? Maternity and the Monstrous-feminine in Superhero Comics." Gibson, Huxley and Ormod 185–196.

Burlingame, Russ. "Megalyn Echikunwoke: Vixen Is a Character I Always Wanted To Exist, and I Didn't Know She Already Existed." *ComicBook.com* 24 Aug. 2015. http://comic book.com/2015/08/25/megalyn-echikunwoke-vixen-is-a-character-i-always-wanted-to-exis.

Campbell, Eddie. "Alan Moore Interviewed by Eddie Campbell." *Egomaina* #2, Dec. 2002. 1–32.

Campbell, Joseph. *The Hero with a Thousand Faces.* Princeton: Princeton University Press, 1973.

Campbell, Joseph, with Bill Moyers. *The Power of Myth.* Ed. Betty Sue Flowers. New York: Doubleday, 1988.

Carter, Lynda, et al. "Beauty, Brawn, and Bulletproof Bracelets: A Wonder Woman Retrospective." *Wonder Woman: The Complete First Season.* Warner Home Video, 2004.

Chatterjee, Rhitu. "India's New Comic Book Hero Fights Rape, Rides on The Back of a Tiger." *NPR*, 16 Dec. 2014. http://www.npr.org/sections/goatsandsoda.

Chocano, Carina. "Tough, Cold, Terse, Taciturn and Prone to Not Saying Goodbye When They Hang Up the Phone." *New York Times.* 1 July 2011. http://www.nytimes.com/2011/07/03/magazine/a-plague-of-strong-female-characters.html.

Colter, Mike. "Luke Cage Speaks: Mike Colter Interview." *Den of Geek* 11 Dec. 2015. http://www.denofgeek.us/tv/luke-cage/251275/luke-cage-speaks-mike-colter-interview.

Cooper, J.C. *An Illustrated Encyclopedia of Traditional Symbols.* London: Thames and Hudson, 1978.

Daniels, Les. *Wonder Woman: The Complete History.* San Francisco: Chronicle Books, 2000.

DiPaolo, Marc Edward. "Wonder Woman as World War II Veteran, Camp Feminist Icon, and Male Sex Fantasy." *The Amazing Transforming Superhero! Essays on the Revision of Characters in Comic Books, Film and Television.* Ed. Terrence R. Wandtke. Jefferson, NC: McFarland, 2007. 151–173.

Douglas, Susan J. *Enlightened Sexism.* New York: Henry Holt, 2010.

Downing, Christine. "Sisters and Brothers." Downing 110–17.

Downing, Christine, ed. *Mirrors of the Self: Archetypal Images that Shape Your Life.* New York: St. Martin's Press, 1991.

Duncan, Randy, and Matthew J. Smith. *The Power of Comics: History, Form, and Culture.* New York: Continuum, 2009.

Edwards, Stassa. "Netflix's *Jessica Jones* Is a Complex Portrait of a Woman Undone." *The Muse,* 23 Nov. 2015. http://themuse.jezebel.com/netflixs-jessica-jones-is-a-complex-portrait-of-a-woman-1744182340.

Emad, Mitra C. "Reading Wonder Woman's Body: Mythologies of Gender and Nation." *The Journal of Popular Culture* 39.6 (2006): 954–984.

Estés, Clarissa Pinkola. *Women Who Run With the Wolves.* New York: Ballantine Books, 1992.

Errico, Marcus. "Meet Patsy Walker (aka Hellcat): Marvel's Newest Female-Led Comic Book and *Jessica Jones* Sidekick." *Yahoo News* 9 Sept. 2015. news.yahoo.com.

Ferguson, LaToya. "The Women of Color Heroes We Both Need and Deserve." *IndieWire* 5 Aug. 2015. http://blogs.indiewire.com/womenandhollywood.

Florence, Brandi L. "Busting Out All Over: The Portrayal of Superheroines in American Superhero Comics from the 1940s to the 2000s." M.S. thesis. University of North Carolina at Chapel Hill, April, 2002.

Formo, Brian. "Why *Jessica Jones* and *Spotlight* Are a Step Forward for Victims of Abuse." *Collider* 9 Dec 2015. http://collider.com/jessica-jones-spotlight-sexual-abuse.

Frankel, Valerie Estelle. *The Avengers Face Their Dark Sides.* Middletown, DE: LitCrit Press, 2015.

_____. *Buffy and the Heroine's Journey.* Jefferson, NC: McFarland, 2012.

_____. *Empowered: The Symbolism, Feminism, and Superheroism of Wonder Woman.* Middletown, DE: LitCrit Press, 2015.

_____. *From Girl to Goddess*. Jefferson, NC: McFarland, 2010.

_____. *Joss Whedon's Names*. Middletown, DE: LitCrit Press, 2014.

Galvan, Margaret. "From Kitty to Cat: Kitty Pryde and the Phases of Feminism." *The Ages of the X-Men: Essays on the Children of the Atom in Changing Times*. Ed. Joseph J. Darowski. Jefferson, NC: McFarland, 2014. 46–59.

Gibson, Mel, David Huxley, and Joan Ormrod. *Superheroes and Identities*. London: Routledge, Taylor & Francis Group, 2015.

Gilly, Casey. "Paul Pope Talks *The Rise of Aurora West*." *CBR* 21 Aug. 2014. http://www.comicbookresources.com/?page=article&id=54962.

Goldman, Carrie. "An Open Letter to Supergirl Stars Melissa Benoist and Chyler Leigh, from an Adoptive Mom." *Chicago Now* 22 Mar. 2016. http://www.chicagonow.com.

Goldman, Eric. "Vixen Animated Series Renewed for Season 2; CW Ponders More in Live-Action." *IGN* 10 Jan. 2016. http://www.ign.com.

Goodrum, M. "'Oh c'mon, those stories can't count in continuity!' Squirrel Girl and the Problem of Female Power." *Studies in Comics* 5.1 (2014), 97–115.

Granshaw, Lisa. "Meet the Inhumans." *BoingBoing* 3 Mar 2015. http://boingboing.net.

Gray, Richard J. II. "Vivacious Vixens and Scintillating Super Hotties: Deconstructing the Superheroine." *The 21st Century Superhero: Essays on Gender, Genre and Globalization in Film*. Ed. Richard J. Gray II and Betty Kaklamanidou. Jefferson, NC: McFarland, 2011. 75–93.

Greven, David. "Throwing Down the Gauntlet: Defiant Women, Decadent Men, Objects of Power, and *Witchblade*." *Action Chicks: New Images of Tough Women in Popular Culture*. Ed. Sherrie A Innes. New York: Palgrave MacMillan, 2004. 123–152.

Gustines, George Gene. "Makeover for Wonder Woman at 69." *New York Times* 29 June 2010. http://www.nytimes.com/2010/06/30/books/30wonder.html.

Hanley, Tim. *Wonder Woman Unbound: The Curious History of the World's Most Famous Heroine*. Chicago: Chicago Review Press, 2014.

Haraway, Donna. "A Cyborg Manifesto." *Theorizing Feminism*. Ed. Anne C. Herrmann and Abigail J. Stewart. San Francisco: Westview Press, 1994. 424–457.

Hatfield, Charles, Jeet Heer, and Kent Worcester. *The Superhero Reader*. Tuscaloosa: University Press of Mississippi, 2013.

Healy, K. "The Secret Origins of Jessica Jones: Multiplicity, Irony and a Feminist Perspective on Brian Michael Bendis's Alias." *Girl-Wonder.org* 2006. http://girl-wonder.org/papers/healey.html.

Henderson, Joseph L. "Ancient Myths and Modern Man." *Jung* 95–156.

"How Jessica Jones Got Rape Stories Right." *TV Guide* 3 Dec. 2015. http://medford.wickedlocal.com.

Huver, Scott. "*Jessica Jones*' Rachael Taylor Would Love to Bring Marvel's Hellcat to Life." *CBR* 1 Feb. 2016. http://www.comicbookresources.com.

Iaccino, James F. *Jungian Reflections within the Cinema*. Westport, CT: Praeger, 1998.

Illidge, Joseph Phillip. "The Color Barrier: Jimenez on Wonder Woman, Sexual Identity, & Racial Politics." *Comic Book Resources* 21 March 2014. http://www.comicbookresources.com/?page=article&id=51620

Inness, Sherrie A. *Tough Girls: Women Warriors and Wonder Women in Popular Culture*. Philadelphia: University of Pennsylvania Press, 1999.

The International Catalog of Superheroes. 2002. http://www.internationalhero.co.uk.

"An Interview with Greg Rucka." Thomas and Ellis.

Jehanzeb. "The Objectification of Women in Comic Books." *Fantasy Magazine* Oct. 2014. http://www.fantasy-magazine.com/non-fiction/articles/the-objectification-of-women-in-graphic-novels.

Jowett, Lorna. "To the Max: Embodying Intersections in *Dark Angel*." *Reconstruction* 5.4 (Fall 2005). http://reconstruction.eserver.org/054/jowett.shtml.

Jung, Carl. *Collected Works*. Vol. 9, pt. 1, 2nd ed. Trans. R.F.C. Hull. Princeton: Princeton University Press, 1990.

_____. "Concerning Rebirth." *Collected Works* 113–147.

_____. "Conscience, Unconscious, and Individuation." *Collected Works* 275–289.

_____. "The Phenomenology of the Spirit in Fairytales." *Collected Works* 207–274.

_____. "Psychological Aspects of the Kore." *Collected Works* 182–206.

_____. "Psychological Aspects of the Mother Archetype." *Collected Works* 75–112.

Jung, Carl, ed. *Man and His Symbols*. New York: Doubleday, 1964.

Kaveney, Roz. *Superheroes! Capes and Crusaders in Comics and Films*. London: I.B. Tauris, 2008.

Keveney, Bill. "Supergirl Learns to Balance Bad Guys with the Everyday." *USA Today: Academic Search Premier*. Web. 12 Nov. 2015.

Knight, Gladys L. *Female Action Heroes: A Guide to Women in Comics, Video Games, Film, and Television*. Santa Barbara: Greenwood, 2010

Kyle, Catherine Bailey. "Her Story, Too: Final Fantasy X, Revolutionary Girl Utena, and the Feminist Hero's Journey." *Heroines of Film and Television: Portrayals in Popular Culture*. Ed. Norma Jones, Maja Bajac-Carter, and Bob Batchelo. Lanham, MD: Rowman and Littlefield, 2014. 131–146.

Inness, Sherrie A. *Tough Girls: Women Warriors and Wonder Women in Popular Culture*. Philadelphia: University of Pennsylvania Press, 1999.

Irwin, William, ed. *Superheroes: The Best of Philosophy and Pop Culture*. Hoboken, NJ: John Wiley and Sons, 2011. Kindle Edition.

Landay, Lori. *Madcaps, Screwballs, and Con Women the Female Trickster in American Culture*. Philadelphia: University of Pennsylvania Press, 1998.

Lee, Stan. *The Superhero Women*. New York: Simon & Schuster, 1977.

Lewis, A. David. "*Qahera* Webcomic Creator Deena Mohamed Talks Superheroes, Gaza, and Women." *Islamicommentary.org* 9 July 2014. http://islamicommentary.org.

Link, Alex. "The Secret of Supergirl's Success." *Journal of Popular Culture* 46.6 (2013): 1177–1197. *Academic Search Premier*.

Liu, Marjorie M. "Mutants." Thomas and Ellis.

Madrid, Mike. *Divas, Dames & Daredevils*. Minneapolis: Exterminating Angel Press, 2013.

_____. *The Supergirls: Fashion, Feminism, Fantasy, and the History of Comic Book Heroines*. Minneapolis: Exterminating Angel Press, 2009.

Mainnon, Dominique, and James Ursini. *The Modern Amazons: Warrior Women On-Screen*. Pompton Plains, NJ: Limelight Editions, 2006.

Marston, William Moulton. "Why 100,000,000 Americans Read Comics." *American Scholar* 13.1 (1943–1944): 35–44.

Mata, Irene. *Domestic Disturbances: Re-Imagining Narratives of Gender, Labor, and Immigration*. Austin: University of Texas Press, 2014.

Matsuuchi, Ann. "Wonder Woman Wears Pants: Wonder Woman, Feminism and the 1972 'Women's Lib' Issue." *COLLOQUY* 24 (2012). www.arts.monash.edu.au/ecps/colloquy/journal/issue024/matsuuchi.pdf

Maya K. "Guest Post: Ms. Marvel, Comics, Diversity and Me." *dcwomenkickingass* 13 May 2014. http://dcwomenkickingass.tumblr.com.

Milik, Anika. "Captain America's Next Top Model." Thomas and Ellis.

Misiroglu, Gina. *The Superhero Book: The Ultimate Encyclopedia of Comic-Book Icons and Hollywood Heroes*. Detroit: Visible Ink Press, 2004.

Mitovich, Matt. "*Smallville's* Allison Mack, Part 2: Here Comes the Bride?" *TV Guide* 8 Oct. 2008. Web. 24 May 2012. http://www.tvguide.com/News/Allison-Mack-Smallville-20069.aspx.

Moore, Anne Elizabeth, and James Payne, eds. *Women's Comics Anthology*. Pressing Concern Books, 2007. https://pressingconcern.files.wordpress.com/womens-comics-anthology-2nd-ed.pdf.

Morse, Ben. "The X-Perts: Kitty Pryde. Jason Aaron, Kieron Gillen, Victor Gischler, Christos Gage and Nick Lowe Discuss the Heart of the X-Men." *Marvelwww* 10 Nov. 2011. http://marvel.com/news/comics/17040/the_x-perts_kitty_pryde.

Morrison, Grant. *Supergods: What Masked Vigilantes, Miraculous Mutants, and a Sun God from Smallville Can Teach Us About Being Human.* New York: Spiegel & Grau, 2011.

Murray, Ross. "The Feminine Mystique: Feminism, Sexuality, Motherhood." Gibson, Huxley and Ormod 173–184.

Najafali, Jaleh. "Spidiversity: Who in the World Is Jessica Drew?" *Superior Spider Talk,* 12 Nov. 2014. https://superiorspidertalk.com/spidiversity-who-in-the-world-is-jessica-drew.

Nelson, Gertrud Mueller. *Here All Dwell Free: Stories to Heal the Wounded Feminine.* New York: Doubleday, 1991.

Neumann, Caryn E. "Babes and Crones: Women Growing Old in Comics." *Aging Heroes: Growing Old in Popular Culture.* Ed. Norma Jones and Bob Batchelor. Lanham, MD: Rowman and Littlefield, 2015. 119–127.

Nevins, Jess. "A Guide to Golden Age Marvel Characters." http://www.reocities.com/jjnevins/widow.html

Packer, Sharon. *Superheroes and Superegos: Analyzing the Minds Behind the Masks.* Santa Barbara: ABC-Clio, 2010.

Pandey, Geeta. "India's New Comic 'Super Hero': Priya, the Rape Survivor." *BBC News, Delhi* 8 Dec. 2014. http://www.bbc.com/news/world-asia-india-30288173.

Parreno, Jamie. "Death's Daughter Rides in October's *Pretty Deadly.*" ImageComicswww 12 Aug. 2013. https://imagecomics.com/content/view/deaths-daughter-rides-in-octobers-pretty-deadly.

Pearson, Carol and Katherine Pope. *The Female Hero in American and British Literature.* New York: R.R. Bowker, 1981.

Perera, Silvia Brinton. *Descent to the Goddess.* Toronto: Inner City Books, 1981.

Pitkethly, Clare. "Wonder Woman." *Icons of the American Comic Book: From Captain America to Wonder Woman* vol. 2. Ed. Randy Duncan and Matthew J. Smith. Santa Barbara: Greenwood, 2013. 824–835.

Radish, Christina. "*Jessica Jones* Cast on Season 2 Possibilities, Sex Scenes, and *Luke Cage.*" *Collider* 28 Jan. 2016. http://collider.com/jessica-jones-season-2-sex-scenes-luke-cage.

Rank, Otto. *The Myth of the Birth of the Hero.* Trans. Drs. F. Robbins and Smith Ely Jelliffe. New York: The Journal of Nervous and Mental Disease Publishing Company, 1914. Sacred-texts.com.

Renaud, Jeffery. "Mark Millar Draws a Bloody Curtain on *Kick-Ass.*" *CBR* 13 May 2013. http://www.comicbookresources.com/?page=article&id=45426.

Reynolds, Richard. *Super Heroes: A Modern Mythology* (Studies in Popular Culture). Tuscaloosa: University Press of Mississippi, 1992.

Rhodan, Maya. "How Melissa Benoist Felt When She Put on Her Supergirl Costume for the First Time." Timewww 2015. *Academic Search Premier.*

Robbins, Trina. *The Great Women Superheroes.* Northampton, MA: Kitchen Sink Press, 1996.

Robinson, Lillian S. *Wonder Women.* New York: Routledge, 2004.

Rogers, Vaneta. "DC Comics Bombshells Creates World Where Women Were Heroes of World War II." *Newsarama* 24 July 2015. http://www.newsarama.com.

Rose, Lloyd. "Burn, Baby Burn." Thomas and Ellis.

Salek, Rebecca. "Spirituality in Comics." *Sequential Tart* Dec. 2003. http://www.sequentialtart.com/archive/dec03/tth_1203.shtml.

Sarkeesian, Anita. "Damsel in Distress (Part 1) Tropes vs Women." *Feminist Frequency* 7 Mar. 2013 http://feministfrequency.com/2013/03/07/damsel-in-distress-part-1.

Schmidt, Victoria Lynn. *45 Master Characters.* Cincinnati: Writer's Digest Books, 2001.

_____. *Story Structure Architect.* Cincinnati: Writer's Digest Books, 2005.

Shoemaker, Deanna. "Cartoon Transgressions: Citlali, La Chicana Super Hero as Community Activist." *Liminalities: A Journal of Performance Studies* 7.1 (2011). http://liminalities.net/7-1/citali.pdf.

Simone, Gail. "Mary Batson and the Chimera Society." Thomas and Ellis.

Singer, Marc. "Time of Harvest." *Grant Morrison: Combining the Worlds of Contemporary Culture.* Tuscaloosa: University Press of Mississippi, 2012. 221–250.

Smith, Zack. "Paul Pope Returns to *Battling Boy* with *Fall of the House of West*." *Newsarama* 31 July 2015 http://www.newsarama.com.
Steinem, Gloria. "Introduction." *Wonder Woman: Featuring Over Five Decades of Great Covers.* New York: DC Comics, Abbeville Press, 1995.
_____. "Wonder Woman." Hatfield, Heer and Worcester 203–210.
Strickland, Carol A. "The Rape of Ms. Marvel." http://carolastrickland.com/comics/msmarvel.
Stuller, Jennifer K. "Feminism: Second Wave Feminism in the Pages of Lois Lane." *Critical Approaches to Comics: Theories and Methods.* Ed. Matthew J. Smith and Randy Duncan. New York: Routledge, 2011. 235–251.
_____. *Ink-Stained Amazons and Cinematic Warriors.* New York: I.B. Tauris, 2010.
"Supergirl: The Last Daughter of Krypton." *Smallville: The Complete Seventh Season.* Warner Home Video, 2008. DVD Featurette.
Thomas, Lynne M., and Sigrid Ellis, eds. *Chicks Dig Comics: A Celebration of Comic Books by the Women Who Love Them.* Des Moines: Mad Norwegian Press, 2012. Kindle edition.
"Toucan Interview with Terry Moore." *Comic-Con.org* 30 Apr. 2013. http://www.comic-con.org/toucan/terry-moore-part-one#sthash.2t92DgqR.dpuf.
Towers, Andrea. "Margaret Stohl Talks *Black Widow: Forever Red*—Plus, Read an Exclusive Excerpt." *Entertainment Weekly* 28 May 2015. http://www.ew.com/article/2015/05/26/margaret-stohl-talks-about-black-widow.
_____. "Meet Marvel's Newest Female Superhero in *Moon Girl and Devil Dinosaur*." *Entertainment Weekly* 13 Aug. 2015. http://www.ew.com/article/2015/08/12/moon-girl-devil-dinosaur-marvel-female-superhero
Tremblay, Kaitlin. "Caught on Between Good and Bad: Catwoman's Feminism." *Comic Book Resources* 11 Aug. 2013. http://goodcomics.comicbookresources.com/2013/08/11/caught-in-between-good-and-bad-catwomans-feminism.
Ursini, James, and Dominique Mainon. *The Modern Amazons: Warrior Women On-Screen.* Pompton Plains, NJ: Limelight Editions, 2006.
Vogler, Christopher. *The Writer's Journey.* Studio City, CA: Michael Wiese Productions, 1998.
Von Franz, Marie Louise. *The Feminine in Fairy Tales.* Boston: Shambhala, 2001.
_____. "The Process of Individuation." Jung 157–254.
Walker, Barbara G. *The Woman's Dictionary of Symbols and Sacred Objects.* San Francisco: HarperSanFrancisco, 1988.
Weinman, Jaime J. "Who's Afraid Of Wonder Woman?." *Maclean's* 127.41 (2014): 60–62. *Academic Search Complete.*
Whaley, Deborah Elizabeth. *Black Women in Sequence: Re-inking Comics, Graphic Novels, and Anime.* Seattle: University of Washington Press, 2015.
White, Brett. "In Your Face Jam: I Love She-Hulk (And You Should, Too)." 9 Oct. 2013. http://www.comicbookresources.com/?page=article&id=48368.
Yabroff, Jennie. "Holy Hot Flash, Batman!" *Newsweek* 5 Jan. 2008 http://www.newsweek.com/holy-hot-flash-batman-87089.
Zeisler, Andi. *Feminism and Pop Culture.* Berkeley: Seal Press, 2008. Print.

Index

9 781476 668789